COMPUTER SYSTEM ORGANISATION

The Author

Dr Naresh Jotwani is serving as Director, School of Solar Energy, PDPU, Gandhinagar. Earlier, he has served as Professor and Dean (R&D) at DA-IICT, Gandhinagar, and as Principal at G H Patel College of Engineering and Technology, Vallabh Vidyanagar.

Dr Jotwani obtained his BTech degree in Electrical Engineering from IIT Bombay and doctorate from Rice University, Houston. His teaching career so far has spanned over twenty five years, in India, Singapore, and the US. He has also worked in computer industry for about five years, in India and Singapore, with brief stints in the US.

Dr Jotwani has carried out several consultancy assignments, written four books and numerous research publications, and delivered several invited lectures. His current research interest is in the field of solar photovoltaics.

COMPUTER SYSTEM ORGANISATION

Naresh Jotwani
Director
School of Solar Energy
PDPU, Gandhinagar
Gujarat

Tata McGraw-Hill Publishing Company Limited
NEW DELHI

McGraw-Hill Offices
New Delhi New York St Louis San Francisco Auckland Bogotá Caracas
Kuala lumpur Lisbon London Madrid Mexico City Milan Montreal
San Juan Santiago Singapore Sydney Tokyo Toronto

Tata McGraw-Hill

Published by the Tata McGraw-Hill Publishing Company Limited,
7 West Patel Nagar, New Delhi 110 008.

ISBN (13): 978-0-07-067876-7
ISBN (10): 0-07-067876-6

Managing Director: *Ajay Shukla*

General Manager: Publishing—SEM & Tech Ed: *Vibha Mahajan*
Sponsoring Editor: *Shalini Jha*
Jr Sponsoring Editor: *Nilanjan Chakravarty*
Jr Editorial Executive: *Tina Jajoriya*
Sr Copy Editor: *Dipika Dey*
Jr Manager—Production: *Anjali Razdan*

General Manager: Marketing—Higher Education & School: *Michael J Cruz*
Product Manager: SEM & Tech Ed: *Biju Ganesan*

Controller—Production: *Rajender P Ghansela*
Asst. General Manager—Production: *B L Dogra*

Typeset at Bluekans Information Systems Pvt. Ltd. B-92, Sector-64, Noida, U.P.

RQLLCRLFRQQLY

*The **McGraw-Hill** Companies*

वागर्थाविव सम्पृक्तौ वागर्थप्रतिपत्तये।
जगतः पितरौ वन्दे पार्वतीपरमेश्वरौ।।

रघुवंशम्

—कालिदास

Contents

Preface

In many universities and institutes, an introductory course on Computer System Organisation is taught in the second year of the BE or BTech degree programme, and in the first year of the MCA programme. In a few engineering degree programmes, this introductory course is taught in the first year, or in the first semester of the third year. The present book does not require any prior knowledge from the student beyond standard XII, and is therefore suitable for such an introductory course on the subject. It will also be a valuable reference for students of BCA, DOEACC 'A' Level, BSc and MSc (Computer Science/IT).

An introductory textbook on the subject of Computer System Organisation should aim to help a student in developing a good understanding of a complete computer system. However, in addition to explaining *how things are organised*, the book should also try to explain *why things are organised in a particular way*. The student need not passively accept everything that is written; he or she should think about the reason behind every element of system organisation. It is only in this way that the student will one day be able to think of innovative system designs, and build a fruitful and satisfying career.

Of course, a student learns the subject only with the help of a teacher. We hope that this approach will also appeal to the teacher. It is always easier to teach a subject which has clear underlying patterns of reasoning, rather than a subject which presents a vast collection of information without bringing out such underlying patterns.

With exponential growth in VLSI technology and advances in processor architecture, the sheer amount of information available on computer system organisation has also grown exponentially. But the basic concepts and principles underlying system organisation do not grow exponentially. Therefore there is a need to distill these concepts and principles in such a way that the student develops sound understanding of all modern computer systems—from the small to the large. Such a system perspective of the subject will also help the student in working with future generations of computer systems.

These are the broad objectives behind writing this book. In keeping with these objectives, it was decided not to use a commercially available processor as a running example. Commercial processors are designed and developed for competitive advantage, not for exemplifying basic concepts and principles of system design. We strongly feel that, with a clear understanding of basic concepts and principles, a student should be able to work with any commercial processor and even, if necessary, carry out a comparative assessment of competing processors.

Moreover, reliance on a commercial processor can limit a student's view of what else is possible. The student may begin to think that *processor* can only mean the latest model of 'Brand X', and may therefore lack in confidence when faced with a processor of 'Brand Y'. The aim of this book is to inject a dose of intelligent inquiry into the study of computer systems, and to make the study *open-ended*. The discussion of commercial processors and systems has therefore been provided in the form of a few case studies, in the last chapter.

NICE—the processor introduced and used in this book—has a fairly simple architecture, which serves both to introduce assembly language programming, and to discuss basic issues related to computer systems. While discussing processor design, the aim once again is to bring out general principles, within a clear framework that stimulates the learning process.

The processor is but one element in a computer system—although no doubt it is central to the system. Since the aim of the book is to explain the computer system, it becomes necessary to place somewhat less emphasis on processor design. In any case, processor design has today become a highly specialised subject, and it is neither possible nor desirable to teach detailed algorithms in an introductory course on computer systems. Of course, we do hope that the essential concepts of processor design have been brought out and discussed as appropriate in an introductory book on the subject.

The book takes a *top down* approach towards the subject. With increasing complexity of designs in VLSI, a top down approach can bring the discussion only to a certain level of abstraction. Beyond this level, the domain belongs to another subject, typically Digital Circuits. For example, for anyone writing system software, knowledge of computer *systems* is essential, whereas knowledge of digital *circuits* is optional.

This point can be stressed with another specific example. From a system point of view, it is essential to understand that by *decoding* some higher order address lines, one can generate an appropriate *enable* signal for a memory element or device. This allows devices and memories to be located in different parts of the processor's address space. Clearly this is a basic concept pertinent to system software.

But while understanding the above point, it is not necessary for the student to also learn that 74138 is the part number of a common decoder chip, and to learn the functions of the various pins on this chip. In a particular programme of studies, if it is decided that a student should indeed learn such details, these can be included in the laboratory component of the course.

Thus there is a limit on the extent to which issues related to implementation can be discussed in an introductory course on computer systems. Another way to look at this point is to imagine that, one day in the future, the binary storage and processing elements are made not from silicon transistors, but from some form of optical devices. In such a system, while the implementation of gates and flip-flops will certainly change, most basic concepts and principles of system organisation will continue to be valid.

The book, over its sixteen chapters, follows an integrated approach to architecture, software and processor design, thus providing an overall perspective of the computer system to the reader. The first chapter gives an overview of computer organisation, including topics such as history of computers, hardware and software, memory, input and output, and data paths. Discussion of basic hardware building blocks has been confined to Chapter 3; subsequent chapters make reference to these building blocks as needed. Chapter 3 does not assume any prior knowledge of Digital Circuits, and of course it does not discuss that subject fully. The aim has been to include only the concepts essential for understanding computer systems. If students have already completed a course on Digital Circuits, Chapter 3 may be skipped, or perhaps given just a quick overview (but with a caution to students not to search for part numbers or pin layouts of IC chips!). Chapter 11 on User Interaction and Chapter 12 on Secondary Storage and Other Devices give a more 'physical' view of the modern computer system to all novice users.

Other pedagogical features of the book include:

- Design-oriented approach
- Concept building through discussions on a general processor
- Tutorial-type treatment to deal with important concepts through solved examples
- Custom processor *NICE* used to enhance understanding of concepts
- A separate chapter dedicated to case studies of commercial products such as Pentium® and Sun UltraSparc T2® processors, JAVA Virtual Machine, 8051 Microcontroller® family, and the PC
- More than 70 solved examples
- 100 simple and clear diagrams to illustrate concepts
- 400 review questions
- More than 150 exercises
- Several assembly language programs

An introductory course on computer systems can serve as a key course in a larger programme of studies, as illustrated by the following diagram:

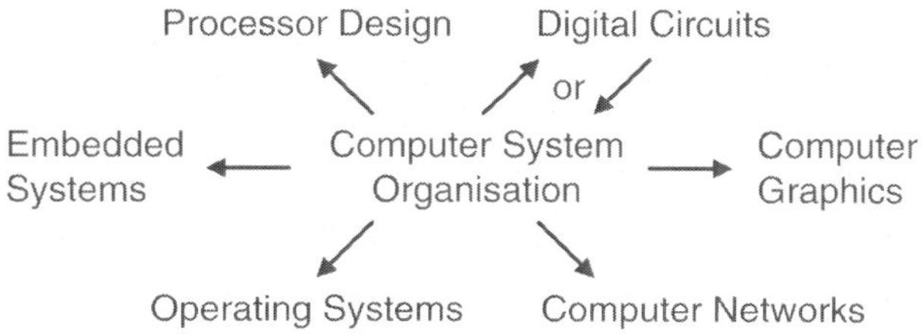

While teaching Operating Systems recently, the author noticed that inadequate understanding of interrupts and direct memory access was creating a difficulty for students in understanding I/O software. A similar situation can arise while teaching Computer Graphics or Embedded Systems. Therefore a course on computer system organisation can be viewed as a key course in such a programme of studies.

This book has been written for a one-semester course on the subject. The teacher will of course determine the degree of emphasis placed on different topics, and the choice of laboratory exercises will vary from place to place, but the core concepts remain the same, and are essential for building a sound understanding of computer systems.

An integrated assembler and simulator for the processor *NICE* has been made available on the website http://www.mhhe.com/jotwani/cso. This software can provide the basis for many useful laboratory assignments associated with the course. Answers to review questions and exercises have also been placed on the same website.

Instructors can avail solution manual, chapter wise PowerPoint slides with diagrams and notes for effective lecture presentations, and an exhaustive test bank at the online learning centre. Resources for students include a sample chapter, additional chapter-wise exercises, and a mini project.

We look forward to receiving from teachers and students their valuable views, comments and suggestions for improvements, all of which may be sent to tmh.csefeedback@gmail.com. Kindly mention the title and author name in the subject line.

Thanks are due to the editorial team at Tata McGraw-Hill—Vibha Mahajan, Shalini Jha, Nilanjan Chakravarty, Tina Jajoriya, Dipika Dey and Anjali Razdan—who helped in bringing the book to its final shape, and to the management at DA-IICT and PDPU—the two places where, in the course of writing this book, the author has worked. DA-IICT students Pradeep Singh, Yogesh Bansal and Sidharth Kumar have worked hard on the assembler-cum-simulator for *NICE*.

A note of acknowledgement is due to the reviewers of the book for their valuable feedback:

Padam Kumar
Indian Institute of Technology, Roorkee

Mukt Bihari
Jaipur Engineering College and Research Centre, Jaipur

Umesh Banodha
Samrat Ashok Technological Institute, Bhopal

Mohd Kashif Qureshi
Aligarh College of Engineering and Technology, Aligarh

Quratul Absar
Amar Singh College, Srinagar

Shuchita Sharma
Inderprastha Engineering College, Ghaziabad

Mahesh Motwani
Jabalpur Engineering College, Jabalpur

Deepak Sukheja
Institute of Engineering and Science, Indore

Amit Jain
Bharat Institute of Technology, Meerut

Ajay Khunteta
Laxmi Devi Institute of Engineering and Technology, Alwar

T P Sharma
National Institute of Technology, Hamirpur

V S Shankar Sriram
Birla Institute of Technology, Mesra

Amiya Kumar Rath
College of Engineering, Bhubaneswar

Prasana Mazumder
Bengal Institute of Technology, Kolkata

Deepak Sharma
K.J. Somaiya College of Engineering, Mumbai

M Kumaresan
Karpagam College of Engineering, Coimbatore

A C Sumathi
Coimbatore Institute of Technology, Coimbatore

Veena Trivedi
Sagar Institute of Research and Technology, Bhopal

R K Gupta
MITS, Gwalior

M Sreelatha
Kakatiya Institute of Technology and Science, Warangal

Munish Khanna
Hindustan College of Science and Technology, Mathura

C Shoba Bindu
JNTU College of Engineering, Anantapur

Jitendra Singh
SRM Institute of Management and Technology, Ghaziabad

Tarun Kumar Ghosh
Haldia Institute of Technology, Haldia

Dr E V Prasad
JNTU College of Engineering, Kakinada

Dr M E Purushoththaman
Hyderabad Institute of Technology and Science, Hyderabad

Finally, two important words for the teacher and student: *Have fun!*

NARESH JOTWANI
Gandhinagar
January 2009

WALKTHROUGH

DESIGN-ORIENTED APPROACH

Concepts underlying the basic system building blocks have been brought out clearly using simple language and diagrams.

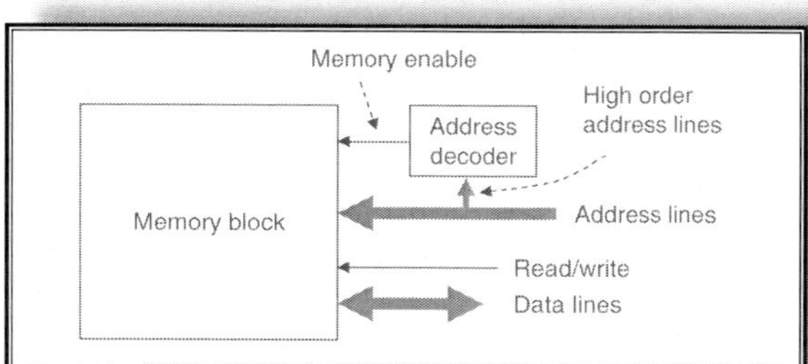

Fig. 3.13 Input and output signals of a typical memory element

TUTORIAL-TYPE TREATMENT

Important concepts are explained using simple solved examples, aimed at leading the student to correct understanding.

Example 2.6

Suppose the stored mantissa of a binary floating point number is 111100000..0, i.e. four '1's followed by all '0's. The implicit 'binary point' is to its left, so that the decimal numeric value of the stored mantissa by itself is calculated as shown below:

$$.111100000..0 \quad 2^{1} \quad 2^{2} \quad 2^{3} \quad 2^{4} \quad 0.9375$$

With an extra hidden '1' to the left ofthe binary point, the value becomes 1.9375.

CONCEPT BUILDING THROUGH DISCUSSIONS ON A GENERAL PROCESSOR

NICE, the simple processor used as a running example, serves well the needs of an introductory course.

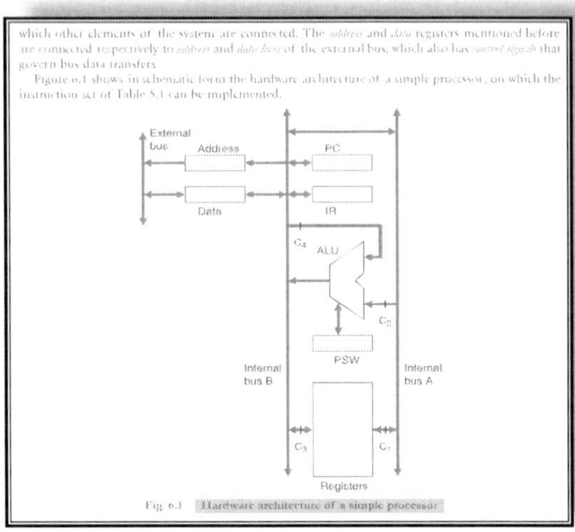

which other elements of the system are connected. The *address* and *data* registers mentioned before are connected respectively to *address* and *data lines* of the external bus, which also has *control signals* that govern bus data transfers

Figure 6.1 shows in schematic form the hardware architecture of a simple processor, on which the instruction set of Table 5.1 can be implemented.

Fig. 6.1 **Hardware architecture of a simple processor**

SIMPLE AND CLEAR DIAGRAMS

Around 100 simple and clear diagrams, interspersed throughout the text, illustrate key system concepts.

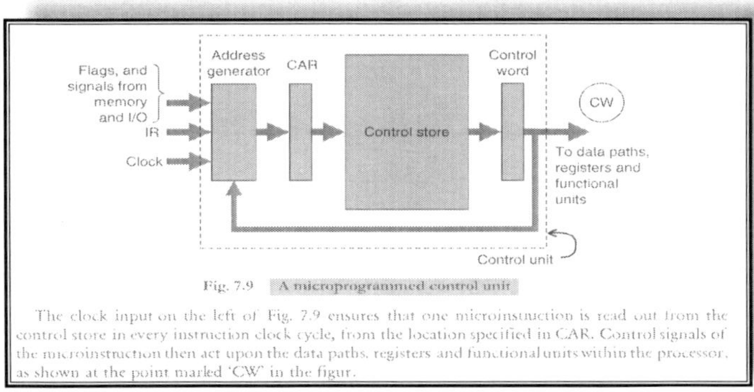

Fig. 7.9 **A microprogrammed control unit**

The clock input on the left of Fig. 7.9 ensures that one microinstruction is read out from the control store in every instruction clock cycle, from the location specified in CAR. Control signals of the microinstruction then act upon the data paths, registers and functional units within the processor, as shown at the point marked 'CW' in the figur.

MORE THAN 150 EXERCISES

Exercises at the end of each chapter provide an opportunity to the student to reinforce his or her learning and gain confidence.

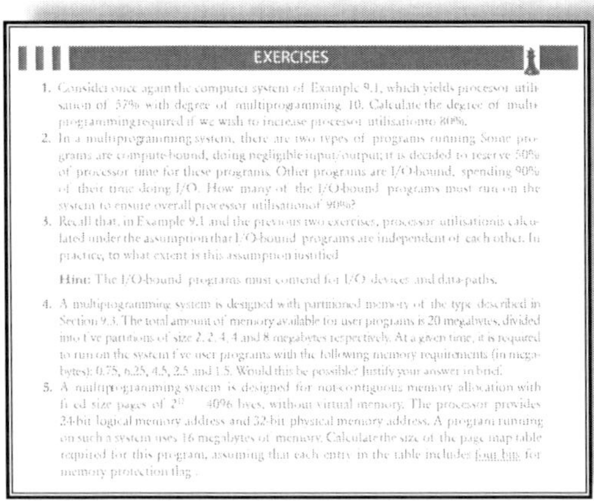

EXERCISES

1. Consider once again the computer system of Example 9.1, which yields processor utilisation of 57% with degree of multiprogramming 10. Calculate the degree of multiprogramming required if we wish to increase processor utilisationto 80%.
2. In a multiprogramming system, there are two types of programs running Some programs are compute-bound, doing negligible input/output; it is decided to reserve 50% of processor time for these programs. Other programs are I/O-bound, spending 90% of their time doing I/O. How many of the I/O-bound programs must run on the system to ensure overall processor utilisationof 90%?
3. Recall that, in Example 9.1 and the previous two exercises, processor utilisationis calculated under the assumption that I/O-bound programs are independent of each other. In practice, to what extent is this assumption justified

   Hint: The I/O-bound programs must contend for I/O devices and data-paths.
4. A multiprogramming system is designed with partitioned memory of the type described in Section 9.3. The total amount of memory available for user programs is 20 megabytes, divided into five partitions of size 2, 2, 4, 4 and 8 megabytes respectively. At a given time, it is required to run on the system five user programs with the following memory requirements (in megabytes): 0.75, 6.25, 4.5, 2.5 and 1.5. Would this be possible? Justify your answer in brief.
5. A multiprogramming system is designed for non-contiguous memory allocation with fixed size pages of 2^{12} = 4096 bytes, without virtual memory. The processor provides 24-bit logical memory address and 32-bit physical memory address. A program running on such a system uses 16 megabytes of memory. Calculate the size of the page map table required for this program, assuming that each entry in the table includes four bits for memory protection flags.

CUSTOM PROCESSOR *NICE*

This simple processor is designed specifically to enhance the student's understanding of concepts. An assembler-cum-simulator for this processor is made available at the website associated with the book, and several assembly language programs are provided at appropriate places in the text.

Program 4.4

```
//
// Program to fin the sum of integers from 1 to 100
//
        MOV     #0, R1      // Initialise R1 to 0
        MOV     #1, R2      // Initialise R2 to 1
//
LOOP:   ADD     R2, R1      // Add R2 into R1
        ADD     #1, R2      // Increment R2 by 1
        COMP    R2, #100    // Compare contents of R2 to 100
        JLE     LOOP        // If less than or equal, jump to
                            // instruction with label LOOP
        HALT                // Halt the program
```

CASE STUDIES

A separate chapter in the book is dedicated to case studies of these commercial products: Pentium® and Sun UltraSparc T2® processors, JAVA Virtual Machine, 8051 Microcontroller® family, and the PC.

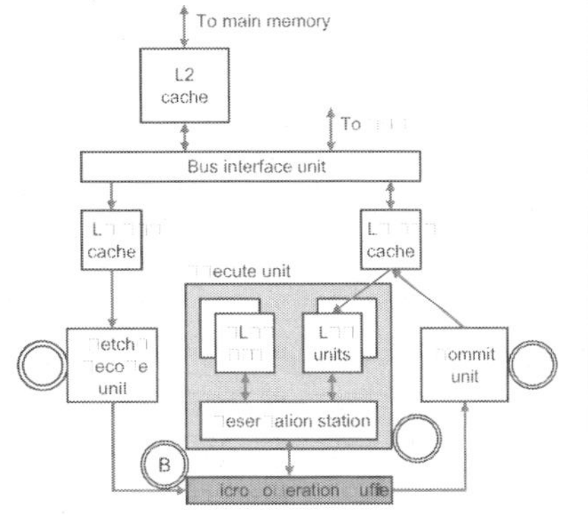

Fig. 16.1 Internal architecture of the Pentium 4 processor

400 REVIEW QUESTIONS

Review questions at the end of each chapter allow a student to review the key concepts and assess his or her understanding.

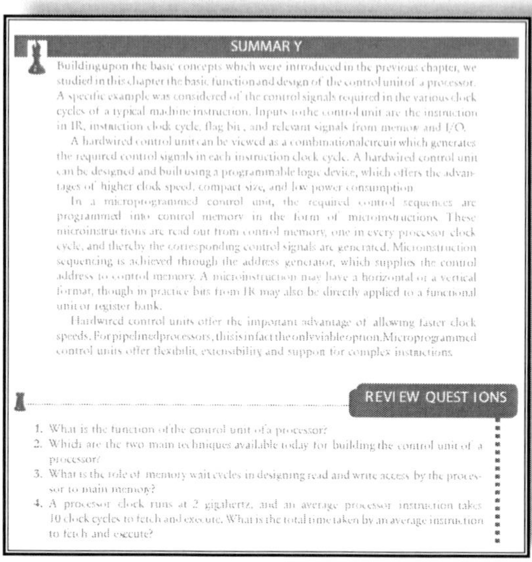

SUMMAR Y

Building upon the basic concepts which were introduced in the previous chapter, we studied in this chapter the basic function and design of the control unit of a processor. A specific example was considered of the control signals required in the various clock cycles of a typical machine instruction. Inputs to the control unit are the instruction in IR, instruction clock cycle, flag bit , and relevant signals from memory and I/O.

A hardwired control unit can be viewed as a combinational circuit which generates the required control signals in each instruction clock cycle. A hardwired control unit can be designed and built using a programmable logic device, which offers the advantages of higher clock speed, compact size, and low power consumption.

In a microprogrammed control unit, the required control sequences are programmed into control memory in the form of microinstructions. These microinstructions are read out from control memory, one in every processor clock cycle, and thereby the corresponding control signals are generated. Microinstruction sequencing is achieved through the address generator, which supplies the control address to control memory. A microinstruction may have a horizontal or a vertical format, though in practice bits from IR may also be directly applied to a functional unit or register bank.

Hardwired control units offer the important advantage of allowing faster clock speeds. For pipelined processors, this is in fact the only viable option. Microprogrammed control units offer flexibilit, extensibility and support for complex instructions.

REVI EW QUEST IONS

1. What is the function of the control unit of a processor?
2. Which are the two main techniques available today for building the control unit of a processor?
3. What is the role of memory wait cycles in designing read and write access by the processor to main memory?
4. A processor clock runs at 2 gigahertz, and an average processor instruction takes 10 clock cycles to fetch and execute. What is the total time taken by an average instruction to fetch and execute?

ESSENTIAL CONCEPTS OF COMPUTER ARCHITECTURE

Using clear diagrams and explanations, essential concepts underlying modern computer architecture are introduced. Interested students are thus ready for a second course focused on computer architecture.

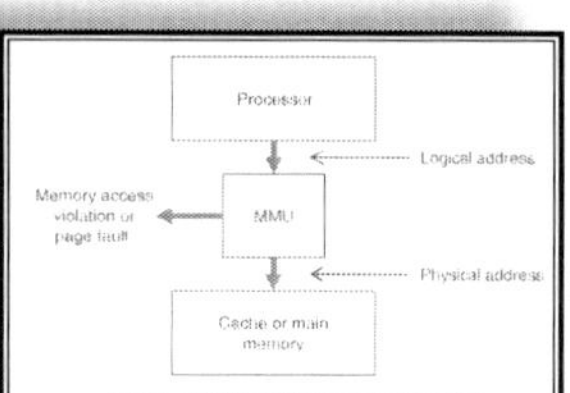

Fig. 9.7 Role of memory management unit

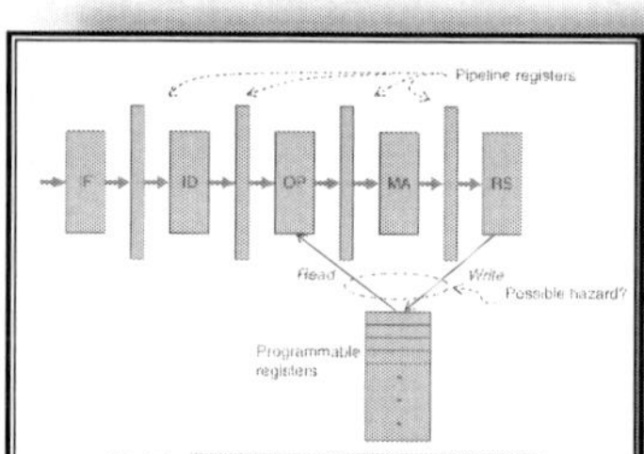

Fig. 6.11 Processor pipeline showing a possible hazard

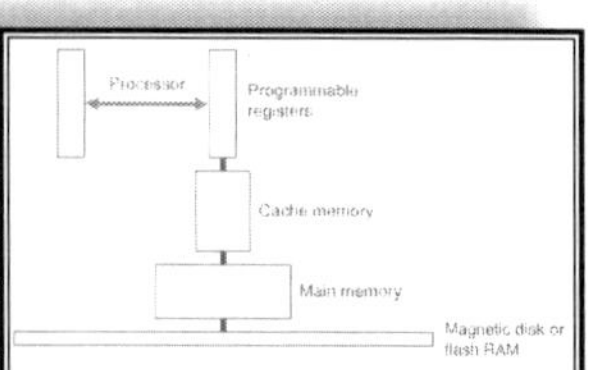

Fig. 9.1 Memory hierarchy in a computer system

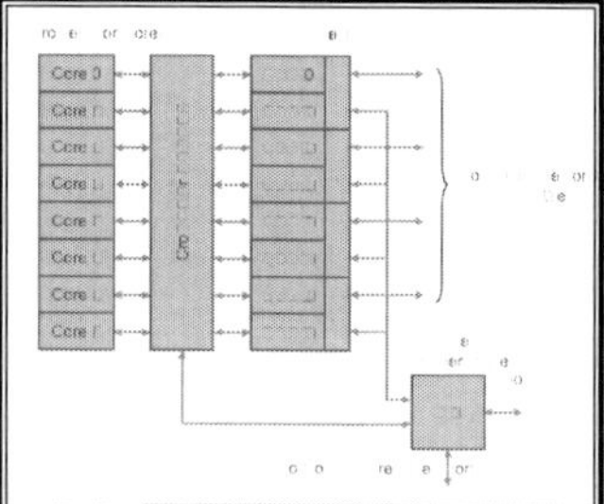

Fig. 16.5 Architecture of UltraSparc T2 'system on a chip'

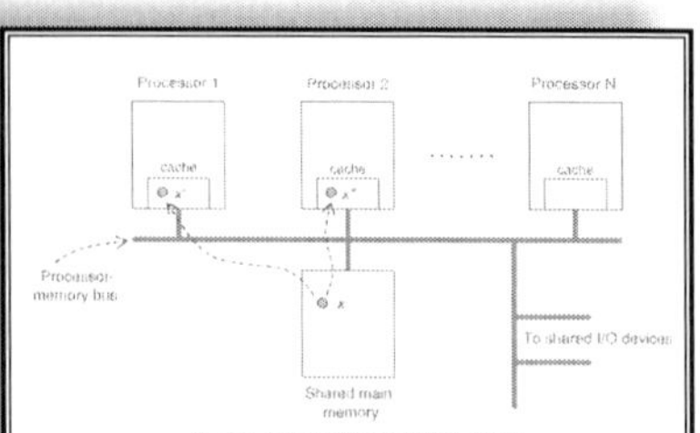

Fig. 14.1 A shared memory multiprocessor

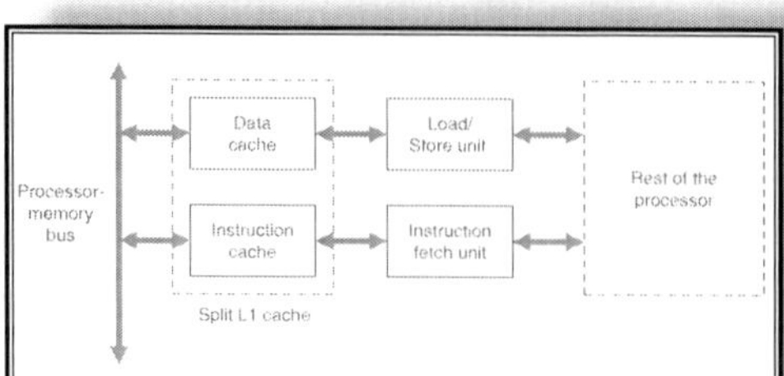

Fig. 9.12 Use of split L1 cache

OVERVIEW

1

1.1 INTRODUCTION

Everyone who uses a computer today is fascinated by the wide range of functions it is capable of performing—such as, for example:

- sending and receiving messages, photos and videos,
- performing complicated calculations,
- making railway or airline reservations,
- creating and storing documents,
- accessing documents from remote systems,
- displaying graphics of amazing colour and clarity

… and the list could go on.

A modern computer is really quite a complex *system*—in the sense that its rich functionality is achieved through the proper interconnection and coordinated operation of a number of separate *sub-systems*, such as the processor, memory, keyboard, disk drive, display, and so on.

This book is about the organisation of a *computer system*, and therefore discusses at some length the various sub-systems of such a system, as also the ways in which these sub-systems are interconnected and operated. Often, though, for the sake of brevity, we may refer to a *computer system* simply as a *computer*.

Note that an end-user does invariably say *computer*, rather than *computer system*. From the point of view of an end-user, this is understandable, because he or she is typically unconcerned with the internal organisation of the system.

The functions listed above represent just a tiny sample of what a modern *general purpose* computer system can do. A typical modern laptop computer is a good example of such a general purpose computer system. But there are also *embedded* computer systems inside many other devices—such as, for example, mobile phones and microwave ovens—which perform specialised functions crucial to the proper working of such devices. Such *embedded computers* are not, however, general purpose, since they are designed and built for specific tasks. One does not expect to send out an e-mail, for example, using the small computer embedded inside a microwave oven.

The earliest computers were conceived and built in the middle of the previous century. These computers represented genuine conceptual breakthroughs achieved by scientists and engineers, because these were the first machines ever built which could be *programmed* to perform mathematical calculations.

Compared to the computers available today, however, these early machines were incredibly less powerful, much more expensive, much larger in size, and also much more difficult to use. Over the subsequent decades, computer technology has grown 'by leaps and bounds'. Today, we can hold in our hands and operate a computer more powerful than one which occupied a large room in the middle of the previous century. In parallel, over the same period, computer networking technology also grew to the point that today we can download in a few seconds a movie clip from half-way around the world.

1.2 BRIEF HISTORY OF COMPUTERS

The earliest programmable computers, which used *vacuum tube* technology, were developed in the middle of the twentieth century. A vacuum tube is an electronic device built from an evacuated glass tube; its typical size being a few centimeters in diameter and length. The picture tubes used in conventional TV sets today use a similar principle, though of course they are much larger in size.

Today's computers use silicon *transistors* to do the work which vacuum tubes did in mid-twentieth century. A transistor used in a computer today measures less than a micron—i.e. 10^{-6} meter—along each dimension. This means that, along each dimension, the transistor is smaller than a vacuum tube by a factor of about 10^{-4}; in terms of volume, this makes the transistor smaller by a factor of 10^{-12}!

To get an appreciation of this scale, consider the dimensions of a typical laptop computer today—approximately 35 cm $\times$ 25 cm $\times$ 3 cm = 2625 cm^3. If we multiply this volume by 10^{12}, the result is a whopping 2.625 $\times$ 10^9 cubic meters! Of course, the earliest computers were not as large as this, but they did occupy whole rooms in laboratories. Their huge size also meant huge power consumption; and because they used primitive input and output mechanisms, they were extremely difficult to program and operate.

The point about an early computer is not that it was reliable, or easy to use, or power efficient—certainly it was none of the above. The point about the early computer is that it represented a major *conceptual breakthrough* to conceive and build a machine which performed actions in accordance with *instructions* fed into it. Two persons whose names are most closely associated with this major conceptual breakthrough were John von Neumann and Alan Turing*.

In 1948, the *transistor*—basically a silicon equivalent of a vacuum tube—was invented. By the 1960s, computers based on transistor technology were in fairly widespread use. If vacuum tube computers represented the *first generation of computers*, then computers based on transistor technology represented the *second generation*. With smaller, more reliable, and more power-efficient building blocks, the computers of second generation boasted of greater reliability, functionality, and ease of use.

In the 1960s, technology was developed to fabricate not only individual devices, such as transistors, but entire electronic circuits on silicon chips. The resulting circuits—which are known as *integrated circuits* (ICs)—provide still higher reliability, smaller size, and more power-efficiency in computers. Computer

*John von Neumann (1903–1957) is known for his major contributions in mathematics, quantum mechanics and nuclear physics. He was amongst the key designers of the earliest computers based on vacuum tubes. Alan Turing (1912–1954) was a mathematician who developed the first theoretical model of computation, known as the *Turing Machine*. During World War II, Turing led a team of mathematicians who broke the cryptographic code used by German armed forces, and thereby contributed to Allied victory.

systems became more sophisticated in their capability, and with this came their differentiation into *minicomputers*, *mainframes*, *supercomputers*, and so on; each meant for different types of applications. Computers built using IC technology are said to constitute the *third generation* of computers.

Integrated circuit technology continued to make rapid advances—which were in fact made possible by the better computer systems that were becoming available for design as well as manufacturing. By the late 1970s, it was possible to fabricate an entire processing unit—i.e. *processor*—on a single IC chip.

By the early 1990s, technology was available to fabricate circuits consisting of a million transistors on a single chip; this technology was dubbed *very large scale integration* (VLSI), and it forms the mainstay of the current *fourth generation* of computers. All of the computer systems and technology we use today—including mobile phones—make use of components which can only be produced using VLSI technology.

1.3 INFORMATION

Basically, a computer system allows us to store, process, display and communicate *information*. But how do we quantify this so-called *information*? How much information do we need to store, process, or communicate in order to carry out a given function?

We communicate or store information by using *symbols*. For example, the letters 'A', 'B', 'C', and so on, allow us to store and communicate textual information, while the numerals '1', '2', and so on, perform similar functions with numeric information.

For quantifying the concept of information, we make use of the very simple *binary alphabet*, which has only the two symbols '0' and '1'. We say that the amount of information carried in any message is nothing but the number of binary symbols—i.e. '0's and '1's—which are required to construct the message.

We denote each binary symbol as a *bit*—which is an abbreviation of *binary digit*; in this context, the word *digit* has essentially the same meaning as *symbol*.

A sequence of symbols of a particular kind—letters of an alphabet, decimal digits, or binary digits—is known as a *string* of symbols. Since we quantify information using the concept of bits, it follows that a string of bits of length n has information content of exactly n bits. But when symbols other than binary are used, we have to perform a little calculation to find its *equivalent number of bits*, as the following example shows.

Example 1.1

Consider a string of four letters 'ABCD'. What is its equivalent number of bits? Or, in other words, how much information content does such a string have?

To answer this question, we must make an assumption about the alphabet from which these four symbols have been selected. Let us assume that the symbols are selected from upper case English letters, which are twenty six in number.

Then, the total number of different strings of length 'four' that we can construct works out to be $26 \times 26 \times 26 \times 26 = 456976$, since each of the four letters in the string can be independently selected in 26 different ways. The string we have here, 'ABCD', is therefore one out of 456976 possible such strings.

Next we ask: How many binary digits—i.e. bits—do we need to be able to construct 456976 distinct binary strings? A little trial-and-error shows us that this number is 19, since 2^{18} is less than 456976, but 2^{19} is greater than 456976.

A string of length four of upper case English letters is thus in this sense approximately equivalent to a binary string of length 19. We may say that binary strings of length 19 give us as much 'expressivity' as strings of length four made up of upper case English letters.

Therefore, the information content of the string 'ABCD', under the assumption made above, is about 19 bits.

As a matter of fact, modern computer systems handle information in millions or even hundreds of millions of bits. For many practical purposes, a single bit proves to be an extremely small unit of information. We therefore say that a *byte* is the equivalent of eight bits of information. Also, we use Latin prefixes *kilo*, *mega* and *giga* to generate larger units, as shown below:

1 *kilo*bit is equal to 1024 or 2^{10} bits.
1 *kilo*byte is equal to 1024 or 2^{10} bytes.

1 *mega*bit is equal to 1024 kilobits or 2^{20} bits.
1 *mega*byte is equal to 1024 kilobytes or 2^{20} bytes.

Similarly, a *giga*bit is equal to 1024 megabits, and a *giga*byte is equal to 1024 megabytes. Since 2^{10} very nearly equals 10^3, and 2^{20} very nearly equals 10^6, the prefixes *kilo*, *mega* and *giga* of the metric system are used in this manner.

How does a computer record—or store—a particular bit as '0' or '1'?

Basically, this is achieved by using the marvels of modern electronic technology, which are in turn based on the special properties of materials known as *semiconductors*, of which silicon is today the preferred choice. Silicon is one of the most abundant elements on our planet; common sand is nothing but a simple compound of silicon.

A basic building block of a computer is an electronic *two-state device*—i.e. a device which remains in one of two stable states. One of these two physical states is used to denote '0', and the other to denote '1'. In fact, which physical state denotes '0' and which denotes '1' is irrelevant, so long as we have reliable means of achieving two distinct states in one device. Such a physical device, which may today occupy less than a square micron of area, thus provides *a single bit of storage.*

If we have a memory element with a capacity of one million bits, for example, then this larger memory element is made up of one million single-bit storage elements—each of which can be individually read or written. Here, *reading a memory element* means determining the pattern of '0's and '1's stored therein, and *writing into a memory element* means recording into it a particular pattern of '0's and '1's.

1.4 HARDWARE AND SOFTWARE

Hardware refers to the various physical sub-systems and components of a computer system. Depending on its context, the word may refer either to *electronic* circuits and elements of a system—such as processor, memory, and so on—or to all its physical components, including mechanical ones such as keyboards, cables and connectors.

For our purposes in this book, *hardware* is to be understood as the electronic circuits and elements making up a computer system. The study of a *computer system* is concerned with its various hardware elements and sub-systems, the way in which these are connected to each other, and the way in which they operate together.

As mentioned above, a computer must be *programmed* to carry out a specific function. A *computer program*, or simply *program*, is a set of instructions which together perform a well-defined function—for example, sending and receiving an e-mail. The function is performed when the instructions making up a program are *executed* by the computer.

From this, we can conclude that a computer system must include at least two different elements in it, namely: (i) a memory element to store the instructions, and (ii) an element to execute stored instructions. These two elements are known, respectively, as *main memory* and *processor**. The processor executes instructions which are stored in main memory, and thereby indirectly controls the operation of the whole system. And, as we shall see, main memory also stores the data on which the instructions operate.

Any modern computer system, even a simple one, in general needs several different programs in order to accomplish its various functions. Depending on its context, the word *software* may mean either:

a. a program or set of programs which perform a specified function, for example, 'software for financial accounting', or
b. collectively all the programs which may run on the system, making up a crucial and vital element of any computer system.

It is in the latter sense that the word *software* was originally used, because information, instructions, and programs are not physical entities like memory chips or keyboards. In fact it is the software on a computer system which alone can make it 'come alive'—but without the right hardware, the software has no way of showing its magic!

The software which can potentially run on a computer system can be broadly divided into two categories: *applications software* and *system software*.

Applications software is designed and developed for specific applications which we wish to carry out using a computer, for example 'financial accounting' mentioned above, or any of the applications listed at the beginning of this chapter.

System software makes it possible for us to design, develop and run applications. In this sense, the relation between system and applications software is analogous to the relation between hardware and software. This is depicted schematically in Fig. 1.1, in which an element shown at a higher level makes use of the capability provided by the element at the next lower level.

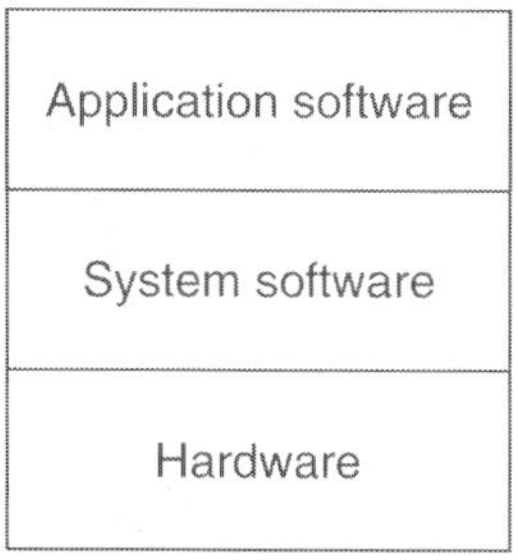

Fig. 1.1 **Relationship between applications software, system software and hardware**

*In earlier days, the processor was more commonly known as the *central processing unit* (CPU), and sometimes simply as *processing unit*. While we treat these terms as synonymous, we shall use the word *processor* in this book (see also Note 6.1 on page 116).

A very useful concept in understanding computer systems is that of an *algorithm*, defined as a clearly specified set of steps to perform a function. For describing an algorithm, we shall often rely on a simple and self-explanatory *algorithmic notation.* The following is an example of an extremely simple algorithm*:

```
repeat the following ten times
{
    read a number from the input device
    multiply it by three
    display the number on output device
}
```

The structure and meaning of this algorithm are self-explanatory. The instruction outside the curly braces causes the three steps inside the braces to be repeated ten times.

In a few places, we may also describe an algorithm using a simple *flow chart,* since its use of graphical notation can sometimes be more effective in communicating the inter-relationship between various steps of an algorithm.

1.5 PROCESSING

On a computer system, we routinely wish to *process information* in various ways, depending on the requirements of our application. As seen above, this is achieved by having the *processor* fetch and execute instructions stored in main memory.

What are the specific functions which a processor needs to perform?

The program—i.e. the sequence of processing instructions—resides in main memory, as does the data which is to be processed. So we may conclude that the processor must carry out the following two steps *repeatedly*:

Step 1: Fetch the next processing instruction from main memory
Step 2: Execute—i.e. carry out—the instruction fetched

The two steps may be called the *Fetch* and *Execute* steps, respectively, in the processing of a single instruction. The basic idea here is that an instruction stored in main memory cannot be executed until it is first fetched—or brought—into the processor. For example, if the instruction fetched is 'ADD A to B', then the *Execute* step of this instruction will result in the indicated numbers being added.

This combination of *Fetch* and *Execute* steps runs as long as the processor is powered up and not explicitly halted. We can therefore describe the working of a typical processor using the following algorithmic notation:

```
repeat forever
{
    fetch the next processing instruction from main memory
    execute—i.e. carry out—the instruction fetched
}
```

**An algorithm is a precise specification of steps according to which data is to be processed. Although algorithms are not the main subject of this book, use of simple algorithmic notation will be helpful in describing the operations performed by a computer system. Brief explanatory notes will be added as appropriate.

The meaning of this notation is clear: The two steps enclosed within the two braces, in that order, are to be repeated indefinitely.

Therefore, if the program—and its required data—are both available in main memory, then by following repeatedly the two steps indicated above, the processor will cause the entire program to be executed. Thus, the processor may be dubbed as the central 'brain' of the computer system—since all actions performed by the system must necessarily take place in response to instructions executed within the processor. We shall look at the processor in much more detail in latter chapters, specifically Chapters 4 to 8.

To gain an understanding of the speeds at which modern processors function, it should be noted that speeds of the order of 10^9 *instructions per second* are quite common in modern processors. We shall also see that, as compared to main memory speeds, a processor today may be at least an order of magnitude faster.

1.6 MEMORY

We see from the discussion above that a computer system needs to be able to *store* information in order to be able to *process* the stored information. Therefore, the two major hardware elements of the system are processor and main memory.

The main memory stores the information which the computer system is going to process, and also the instructions which govern how that information is to be processed. Given a list of a hundred numbers, for example, are we going to add them, or sort them in ascending order, or do something else with them?

Since a computer program is nothing but a sequence of instructions, we can say that the main memory stores *program(s)* as well as *data*. At this stage of development, our simple computer system has the form shown schematically in Fig. 1.2. The *data path* shown between main memory and processor provides for the transfer of instructions and data between the two elements.

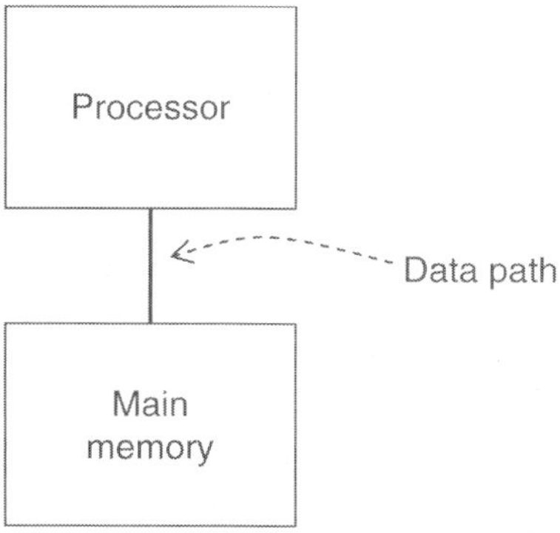

Fig. 1.2 **Simple computer with main memory and processor**

But of course there is more. Modern technology provides us with several different types of storage media. Some are fast, relatively expensive—and *volatile*, in the sense that all the stored information is lost, if we switch off power to the memory. Other media are slower, inexpensive—and *non-volatile*, in the sense that they preserve the information stored even when power is switched off.

Example 1.2

A typical desk-top calculator with memory loses its contents when we switch it off or remove its battery, whereas a music cassette preserves its contents outside the tape recorder, i.e. without any source of power. Thus, we see that the memory element inside the calculator is volatile, whereas the cassette tape provides non-volatile storage.

Today, we cannot afford to lose all the contents of a computer memory when power is switched off. In fact, well-organised and long-term storage of information is one of the very important functions of a modern computer system.

At the same time, we do also wish to process information as fast as possible. We do not want a fast processor to be slowed down because it has been hitched to slow main memory—even if the latter is non-volatile.

In other words, to gain the benefit of speed as well as non-volatile storage, we would like to have in our computer system both of the following:

a. faster main memory for storing programs and data which are being processed, even though this memory may be volatile, and
b. a non-volatile storage element, to provide long-term storage, even though this may be slower than main memory.

With this type of a dual-memory system, our computer system takes the form shown schematically in Fig. 1.3. The non-volatile long-term storage is usually referred to as *secondary memory* or *secondary storage.*

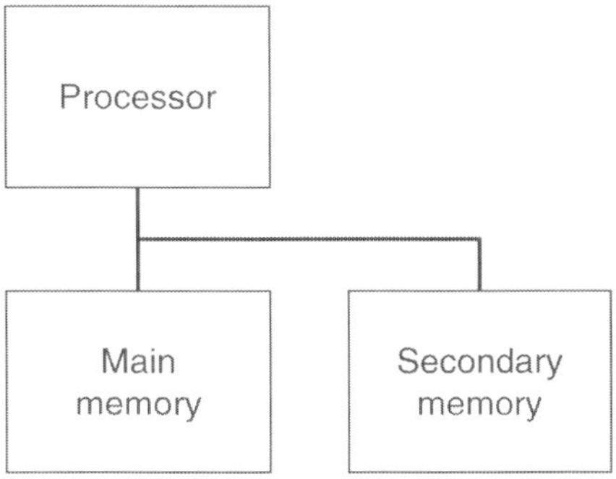

Fig. 1.3 **Simple computer with main memory, secondary storage and processor**

Main memory, which holds programs and data currently under process, is built using semiconductor technology. Semiconductor memory today is fast, of very small size, and inexpensive; however, in its tiniest and most inexpensive version, this memory is volatile.

Secondary storage, used for long-term storage of large volumes of programs and data, is also today extremely compact and inexpensive. The most common form of it is *magnetic disk*, which utilises a magnetic storage medium—similar in principle to what a music cassette uses—organised as a rigid circular disk rotating at a high speed.

A typical personal computer today may have 512 megabytes or more of semiconductor main memory, and 100 gigabytes of magnetic disk storage. Larger systems, such as those deployed in large companies and in support of major websites, would have much larger amounts of main memory and secondary storage available.

An important factor which determines the effective processing speed of a computer system is the speed at which instructions and data can be accessed from its main memory. Main memory systems today have access times less than 100 nanoseconds—i.e. less than 10^{-7} second, since one nanosecond equals 10^{-9} second.

Typical disk storage systems have much longer access times, of the order of 10 milliseconds, i.e. 10^{-2} seconds. Thus a typical disk access may be a hundred thousand times slower than a typical main memory access. These performance characteristics play a key role in the design and operation of computer systems.

1.7 INPUT AND OUTPUT

A computer system must interact with its user(s), with other computer systems, and with various other useful devices connected to it—such as a printer, a CD drive, a digital camera, or a music player.

For interacting with users, a typical computer system is provided with a keyboard, a mouse, and a display screen. The first two of these are *input devices*, while the display screen is an *output device.*

Thus, the processor and memory systems depicted in Figs. 1.2 and 1.3 must be somehow enhanced to indicate these capabilities, known collectively as the *input and output* functionality of a computer system. The range of input and output devices which we may wish to connect to a computer system spans a wide variety—for example, from the relatively slow keyboard and mouse to the much faster CD drive.

The magnetic disk—or any other secondary storage device—must also provide for both input and output, i.e. reading data from the device, and writing data to it. And therefore the interconnections which must be provided to secondary storage device(s) must also be considered a part of the input and output functionality of a computer system.

When we put all these elements together, the computer system depicted in Fig. 1.3 becomes enhanced and takes the general shape depicted schematically in Fig. 1.4.

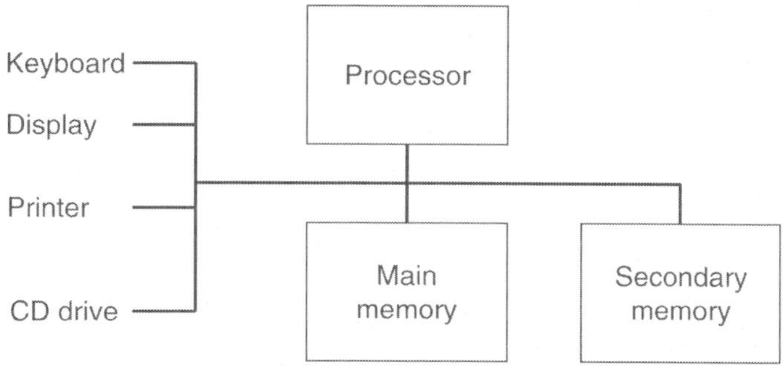

Fig. 1.4 **Computer system with input and output functionality added**

The diagram of Fig. 1.4 depicts the *schematic*, or *logical* organisation of a computer system—so called because it does not bear any essential resemblance to the final *physical* organisation of the system. However, many computer systems, from the very small to the very large, do follow a broadly similar logical organisation.

Example 1.3

A *microcontroller* is essentially a small computer system—including processor, memory, and some input/output capability—in a compact package, especially designed for use in embedded applications.

A microwave oven needs to be provided with simple user interaction functions, timing functions, and the ability to turn microwaves on and off. An embedded microcontroller is the right choice for such an application because of its low cost, compact size, reliability, and the ability to re-program the device for better functionality.

The main subject of this book is the *logical* organisation of computer systems. Many important physical aspects of computer systems—such as *power supply*, *heat dissipation*, and *packaging*—will therefore not be discussed. However, in Section 1.10, we do take a very brief look at how the logical organisation gets translated into a complete physical implementation—a product which can be manufactured, sold and used.

The input and output devices which can be connected to computers today make up a rapidly growing variety in terms of functionality, size, speed, cost, and so on. Given that computer industry today is in every sense a global industry, what is the mechanism to ensure that an input device manufactured in one country works correctly with a computer system manufactured half-way around the world?

Basically, this is done by professional and industry associations which develop *interface standards* for how various kinds of devices and sub-systems are to be interconnected and operated together. As long as two manufacturers build their products according to the relevant standards, their products should be able to work together.

1.8 von NEUMANN MODEL

In the computer system which we have been discussing, the main memory stores both instructions and data in a uniform manner. The hardware does not, for example, reserve one part of main memory for instructions and another part for data.

As a program runs, the processor fetches its instructions from main memory. Execution of instructions within the processor causes data to be *read* from main memory to the processor, or *written* from processor to main memory.

This basic design of a computer system is known as the *von Neumann model*, after the name of one of the main contributors to the early development of computers (see Section 1.2). A single processor and common main memory for programs and data characterise this model.

von Neumann model is not the only conceivable model for a computer system. This can be seen by considering alternative models. In one such alternative model, two different memory elements are provided—one reserved for instructions, and one for data. Such a model can be used for specialised applications such as *digital signal processing*. Another type of system which extends the original von Neumann model is one with multiple processors sharing common main memory, which we shall discuss in Chapter 14.

A fundamentally different model, the so-called *data flow architecture*, has also been proposed with the aim of achieving faster processing rates through systems*. But with the revolutionary advances in VLSI and processor technologies over the last two decades, this particular alternative model has not been able to prove itself.

Thus, almost six decades after it served as the first 'blueprint' of early computers, the simple von Neumann model continues to be employed in most computer systems around the world. This fact testifies both to the basic simplicity of the model and to the creative genius of its original designers and developers.

*The name of Jack Dennis, Emeritus Professor of Computer Science and Engineering at MIT, is most closely associated with this type of architecture.

1.9 DATA PATHS, DATA RATES AND INTERFACES

In the various diagrams seen so far, different sub-systems of a typical computer system are shown interconnected by straight lines. Figure 1.5 is just another rendering of Fig. 1.4, with the interconnections emphasised, and the various sub-systems themselves shown in a lighter shade.

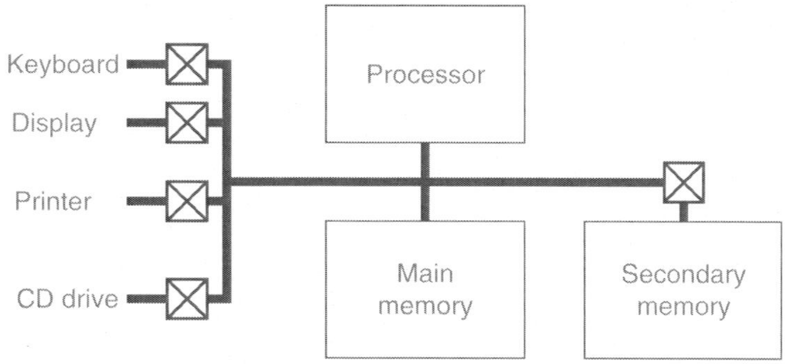

Fig. 1.5 **Computer system of Fig. 1.4, with emphasis on the interconnections between sub-systems**

These interconnections in our diagrams represent electrical connections between the various sub-systems, which transfer information between sub-systems in the form of voltages and currents. Each thick interconnection line in Fig. 1.5 includes in general many single-bit connections, and thus the interconnection carries multiple bits of information *in parallel*. Some of these connections carry so-called *timing and control signals* which are required to accomplish each transfer. Functionally, therefore, these interconnections serve as *data paths* between the various elements or sub-systems.

Also shown in Fig. 1.5 are certain extra components along each data path to an input or output device, each depicted as a small square with a cross inside. These are specialised components which bridge the technical differences between the processor and individual input/output devices. These components are known as *device controllers*; they manage the operations of the devices, under control of the program running on the processor. Often the device controllers also *buffer* data as it is being transferred between the device and the processor or main memory.

A magnetic disk, for example, is a fundamentally different type of a device as compared to the processor or main memory. A *disk controller* makes it possible for a processor to make use of a magnetic disk.

Example 1.4

Suppose two sub-systems, say A and B, are to be connected in such a way that at one time we can transfer 32 bits of information from A to B, or *vice versa*. Then the data path between A and B can be depicted as in Fig. 1.6 (a), where we have placed a small stroke across the line and written the number '32' near the stroke.

This means that the data path between A and B has a *width* of 32 bits. The data path can transfer 32 bits at one time from A to B, or from B to A. If the data path is capable of completing a million such transfers in a second, then clearly it has a capacity of transferring 32 million bits per second.

Most data paths we shall see in this book are *bi-directional*, in the sense of being capable of transferring data between any two devices connected to them, in either direction.

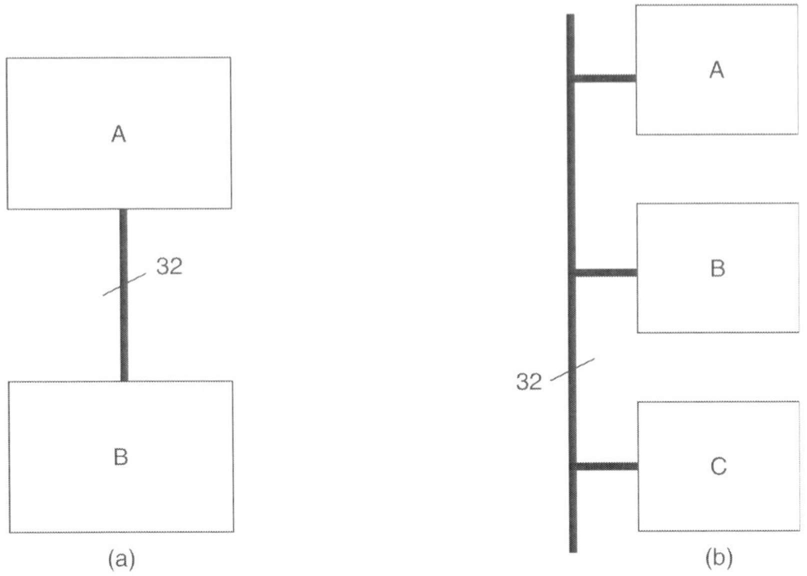

Fig. 1.6 **(a) A data path of width 32 bits between sub-systems A and B, and (b) A bus of width 32 bits with sub-systems A, B and C connected to it**

When an interconnection is capable of connecting together multiple elements or sub-systems, as in Fig. 1.6 (b), it is known as a *bus*. At one time, only one element or sub-system places data on the bus—but one or more elements or sub-systems can 'take in' the data placed on the bus. In this sense, therefore, the bus is a data path which supports transfer of data into multiple destinations in parallel.

Example 1.5

In a computer system, suppose that the main memory is capable of supplying instructions and data to the processor at a rate of 10^9 bytes per second, and that the processor is capable of processing data at this same rate.

Suppose, however, the data path between the two can support data transfers at only half of this rate, i.e. 0.5×10^9 bytes per second. In such a situation, the data path is not able to 'keep up' with the speeds of main memory and processor. We may say that the data path is the 'weak link' in the system.

Such a system would be limited in its performance not by the processor or main memory speeds, but by the limited capacity of the data path between them.

Example 1.5 attempts to show that the various parts of a computer system must be balanced in terms of their performance capability. The overall performance of a system requires its various sub-systems to work in coordination—which therefore means that no single sub-system should become a performance limiting factor.

An analogy may be helpful here. Suppose there is a four-lane highway between cities A and B, but only a single lane road onwards from B to C. Then the limiting factor in traveling from A to C will be the 'slower stretch' of the road, from B to C. To put it in different words, we may say that a chain is only as strong as its weakest link.

In a computer system, the designers must take care that gross imbalances between sub-systems do not become limiting factors in system performance. When two sub-systems, say A and B, are connected together, the data path between them must be designed in such a way that

(i) The data path itself does not become a limiting factor in the performance of A and B, and
(ii) It is possible to substitute another version of one sub-system—for example, sub-system A—without changing either the data path or the sub-system B. This requirement is especially important for the external devices which may be connected to a system.

The second requirement is a form of *modularity*; it is a critical requirement in computer industry, because the various components, sub-systems and devices in a complete system are made by many different companies located around the world.

Therefore it is crucial that various interconnections which may be made to a computer system should be standardised. Electronics and computer industry associations come out with various *interface standards* for different parts of a computer system. The familiar USB—or *Universal Serial Bus*—interface, which is commonly seen on digital cameras, memory sticks, and mobile phones, is an example of such a standard.

To understand the *logical* principles of computer system organisation, a detailed study of interface standards is not essential. However, it is desirable to develop an appreciation of the crucial role of interconnections and the necessity of interface standards.

Example 1.6

If a laptop computer is to be acceptable to a user, it must satisfy several critical user expectations in term of size, weight, quality of display, quality of software, battery capacity, and so on. These user expectations translate into extremely stringent technical requirements which must be satisfied, if the product is to succeed in the marketplace.

In a typical laptop computer, the LCD (or *liquid crystal display*) screen is built into the foldable top cover. For animated graphics, the processor and main memory, which are seated underneath the keyboard, must supply data to the display at a rate which can be of the order of tens of megabytes per second or more.

The interconnection from the processor and main memory to the display screen must necessarily pass through the mechanical hinges provided on the top cover. This mechanically flexible interconnection must continue to function, for example, even when a user is changing the tilt angle of the display screen.

This particular interconnection, therefore, apart from meeting stringent requirements of transfer speeds, must also meet the mechanical requirements of being flexible, rugged, and of a shape which can be passed through from the base to the hinged top cover.

1.10 A COMPLETE SYSTEM

Depending on requirements, computers systems come in many sizes and shapes. As mentioned above, however, all of them have the general *logical* organisation of the type shown in Fig. 1.4. In terms of the *physical* design and packaging, there are of course large differences between computer systems.

Differences between computer systems may be in terms of:

- rate at which information can be processed,
- amount of main memory and secondary memory available,
- variety of input and output devices available,
- quality of graphical display unit,
- power consumption,
- size and portability,
- expandability, i.e. range of 'add-on' options available,
- range of applications possible.

At the small end, computer systems, such as those embedded within mobile hand-sets, take up a few cubic centimeters of space and consume only a trickle of power. At the large end, so-called *mainframe* computers and *supercomputers* may occupy several square meters of floor-space and may have special cooling requirements.

For mobile and hand-held systems, in particular, power consumption is a critical issue, since it determines the time for which the system can be used without a recharge.

In Fig. 1.7, we have outlined in a simple way the *physical* design of a typical modern laptop computer system, which may be said to occupy the middle-ground between the two examples cited above. Apart from 'raw performance', other characteristics—such as ease-of-use, size and weight, power consumption, cooling, robust packaging, and price—play a crucial role in the design of such a laptop computer.

In an introductory text-book on computer organisation, it is neither possible nor desirable to discuss the various ways in which designers can go about addressing these issues. Some of the issues (for example, packaging) require an understanding of other subjects, such as properties of materials and of various manufacturing techniques. Similarly, ease of use is a fascinating issue which requires understanding of subjects known as *ergonomics* and *human factors*.

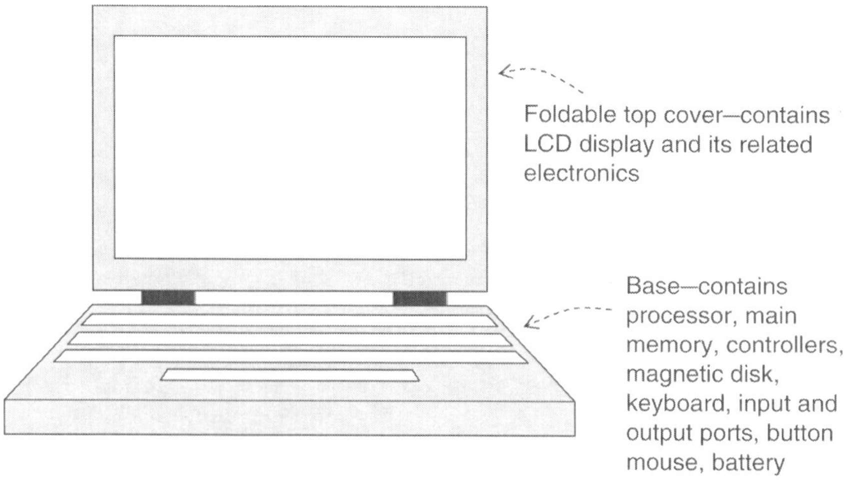

Fig. 1.7 **A laptop PC, an example of a complete system**

Certainly, a student of logical computer organisation should not be expected to also study all these subjects side by side. However, it is desirable that he or she develops at least some awareness about the issues that become relevant when a logical design is translated into complete physical design, on its way to becoming a saleable product.

It is also essential for the student to appreciate that the *logical* principles he or she is studying are applicable to a very wide range of systems, since he or she would work with many different computer systems in the course of a working life.

In the remaining chapters of this book, we shall look at the various important sub-systems which make up a typical computer system. The processor is the central, the most important, and potentially the most complex such sub-system, and therefore a full five chapters of the book are devoted to various aspects of its design and operation.

Before looking at the various specific sub-systems of a computer system, however, we must study how the humble and almost insignificant *bits* can be used to represent— or *encode*—the wide variety of different data types which we expect to process using a computer system. This important topic, known as *data representation*, is the subject matter of the next chapter.

SUMMARY

In this chapter, we took a broad overview of computer systems. After a brief summary of the history of development of computer systems, the basic concepts of *information*, *hardware*, *software* and *algorithm* were introduced. We saw that machine instructions making up a program are fetched by the *processor* from *main memory* and executed.

The various sub-systems making up a computer system were discussed in brief; these include the *processor*, *main memory*, *secondary memory*, *input and output* facilities, and the *data paths* which connect these sub-systems together.

The original *von Neumann* model of computer systems, which is still the most common model in use, was discussed in brief. The design of a complete computer system involves many issues other than the *logical* organisation of a system, and this point was sought to be brought out with a brief description of interface standards, and of a typical laptop PC as an example of a complete system.

REVIEW QUESTIONS

1. When were the earliest programmable computers first developed?
2. Which was the electronic device used in the earliest programmable computers?
3. Which is the electronic device used in computers today in place of the device used in the earliest computers?
4. List three advantages of the electronic device you named in answer to the previous question, as compared to the device used in the earliest computers.
5. Explain in simple words the idea of an 'integrated circuit'.
6. What does the acronym 'VLSI' stand for? How does this relate to the answer to the previous question?
7. What are the two symbols of a binary alphabet?

8. Which is the semiconductor material most commonly used in building electronic circuits today?
9. What are the two basic operations one can perform on a single bit storage element?
10. Which are the two very basic hardware elements of a computer system?
11. What is the difference between application software and system software?
12. Define in simple words the notion of an algorithm.
13. List the two basic steps which a processor performs repeatedly.
14. Which is the part of a computer system which stores running programs and the associated data?
15. What is the difference between a volatile and a non-volatile memory element?
16. What is the role of secondary storage in a computer system? Which is the technology commonly employed in secondary storage devices used today?
17. What is a microcontroller?
18. List some of the physical aspects of a computer system which are not encompassed in a study of logical organisation of computer systems.
19. What is the role of interface standards in designing and operating a computer system?
20. What is the characteristic of the von Neumann model of a computer system?
21. List one model of computer system other than the von Neumann model.
22. What is the role of data paths in a computer system?
23. What is the role of device controllers in a computer system?
24. List at least half a dozen criteria by which two computer systems may differ.

EXERCISES

1. One page of a book contains on an average 300 words, and a word contains on an average 6 characters. On a computer system, such a book is stored in such a way that each character occupies two bytes. How many pages of text can we store in one megabyte of secondary storage on the system?
2. For an application, we need to represent an integer quantity—for example, the serial number of a product—which is in the range from 1 to 999. What is the minimum number of binary digits (i.e. bits) we need to represent this quantity?

   [**Hint:** A single bit can be in one of two possible states, '0' and '1'. A set of two bits can be in one of four possible states, and in general, a string of bits of length k can be in one of 2^k possible states. Find the smallest k such that $2^k \geq 999$.]
3. A product code is to be defined as an upper case English letter followed by two digits, as 'A24' or 'P66', for example. How many distinct such codes can we generate? What is the minimum number of bits we need to represent this code in binary?
4. For an application, we need to represent upper case English letters, lower case English letters, decimal digits, and about forty special symbols (such as punctuation symbols, arithmetic symbols, parentheses, and so on). Thus, the total number of distinct symbols required works out to 100. What is the minimum number of bits required to represent such symbols?

5. Figure 1.8 shows how a 7 × 5 grid of squares can be used to represent English letters, by darkening selected squares in the grid. Examples of letters 'T' and 'g' are shown. Using the same grid, show how you would represent a few more letters (including at least one lower case letter with a *descender*), and a few decimal digits.

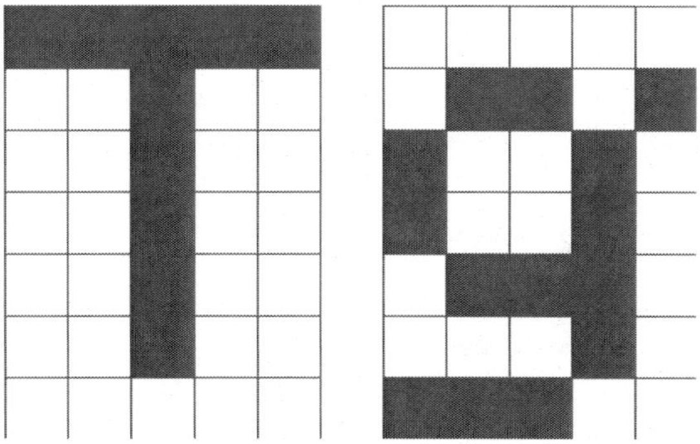

Fig. 1.8 A 7 × 5 grid of squares, with letters 'T' and 'g'

6. The main memory of a computer can read or write one 'word' of four bytes every 50 nanoseconds. What is the maximum sustained transfer rate, in megabytes per second, which this main memory can support?
7. A data transfer bus—similar to the one shown in Fig. 1.5 (b)—is 64 bits wide, and has a 'cycle time' of 10 nanoseconds. What is the maximum data rate this bus can sustain between any two sub-systems connected to it?
8. Consider a microcontroller which is embedded within a digital camera. What are the input and output devices within this system? List a few typical functions which must be programmed into this system.
9. A computer is to be used in a building security application in the following manner:

   Every visitor to a building places his or her right thumb against a device. The device scans the 'thumb-print' and matches it against a stored database of thumb-prints of authorised visitors. If the scanned thumb-print is that of an authorised user, the entrance door to the building opens, with a message 'Welcome to High-Tech Building'. The system keeps a record of all visitors and can print reports.

   What are the input and output devices of this computer system?
10. Operation of a laptop computer consumes 40 watts of power. The battery of this computer is charged for two hours at the rate of eighty watts. How many hours of operation can we expect?

    In calculating your answer, did you have to make any assumption about battery capacity?
11. On the website of your choice, look up the technical specifications of a popular brand of laptop computer. Try to understand as many of the specifications as possible, and classify these specifications as pertaining to either to processor, main memory, secondary storage, or an input/output device.

12. Consider the following simple algorithm:

```
initialise answer to zero
for values of N from 1 to 100
{
   if the value is a prime number
         add value of N to the answer
}
display answer
```

Execute the steps of the algorithm by hand and determine the answer that will be displayed.

13. Consider the following simple algorithm:

```
initialise answer to zero
for values of N from 1 to 10
{
   add value of N to the answer
}
multiply the answer by 2
display answer
```

Execute the steps of the algorithm by hand and determine the answer that will be displayed.

REPRESENTATION OF DATA IN BINARY

2

2.1 INTRODUCTION

We can represent information using the two binary symbols '1' and '0', and we can also find ways to arrange millions of such binary digits—i.e. bits—in a piece of silicon or on a magnetic medium. But a moment's reflection will convince a student that more needs to be done before we have on our hands something useful.

Imagine that Fig. 2.1 depicts a pile of millions of bits of information. The physical size of the pile is irrelevant—the pile could be smaller than a pin-head, as big as a cupful of sugar, or much bigger than that. What is relevant for the present is that we imagine this pile of bits to be completely unorganised.

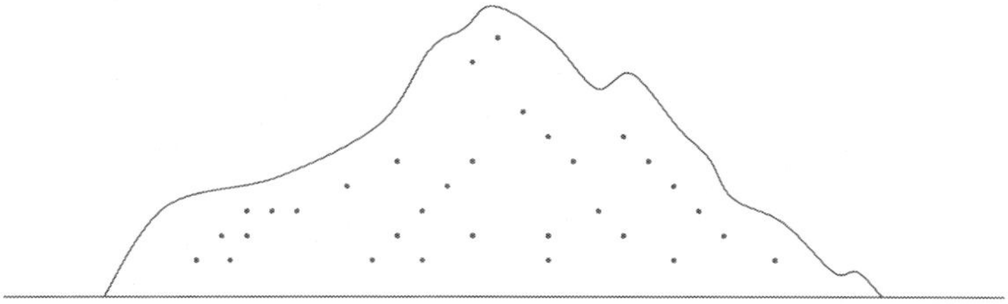

Fig. 2.1 **A 'pile' of bits**

Suppose we know that someone's examination result is somehow 'stored' within this pile, and we need to find it. Can we ever hope to find it? Can we hope to distinguish this useful piece of information from much else which must also be in the pile?

The answer to both these questions is an emphatic NO, and the reason is twofold.

Firstly, how do we know where within this pile of millions of bits lies the important examination result? In other words, how do we find this one piece of information from amongst many others?

Secondly, even if we find the right piece of information, how do we know whether it says 80% (good) or 40% (not so good)?

The first question refers to locating—i.e. *addressing*—the right information within the pile, while the second question refers to knowing its *representation.*

As was mentioned in Chapter 1, we usually deal with information in units much larger than a single bit—thus we may refer to a byte, or a hundred bytes, or a megabyte, and so on. So perhaps we can say that the millions of bits in our pile are really piled up as so many bytes. But then even these bytes need to be organised in some way—because a pile of bytes will not be much more useful than a pile of bits.

So we shall first arrange our millions of bits as a *linearly ordered* set of bytes. This means that, for example, if we have 100000 bytes of storage, these bytes are uniquely identified as byte number 0, byte number 1, and so on, up to byte number 99999. The number which uniquely identifies a byte will be known as its *address**, while the particular bit pattern stored in a byte will be known as its *content.*

Now comes the second question. How do we know that a particular byte, or group of bytes, contains the examination result that we are concerned about?

The answer is: Ultimately only the computer program processing the data can—and must—keep track of the addresses at which specific items of data are to be found. Suppose that the examination score we are looking for is 80; in binary representation, as a single byte, this will look like '**01010000**'. But how do we say that this is not somebody's bank balance, or a house number on a street, or even the letter 'P'?

If the computer program locates and interprets the bit pattern correctly, it will produce the right result; otherwise, the program will make an error. One of the main aims of computer scientists is to develop computer programs which are provably correct; and locating correctly the required item of data, possibly amongst millions of others, is an important issue faced by them in achieving this aim.

In this chapter we shall study how, depending on our requirements, different *types of data* can be represented in binary. By *types of data*, we mean letters of an alphabet, including punctuation marks and other special symbols; positive and negative integers, and fractional numbers. We shall also take a brief look at how graphics, audio, and video information is represented in binary.

In Chapter 3, we shall study how the main memory of a computer system is organised as a linear arrangement of bytes, and in Chapters 4 and 5, we shall study how in fact a computer program locates and processes the data stored in main memory.

2.2 NUMBER SYSTEMS

In mathematics, a *number* is defined as an element of a set on which operations such as addition and multiplication have been defined. Thus the different sets of numbers we know as integers, real numbers, and rational numbers can be defined. A *number system* can be defined as a system of *representation* of numbers using numeric characters, such as '0', '1', '2', and so on.

The simplest number system imaginable is the so-called *unary number system* for positive integers, in which a single character is repeated as many times as the numeric value to be represented. Thus, in this system, the string of characters '|||||||' may represent the integer seven. Naturally, while this system might have worked well for the early man, it is not useful in today's world. The Romans developed another system, in which—to take one example—the decimal number we write as 2008 is represented as MMVIII.

Mathematicians in India developed the decimal *positional* or *place value system*, in which the numeric value of a decimal digit depends on its position or place in the number being represented. This number system requires the use of special digit '0', with numeric value zero, which the Roman number system did not have.

*Why we have numbered the bytes from 0 to 99999, and not from 1 to 100000 as we do in daily life, should become clear very soon.

The decimal place value system is the one we use today in daily life. In the number 505, for example, the first '5' has place value 500, while the second '5' has place value 5. In general, if a number is represented by the string of decimal digits $d_k d_{k-1}..d_1 d_0$, then the digit d_i is multiplied by 10^i to obtain its place value.

In a computer system, we must make use of *binary* representations rather than *decimal* ones. However, as we shall see in the next section, the basic idea of place values holds good in the case of binary numbers as well.

For representing fractional numbers in decimal, we make use of the *decimal point.* The 'point' separates the integer part of the number from its fractional part. Digits appearing after the decimal point have progressively smaller place values—as 10^{-1}, 10^{-2}, and so on. This basic idea can be used to define binary representations of fractional numbers also, except that the 'point' used in binary fractional numbers is called the *binary point.*

In the next few sections, we shall study in some detail the binary representations of numbers. Numerical computations constitute a large part of the work performed by computer systems, and therefore, it is useful to understand the characteristics as well as limitations of these number representations.

2.3 UNSIGNED INTEGERS

Unsigned integers make up the data type which can be represented in binary using the simplest possible technique. To begin with, let us say that we wish to use eight bits—i.e. a byte—to represent unsigned integers. With eight bits, we get a total of $2^8 = 256$ possible binary patterns, since each of the eight bits can be selected in two possible ways. The simplest way to enumerate these 256 patterns is to count up in binary from eight '0's to eight '1's—i.e. from 00000000 to 11111111.

In binary number system, the rightmost bit in an eight-bit number has place value $2^0 = 1$, the second rightmost bit has place value $2^1 = 2$, and so on, until we get to the leftmost bit with place value $2^7 = 128$. Thus 00000000 represents the numeric value zero, while 11111111 represents the numeric decimal value 128 + 64 + ... + 2 + 1 = 255. Thus an eight-bit binary number can represent in a very natural way an unsigned—and therefore non-negative—integer from zero to decimal 255.

Note that the decimal number 255 seen above can be written as:

$$\sum_{i=0,7} 2^i = 2^8 - 1$$

For any other numeric value in the range 0 to 255, the general bit pattern will be:

$$b_7 b_6 b_5 b_4 b_3 b_2 b_1 b_0$$

where each of the b_i's will be either 0 or 1. Therefore the numeric value corresponding to such a binary number will in general be given by:

$$\sum_{i=0,7} b_i 2^i$$

In such a binary representation, b_0 is referred to as the *least significant bit* (or LSB), and b_7 is referred to as the *most significant bit* (or MSB).

Example 2.1

Let us calculate the numeric value in decimal corresponding to the eight-bit unsigned binary number 00100101.

We see here that $b_5 = b_2 = b_0 = 1$, and all the other bits are 0. Substituting these values in the above summation, we get the numerical value in decimal as $2^0 + 2^2 + 2^5 = 37$.

Example 2.2

Now, as an example of the reverse conversion, we shall calculate the 8-bit binary number corresponding to the decimal number 113.

The first step is to write 113 as a sum of powers of 2, which can be done by successively dividing the given number by 2. Through this process, we see that $113 = 64 + 32 + 16 + 1 = 2^6 + 2^5 + 2^4 + 2^0$.

In our notation, this means $b_6 = b_5 = b_4 = b_0 = 1$, and all the other bits are 0. From this, we see that the 8-bit binary equivalent of 113 is 01110001.

When we have binary numbers with more than eight bits, exactly similar reasoning applies. For an n-bit quantity, the bits are numbered from 0 for the rightmost bit (LSB), to $n - 1$ for the leftmost bit (MSB), and thus the place value of the ith bit is 2^i. The range of subscript i in the summation above then goes from 0 to $n - 1$.

Thus a ten-bit unsigned integer can represent a number from zero to:

$$\sum_{i=0,9} 2^i = 2^{10} - 1$$

which equals decimal 1023. In computer jargon, the number 2^{10} = decimal 1024 is known as 1K, where K originates from the Latin prefix *kilo*.

Similarly, a sixteen-bit unsigned integer can represent a number from zero to:

$$\sum_{i=0,15} 2^i = 2^{16} - 1$$

which equals decimal 65535. In computer jargon, the number 2^{16} = decimal 65536 is represented as 64K. In the same way, a 32-bit unsigned integer can represent a number from zero to $2^{32} - 1 =$ 4294967295.

This natural method of binary representation of unsigned integers explains why computer scientists find it most natural and convenient to enumerate any N items from 0 to $N - 1$—rather than from 1 to N.

But clearly there are also difficulties with this type of number representation. For example, the integers 100 and 200 can both be represented in eight bits, since they are within the range of 0 to 255. But their sum 100 + 200 cannot be represented in eight bits. What happens when we try to perform such an addition using eight-bit integers?

To answer this question, it helps to resort to a schematic diagram such as that shown in Fig. 2.2. For clarity of presentation, this diagram only shows <u>four</u>-bit unsigned integers, but it does illustrate the principle which holds good even with a larger number of bits in the representation.

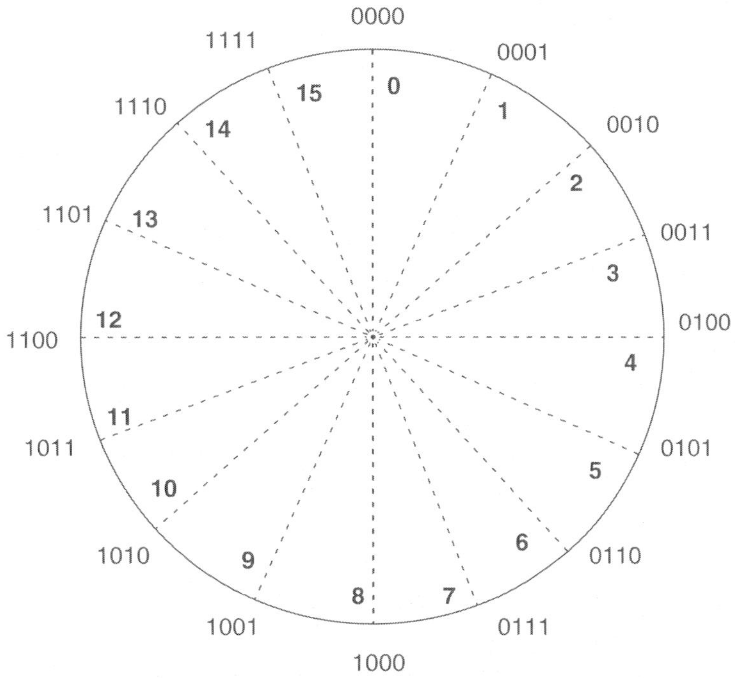

Fig. 2.2 **Four-bit unsigned integers represented along a circle**

With four bits, the sixteen unsigned numbers which can be represented run from 0 to 15. These are shown in Fig. 2.2 along the periphery of a circle, starting from the top and increasing clockwise. Outside the circle, the binary bit patterns have been shown; and just inside the circle, in bolder numerals, are shown the corresponding unsigned numbers in their usual decimal representation.

Suppose we wish to find the value of 3 + 4 on this circle. Naturally, we first locate 3 on the circle, and then count off four more numbers on the circle in the clockwise direction, to arrive at the correct answer 7.

Now suppose we wish to find the value of 8 + 10, which exceeds 15. We locate 8, and then count off ten more steps in the clockwise direction. However, this time we are forced to cross 0 from left to right, so that, after 15, our count becomes 0 rather than 16! Here it seems we take a 'loss' of 16 while crossing 0 from left to right! And therefore our answer comes out as 2, rather than the 18 that we would have liked to see.

In fact, what has happened is that decimal 18 has the binary equivalent 10010, which cannot be represented in four bits. In the process of addition, the leftmost '1' fell off, and we were left with the answer 0010, which is decimal 2. Since the leftmost '1' in 10010 has place value 16, this meant a 'loss' of 16. More technically, the answer is obtained by taking the remainder of 18/16, which is 2. In mathematics, this type of remainder is also known as the result of a *modulo* operation, so that we can say that the result is nothing but (8 + 10) *modulo* 16.

Thus we see that a '1' bit did fall off from the left when 8 + 10 was calculated using four-bit representation; but we must give a more technical name to this 'bit falling off'. In performing binary arithmetic with a limited number of bits, we may even wish to somehow record this fallen off '1' bit, so that we can correct any possible error in the answer. The technical name for this fallen off '1' bit is *carry* or *overflow*. For unsigned integer arithmetic, these two have the same meaning; when we look at signed arithmetic, we will in fact need to distinguish between *carry* and *overflow*.

A similar situation arises when we subtract two 4-bit integers. We find 7 − 4, for example, by locating 7 on the circle and then counting off 4 in the counter-clockwise direction. If we happen to cross 0 from right to left, the answer would be too high by 16. In technical terms, this would once again show up as *borrow* or *overflow*.

The student may note that, when we 'close the circle' at the top from 15 to 0, we go through a discontinuity or 'jump' in the value of the number. The jump is −16 if we go from left to right, in the sense that the next number seen after 15 is 0 rather than 16; similarly the jump is +16 if we go from right to left. Clearly, the discontinuity occurs because the result in either case is not in the range from 0 to 15.

These basic concepts remain unchanged when we perform unsigned integer arithmetic using 8, 16 or 32 bits, except that it becomes very difficult to draw a schematic circle with 2^8 unsigned integers along its periphery! If that task is attempted, the diameter of the circle has to be made large, since the angular separation between successive numbers would be only 360/256 = 1.4 degrees. With 2^{16} or 2^{32} integers, this task should only be attempted in imagination.

2.4 SIGNED INTEGERS

In practice, of course, we also have to deal with negative integers. In mathematics, we indicate such integers with a minus sign '−' in front, as in −20, −330, and so on, with the tacit understanding that an absence of sign indicates a positive number.

Conceptually, the simplest method for indicating the sign of a number in binary is to provide an extra *sign bit* in front of the number—with the understanding that '0' in this bit represents a positive number, and '1' represents a negative number. Such a number representation is known as *sign and magnitude* representation, since we separate the sign of the integer from its magnitude.

Sign and magnitude integer representation has the odd feature of having two forms of zero, since +0 and −0 both in fact refer to the one and only zero of mathematics. Another oddity of the representation is this: Say x is a positive integer. In mathematics, $-(x - 1)$ is obtained from $-x$ by adding 1 to it; for example $-7 = (-8) + 1$. But in *sign and magnitude* representation, $-(x - 1)$ is obtained from $-x$ by subtracting 1 from the magnitude.

For these reasons, in designing hardware circuits for integer arithmetic operations, *sign and magnitude* representation proves to be somewhat unwieldy, and is not much used.

A second method of representing negative integers is to use the *bit-wise complement* of an integer to denote its arithmetic negative. In eight bits, for example, 00110000 equals decimal 48, and therefore we can say that 11001111 will represent decimal −48. Note here that '0' and '1' are the bit-wise complements of each other.

This representation, known as *one's complement*, has the same problem of two zeros—for example, in eight bits 00000000 would be +0 and 11111111 would be −0. For such reasons, this method also proves to be slightly unwieldy in hardware implementation.

In view of the shortcomings of these two methods, over the years the preferred method for representing signed integers in computer systems has come to be the so-called *two's complement* method. We shall therefore study this method in more detail.

Two's complement of an n-bit binary quantity x is defined as the n-bit binary quantity given by $2^n - x$. Note here that 2^n is an $(n + 1)$ bit integer, and that $2^n - x$ denotes bit-by-bit subtraction of the given n-bit binary quantity x from 2^n. The subtraction must be carried out in binary, with a *borrow* from the next higher order bit position in the case that 1 is subtracted from 0 in a bit position.

Example 2.3

Consider once again the eight-bit integer $x = 00110000$, which has decimal value 48. Taking $n = 8$, we get the two's complement of this 8-bit integer as the integer 11010000, as shown in the binary subtraction below:

```
  100000000   9-bit integer 2^8
-  00110000   8-bit integer x
-----------
   11010000   two's complement of x
```

Note that the first quantity above is a 9-bit integer. The student may verify this subtraction by adding once again 00110000 and 11010000; the result will of course be the 9-bit integer 100000000, i.e. 2^8, which is 256 in decimal.

Note that, as an unsigned 8-bit integer, we would say that 11010000 represents decimal 208, but as a *signed two's complement* 8-bit integer it represents the decimal value −48 rather than 208.

This brings us again to the point made at the beginning of this chapter: What the bit pattern 11010000 represents—the unsigned integer 208, or the two's complement integer −48, or even something else—depends finally on the program which processes this bit pattern. Naturally, this means the computer programmer must ensure that his/her program operates on each data type using operations which are appropriate to the data type.

From the definition of *two's complement*, it can also be seen easily that the two's complement of two's complement of x will again be x. This of course agrees with the simple arithmetic property that $-(-x) = x$.

The circle of Fig. 2.3 shows four-bit integers in signed two's complement representation. Once again, outside the circle, the same binary bit patterns have been shown as in Fig. 2.2. Inside the circle, in bolder numerals, are now shown the corresponding signed integers in decimal representation. The range of integers now represented runs from −8 (at the bottom), in the clockwise direction, to +7. Note that the leftmost bit remains 1 for negative numbers and 0 for non-negative numbers—and therefore the leftmost bit is considered to be the *sign bit.*

Suppose we wish to find the value of 3 + 4 on this circle. Naturally, we first locate 3 on the circle, and then count off four more numbers on the circle in the clockwise direction, to arrive at the correct answer 7.

But, in the same way, if we try to find 3 + 5, we get the answer −8 rather than 8! This is because the discontinuity in numeric values is now occurring at the bottom of the circle: +7 is followed by −8, rather than by +8. This is a jump of +16 or −16, depending on the direction in which we move.

With four-bit signed integers, we now have a range of representation from −8 to +7. In general, with n bit representation, the range would be from -2^{n-1} to $2^{n-1} - 1$. Thus, for example, 16-bit signed integers would have the range −32768 to +32767.

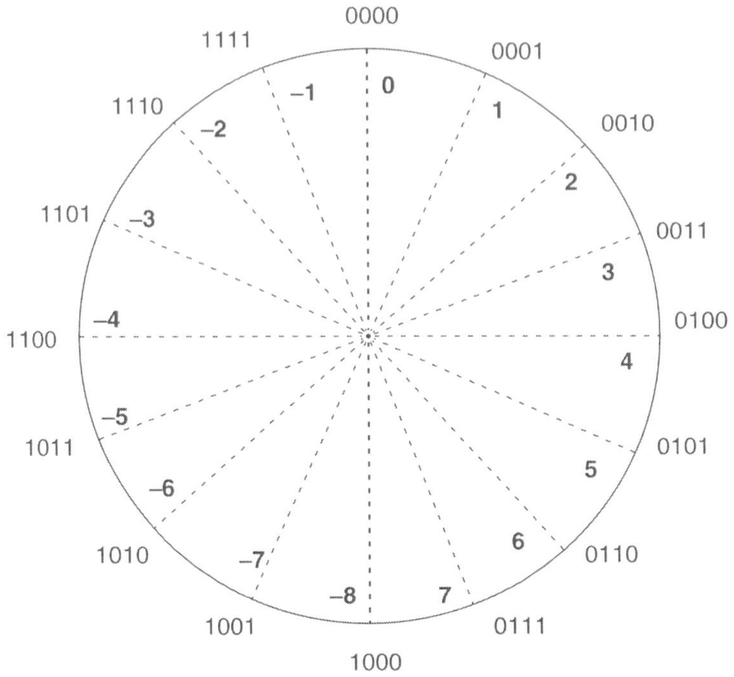

Fig. 2.3 **Four-bit signed two's complement integers represented along a circle**

With signed integer representations, *carry* and *overflow* do not refer to the same condition in an addition or subtraction operation. As we saw before, when we add 1 to the 4-bit integer 1111, which is -1 in two's complement, we get the four-bit integer 0000 with a '1' falling off on the left. This condition is known as *carry*, and it proves useful in implementing arithmetic operations on larger size signed integers. However, no *overflow* occurs in this case because both -1 and 0 are within the range of representation.

However, in two's complement form, when we add 1 to 7, the resulting bit pattern 1000 represents the number -8 rather than $+8$; and a similar thing happens when we subtract 1 from -8. This condition is known as *overflow*, since the correct results $+8$ and -9 are out of the range of representation. *Overflow* usually indicates an error in the result, and the programmer needs to guard against such an error.

Thus we see that carry occurs when we move between 1111 and 0000 (in either direction) on the circle of Fig. 2.3; overflow occurs when we move between 0111 and 1000 (in either direction) on the circle.

Given an integer x, its *two's complement* can also be found in two alternate simple ways.

(i) Find the bit-wise complement of x, and then add 1 to it.

(ii) Starting from the rightmost (LSB) bit of x, scan the bits from right to left. Leave unchanged all the initial 0's on the right, as well as the first 1 coming from right to left. Complement bit-wise all the remaining bits in x.

Example 2.4

Consider once again the eight-bit integer x = 00110000 of Example 2.1.

(i) *Method 1*: The bit-wise complement of x is 11001111. When we add 1 to it, we get 11010000, the answer obtained earlier.

(ii) *Method 2*: Scanning the bits of x from right to left, we leave unchanged the four 0's as well as the first 1 immediately to the left of the four 0's. We then complement bit-wise the left-most remaining three bits 001 of x. Their complement 110 along with the unchanged five bits 10000 again yields the same answer as the two's complement of x.

It can be shown easily that the original definition $2^n - x$ is equivalent to each of these two simple methods for finding the two's complement of x.

Example 2.5

Let us find the decimal equivalent of the eight-bit integer x = 10111100.

(i) *Method 1*: The bit-wise complement of x is 01000011. When we add 1 to it, we get the two's complement of x, which is 01000100, with decimal value $64 + 4 = 68$. Therefore the given number x represents -68 in decimal.

(ii) *Method 2*: Scanning the bits of x from right to left, we leave unchanged the two 0's as well as the first 1 immediately to the left of the two 0's. We then complement bit-wise the left-most remaining five bits 10111 of x. Their complement 01000 along with the unchanged three bits 100 again yields 01000100 as the two's complement of x. Since the two's complement of x has value 68, the value of x is -68.

Two's complement representation is preferred in computer systems for a simple reason—the basic arithmetic operations of addition and subtraction remain unchanged between unsigned integers and signed integers in two's complement form. This important property simplifies the design of the required hardware circuits for carrying out integer arithmetic operations, as we shall see in Chapter 8.

With two's complement representation, the only difference between operations on signed and unsigned integers is the one mentioned earlier—namely, that the resulting *overflow* condition, if any, is interpreted differently in the two cases. The representations of Figs 2.2 and 2.3 should help make this point clear.

2.5 FLOATING POINT NUMBERS IN DECIMAL

We have seen how positive and negative integers, albeit within a finite range, can be represented in binary using a specified number of bits, say 16 or 32. In practice, of course, we also work with numbers which are not integers. Someone may have a bank balance of Rupees 892.50, and a mechanical part may have a weight of 0.752 kg. In science, we even run into quantities such as 1.6×10^{-19} and 6.23×10^{23}.

Range and *precision* are two important aspects of such quantities which need to be understood before a suitable binary representation can be found for them.

The last two quantities above show that our numbers may be extremely small, and also extremely large. Thus these two quantities hint at the kind of *range* we must achieve with our number representation.

Precision in a number representation is viewed in terms of *significant digits* we can accommodate. When we say that a weight is 0.752 kg, what we are really saying is that the weight is closer to 0.752 kg than it is to 0.753 kg or 0.751 kg*. The weight is being reported in this case to the nearest gram.

Suppose instead that the weight is reported as 0.75 kg, which now means that the weight is closer to 0.75 kg than it is to 0.76 kg or 0.74 kg. Now the weight is being reported only to the nearest 10 grams. Thus this second report of weight 0.75 kg has <u>less precision</u> than the first report 0.752 kg. We can imagine that the second report came from a weighing instrument which had less precision.

We say the first report of weight 0.752 kg has three *significant digits*, while the second report 0.75 kg has two *significant digits*. Similarly, the quantities 1.6×10^{-19} and 6.23×10^{23} have, respectively, two and three significant digits.

Considering a suitable number representation for such quantities, we can conclude that it needs to provide sufficient *range* as well as *precision*, since we would not like to be handicapped in either respect when working with numerical quantities.

Let us now examine the two quantities 0.7291×10^{-24} and 0.7291×10^{24}. Note that in both cases the *precision* is signified by the four digits 7291. The position of the decimal point is not really significant, because, for example, the same two quantities can also be written as 7291×10^{-28} and $7291 \times 10^{+20}$ respectively.

Clearly the numerical *range* between these two quantities—from 10^{-24} to 10^{+24}—is signified by the two *exponents* -24 and $+24$. The base 10 in either case has no significance, because it is always implied in any decimal representation.

Just as the base (or *radix*) 10 is implied, we may also similarly make implicit the position of the decimal point. Then these two numbers can also be written in the form of pairs of numbers, say $<7291,-24>$ and $<7291,+24>$. The first element in each pair contributes to *precision*, while the second number contributes to *range*. The decimal point here is assumed to be immediately to the left of the digits 7291.

In technical terms, the first number in such a pair is known as *mantissa*, and the second number is known as *exponent*. When these two are paired together, the resulting number representation allows us to achieve the required range as well as precision. In addition, of course, this number representation must also provide for a separate sign, so that a number such as -0.7291×10^{-24} can also be represented.

Such a number representation is known as *floating point* number representation, since a change in the exponent value causes the implied decimal point to effectively move left or right within the significant digits contained in the mantissa.

It is easier to first understand thus the concept of floating point number system in decimal, since all of us are more familiar with and comfortable with decimal numbers. For building computer systems, however, we must turn our attention next to floating point number representation in *binary*.

---

*This is equivalent to saying that the weight is 0.752 ± 0.0005 kg or 752 ± 0.5 gm.

Note 2.1

A word about *fixed point* number representation is in order here. This representation can in fact be understood as a number system with only mantissa, and no exponent, with the implied decimal or binary point at some *fixed* place within the mantissa.

Financial accounts are usually maintained using such a system. Suppose that the highest amount we wish to record is Rupees 999999, and that we wish to record amounts to the last Paisa. Then our number representation must be of the form $d_7d_6d_5d_4d_3d_2 . d_1d_0$, i.e. with eight significant decimal digits, with the explicit or implicit decimal point two places from the right.

Suppose a school or a college records the average marks of every student to the nearest one tenth of a percent, which means that the average marks of every student are *rounded off* to the nearest tenth of a percent. Allowing for the highest possible average of 100.0, a decimal fixed point representation of the type $d_3d_2d_1 . d_0$ will serve the purpose.

For all practical purposes, *fixed point* arithmetic has characteristics which are similar to those of integer arithmetic. In fact integer arithmetic can be viewed as a special case of fixed point arithmetic, and therefore designers of computer hardware do not usually treat fixed point arithmetic as a separate category.

2.6 IEEE FLOATING POINT STANDARD

When we represent floating point numbers in binary, exactly the same considerations apply, except that the mantissa, the exponent, and the sign must all be represented in binary, using the total number of bits available for the number. Recall here the basic principle that mantissa provides precision, while exponent provides range. Also, in binary, it is advantageous to choose the radix as 2, or an integer power of 2.

To ensure compatibility of data representation used by different suppliers of hardware and software, an international standard for binary floating point number representation was adopted in 1985. In this section, we shall study some key features of this standard, which has become known as the *IEEE Floating Point Standard**.

The two standard floating point number representations in common use, known as *single-precision* and *double precision*, make use of 32 and 64 bits respectively. Of these, we shall first study the single-precision 32-bit floating point number representation.

The stored mantissa in the 32-bit floating point number consists of 23 bits, with the implicit 'binary point' to the left of it. In addition, for reasons which will become clear soon, an extra 'hidden' bit is also implicitly present to the left of the binary point.

It is easy to see that the 'binary point' can be made implicit. Since it is always going to be present in the number at a fixed location, we do not ever need to store it. What this means is that any hardware or software processing such a number must always behave as though there was a 'binary point' to the left of the stored mantissa.

*This international standard is known formally as IEEE Standard for Binary Floating-Point Arithmetic (ANSI/IEEE Standard 754–1985). IEEE stands for *Institution of Electrical and Electronic Engineers*, and ANSI stands for *American National Standards Institute.*

Example 2.6

Suppose the stored mantissa of a binary floating point number is 111100000..0, i.e. four '1's followed by all '0's. The implicit 'binary point' is to its left, so that the decimal numeric value of the stored mantissa by itself is calculated as shown below:

$$.111100000..0 = 2^{-1} + 2^{-2} + 2^{-3} + 2^{-4} = 0.9375$$

With an extra hidden '1' to the left of the binary point, the value becomes 1.9375.

But it requires a little more effort to understand that an extra hidden '1' bit to the left of the binary point can always be assumed to be present.

Consider for example a 24-bit mantissa 011110000..0, in which the leftmost bit is seen to be '0'. The binary point is assumed to the right of the leftmost '0'. Now how can the leftmost '0' bit become '1'?

The answer lies in the following simple observation:

Recall that the mantissa is always paired with an exponent. In the floating point standard, the exponent is taken with an implicit radix of 2. Therefore the mantissa '011110000..0' with some exponent x represents the same number as the mantissa '11110000..0' with exponent $x - 1$. To see this, we need only note that the numerical value of '11110000..0' is exactly twice as large as the numerical value of '011110000..0'.

This means that we can always drop the *leading* '0' bits from a mantissa, by subtracting 1 from the exponent for every dropped '0', until the leading—i.e. leftmost—bit in the mantissa becomes '1'. While dropping the '0' bits from the left of the mantissa, we insert an equal number of '0' bits at its right end. This process can be carried out with the binary point always being assumed immediately to the right of the leftmost bit.

Of course, this procedure does not work if the mantissa has all '0' bits. Therefore, in the IEEE standard, the all '0' mantissa in the standard indicates either the mathematical zero or a special symbol 'infinity', depending on the value of the exponent.

A floating point number which has the implicit '1' to the left of the binary point is known as a *normalised* floating point number. Since this bit is not stored explicitly with the number, in a *normalised* floating point binary number, a 23-bit stored mantissa provides the precision of a 24-bit actual mantissa.

The radix in the IEEE standard floating point representation is chosen to be 2, and in a single-precision number, 8 bits are used to store the exponent. Thus, the unsigned numerical range of this stored 8-bit exponent varies from 0 to $2^8 - 1 = 255$.

Since negative exponent values are also required, the actual exponent is taken as the stored 8-bit exponent minus 127. The stored exponent values of 0 and 255 are reserved to for zero, and the special 'infinity' and 'not a number' symbols; therefore the actual exponent value lies in the range from the smallest value $1 - 127 = -126$ to the largest value $254 - 127 = +127$. Since the stored value of the exponent is 127 greater than its actual arithmetic value, this exponent is said to be in *excess 127* format.

Example 2.7

Consider once again the floating point number of Example 2.4, which has mantissa with equivalent numerical value 1.9375. Suppose now that the actual exponent of this number is 3, which means that the magnitude of the number being represented is:

$$1.9375 \times 2^3 = 15.5$$

Since the actual exponent is 3, the stored value in the 8-bit exponent of the floating point number must be made 127 + 3 = 130. In binary, this value is 10000010.

Now that we have both the mantissa and the exponent, the only bit remaining undecided in the number is its sign bit. If our number is −15.5, say, then the sign bit is '1' and the full 32-bit floating point number is:

Note that—purely for convenience—the 32 bits of the number here have been divided into sign bit, 8 bits of exponent, and 23 bits of stored mantissa. This is the order in which the 32 bits of the single floating point number are stored: i.e. the sign bit, followed by the 8 bits of exponent, and then the 23 bits of mantissa.

Example 2.8

Now let us find the single-precision floating point number equal in value to the decimal number 20.5.

We first write the given number as 41/2. Note that the hidden bit of the mantissa, to the left of the binary point, ensures that the equivalent value of the mantissa lies between 1 and 2. Therefore we factorise the given number as $41/32 \times 16 = 41/32 \times 2^4$.

Now 41/32 will give us the mantissa, while 2^4 will give us the exponent.

We write 41/32 as 1 + 9/32, and then express 9/32 in negative powers of 2 as:

$$9/32 = 1/4 + 1/32 = 2^{-2} + 2^{-5}.$$

Thus the mantissa, including the hidden bit, will be 1.010010…0, and therefore the stored mantissa without the hidden bit will be 010010…0.

The exponent needed is 4, and therefore the stored exponent is 127 + 4 = 131, which in 8 bit binary is 10000011.

Putting together the sign bit, stored exponent, and stored mantissa, we get the answer:

0 10000011 01001000000000000000000

Note again that—purely for convenience—the 32 bits of the number here have been divided into sign bit, 8 bits of exponent, and 23 bits of stored mantissa.

Note here that, if we exclude the sign bit, we have a total of 31 bits in single-precision floating point number representation for the mantissa and exponent. From the discussion in the previous section, we know that the mantissa contributes to precision, while the exponent contributes to range.

What then are the factors which determine that the mantissa must be 23 bits and the exponent 8 bits? This choice in fact involves a *trade-off* between precision and range—i.e. more bits can be devoted to one only at the expense of the other; the sum of these two in single precision being restricted to 31.

Based on the experience of many scientists and mathematicians who had carried out extensive numerical computations using computers, the single-precision standard was defined with these particular sizes for mantissa and exponent.

Numerically, the largest possible mantissa is the one in which all bits are '1', and this mantissa has numerical value of almost 2.0, after we add 1 for the hidden bit. Similarly, the largest possible exponent is $254 - 127 = 127$. The number 2×2^{127} is approximately equal to 10^{38}. Thus the largest number we can represent in single precision is approximately equal to 10^{38}.

The smallest exponent is $1 - 127 = -126$, and correspondingly the smallest normalised number we can represent in single precision is approximately equal to 10^{-38}. As a special case, the zero of mathematics is given the representation of all 32 '0' bits.

With 23 and one hidden bit in mantissa, the single-precision floating point standard provides a precision of approximately $24/\log_2 10$ = seven decimal digits.

In many applications of science and engineering, the precision and range provided by single-precision numbers are not sufficient. For such applications, the standard defines 64 bit *double-precision* floating point number representation, with 52 bit mantissa and 11 bit exponent, with the same concepts of normalisation, hidden bit, etc. The precision provided by double-precision numbers is about 16 decimal digits, while their approximate range is from 10^{-308} to 10^{+308}.

Several other useful features are included in the standard floating point number representation, such as 'infinity' and 'not a number' symbols, rounding modes, guard bits, overflow, underflow, etc. Also included with the standard is the definition of so-called extended precision format. The interested student may refer to the above-mentioned standard for details.

2.7 LIMITS OF REPRESENTATION

In mathematics, both integers and real numbers define sets which contain infinite number of elements. The set of integers is said to be 'countably infinite', whereas the set of real numbers can in fact be shown to be 'uncountably infinite'.

The concept of 'uncountable infinity' of real numbers can be understood in this way: Between any two distinct real numbers, no matter how close they may be, there exist once again infinitely many other real numbers. Most of these real numbers, for example π or $\sqrt{3}$, cannot even be represented using a finite number of digits.

In a computer system, we make use of a finite number of bits to store numbers, either as integers or as floating point numbers. Suppose we are using a 32-bit number representation. Clearly, with such a choice, we can represent at most 2^{32} distinct integers or real numbers—since that is the number of distinct bit patterns possible with 32 bits.

Now 2^{32} is a fairly large number—about four billion—but it is finite. Therefore it follows that infinitely many integers and real numbers of mathematics cannot even be represented in 32 bits. Thus there are limits to our representation of numbers, and it is necessary to have some understanding of what these limits are.

In the case of integers, the answer is simple. If we use unsigned integer representation, and use k bits to store one integer value, then the range of representation is from 0 to $2^k - 1$. Any possible result outside this range generates *overflow* condition. Similarly, in signed two's complement representation, the range is from -2^{k-1} to $+ 2^{k-1} - 1$, and an out of range result generates *overflow*.

In the case of floating point number representation, the situation is a little more complex. The size of the exponent determines the range of representation. We have seen that for single-precision numbers, the range is approximately 10^{-38} to 10^{+38}, whereas for double-precision numbers, it is approximately 10^{-308} to 10^{+308}.

As already explained, the precision of a floating point number representation is determined by the size of mantissa. Accordingly, for single- and double-precision floating point numbers, the precision equals about 7 and 16 decimal digits, respectively.

The smallest magnitude X_{min} which can be represented in single precision is about 2^{-126}, i.e. about 10^{-38}. What then is the fate of the infinitely many real numbers between $-X_{min}$ and zero, and between zero and $+X_{min}$?

Naturally, we should expect that any arithmetic operation that generates a number between $-X_{min}$ and zero must *round* it correctly to one of these two numbers; and similarly any arithmetic result between zero and $+X_{min}$ must be rounded correctly to one of these two numbers. If, for the practical purpose at hand, such *round-off errors* are acceptable, then there is no problem. After all, the computer is a device for practical work, and its results must be judged by that criterion.

The same argument applies to any other real number which cannot be represented exactly in floating point. Irrational numbers such as π or $\sqrt{3}$, and even fractions such as 1/3—in which the denominator is not a power of 2—cannot be represented exactly in single or even double precision. But as long as the round-off error involved is acceptable, the computations can go ahead. In a similar way, any magnitude larger than the largest representable number may be deemed to be 'infinity'.

Within these inevitable limits of representation, any operation on integer or floating point operands can be carried out on a computer system—either in hardware or in software. The processor in any computer system provides some basic arithmetic operations in hardware; even the simplest processors must provide at least 8-bit integer addition and subtraction operations. If an application needs to work with larger size operands than what is available on the processor, then the rest of the work must be done in software.

For example, on a processor with only 8-bit integer addition and subtraction, one can write software to carry out 64-bit—i.e. double precision—floating point operations, including multiplication and division. Such operations will take up many instruction cycles on the processor, and as a result they will be slower in execution. But in some cases, the slower speed may well be acceptable for the requirement at hand.

2.8 OCTAL AND HEXADECIMAL REPRESENTATION

Computer systems store and process all data in binary. Therefore, any data item stored in a computer, of whatever type or size, can be understood and displayed as a sequence of '0' and '1' bits. However, we have also noted that in practice a single bit is a tiny unit of information, and we defined a byte as eight bits of storage.

Similarly, for achieving compactness in displaying binary data, it is convenient to define digits which are 'more expressive' than the two binary digits '1' and '0'. Two systems of representation are commonly used for this purpose:

If we group three binary digits together, we create an *octal* digit, while if we group four binary digits together, we create a *hexadecimal* digit*. A simple example will make this idea clear.

Example 2.9

Let us say the eight-bit binary quantity 11010111 is to be represented in octal as well as hexadecimal.

For octal representation, starting from the right, we divide the given eight bits into groups of three each, adding an extra '0' to the left, as shown:

011 010 111

Now, we encode the resulting groups of three bits into the *octal* digits from '0' to '7' in a straight-forward manner: bits 000 are encoded as octal digit '0', bits 001 are encoded as octal digit '1', and so on, so that bits 111 are encoded as octal digit '7'.

Thus, the given eight bits above have octal representation 327. Note that an extra '0' bit is assumed to be present to the left of the leftmost bit, so as to give us the three bits 011 which map into the single octal digit '3'.

For hexadecimal representation, starting from the right, we divide the given eight bits into groups of four bits each, as shown:

1101 0111

Now we encode groups of four bits into the *hexadecimal* digits from '0' to '9' and then 'A' to 'F' in a straight-forward manner: bits 0000 are encoded as hexadecimal digit '0', bits 0001 are encoded as hexadecimal digit '1', and so on, so that bits 1111 encoded as hexadecimal digit 'F'.

With this encoding, the given eight bits have hexadecimal representation D7.

Example 2.10

a. Let us now convert the octal string 150274 into its equivalent 16 bit binary quantity.

In this case, the rightmost five octal digits generate their equivalent $5 \times 3 = 15$ bits, in a manner which is exactly the converse of what we did in the previous example—i.e. octal digit '0' generates bits 000, and so on. So the rightmost 15 bits of our result are:

101 000 010 111 100

The leftmost sixteenth bit of the result comes from the leftmost octal digit '1'—i.e. the leftmost bit of the result must be made 1. Thus, the required sixteen bit result is:

1 101 000 010 111 100

(For clarity, extra spaces have been added between groups of three bits).

b. Let us convert the hexadecimal string ABCDEF01 into 32-bit binary.

In this case, we simply convert each hexadecimal digit into its 4-bit equivalent binary. As seen above, 'A' becomes binary 1010 (i.e. decimal 10), 'B' becomes binary 1011, and so on. When we do this, the required 32 bit result is:

1010 1011 1100 1101 1110 1111 0000 0001

(For clarity, extra spaces have been added between groups of four bits).

*The words *octal* and *hexadecimal* are derived from Latin words for eight and sixteen, respectively.

Octal and hexadecimal representations may be viewed simply as convenient and compact means of displaying bit strings, since the required information is displayed in a smaller number of digits. Octal and hexadecimal digits can also form the basis of *base 8* and *base 16* integer arithmetic respectively; for our purposes, however, it is not necessary to explore those possibilities.

Note 2.2

Binary coded decimal (BCD) is a representation for decimal integers and fixed point numbers which was commonly supported in the instruction sets of computers of earlier generations. Nowadays, however, with better technologies of processor design and more powerful software development tools, this representation is not always supported in newly designed processors. Section 8.7 discusses in brief BCD number representation and also some issues related to BCD arithmetic.

2.9 CHARACTERS

'Text' in any language is the sequence of characters which make up a piece of writing. For example, the text part of this book, which excludes diagrams, makes up well over half a million characters, while the word 'computer' has eight characters.

What a reader sees of a character is its displayed form. In Fig. 2.4, for example, we see the word 'Computer' displayed in three different combinations of *fonts*, *font sizes* and *font styles*.

Computer	*Computer*	Computer
Times Roman font, size 12	Arial font, size 16, in italics	Arial font, size 20, with 'engraved' appearance

Fig. 2.4 **The word 'Computer' in different fonts, font sizes and font styles**

When seen as 'bare' characters, however, each of the three different visual forms of the word 'Computer' in Fig. 2.4 consists of the same eight characters 'C', 'o', 'm', 'p', 'u', 't', 'e' and 'r'. Since computer systems must store and process such characters in large quantities, clearly a technique has to be found to represent—or *encode*—characters in binary. This is a requirement not only for English, but for all the languages around the world, including languages such as Chinese and Japanese in which the concept of a 'character' is in fact similar to the concept of a 'word' in English.

One basic principle invariably followed in representing characters is this: The displayable attributes of a character—such as *font*, *font size*, *font style*—are considered to be separate from the character itself. In other words, if we take character 'C' as an example, the binary code of 'C' remains the same, no matter in which style or size we may wish to display it. Our discussion, therefore, will focus on 'bare' character codes, and not on the visual ornamentation we add to characters for various practical purposes*.

Taking English as an example language, let us first consider the question of the total number of characters we need to encode in binary.

There are twenty six letters in the English alphabet, each of which may be depicted in either upper case or lower case, giving fifty two characters. Then there are ten decimal digits, 'space' (or 'blank') character, and various punctuation marks, quotation marks, and three different pairs of 'open bracket' and 'close bracket' symbols. In addition, we need basic arithmetic and other symbols such as the plus sign, asterisk, ampersand, percent sign, and so on. The total number of characters comes to just under a hundred, which means that seven bits are needed to encode this set of characters.

In addition to these, certain *control characters* also need to be included with the set, since they can help a computer system to (a) send and receive data from another system, and (b) control the operations of an output device such as a printer. Associated with the printer, for example, is a control character known as *form feed*, which causes the printer to eject the current page and bring in a fresh page, on which it will print subsequent output from the computer.

Taking into account all such control characters, a seven-bit character code known as the American Standard Code for Information Interchange (ASCII) has been defined since the early years of computer industry, with a total of 127 characters. The binary value zero is reserved for a character known as *null*, which has no assigned function, but a programmer is free to assign it a role depending on specific needs of the software. In several programming languages, for example, the *null* character is used to indicate the end of a sequence of non-*null* characters.

Table 2.1 shows the table of all 128 ASCII characters. Other than the header row, this table has 32 rows, and it has twelve columns. In fact, the columns should be seen as forming four groups of three columns each. In each such group of three columns, the header row has the three headings **Dec**, **Hex** and **Char**.

The values under heading **Dec** in the first column run from decimal 0 to 31; the next column **Hex** has the same values represented in hexadecimal, which are therefore seen to run from 00 to 1F. The third column **Char** shows the character which has been assigned the code seen in the **Dec** and **Hex** columns to its left. The control character *form feed* mentioned above, for example, has the code decimal 12 or hexadecimal 0B.

The next three columns of the table once again have headings **Dec**, **Hex** and **Char**. The decimal values now run from 32 to 63, corresponding to hexadecimal 20 to 3F. In these columns, our familiar decimal digits '0' to '9' are seen to have hexadecimal codes from 30 to 39 respectively. These chosen code values have the advantage that the binary value corresponding to a decimal digit can be obtained by simply *masking out*—i.e. making 0—the higher order three bits from the seven-bit character code.

*While there is a great deal of standardisation globally in character codes, that is not always the case with respect to their other attributes such as fonts, sizes, and styles. The latter may vary from one piece of software to another—but the 'bare' character codes remain the same, in the interest of interchangeability of data around the world.

Table 2.1 Table of ASCII Characters

Dec	Hex	Char	Dec	Hex	Char	Dec	Hex	Char	Dec	Hex	Char
0	00	NUL	32	20	(space)	64	40	@	96	60	`
1	01	SOH	33	21	!	65	41	A	97	61	a
2	02	STX	34	22	"	66	42	B	98	62	b
3	03	ETX	35	23	#	67	43	C	99	63	c
4	04	EOT	36	24	$	68	44	D	100	64	d
5	05	ENQ	37	25	%	69	45	E	101	65	e
6	06	ACK	38	26	&	70	46	F	102	66	f
7	07	BEL	39	27	'	71	47	G	103	67	g
8	08	BS	40	28	(	72	48	H	104	68	h
9	09	TAB	41	29	)	73	49	I	105	69	i
10	0A	LF	42	2A	*	74	4A	J	106	6A	j
11	0B	VT	43	2B	+	75	4B	K	107	6B	k
12	0C	FF	44	2C	,	76	4C	L	108	6C	l
13	0D	CR	45	2D	-	77	4D	M	109	6D	m
14	0E	SO	46	2E	.	78	4E	N	110	6E	n
15	0F	SI	47	2F	/	79	4F	O	111	6F	o
16	10	DLE	48	30	0	80	50	P	112	70	p
17	11	DC1	49	31	1	81	51	Q	113	71	q
18	12	DC2	50	32	2	82	52	R	114	72	r
19	13	DC3	51	33	3	83	53	S	115	73	s
20	14	DC4	52	34	4	84	54	T	116	74	t
21	15	NAK	53	35	5	85	55	U	117	75	u
22	16	SYN	54	36	6	86	56	V	118	76	v
23	17	ETB	55	37	7	87	57	W	119	77	w
24	18	CAN	56	38	8	88	58	X	120	78	x
25	19	EM	57	39	9	89	59	Y	121	79	y
26	1A	SUB	58	3A	:	90	5A	Z	122	7A	z
27	1B	ESC	59	3B	;	91	5B	[	123	7B	{
28	1C	FS	60	3C	<	92	5C	\	124	7C	|
29	1D	GS	61	3D	=	93	5D	]	125	7D	}
30	1E	RS	62	3E	>	94	5E	^	126	7E	~
31	1F	US	63	3F	?	95	5F	_	127	7F	□

Example 2.11

Suppose the numerical character decimal '7' in ASCII code has to be converted to its equivalent value in binary.

Table 2.1 shows that the code for '7' is hexadecimal 37, which in seven bit binary is equal to 0110111. When we *mask out* the higher order three bits from these seven bits, we get 0000111, which is nothing but the decimal value 7 represented in binary.

Of course another simple way to calculate the numerical value of the character '7' is to simply subtract the code of '0' from the code of '7'. This method works because the code values of decimal digits are assigned consecutively, in increasing order, from hexadecimal 30 to 39.

The next three columns of the table have decimal values running from 64 to 95, corresponding to hexadecimal 40 to 5F; these columns have the twenty six upper case English letters and some other characters. The last three columns of the table have decimal values running from 96 to 127, corresponding to hexadecimal 60 to 7F; these columns have the lower case English letters and some other characters.

As we have seen, an eight-bit *byte* is a common and convenient unit of storage in computer systems. Since ASCII is a seven-bit code, the question naturally arises: How are seven-bit ASCII characters stored in eight-bit bytes?

In other words, suppose we have seven bytes, i.e. $7 \times 8 = 56$ bits, of storage available. In theory, these seven bytes can store eight ASCII characters. But this type of storage would create the problem that stored characters would cross *byte boundaries*—requiring tricky handling in software, since almost all computer instructions operate within byte boundaries.

Instead, it is much simpler to store just seven ASCII characters in these seven bytes of storage, following the simple rule of one character per byte. This means that the higher order one bit in each byte is unused, but that is a small price to pay for the simplicity achieved. Besides, any software is free to use this one unused bit in an innovative way, depending on its specific requirements.

So much for English. As we know, there are many other languages in use around the world, using different alphabets. If the letters of any such alphabet, including the special symbols seen above, can be encoded in seven or eight bits, then in theory all we need is a different code table for each such language, similar to the one shown in Table 2.1. The software making use of text data must be informed, of course, about the language being used, so that the correct code table for the language is employed by the software.

For languages such as Chinese and Japanese, however, an eight-bit code does not suffice. The number of characters to be represented in these languages runs into thousands, since each complex 'character' in effect performs the role of a word in English, and cannot be compared to a mere letter of an alphabet. To accommodate such writing systems, and also many alphabet-based languages such as Hindi and Telugu, a code known as Unicode has been standardised*. Using two byte code, Unicode can accommodate up to $2^{16} = 65536$ characters, and there is also provision for extending the code to three bytes.

*Information and resources are available at www.unicode.org.

2.10 AUDIO, VIDEO AND GRAPHICS

A computer system handles more than just data in the form of integers and characters, and therefore it is necessary to take at least a cursory look at how a computer system represents information which is in the form of graphics, voice and video images.

Sound is generated and received in the form of acoustic waves in air, the natural medium for carrying sound. The human vocal tract and ears are the wonderful biologically evolved mechanisms to generate and receive sound. Compared to the human vocal tract, musical instruments can generate sound over a higher frequency range. For storing and processing in a computer system, and for sending it over a communication network, the acoustic sound signal is converted to electronic form and *digitised*, which means that the original sound signal is converted to a sequence of electronic '1's and '0's.

The quality of sound reconstruction needed may vary from one application to another; for example, we need only 'telephone quality' sound from a phone system, but 'high fidelity' sound from an expensive music system. Depending on the sound quality and fidelity required, one second of digitised sound requires from a few kilobits to a few tens of kilobits of storage. The basic aim of the science of representation in this case is to get the required quality of sound with as little storage as possible. Any saving achieved here gives an added advantage—more compact storage also means less cost in sending such a digitised signal across a communication system.

Similar considerations apply when we consider 'video'—i.e. visual—information, but with two crucial differences:

a. Visual information may be required either in *static* or in *animated* form—i.e. still pictures or moving pictures, whereas there is no such thing as a *static* sound signal.
b. One second of digitised video signal requires a much large number of bits to represent—i.e. *encode*—than one second of sound.

From the earliest days of cinema, almost a hundred years ago, we have known about human *persistence of vision*—if twenty five or thirty static but gradually changing picture frames are shown to a person in one second, the perception is that of seeing an animated 'film'. This principle is at the heart of all film and television production.

Therefore, an animated film is nothing but twenty five or thirty successive static picture frames shown per second. We may therefore say that if one static picture requires n bits of storage, then one second of film will require of the order of $30n$ bits of storage. Once again, the science of representation tries to achieve the required video quality with the smallest possible number of bits used per frame, or per second of film.

By graphics, we mean here computer-generated graphics, which may be simple diagrams, such as those in this book, or much more complex graphics, such as an animated model of a sports car displayed on a computer screen. In essence, any such graphic can be viewed as being defined by so many line segments, each with its own two end-points. Areas enclosed by such line segments are filled with the required colors.

This means that the information required to generate such a graphic consists of (i) geometrical coordinates of end-points of line segments (in two or three dimensions), and (ii) color codes for the various parts of the graphic. Thus, the information required to generate the graphic becomes numerical—for example, every end-point of a line segment is represented using integer or floating point format. It is then the job of so-called *rendering software* to display such an encoded graphic correctly on the display screen of the computer, or to print it out on a printer, etc.

We have taken here only a cursory look at how graphics, audio and video signals are represented in digitised form. For more details, the student may look up a good book on *Computer Graphics* or on *Multimedia Systems*.

We may however, note here one feature that all such representations have in common. There is no single unified encoding standard for graphics, audio and video signals. It is the application software—for example, the media player or design software on a PC, or the software inside a digital camera—which must correctly *encode* or *decode* the graphics, audio or video signals, as the case may be.

2.11 ERROR DETECTION AND CORRECTION

Computer systems today store, process and communicate various types of data, each in its appropriate binary representation. Within the system, all binary data is represented in the form of voltages, currents, or patterns of magnetisation on a medium.

As a computer system operates, such data is read, written, transferred over internal data paths, or communicated from one system to another. Electronic signals carrying the data are, however, subject to several forms of unwanted disturbances of random nature, which are collectively known as *noise*. For example, if a TV set is switched on near a computer, electromagnetic noise from the TV set will reach the electronic circuits within the computer. System designers must therefore protect the system and its operations from adverse effects of such noise.

The basic effect of noise on data is that the process of data transfer or communication from one point to another may not take place with perfect integrity. In other words, some bits in the data may be in *error* when they are received at the other end. Since this is not acceptable, the following two basic techniques are employed to reduce the probability of such errors in a system:

(i) Circuits and data paths within the system are designed in such a way that, to the extent possible, they are *shielded* from the physical effects of noise. This technique lies within the domain of electronic and physical design of circuits.

(ii) In the coding of data in binary, extra care is taken so that, at the receiving end, errors in the data may be *detected* and also, if possible, *corrected*. Mathematical techniques have been developed over the decades to achieve such *error detection and correction*. In this section, we shall take a brief look at the basic concepts used in these techniques.

Let us assume that a *message* of length k bits is to be sent from source A to destination B. Due to the effects of noise, one or more bits of the message may be received in error at B. Our aim is to detect if such a thing has happened and, if possible, to correct the error.

The basic point to note in this context is that no error detection is possible unless some *redundancy* is introduced into the message when it is sent from A to B. This is the key concept here, and it can be understood in the following way:

At the source A, with message length of k bits, the total number of possible messages is 2^k. Each one of these 2^k messages is *valid*, in the sense that A can select any one of these messages to send to B.

Suppose that, on its way from A to B, due to the effects of noise, a valid message M_1 gets changed to another valid message M_2.

At the destination B, if a valid message M_2 is received, there is absolutely no logical basis for the receiver to conclude that an error caused some unknown M_1 to be changed to M_2. The only logical decision at B is to conclude that the message sent was M_2. In other words, if a valid message is received at B, the error must go undetected.

Therefore, simple logic tells us that, in order to conclude that an error has occurred, B must receive something other than a valid message. Clearly, if B receives a 'garbled' message which is not even defined as a valid message, then B can conclude that an error has occurred, because A is going to send only valid messages.

Therefore the set of 'receivable messages' at B must include valid as well as 'garbled' messages, i.e. the set must be larger than 2^k. Assume that we add r extra bits—known as *redundancy bits*—to every valid message sent from A, in such a way that the r extra bits are computed from the k bit message. We say that the k bit message and the r extra bits together make up a *codeword* of length $n = k + r$.

Now, the number of codewords receivable at B is $2^n = 2^k \times 2^r$. Of these, however, only 2^k codewords represent possible error-free valid messages sent by A. Any other codeword received at B must indicate an error, i.e. this scheme gives us error detection. Note here that, for every valid codeword, there are $2^r - 1$ possible invalid codewords.

Example 2.12

The simplest possible way in which we can add redundancy to a k-bit message is to add an extra *parity* bit to the message according to the following rule:

$$\text{parity bit} = \begin{cases} \text{'1'} & \text{if number of '1' bits in message is odd} \\ \text{'0'} & \text{otherwise} \end{cases}$$

The parity bit added to the message is '1' if the number of '1' bits in the original message is odd, and '0' otherwise. Therefore, with this added parity bit, a valid codeword always has an even number of '1' bits; we say that it has *even parity*.

If an invalid codeword—i.e. one with odd parity—is received at B, we must conclude that at least one bit in the received codeword is in error. This means that we have been able to detect a single bit error; however, since we do not know which bit is in error, we have no means to correct the error.

If a codeword with even parity is received at B, it must be assumed that no error has occurred in transmission of data from A to B. This means that, if the transmission of data caused two bits to be in error, the double-bit error will go undetected.

Thus, the technique of using a single parity bit gives us the capability to detect single-bit errors, but no capability to detect multiple errors or to correct any errors.

For achieving error correction, the computation of the r redundancy bits is in effect repeated on the codeword received at B. The result of this computation determines the most probable valid codeword to have been sent from A—and this codeword is accepted as the corrected version of the codeword received.

When an uncorrectable error is detected in data at the receiving end, one possible strategy to deal with the error is to request re-transmission of the data.

Within a computer system, suitable form of error detection and correction is applied to data stored in main memory and on secondary storage devices, and on data transmitted and received over communication links. Internal data paths within the system also have some form of error detection and correction built into them.

Error correction is not feasible when larger blocks of data are transmitted, for example, blocks containing a few thousand bits or more; but it is necessary to detect multiple-bit errors in such blocks. In such cases, redundancy is added to the transmitted block in the form of a *check sum*; this check sum is re-calculated at the receiving end, and any mismatch with the transmitted check sum indicates an error.

When audio and video data is transmitted across a computer network, occasional errors in the received data are acceptable. Sound and pictures usually contains plenty of inherent redundancy; and, based on past learning, the human mind can perform excellent error correction on received messages. For example, every reader of this book will be able to correct the error deliberately made in the word 'cmoputer'.

We also make use of message redundancy in daily life. When communicating over a noisy or a weak phone connection, we say "N for New Delhi", rather than simply "N"—since the 'redundant' information added helps the person at the other end to understand the received sound correctly.

SUMMARY

Computer systems today deal with a vast variety of data. Since the hardware and software of computer systems can operate only on binary representations of data, it becomes necessary to encode all forms of user data into binary. In this chapter, we discussed the key principles of how this is done.

In particular, we studied the techniques for binary representation of integers, floating point numbers, and characters. Integers and floating point numbers provide the basis for all mathematical operations performed on computers, and also for the representation of more complex types of objects—such as, for example, computer-generated graphics.

For signed integers, we make use of two's complement representation. Floating point numbers are represented using separate sign bit, exponent, and mantissa. IEEE Floating Point Standard defines the commonly used single-precision and double-precision formats, which make use of 32 bits and 64 bits respectively. The two important attributes of a floating point number representation are range and precision.

We also discussed in brief the important issue of the limits of binary representation of data. Later in the chapter, we took a brief look at the basic techniques of encoding graphics, audio and video data in binary.

Noise in an electronic system can cause errors in data while it is stored or when it is transferred from one part of the system to another. Some error detection and correction techniques must therefore be employed within the system, and we took a brief overview of the very basic concepts underlying these techniques.

REVIEW QUESTIONS

1. List the two important conditions which must be satisfied in the organisation of any useful medium of storage of binary information.
2. List the different types of data which a user may need to work with on a modern computer system.
3. What is a 'number system'? Give an example.
4. Calculate the numeric value corresponding to unsigned 8-bit integers (i) 00001111 and (ii) 11110000.
5. What is the largest unsigned integer which can be represented in 12 bits?
6. What is the largest unsigned integer which can be represented in 14 bits?
7. What is the smallest signed integer which can be represented in 14 bits using two's complement representation?
8. Note that two diametrically opposed numbers in Fig. 2.2 differ in value by 8. Note the difference in bit patterns between two such numbers, say 3 and 11.
   Now imagine a similar circle drawn for 8-bit unsigned numbers. On this circle, what will be the number located diametrically opposite 0? Opposite 20?
9. What is the decimal value of the 5-bit quantity 10101 in sign and magnitude representation?
10. What is the decimal value of the 5-bit quantity 10101 in one's complement signed representation?
11. State the basic reason why two's complement representation of signed integers is used in computer systems.
12. Draw the circle representation similar to Fig. 2.2 for (i) 3-bit and (ii) 5-bit unsigned integers.
13. Draw the circle representation similar to Fig. 2.3 for (i) 3-bit and (ii) 5-bit two's complement signed integers.
14. State two important attributes which a number representation should have so as to allow fractions as well as very large and very small quantities to be represented.
15. If the temperature T of a fluid is reported as being 15.2° centigrade, what is the specific range of values within which T lies? What is the number of significant digits in this temperature reading?
16. If the weight W of a machine part is reported as being 0.47 kg, what is the specific range of values within which W lies? What is the number of significant digits in this reported weight?
17. What are the two parts other than sign of a number in floating point representation?
18. Of the two parts other than sign of a number in floating point representation (see previous question), which one contributes to the range of representation, and which one contributes to its precision? Why?
19. What is the size in bits of an IEEE standard floating point number in (i) single-precision representation, and (ii) double-precision representation?
20. What is a normalised binary floating point number?

21. Define the excess-127 format of the exponent in IEEE standard single-precision floating point number representation.
22. What is the basic trade-off involved in choosing the sizes of the mantissa and the exponent in a floating point number representation?
23. What are the approximate ranges of numbers which can be represented in IEEE standard single-precision and double-precision formats? Justify the answers in brief.
24. What is the approximate precision of numbers which can be represented in IEEE standard single-precision and double-precision formats? Justify the answers in brief.
25. List the main categories of characters which must be encoded in the English alphabet. Show that six bits are insufficient and that seven bits are sufficient for representing all these characters.
26. What is the full form of 'ASCII', the most widely used character code?
27. Let *ASCII*(x) represent the numerical value of the ASCII code of character x, and let X and x respectively represent the upper and lower case versions of a character of English alphabet. Verify using Table 2.1 that *ASCII*(X)-*ASCII*(x) has the same value for all letters of the alphabet.

EXERCISES

1. Find sixteen-bit binary representations of the following unsigned decimal integers:

   15, 23, 31, 32, 1023, 4095, 4096

2. Find the sixteen-bit two's complement representation of the arithmetic negatives of the integers of Exercise 1.
3. Find the decimal equivalent of the following sixteen-bit binary integers assuming that they are (a) unsigned integers, and (b) signed two's complement integers.

   0000000011110000, 0000111100000000, 1111000000000000, 1111000011110000

4. A particular computer system makes use of eighteen-bit binary quantities as (a) unsigned integers and (b) signed integers in two's complement representation. Find the range of integers which can be represented in each case.
5. Find the standard single-precision binary floating point representation of the following decimal numbers:

   $0.75, 13.75, 2 \times 10^6, 256 \times 10^6, 0.2$

   Note: The last of these numbers cannot be expressed exactly as a sum of powers of 0.5. Therefore, its nearest approximation will have to be found in terms of powers of 0.5; this will become tedious, but an attempt should be made.
6. A particular computer system makes use of a non-standard floating point number representation, with a 25-bit mantissa and 10-bit exponent stored in excess 511 form. The implicit extra '1' bit of the mantissa is also utilised. Find the approximate precision and range provided by this representation.

7. Convert the following twelve-bit binary strings to (a) octal, (b) decimal, and (c) hexadecimal representation:

010101010101, 101010110111, 100110101111

8. Convert into 16-bit binary equivalent, the octal strings given in (a) and the hexadecimal strings given in (b) below:
a. 145327, 177777, 77777, 100000, 22
b. AB71, 16FF, FFFF, A89E, FF

9. Convert into unsigned decimal equivalent, the binary strings obtained in answer to parts (a) and (b) of the previous exercise.

10. The string of four ASCII characters 'ABPQ' is given to you. Looking at Table 2.1, outline how you would convert such a string to its *lower case* equivalent, i.e. 'abpq' in this case.

Hint: Consider the difference Δ between the numerical code of 'a' and the numerical code of 'A', and apply this amount of 'correction' to each character of the given upper case string. See Review Question 27 above.

11. The string of three ASCII characters '327' is given to you. Since all three characters in this string are octal digits, it should be possible to convert this string into its equivalent nine-bit binary string, which in this case is '011010111'. Verify this, and then outline a procedure by which you will be able to convert any such ASCII string $d_2d_1d_0$ of three octal digits into its equivalent binary string.

Hint: By dropping higher order bits, first convert each of the three ASCII digits to its three-bit binary equivalent—i.e. character '3' becomes binary 011, and so on. Concatenate the resulting bits.

12. The string of four ASCII characters 'A387' is given to you. Since all four characters in this string are hexadecimal digits, it should be possible to convert this string into its equivalent 16-bit binary representation. Verify this, and then outline a procedure by which you will be able to convert any such ASCII string $d_3d_2d_1d_0$ of four hexadecimal digits into its equivalent 16-bit binary string.

13. The string of four ASCII characters '4387' is given to you. Since all four characters in this string are decimal digits, it should be possible to convert this string into an equivalent 16-bit binary representation. Verify this, and then outline a procedure by which you will be able to convert any such ASCII string $d_3d_2d_1d_0$ of four decimal digits into its equivalent 16-bit binary string.

Hint: Concatenation of bits, as in the previous two examples, will not work!

14. In an error detection and correction system, every message of length k bits is provided with r redundancy bits. Show that, for every valid codeword, there are $2^r - 1$ invalid codewords in the system.

HARDWARE BUILDING BLOCKS

3

3.1 INTRODUCTION

In this chapter, we take a look at the basic building blocks of computer hardware. This is in fact a vast subject, to which a lifetime of fruitful study and research may well be devoted. But our purpose here is limited, and defined mainly by the following two somewhat conflicting constraints.

On the one hand, it is not possible to study computer organisation without paying at least some attention to these hardware building blocks. But, on the other hand, a detailed study of these building blocks would take us into the subject matter of electronics, which is not the aim of this book. Therefore, we have to chart a careful middle course—to understand sufficiently well the functions of these hardware building blocks, without losing our way and wandering into the magical world of electronics.

Of course, a little peek into the magical world of electronics is certainly in order.

3.2 ELECTRONICS

An electron is an elementary particle, which means an incredibly tiny, indivisible constituent of all matter. Physical properties of the matter around us are determined by the arrangement of elementary particles within it—mainly the electron, the proton and the neutron. These three combine to form atoms, which in turn combine to form molecules of many different substances, for example, oxygen, water, starch, and DNA.

Amongst the three elementary particles mentioned, only the electron has the double benefit of being extremely light as well as electrically charged. What this means is that useful things can be done by making electrons move about—or <u>not</u> move about—in various well-defined ways. For example, a microphone is a device which senses sound waves and converts them into corresponding movement of electrons.

Movement of electrons through any medium is known as electric *current*. But electrons can also be forced to bunch up together without moving, resulting in the creation of what is known as electric potential, or *voltage*. Thus *voltage* and *current* can be thought of as two basic and complementary ways in which the behavior of electrons can be measured and controlled, the aim being to obtain something useful in return.

Electronics is the name given to the art, science and technology of getting electrons to do useful things, such as having music played through a speaker, or having moving pictures shown on a television screen. The subject matter of electronics is, in other words, to learn how electrons behave in different media, and then to exploit that knowledge in clever ways to achieve various ends.

Until about a century ago, physicists were not even aware that there existed in nature a light, charged particle such as an electron. However, since its discovery and the subsequent in-depth study of its properties, increasingly ingenious ways have been found to harness these properties in ways which were quite literally unimaginable to earlier generations. Modern computer and communication systems—which have transformed the world we live in—are among the many products of the historically amazing burst of ingenuity which followed the discovery of the electron.

Materials through which electrons can flow freely are known as *conductors*, and materials which totally block the flow of electrons are known as *insulators*. But, between these two extremes, there are also materials—known as *semiconductors*—through which the flow of electrons can be regulated fairly accurately. These materials constitute the bulk of electronic technology today, the most prominent semiconductor material in this respect being silicon.

As we saw in the previous two chapters, all possible forms of information can be represented—or encoded—in appropriate patterns of binary symbols, i.e. '0's and '1's. Now suppose, we could achieve each of the following objectives using electronics:

a. Utilise two distinct electronic states to represent, respectively, the binary symbols '1' and '0', to provide a physical realisation of the notion of *one bit of information.*
b. Build an electronic system in which a large number of bits—hundreds of millions, for example—could be reliably stored, written as input, or read as output.
c. Provide the system of (b) above with the means of *processing* the information stored according to well-defined instructions.

If these objectives can be achieved, we have in our hands an electronic information processing system. As we all know, not only have these objectives been achieved, but the resulting systems are becoming more and more efficient and powerful by the year. These resulting systems—which are commonly known as *computer systems*—form the core subject matter of this book.

Clearly objectives (b) and (c) can be achieved only after we have a reliable way of achieving (a). Therefore, we must take a brief look at how, using electronics, two distinct states can be achieved which can represent the binary symbols '1' and '0'.

One of the most useful of all electronic devices is the *transistor*, and this device can be operated *electronically* as a simple ON–OFF switch. Note that such a switch is basically a two-state device. When we connect its two ends to two different voltages (say 5 volts and 0 volt), the voltage at the output of the switch takes on one of these values, depending on whether the switch is in one state or the other, as shown in Fig. 3.1.

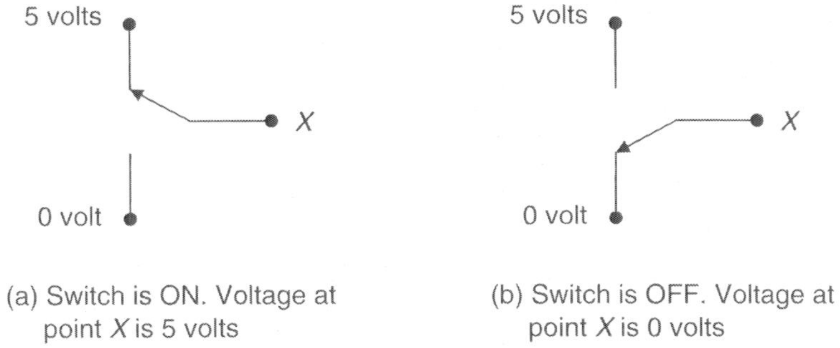

Fig. 3.1 **An ON–OFF switch and its two possible output voltages**

So basically the electronic device which gives us the answer to objective (a) above is the transistor, operated electronically as an ON–OFF switch.

How do we go about achieving objectives (b) and (c)?

For achieving electronic storage of a large number of bits, transistors are arranged in a rectangular array, or grid. At each intersection of a row and a column in this grid, a single bit of storage is provided. Of course, appropriate means have to be provided to *read* or *write* any single bit in this grid. A typical semiconductor memory element built on such a principle is discussed in Section 3.6.

For objective (c), i.e. processing the information stored, we must first consider two further basic questions: (i) how a single bit can be processed, and (ii) how two or more bits can be processed together. We address these questions in Sections 3.2 and 3.3.

The type of electronics we utilise to address the objectives (a), (b) and (c) listed above, and also the two basic questions (i) and (ii), is known as *digital electronics*—the reason being that here we work with the electronic counterparts of the *binary digits* '1' and '0'.

Note 3.1

Electronic circuits which work with continuously varying quantities, such as sinusoidal functions, make up the subject matter of *analog electronics*. When we work with a continuously varying quantity, such as $y = \sin(2\pi t)$, we consider both the value of time t and the value of voltage or current y to be real variables.

Analog electronic circuits require circuit models, analysis and design techniques which are very different from the models and techniques employed for digital circuits. The design of a high fidelity and high power audio amplifier, for example, would require a correspondingly high degree of mastery of analog electronics.

Within the large community of practitioners of electronics around the world, many are passionate aficionados of either *analog* or so-called *mixed signal* design. Given our purposes, however, any further discussion of these subjects is not really justified.

3.3 LOGIC GATES

In how many different ways can a single bit of information be processed?

Let a binary variable X represent a single bit of information, i.e. X may have value 1 or 0.

We wish to *process* X to produce binary variable Y. In mathematical notation, we say that we are looking for a *function*, say f, such that $Y = f(X)$. We say that X is the *input* to function f, and Y is the *output* of function f. Figure 3.2 shows this schematically.

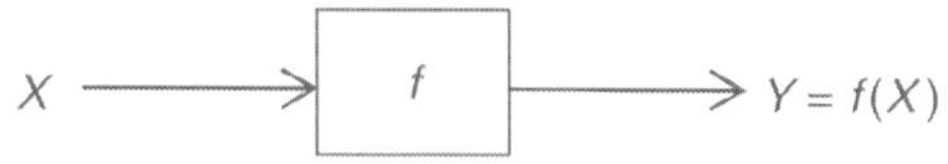

Fig. 3.2 A binary function f of one binary variable

For a single binary input such as X, each of the values $f(0)$ and $f(1)$ can independently be chosen in two possible ways, i.e. either 1 or 0. Therefore, there are $2 \times 2 = 4$ possible ways to define the function f.

Of the four possible definitions of f, one represents the *identity function*, i.e. $f(0) = 0$ and $f(1) = 1$, which means $Y = X$. In this case, since output Y is identical to X, the function f does not really represent any processing of the input. Two other possible functions are the constant functions $f(X) = 1$ and $f(X) = 0$. In these cases, since output Y is independent of input X, once again the function f does not really represent any processing of the input.

The only other possible definition of f, for single binary input X, is the one shown in Fig. 3.3 (a). This is the function known as *inverter* or *not*, i.e. the value of binary output Y is the *inverse* of the value of binary input X. Fig. 3.3 (b) shows the standard graphical symbol of the *not* function.

Value of input X	Value of output Y
1	0
0	1

(a) Tabulation of $Y = f(X) = \neg X$

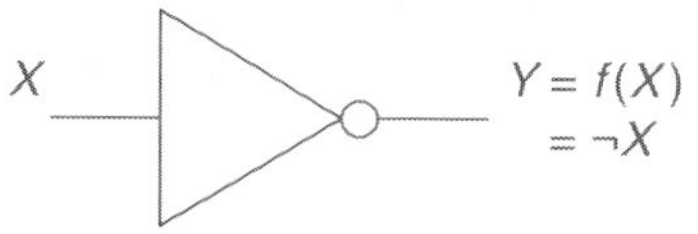

(b) Graphical notation

Fig. 3.3 The *inverter* or *not* function

Now let us extend our inquiry to the following question: In how many different ways can two bits of information be processed?

Refer to part (a) of Fig. 3.4. We see that the input to function f is now a set of two binary variables, say X_1 and X_2. The output of f is still a single bit, Y, so that we may say $Y = f(X_1, X_2)$.

From part (b) of Fig. 3.4, we see that a definition of f now requires us to fill out four possible values of Y, corresponding to the four possible combinations of inputs X_1 and X_2. Let us denote these four values of Y as y_0, y_1, y_2 and y_3. Thus we may say:

$$y_0 = f(0,0)$$
$$y_1 = f(0,1)$$
$$y_2 = f(1,0)$$
$$y_3 = f(1,1)$$

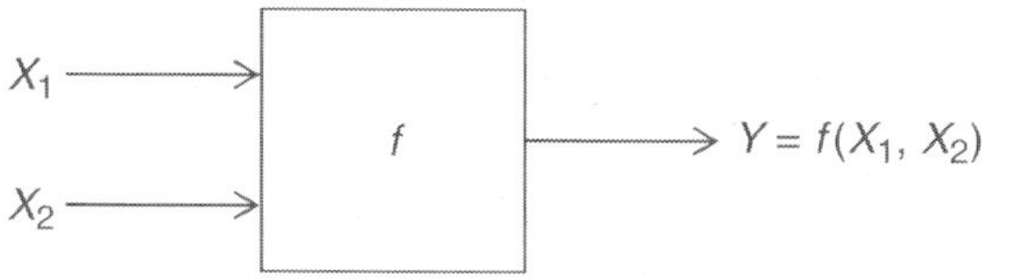

(a) Block diagram

Value of input X_1	Value of input X_2	Value of output Y
0	0	0 or 1
0	1	0 or 1
1	0	0 or 1
1	1	0 or 1

(b) Tabular representation

Fig. 3.4 Function of two binary variables $Y = f(X_1, X_2)$

Now, each of these four values can be chosen in one of two different ways, i.e. either 1 or 0, and the four choices can be made independently of each other. Therefore, the total number of different ways in which *f* can be defined is $2^4 = 16$. These are all the sixteen different ways in which a function *f* of two binary variables can be defined.

It turns out, however, that by using combinations of just two of these sixteen functions, along with the *not* function seen earlier, we can build any desired function *f* of two binary variables. These two 'special' functions of two binary variables are the so-called *and* and *or* functions, as shown in Fig. 3.5.

Value of input X_1	Value of input X_2	Value of output Y
0	0	0
0	1	0
1	0	0
1	1	1

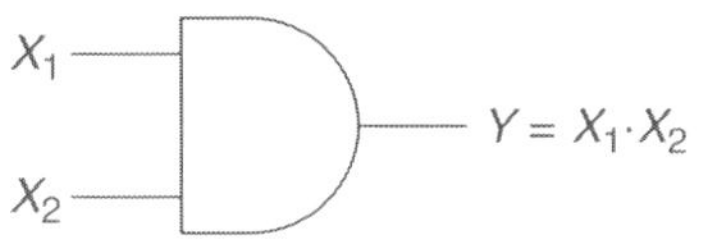

(a) Table and graphical notation of function *and*

Value of input X_1	Value of input X_2	Value of output Y
0	0	0
0	1	1
1	0	1
1	1	1

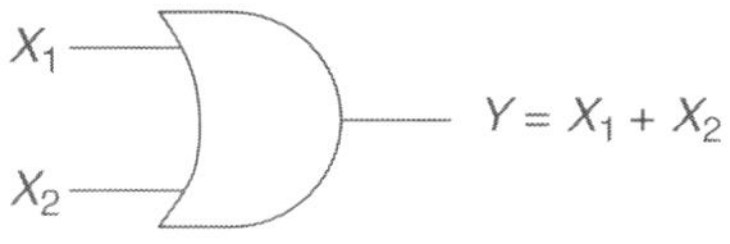

(b) Table and graphical notation of function *or*

Fig. 3.5 The functions *and* and *or*

Note here the following characteristic of these two basic functions:

(i) *and* function, which is also known as *conjunction*, has output 1, if and only if both of its inputs have value 1.

(ii) *or* function, which is also known as *disjunction*, has output 1, if and only if at least one of its inputs has value 1.

Using suitable compositions of *and*, *or* and *not* functions, one can implement any other function of two—or even more—binary input variables. Thus, these three functions can serve as one possible set of general-purpose building blocks for building any other required functions of binary variables.

By using appropriate combinations of transistors, these three functions can be implemented in silicon. In their *avatar* as electronic building blocks, these three basic functions—and others like them—are known as *logic gates*.

Using suitable interconnections of these three basic logic gates, it is possible to implement any binary function of two or more binary variables. When two or more gates are thus interconnected to implement another function, they form a *digital circuit*.

In the following section, we will discuss in some more detail one useful class of digital circuits, known as *combinational* circuits.

3.4 COMBINATIONAL CIRCUITS

We shall begin our discussion of combinational digital circuits with a simple example of a digital circuit which has three inputs.

Example 3.1

Consider a digital circuit with three input variables X_1, X_2 and X_3, and output variable Y, defined using *and*, *or* and *not* gates in the following way:

$$Y = or\,(X_3,\ and\,(X_1,\ not\,(X_2)))$$

Note here that:

(i) The output of *not* is one of the inputs of *and*; the second input of *and* is X_1.
(ii) The output of *and* is one of the inputs of *or*; the second input of *or* is X_3.

If we replace this function notation by *operator* symbols +, ·, and ¬ for functions *or*, *and* and *not* respectively, we may write the above definition equivalently as:

$$Y = X_3 + X_1 \cdot (\neg X_2)$$

In graphical notation, the corresponding digital circuit appears as in Fig. 3.6.

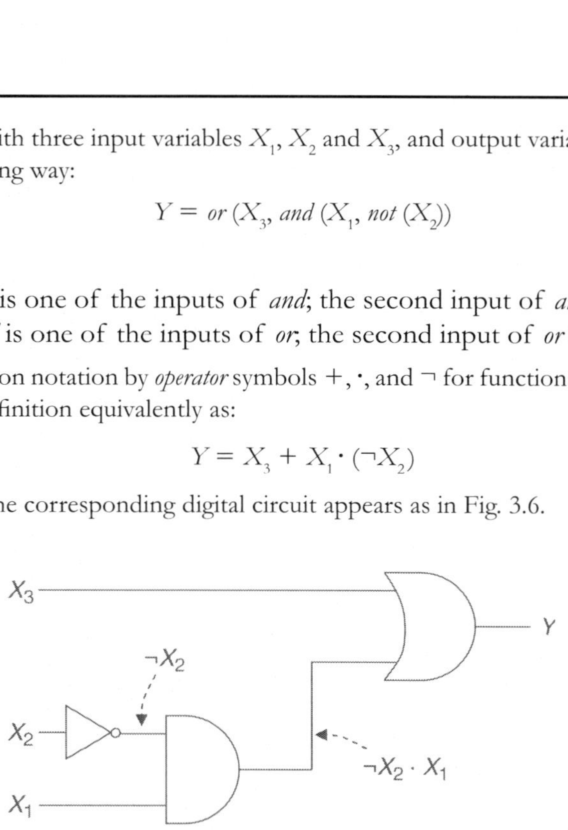

Fig. 3.6 **The combinational circuit of Example 3.1**

As we tabulated *and* and *or* gates in Fig. 3.5, this composite function defined by the circuit can also be tabulated. Since the function has three inputs, its tabulated version will have $2^3 = 8$ rows, and four columns corresponding to X_1, X_2 and X_3 and Y. The tabulated version of such a binary function of binary variables is known as its *truth table* (see Exercise 2 at the end of the chapter).

In the circuit of Fig. 3.6, we see that the output of the *inverter* is connected to one input of the *and* gate, and the output of the *and* gate is connected to one input of the *or* gate. It is through such interconnections that the functional notation seen above is translated into the graphical notation corresponding to digital circuits.

In the language of digital circuits, a variable is more commonly known as a *signal.* The various interconnections in the circuit may then be labeled with the names of the signals they represent.

In the circuit of Fig. 3.6, we may observe a total of six signals. Of these, X_1, X_2 and X_3 are *input signals* of the circuit, Y is its *output signal*, and the remaining two—namely $\neg X_2$ and $\neg X_2 \cdot X_1$—may be called *internal signals* of the circuit.

An interconnection in a circuit is often referred to as a *signal line* or simply a *line.* Such a line usually connects the output of one gate to the input(s) of one or more gates*.

The designer of a digital circuit employs terms such as *signals*, *lines* and *gates*, rather than *variables* and *functions.* But, as this example should make clear, the aim in either case is to define the basic building blocks for processing any information which is represented using the binary symbols '1' and '0'.

In the circuit of Fig. 3.6, as we trace the path from input X_2 to output Y, we see that the path goes through the *inverter*, *and* gate, and *or* gate. When such a circuit is implemented using transistors, any change in input X_2 will be reflected in output Y only after a certain time delay, since all physical processes have some inertia associated with them.

The time delay seen between a change in X_2 and the corresponding change in Y will be determined in the main by two factors:

a. the *gate delay* of each gate in the path, which is determined by the technology used to build the transistors in the circuit, and
b. *propagation delay* caused by the interconnections within the circuit, which will depend in general on the length and other characteristics of the interconnections.

In general, the speed at which a digital circuit can be operated is determined by the gate delays and the propagation delays within the circuit. With the VLSI technology today, gate delays are down in the range of mere picoseconds (10^{-12} seconds). The speed of propagation of signals through circuits is of the order of 20 centimeters per nanosecond, which is about two thirds the speed of light through vacuum.

As was mentioned in the previous section, any binary function of two or more input variables can be implemented using the *inverter*, *and* and *or* gates. Furthermore, in theory any such function can be implemented with no more than two gate delays between input and output. This point is worth noting, since in our computer system we may in general decide to make use of a function Y of, say, n input variables $X_1, X_2 \ldots X_n$:

$$Y = f(X_1, X_2 \ldots X_n)$$

For any such function f, we thus have a reliable upper bound on the total gate delay between any input X_i and output Y. We will make use of several such functions as our building blocks, with the understanding that any such function can be implemented using the gates we have seen**, and that too with known bounds on gate delay.

---

*While building an electronic circuit, one has to be more careful if the outputs of two or more gates are to be 'wired' together with the inputs of one or more gates. In such cases, an implicit *or* function is usually intended between the multiple outputs. In this book, however, since the emphasis is not on electronics, we assume that an explicit *or* gate is used in all such cases.

**In practice, *nand* and *nor* gates are often used, but the basic point made here about combinational circuits remains valid. A *nand* gate may be viewed as an *and* gate with inverted output, and a *nor* gate as an *or* gate with inverted output.

The class of circuits we discussed in this section, as exemplified by the functional equation of output Y in terms of inputs $X_1, X_2 \ldots X_n$, is known as *combinational circuits*. In these circuits, the output does not in any way depend on *prior* inputs. Ignoring gate delays and propagation delays, we may say that the output at time t is only a function of the inputs at time t. Such circuits can have 'no memory' of prior inputs.

While combinational circuits form key elements of any computer system, the system also needs circuits 'with memory'. We must, therefore, turn our attention to such circuits, which are known as *sequential circuits*.

3.5 SEQUENTIAL CIRCUITS

A combinational function such as $Y = f(X_1, X_2 \ldots X_n)$ has 'no memory', because the output is determined solely by the inputs. If a circuit had memory, then surely it could record one or more bits of information within it in such a way that these recorded bits also affect subsequent circuit outputs.

In other words, the function represented by a circuit with memory would be of the type:

$$\text{output} = f(\text{ inputs, recorded bits within the circuit })$$

But, of course, the recorded bits themselves may change with inputs, in the following manner:

$$\text{recorded bits at time } t + \Delta t = g(\text{ inputs at time } t, \text{ recorded bits at time } t)$$

Note that we have been forced to introduce *time* into the function g because, as the recorded bits within the circuit change, we need to observe their behavior as a function of time. This is the reason why such circuits are known as *sequential circuits*.

What does the symbol Δt here represent? As was mentioned above, any physical system has some inertia, and therefore no change can happen in zero time. We assume here that Δt is a time interval which allows one round of changes to be completed within the circuit, so the circuit is ready for another round. Equivalently, we may say that, after any change, the various signals of such a circuit reach their valid or correct values only at the *discrete* time instants $t_0 + \Delta t$, $t_0 + 2\Delta t$, and so on, starting with some initial instant t_0.

In other words, changes can only happen in such a circuit at the rate of once per Δt seconds. In practice, Δt is the time period of the *clock signal* driving the circuit, and $1/\Delta t$ is therefore the frequency of this clock signal. We shall discuss the clock signal in some more detail later, in Section 3.6.

But we must first see how a single bit can be recorded electronically. The typical electronic circuit which can record one bit is known as the *flip-flop*, which is built using a so-called 'back-to-back' arrangement of two transistors. Of course, the details of how to design and build a *flip-flop* circuit are not relevant here, but we do need to study its behavior, since it will serve as a building block of other system elements.

Refer to Fig. 3.7, which shows a flip-flop with an input line, an output line, and a clock input at the bottom. Once in every *clock cycle*, at an appropriate clock *transition* or *edge*—about which we shall see more in Section 3.6—the flip-flop records the state of the input. If the input is 0 at the appropriate clock transition, the flip-flop records a 0; and if the input is 1, the flip-flop records a 1.

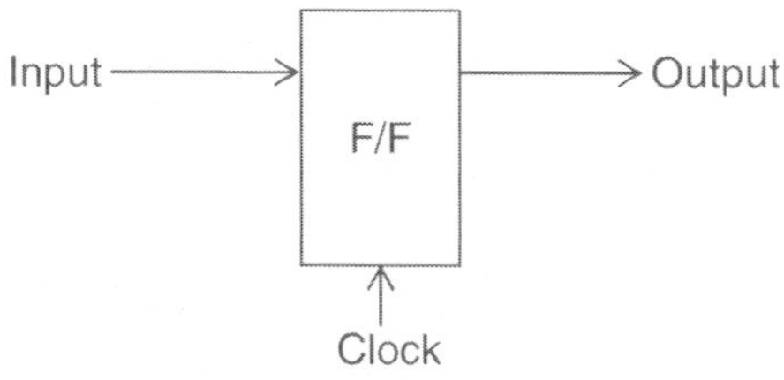

Fig. 3.7 **A *flip-flop*, providing one bit of storage**

When a flip-flop changes state from 0 to 1, it is said to be *set*, and when it changes state from 1 to 0, it is said to be *reset*. In fact, another type of flip-flop circuit has two inputs, one for *set* and one for *reset*, and yet another type of flip-flop works in so-called *toggle* mode. Usually a sequential circuit is designed using the type of flip-flop appropriate to it, but their basic principles of operation are essentially the same.

A flip-flop is thus our one bit of memory. By arranging N such flip-flops in a linear array, we obtain N bits of memory. But when we need a much larger amount of memory—for example 2^{16} bits—the linear arrangement is no longer feasible, and we need to arrange the flip-flops in a square grid, as we shall see later.

Figure 3.8 shows in a general way how a sequential circuit makes use of such memory elements. It turns out that such a circuit can be viewed as having a combinational element and a separate memory element. The conceptual pattern of interconnections between these elements is shown in the figure using thick lines and arrows.

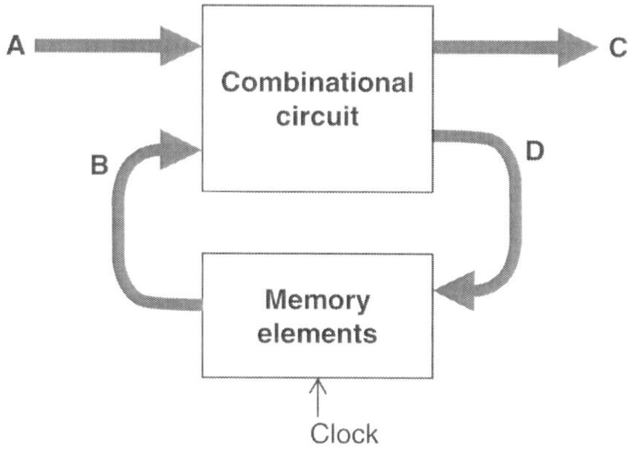

Fig. 3.8 **General model of a sequential circuit**

In Fig. 3.8, upper case letters A, B, C and D have the following meaning:

A Input signals to the sequential circuit
B State of the circuit at time t
C Output signals of the sequential circuit
D State of the circuit at time $t + \Delta t$

Note that here we have used the words *state of the circuit* instead of 'recorded bits within the circuit'. *State* is technically the more correct description, while 'recorded bits' has the advantage of being less abstract, and therefore easier to understand.

A circuit with K bits of memory can have at most 2^K distinct states, although some of them may not in fact be 'reachable'.

Example 3.2

A *counter* is one of the simplest examples of a sequential circuit. Consider a single digit decimal counter which can count from 0 to 9, like a single decimal digit in the odometer of a car. Naturally, after the counter counts to 9, the next count it reaches would be 0 again. If there was a more significant digit to its left, that digit would then go up by one; for example, the count of 49 is followed by 50, and 299 is followed by 300.

But here we are considering only a single digit decimal counter, which can also be considered a *modulo 10* counter, since in general *modulo N* arithmetic is defined on integers from 0 to $N - 1$.

A counter circuit with a clock input basically counts the number of times it 'senses' its input signal to be 1, given that it senses the input signal only at the appropriate clock transition, once in every clock cycle.

How many bits of memory does our counter need? Recall the examples seen in Chapter 1. With three bits, the circuit can have at most $2^3 = 8$ distinct states. Obviously, this is not sufficient if we wish to count from 0 to 9. With four bits, we can have up to $2^4 = 16$ distinct states. Since we need only 10 distinct states, we can manage with four bits. In fact $16-10 = 6$ states of such a circuit will be unutilised in a decimal counter.

The output of such a counter, corresponding to the set C in Fig. 3.8, would consist of four signals, which go from 0000 (zero) to 1001 (nine) and then again back to 0000.

For all counters in general, the sets C and D shown in Fig. 3.8 are identical.

Example 3.3

Suppose we wish to design a sequential digital circuit which functions as a 24 hour 'time of day' clock, showing its output in the form *hh:mm:ss*. Let us assume that a clock signal with time period of 1 second is driving such a circuit, and let us determine the number of flip flops this circuit will require.

Approach 1:
There are $60 \times 60 \times 24 = 86400$ seconds in a day, and we know that $2^{16} < 86400 < 2^{17}$. Therefore a 17-bit counter, which must be reset to 0 in the next second after it reaches 86399, can in theory serve our purpose. However, for display, the 17-bit output of this counter must be converted to *hh:mm:ss* format—and this requires a fairly complex combinational circuit. This approach therefore becomes impractical for the given application, and we must try a different approach.

Approach 2:
We can separately maintain counters for hours, minutes, and seconds—the first one counts from 0 to 23, while each of the other two count from 0 to 59. The seconds counter is driven by the 1 second clock signal supplied to the circuit. The minutes counter is incremented every time the seconds counter turns over from 59 to 0, while the hours counter is incremented every time the minutes counter turns over from 59 to 0.

The hours counter needs five bits, since $2^4 < 24 < 2^5$, while the minutes and the seconds counters need 6 bits each*. Therefore, the total number of flip flops required is again $5 + 6 + 6 = 17$; however, this second approach has the advantage over the first approach that the combinational part of the circuit will be smaller and simpler.

Approach 3:
We provide a separate counter for each of the six digits of *hh:mm:ss*. Let us designate these digits as h_1, h_2, m_1, m_2, s_1 and s_2 respectively. Values of h_1 run from 0 to 2, values of m_1 and s_1 run from 0 to 5, and values of h_2, m_2 and s_2 run from 0 to 9. Therefore, we need 2 bits for h_1, 3 bits each for m_1 and s_1, and 4 bits each for h_2, m_2, and s_2*. The total number of bits needed is therefore $2 + 6 + 12 = 20$.

Thus, the total number of flip flops needed under the third approach is slightly larger—but the combinational part of the circuit now will be much simpler even than that required under the second approach, and the six required digits are produced directly as the outputs of respective counters.

Systematic and efficient methods have been developed over the years for the design of combinational and sequential circuits. These methods are usually available in the form of *circuit design software* which can handle complex circuits. A decimal counter, such as the one of Example 3.2, is usually a favourite design example for sequential circuits.

Since our aim is not the design of such circuits, but rather their use in a computer system, we need to understand only the broad characteristics of digital circuits. We shall therefore not pursue any further the design issues of combinational or sequential circuits.

*In each such instance, the student is encouraged to verify the statement made in the text, using one or two steps of simple mathematics.

3.6 INTEGRATED CIRCUITS

We saw in Chapter 1 that the newly developed *integrated circuit* (IC) *technology* of the 1960s resulted in computer systems making a major 'evolutionary change' from the second to the third generation. IC technology allowed entire circuits to be integrated into tiny silicon chips—as compared to the earlier and bulkier methods of assembling circuits from discrete components such as transistors and resistors.

IC technology resulted in circuits becoming smaller, faster, less expensive, more power-efficient, and more reliable. Each one of these factors, in itself, is of major significance in system design. Together, these advantages of IC technology resulted in a major step forward in the development and spread of computer systems.

As developments in IC technology continued at a fast pace, the advantages listed above continued to grow year after year—ICs continued to become ever smaller, faster, less expensive, more power-efficient, and more reliable. By the late 1970s, it became possible to fabricate an entire processor on a single chip, the resulting chip becoming known as the *microprocessor*. The so-called personal computer revolution of the late 1970s and early 1980s was made possible by the development of the microprocessor. Bit-densities of memory chips also continued to grow over the years.

In the very early years of the technology, an IC chip contained perhaps a few dozen components. Starting with the original *small scale integration* (SSI) , IC technology graduated to *medium scale integration* (MSI) , *large scale integration* (LSI) , and then finally *very large scale integration* (VLSI)—with the capability to fabricate millions of transistors on a single chip.

We shall now take a very brief peek at the techniques which allow electronic circuits to be integrated on a tiny silicon chip.

It was mentioned in Section 3.1 that the flow of electrons through a semiconductor material can be controlled fairly accurately. As mentioned above, the basic device which achieves this control is the *transistor*—a three-terminal circuit element made from silicon. In one type of transistor, the current flowing between *emitter* and *collector* is controlled by the voltage applied to the *base*; in another type of transistor, the current flowing between *source* and *drain* is controlled by the voltage applied to the *gate*.

An integrated circuit has components such as transistors, resistors and capacitors, with thin strips of conductors connecting them. These components are created on a thin silicon substrate by diffusing or implanting into it—in well-defined geometries—the so-called *p*-type and *n*-type impurities*. Connections between components are created by tracks of metal deposited on the silicon, and electrical isolation between components is achieved by creating insulating layers of silicon dioxide.

Thus, all the required circuit elements can be defined on a silicon substrate through processing steps such as diffusion, oxidation, metal deposition, and so on. Since the circuit elements are extremely small in size, each of these steps must be carried out with very precisely specified geometry. To define required geometries on the silicon substrate, two-dimensional optical masks are placed over it during the processing steps—a process known as *photolithography*. All the processing steps are precisely controlled using automated equipment.

A single silicon chip, with an integrated circuit fabricated on it, may measure a few millimeters on a side. But it must be provided with *leads* for making connections to other chips and components,

*Actually very pure boron and phosphorous, respectively.

and packaged durably in ceramic or plastic. A buyer is provided with *data sheets* which set out the full functional and electrical specifications of the IC. ICs are available for a vast range of useful functions, including logic gates, counters, decoders, timers, memory chips, processors, and device controllers.

IC technology is not restricted to digital ICs. Analog ICs are also available such as amplifiers, voltage regulators, clock generators, and so on. Conveniently packaged ICs are also available for analog to digital and digital to analog conversion.

Within a computer system, ICs are mounted on *printed circuit boards* (PCBs)—on which pre-defined metallic interconnections between ICs are 'printed'. An IC may have leads which go through the PCB, or the IC may be surface mounted on one side of the PCB. The number of leads on an IC may run from as few as twelve on a simple device, to hundreds on a modern processor chip.

3.7 CLOCK SIGNAL

In theory, sequential digital circuits can be designed to work with or without a *clock signal.* However, the example circuits we saw in the previous section did make use of a clock signal, and in general the circuits employed in today's computer systems almost invariably do employ a clock signal.

For example, when we read that a processor 'runs at 2 GHz', what it means is that the clock signal 'driving' the processor has a frequency of 2 gigahertz, i.e. 2×10^9 cycles per second. For a better understanding of the operation of digital circuits, it is necessary to understand the role of the clock signal.

In Fig. 3.9, we have shown in a simplified way three cycles of a typical clock signal. The horizontal axis represents time, while the vertical axis represents clock voltage. As seen, the voltage changes in a regular pattern between 0 volts and (in this case) 3 volts. In every time period, the clock signal exhibits two *transitions* or *edges*. In the figure, these two transitions are labeled as *rising edge* and *falling edge*. The reason why these two edges are not perfectly vertical is that the voltage cannot change in zero time.

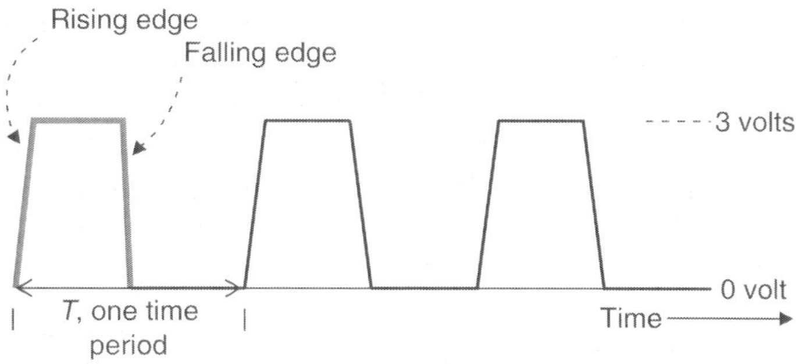

Fig. 3.9 **Three cycles of a clock signal**

Within one time period, the part of clock signal between the rising edge and the falling edge is known as a *clock pulse*. In the figure, the clock pulse within the first time period has been marked using a thick brown line.

Typically, a flip-flop—or in general any sequential circuit—utilises one of the two edges of a clock pulse as an instant of transition. In other words, if a flip-flop is going to switch from state 1 to state 0, and it is designed to operate on the rising edge, then the change from state 1 to state 0 will take place at the rising edge of the next clock pulse.

Naturally, the frequency of the clock signal is inversely related to its time period. For example, if the clock signal of Fig. 3.9 has frequency 2 GHz, then its time period is 0.5 nanosecond.

Suppose the clock signal of Fig. 3.9 is driving the single digit decimal counter which we studied in Example 3.2, such that the count is incremented at every clock pulse. Then the counter will repeatedly count from 0 to 9, and then back again to 0. In other words, after counting up from 0 to 9 in ten cycles, the counter will switch back from 9 to 0 once in every ten clock cycles.

Now suppose that we use only this 9-to-0 transition of the counter as yet another clock. The frequency of this second clock will then be one tenth the frequency of the clock we apply to the decimal counter. Thus the decimal counter allows us to scale down the clock frequency from the original 2 GHz to one tenth of that value, i.e. 200 MHz.

In general, in this way, from one *master clock*, circuit designers are able to derive other lower frequency clocks. Since different parts of a computer system may in fact need to operate at different clock speeds, this becomes a very useful technique.

From the discussion above, it should be clear that any processing step in a computer system happens only at the rising or falling edge of a clock pulse, of which there is only one in every clock period. Suppose we have two circuits C1 and C2 which process data, which are identical in every respect except this one: C1 is operated with a clock which is twice as fast as the clock of C2. Since the two circuits are otherwise identical, we can say that C1 will process data twice as fast as C2.

It is important to view the clock signal as a *physical signal*, and not as one of the *logical* input or output signals of the circuit. This is the reason why, in the functional equation of any circuit, such as $Y = f(X)$, the clock signal does not make an appearance.

Clock generation and distribution is one of the key issues in the hardware design of computer systems and VLSI circuits. Several manufacturers have specialised clock generator circuits in their product line, which system designers can use as building blocks. In latter parts of this book, for a proper understanding of how system hardware operates, we may at times need to make use of terms such as clock signal, clock frequency, clock pulse, or an edge of the clock pulse.

3.8 REGISTERS

We have seen that a flip-flop is a basic circuit which can store one bit of information. Our computer systems need to process information in larger units—such as bytes and words—and they also need to store hundreds of millions of bytes. Therefore we need to understand how larger units of memory can be organised, which may be used as components or even sub-systems of a computer system.

When an array of, say, N flip-flops is designed and used as a single unit of storage, we call the resulting element an *N-bit register*. If a register is used primarily as a counter, we may also call it an *N-bit counter*. As we have seen above, the unsigned integer count in an N-bit counter goes from 0 to $2^N - 1$, after which it is again reset to 0.

Often, several related registers are grouped together to form a *register bank*. In Fig. 3.10, we see a bank of eight *N*-bit registers, where *N* may have the value, say, 16 or 32.

An important question at this stage is: How does such a *register bank* get connected to the rest of the system?

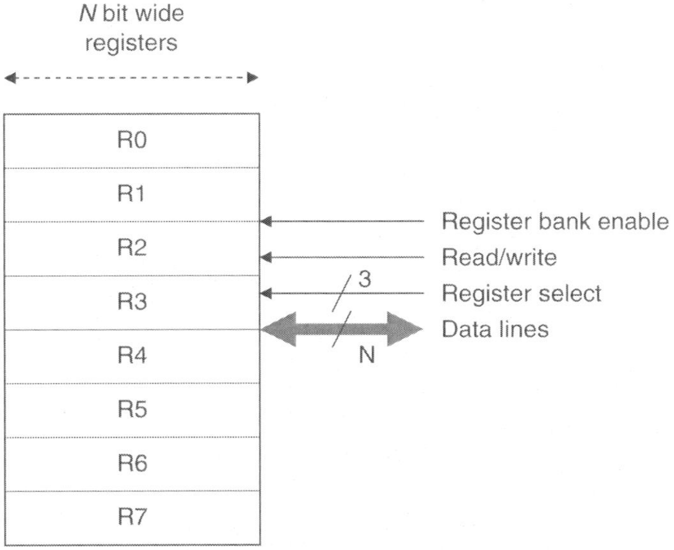

Fig. 3.10 A register bank of eight *N*-bit registers

On the right in Fig. 3.10, we see the interconnections required. The thick line shows *bi-directional data lines* which would connect this register bank with some other part of the system. The word *bi-directional* here means that data can be passed in either direction along the data lines, corresponding to a *read* and a *write* operation on a register. The *width* of this data path is naturally the same as the register size, i.e. *N* bits.

Just above the data lines, we see a group of three lines labeled *register select*. In this case, any operation on the bank targets one of the eight registers, so we need three bits of information to select a register for a *read* or a *write* operation.

Just above the register select lines, we see a signal line labeled *read/write*. In a given clock cycle, we may perform a *read* or a *write* operation on a register. The *read/write* signal decides which operation is going to take place. This implies that some circuit element external to the register bank determines, in a given clock cycle, whether a *read* or a *write* operation will be performed on the selected register. A '1' on this line may signify a *read* operation, for example, and a '0' a *write* operation.

Finally, at the top, we see a signal labeled *register bank enable*. In general, there will be other devices connected to the data lines. In a given clock cycle, it may well be that this register bank has to do nothing—which may also mean that some other devices are in fact making use of the shared data lines. Therefore, we must *enable* this register bank only when performing an operation on it, and not otherwise. Typically, a '1' on this line would enable the register bank for a read or write operation.

On the selected register in the register bank of Fig. 3.10, we read or write *N* bits in one clock cycle—i.e. the *N* bits of the register are read or written *in parallel*.

On a single register, it is also possible to provide a *serial* mode of operation. Figure 3.11 shows a 16-bit register provided with both parallel and serial modes of operation.

In serial mode, register bits are read in or written out one bit per clock cycle, in serial order. This is shown at point 'B' in the figure; clearly therefore, on an N-bit register, a complete serial read or write operation takes N clock cycles. Serial mode of operation is required if a device with which data is being exchanged does so only in serial mode—i.e. one bit at a time. Since communication devices send and receive data in serial mode, an arrangement of the type shown is required in their controllers.

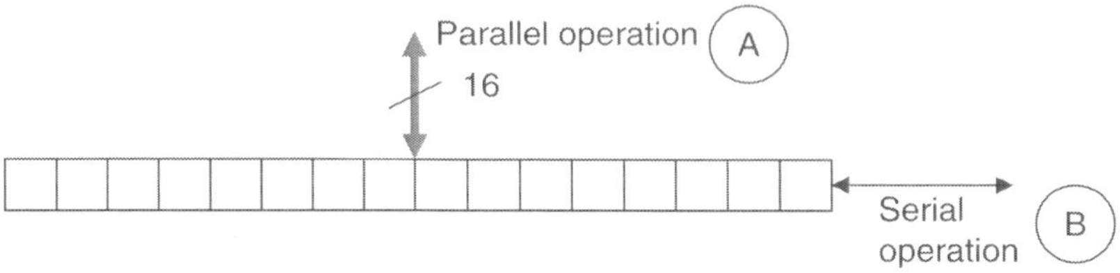

Fig. 3.11 Parallel and serial operation on a 16-bit register

A *shift register* is a register whose contents can be shifted left or right by a specified number of bits. The operation of the register of Fig. 3.11 can therefore be either (i) a parallel write at 'A', followed by serial shift of the data out from 'B', or (ii) serial shift of the data in from 'B', followed by parallel read at 'A'.

In Chapters 4 and 5, we shall see the many useful ways in which a program running on the processor makes use of so-called *programmable registers* within the processor. We shall also study the important role of special processor registers such as *instruction register*, *program counter* and *stack pointer*.

3.9 MEMORY ELEMENTS

When larger blocks of memory are to be built—say a million bytes or more—then the storage cannot be organised in the same manner as in the register bank. Recall that such larger memory blocks make up the main memory of typical computer systems.

For flexibility and efficiency in programming, the main memory of a system is almost invariably made *byte addressable*, which means that every *memory address* points to one eight-bit byte in the memory block. At the same time, such memory is also made capable of multi-byte operations—i.e. reading and writing, say, four or eight bytes of memory in one memory cycle.

Figure 3.12 shows a schematic organisation of byte addressable memory. If a word equals four bytes, then every fourth byte of memory defines a so-called *word boundary*. Counting memory bytes from 0 onwards, we then have word boundaries at the end of bytes 3, 7, 11, and so on, as shown in the figure.

Usually, word operations on main memory are constrained to be aligned with word boundaries, and likewise for *half-word* and *double-word* operations.

Since any randomly selected byte or word in such a memory element can be accessed in one memory cycle—either for a *read* or for a *write* operation—such memory is referred to as *random access memory*, or RAM.

The cycle time of memory elements used as main memory of a system is typically at least an order of magnitude longer than the cycle time of the processor. However, for special purposes such as *cache memories* (see Sections 6.9 and 9.9), faster memory elements are built, which have cycle time of the same order as that of the processor. Due to constraints of size, power consumption and cost, however, such faster memory elements cannot be employed in the main memory of a computer system.

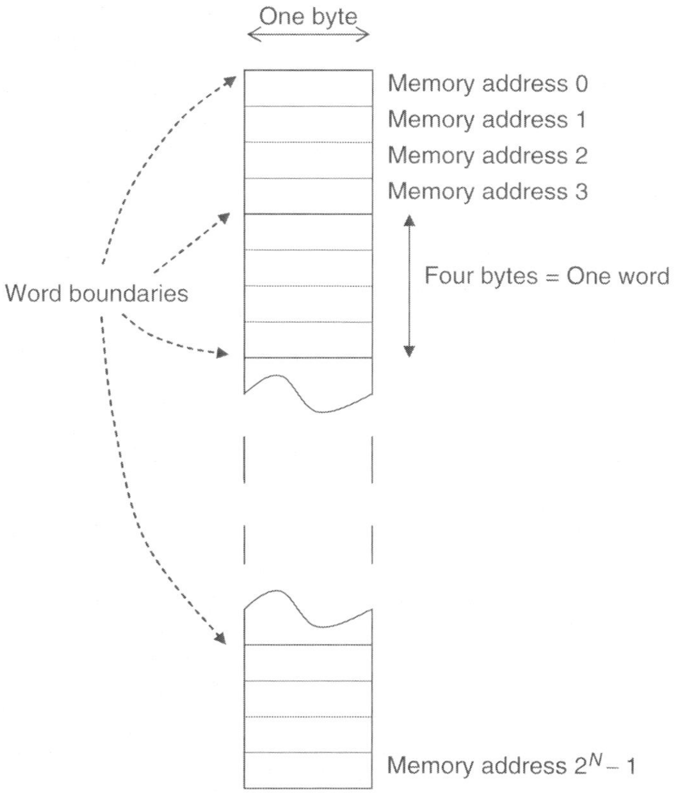

Fig. 3.12 **Organisation of byte-addressable memory**

Figure 3.13 shows a simplified diagram of the input and output signals of a typical memory element. Let us assume that the memory element depicted in the figure can store 2^{20} bytes, i.e. one megabyte. For selecting one byte within the element, we therefore need twenty address lines. But the computer system will in general make use of several such memory elements—and therefore the processor may in fact be having, say, thirty two address lines, for a total addressability of 2^{32} bytes, i.e. four gigabytes.

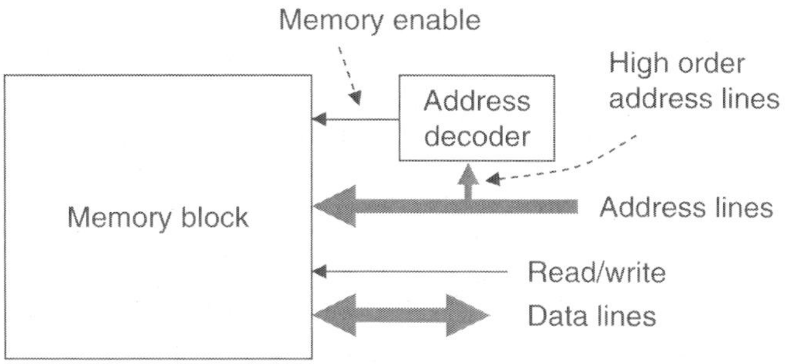

Fig. 3.13 **Input and output signals of a typical memory element**

So the important question here would be: Which of the thirty two address lines of the processor do we supply to this particular memory element?

The answer is twofold:

a. Connect the lowest order twenty bits of the system address lines to this memory element, and
b. Use the remaining higher order bits of the address lines to determine which system addresses will *enable* this memory element.

This means that one or more of the remaining higher order twelve bits of the system address lines must be appropriately *decoded* to generate the correct *enable* signal for this memory block. This is shown in Fig. 3.13 in the form of an *address decoder* element—i.e. a combinational circuit which generates the *enable* signal for the memory element when the higher order address lines have the value defined for this memory element.

By using this mechanism, the system designer can provide the system with the required amount of memory—and that too at the appropriate address within the *logical address space* of the processor.

The following two examples should be able to clarify this idea.

Example 3.4

Assume that a processor in a computer system provides 32-bit memory address. This processor—and therefore the computer system—would thus have an addressable memory space of 2^{32} bytes, i.e. four gigabytes.

However, assume that for the system under design we need only 256 megabytes of memory. In such cases, the system designer needs to determine which part or parts of the total four gigabyte addressable memory space is occupied by the actual—i.e. physical—memory of 256 megabytes being provided.

Conceptually, the simplest arrangement will be for the physical memory of 256 megabytes to occupy the lowest addresses within the logical address space. Since 256 megabytes equals 2^{28} bytes, this means that the lower order 28 bits of the system bus must be connected to the 28 physical address lines of the memory block.

The higher order $32 - 28 = 4$ bits of the system bus must all be 0 when this memory element is selected, and therefore a logical *or* of these four higher order bits followed by an inverter can generate the required *enable* signal for the memory block*.

Note that here we have assumed that we are using a single physical memory element—i.e. a single *integrated circuit* (IC) *chip*—for the required 256 megabytes.

Example 3.5

In the system of Example 3.4, suppose that we are using not one memory chip of 256 megabytes, but four memory chips of 64 megabytes each. Each of these four chips now needs to be connected to the lower order 26-bits of the system address bus, since 2^{26} bytes equals 64 megabytes.

The highest order four bits must still be 0, as before, but the next two higher order bits of the address must now be *decoded* to generate the four different *enable* signals we need for the four physical memory chips. This is indicated schematically below, where the 32 bits of the address are grouped as 4 + 2 + 26.

*The student is encouraged to verify this statement using the basic concepts of logic gates.

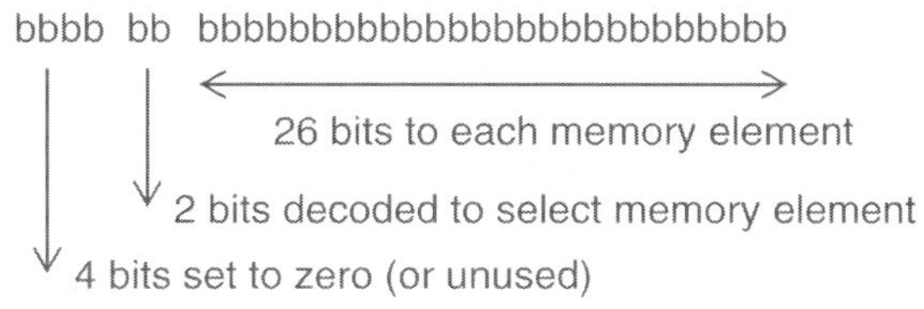

The four possible values of 00, 01, 10 and 11 in the two decoded bits must enable the respective four memory chips. A simple combinational circuit can do this job.

Many systems, including the common PC, provide several *sockets* for memory chips, along with the required interconnections and also decoding circuits. It then becomes a simple matter to add memory chips of appropriate size to such systems.

Semiconductor memory designers strive constantly to design faster and denser memory chips. For this reason, in the main memory of a computer system, the single-bit memory element used is often not the flip-flop circuit that was mentioned earlier. In place of the flip-flop, which makes use of several transistors, the single-bit memory element commonly used in the main memory is built from only a single transistor.

Of course there is a price to be paid for using this smaller, single transistor memory element—such memory elements 'lose memory' over time, and therefore need a periodic *refresh* operation. Such memory elements are labeled as *dynamic.*

In contrast, a flip-flop is referred to as a *static* memory element, since it can hold its content for indefinite time. Correspondingly, the two types of random access memories are known as DRAM and SRAM respectively. Static RAMs can be built to be faster, but dynamic RAMs are denser and consume less power.

Both these types of memory elements find their uses in a typical system. A register bank and cache memory in the processor, for example, would use the faster static memory, while the main memory is usually built using DRAMs.

A type of *non-volatile* memory element sometimes used in a computer system is the *read only memory* (ROM) , and its *programmable* variants such as EEPROM—which is an *electrically erasable programmable* ROM. These various types of *programmable* ROM memory elements follow the same logical and physical organisation shown in Figs. 3.12 and 3.13. Of course, a volatile RAM element with battery backup also becomes a non-volatile memory element, and is sometimes used in that manner.

A *flash memory*, used in digital cameras, mobile handsets and pen drives, is also a type of EEPROM, but it can only be read or written one block at a time, rather than one word at a time. Therefore such a device is only suitable as a secondary memory element, and not as main memory; we shall take a brief look at *flash memory* in Chapter 12.

While we saw in this section how a single memory block can be connected to a system, we will come back to this topic in Chapter 9. At that stage, we will examine some other important system requirements which the memory sub-system must also satisfy.

3.10 OTHER USEFUL ELEMENTS

Connecting the various elements of the system together are one or more appropriately designed *data buses*. The job of a *bus* is to carry out a complete data transfer operation in one *bus cycle* between any two elements connected to it. For this purpose, a typical bus may consist of data lines, address lines, read/write signal, various other control signals, clock signal, supply voltage, and ground.

Another significant element in any computer system is the hardware which takes care of its input, output and secondary storage requirements. Basically this hardware is also made up of elements such as registers, counters, data buses, and some combinational and sequential circuits. These elements are combined together to provide specific input and output mechanisms, as we shall see in some detail in Chapters 10, 11 and 12.

The address lines of the system typically extend from the processor to all memory elements and input/output device controllers. We saw earlier how some of these address lines are decoded to generate the *enable* signal for a memory element (Fig. 3.13) . *Decoder* ICs are commonly available to simplify this work. Figure 3.14 shows a schematic diagram of the so-called *3-to-8 decoder*.

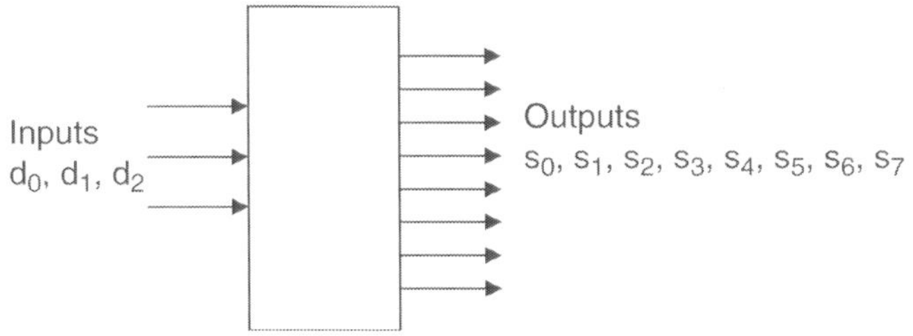

Fig. 3.14 **A 3-to-8 decoder**

Clearly the three inputs to such a decoder can have one of $2^3 = 8$ possible values, namely 000, 001, 010, 011, 100, 101, 110 and 111. Accordingly, exactly one of the eight output lines will have value 1, while all others are 0. We could say that the 3-bit binary number on the input determines which single one of the eight outputs has value 1. For example, if three higher order address lines of the system are provided as inputs to such a decoder, its eight outputs can be connected to enable eight different memory chips.

Table 3.1 is the truth table of 3-to-8 decoder, shown in a slightly simplified format in the interest of clarity.

Table 3.1 **Truth table of a 3-to-8 decoder**

Inputs* d_0, d_1, d_2	**Outputs*** s_0, s_1, s_2, s_3, s_4, s_5, s_6, s_7
0,0,0	1,0,0,0,0,0,0,0
0,0,1	0,1,0,0,0,0,0,0
0,1,0	0,0,1,0,0,0,0,0
0,1,1	0,0,0,1,0,0,0,0
1,0,0	0,0,0,0,1,0,0,0
1,0,1	0,0,0,0,0,1,0,0
1,1,0	0,0,0,0,0,0,1,0
1,1,1	0,0,0,0,0,0,0,1

*We may assume that, in Fig. 3.14, input and output signals are numbered in increasing order as we go from top to bottom.

An *encoder* works in a manner which is exactly the converse of the *decoder.* An 8-to-3 encoder has eight inputs, exactly one of which must be set to 1 at any time. Its three output lines have a value from 000 to 111, depending on which input line is set to 1. Figure 3.15 shows a schematic diagram of an 8-to-3 encoder. Naturally, the truth table of an 8-to-3 encoder will be similar to that shown in Table 3.1, but with the roles of input and output lines reversed. The encoder must be operated under the constraint that exactly one of its inputs has value 1 at any time. (See Exercise 10 at the end of this chapter.)

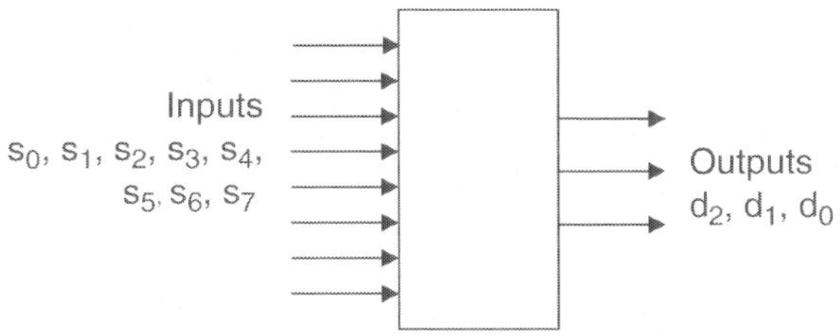

Fig. 3.15 **An 8-to-3 encoder**

A *comparator* is a combinational circuit which compares two binary values, say A and B, and generates output according to the result of the comparison. The result on the output indicates one of the three possible results of comparison: A < B, A = B, or A > B.

A *multiplexer* is a circuit with several sets of inputs, exactly one of which is connected to the outputs, depending on the control signals applied. Figure 3.16, for example, shows a 4-line, 4-to-1 multiplexer. The two control signals shown at the bottom of the device can have value 00, 01, 10 or 11. Accordingly, data from the corresponding set of four input lines appears the four output lines.

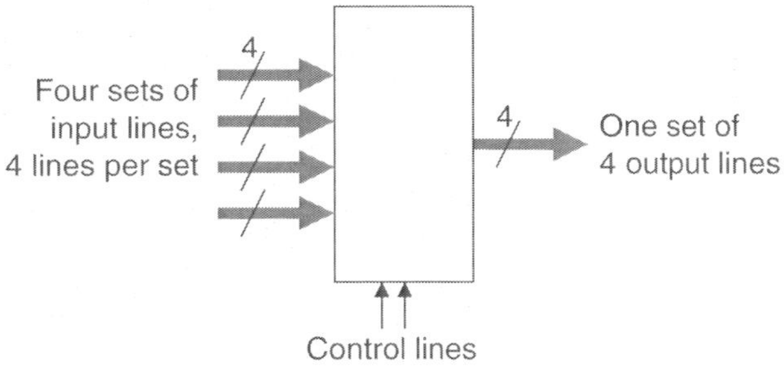

Fig. 3.16 **A 4-line, 4-to-1 multiplexer**

Table 3.2 is the truth table of 4-to-1 multiplexer, shown in a slightly simplified format in the interest of clarity.

Table 3.2 **Truth table of a 4-to-1 multiplexer**

Control inputs* c_0, c_1	Output set*
`0,0`	`=input set A`
`0,1`	`=input set B`
`1,0`	`=input set C`
`1,1`	`=input set D`

*Assume that, in Fig. 3.16, control inputs are named c_0 and c_1, and data input sets are named A, B, C and D as we go from top to bottom.

A *demultiplexer* performs a function which is the converse—the single set of input lines is connected to exactly one out of several sets of output lines. As an example, Fig. 3.17 shows a 4-line, 1-to-4 demultiplexer. The two control signals shown at the bottom of the device can have value 00, 01, 10 or 11. Accordingly, data from the set of four input lines appears on exactly one of the four sets of output lines.

Table 3.3 is the truth table of 1-to-4 demultiplexer, shown in a slightly simplified format in the interest of clarity.

Table 3.3 Truth table of a 1-to-4 demultiplexer

Control inputs* c_0, c_1	Input data appears on output set*
0,0	A
0,1	B
1,0	C
1,1	D

*Assume that, in Fig. 3.17, control inputs are named c_0 and c_1, and output sets are named A, B, C and D as we go from top to bottom.

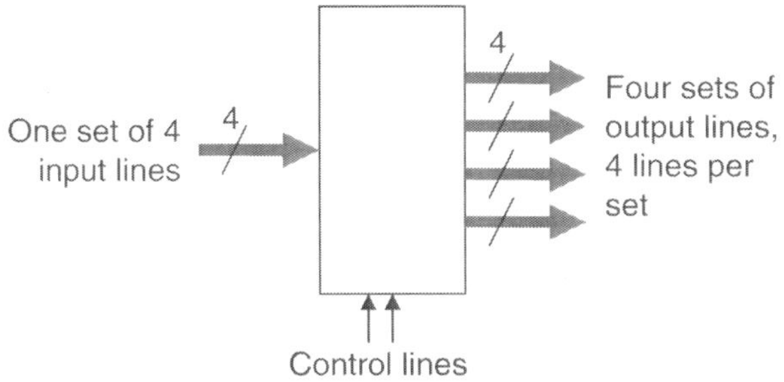

Fig. 3.17 A 4-line, 1-to-4 demultiplexer

Example 3.6

Suppose we are given a set of 2-to-1 multiplexers, and by connecting several of them together, we wish to achieve the functionality of a 4-to-1 multiplexer. Figure 3.18 shows how this can be achieved using three 2-to-1 multiplexers.

Note first of all that a 2-to-1 multiplexer has one control line to select which of its two sets of inputs is connected to the output.

The four sets of inputs of our required 4-to-1 multiplexer are denoted in the figure as A_I, B_I, A_{II} and B_{II}, respectively. Input sets A_I and B_I are connected to the inputs of 2-to-1 multiplexer I, while input sets A_{II} and B_{II}

are connected to the inputs of multiplexer II. The first of two control signals is applied to both the multiplexers I and II

By applying the correct value—0 or 1—to the first control signal, we can select either (i) A_I as the output of I and A_{II} as the output of II, or (ii) B_I as the output of I and B_{II} as the output of II. Thus either (i) A_I and A_{II}, or (ii) B_I and B_{II} reach the input of multiplexer III.

In case (i), by applying the correct value—0 or 1—to the second control signal, we can select either A_I or A_{II} as the output of multiplexer III, i.e. as the final circuit output.

In case (ii), by applying the correct value to the second control signal, we can select either B_I or B_{II} as the output of multiplexer III, i.e. as the final circuit output.

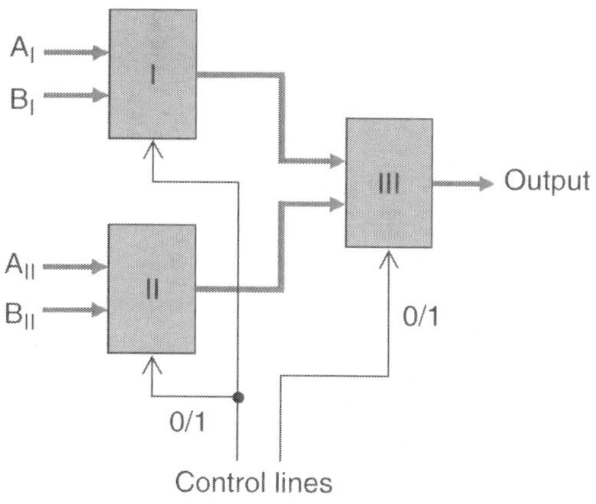

Fig. 3.18 **Circuit of Example 3.6**

In this way, by an appropriate choice of the two control signals, we can select one of the four sets of inputs as the final output of our synthesised 4-to-1 multiplexer.

Often, in a system, a single pulse or a transition on a line needs to be 'captured' into a flip-flop, so that the state of the flip-flop records a prior occurrence of the pulse or transition. A *latch* is basically a flip-flop employed for such a purpose. Similarly, an *8-bit latch* is a device with eight flip-flops which can record at one time the presence or absence of prior pulses (or transitions) on eight input lines. Such devices also have a *clear* input which resets all the flip-flops.

A *buffer* is a device which does not alter the logical value—1 or 0—of its input lines, but strengthens the electronic signals, so that they can perform their intended function when connected to another device. Physical distance, and also the number of devices connected to a signal line, tend to weaken the signal as it traverses along a circuit path. At times, therefore, the system designer may need to insert such a buffer circuit on the path.

A *timer* is a device similar to a counter. A timer device may have an internal or external clock; based on its pre-defined 'timer count', the device generates an output pulse once in that many clock periods. Often, the timer count is initially written into the timer device by the programmer, and therefore such timers are known as *programmable* timers. Since every computer system has at least one clock signal of known frequency, often the timer function can also be achieved in software.

Armed with all this knowledge of various hardware elements which store and manipulate binary information, it is time for us to get on with the subject of processing information according to the instructions making up a computer program.

Clearly the key element in any computer system is the processor—the 'brain' of the system. The processor is also made up of the basic building blocks described in this chapter. However, to better understand how a typical processor operates, it is necessary to first understand how it is programmed. The next two chapters describe a programmer's view of the processor, which is defined by its *instruction set*. Hardware design of the processor is then discussed in Chapters 6, 7 and 8.

SUMMARY

Electronic technology provides us the basic building blocks using which the various sub-systems of a computer system are designed and built. In this chapter, we studied these building blocks from a purely *functional* point of view—i.e. in terms of the functions which the building blocks perform.

We studied the basic principles of the transistor serving as an ON–OFF switch, logic gates, combinational circuits, flip-flops, and sequential circuits. Any combinational function can be implemented using *and*, *or* and *not* gates, while the flip-flop is the basic circuit element which stores one bit of information.

The output of a combinational circuit at a given time depends only on its inputs at that time. In a sequential circuit, on the other hand, the output depends on its inputs as well as the state of the circuit. In this sense, combinational circuits are without memory, while sequential circuits have memory elements within.

We took a brief look at the powerful integrated circuit technology, which—in the form of VLSI—has been driving the ongoing technology revolution around the world.

After studying the crucial role of the clock signal in computer circuits, we looked at other useful building blocks of computer systems, including registers and register banks, memory blocks, encoder, decoder, multiplexer, demultiplexer, and others.

REVIEW QUESTIONS

1. Which is the common electronic element used as a basic ON–OFF switch in a digital circuit?
2. What is the defining characteristic of a combinational digital circuit?
3. List the three basic logic gates which, when suitably interconnected, allow any combinational digital circuit to be implemented.
4. What do you understand by the truth table of a binary function of binary variables?
5. List the two main factors contributing to the total time delay in a combinational circuit between a change in an input signal and a corresponding change in its output signal.
6. What are the typical values of time delays in a combinational circuit implemented in VLSI?
7. Define *nand* and *nor* gates in terms of *and*, *or* and *not* gates.
8. What is the name given to digital circuits 'with memory'?
9. What are the two separate functions which together define the overall function of a sequential digital circuit?
10. Name the basic electronic circuit which can store—i.e. record—one bit of information.
11. Draw the general model of a sequential circuit and explain the various relevant groups of signals.
12. What is the meaning of set and reset operations on a flip-flop?

13. A sequential circuit has k flip-flops in it. What is the maximum possible number of distinct states of this circuit?
14. We need to design a counter which can count from 0 to 99, after which the count is reset to 0. How many bits of storage—i.e. flip-flops—does the counter need?
15. We need to design a counter which can keep track of 'day of month'—i.e. from 1 to 31 or less, depending on the month. How many bits of storage—i.e. flip-flops—does this counter need?
16. List the advantages of integrated circuits (ICs) over circuits which are assembled out of discrete components.
17. What is a microprocessor?
18. What is the full form of the acronym VLSI?
19. What is a printed circuit board?
20. How many 'edges' does a single clock pulse have? What is the name given to these edges?
21. What is the time period of a clock signal running at 400 megahertz?
22. The clock signal of the previous question is applied to a 3-bit counter which counts from 0 to 7, and then back to 0. The 7-to-0 transitions of this counter are used as a second clock signal derived from the first. What are the frequency and the time period of this second clock signal?
23. List the signals which will be required to connect a bank of 16 registers, each of width 32 bits, to the rest of the computer system.
24. What are the two possible modes of data transfer between an N bit register and any other element of the system?
25. What is the meaning of a left or right shift operation on the contents of a register?
26. In a memory element, what is the meaning of (i) byte addressability, (ii) multi-byte operations, and (iii) word boundary?
27. A computer system is designed with 24 memory address lines, and a particular memory element has size 1 megabyte. How many address lines does this memory element have? Which bits of the system address must be decoded to produce the *enable* signal for this memory element?
28. What are some key differences between static and dynamic RAM?
29. State in one line each the functions of these devices: decoder, encoder, multiplexer, and demultiplexer.
30. State in one line each the functions of these devices: buffer, latch, timer, and programmable timer.

EXERCISES

1. Consider $f(X,Y)$, a binary function of two binary variables. It is known that f is symmetric with respect to its two inputs, which means $f(1,0) = f(0,1)$. It is also known that f is not identically equal to 1 or 0. In how many different ways can such a function f be defined?

2. Construct the truth tables of the three input combinational circuits of Figs. 3.6, 3.19 (a) and 3.19 (b).

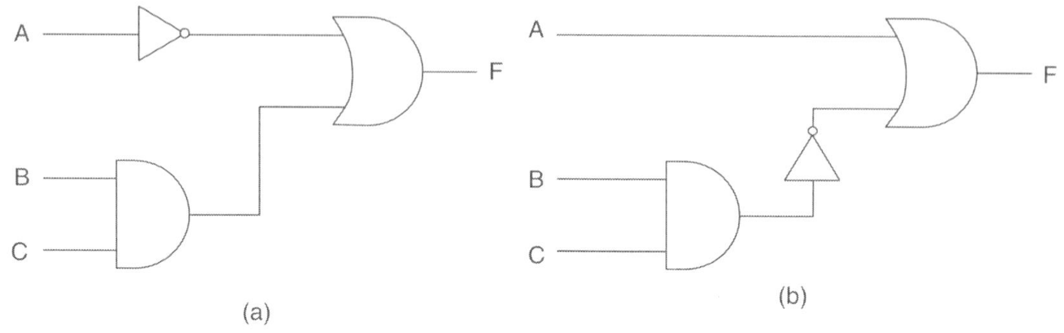

Fig. 3.19 **Digital circuits for Exercise 2**

3. By constructing appropriate truth tables, show that:

   (i) A + (B + C) = (A + B) + C
   (ii) A · (B · C) = (A · B) · C
   (iii) A · (B + C) = A · B + A · C
   (iv) A + (B · C) = (A + B) · (A + C)

   The first two of these identities represent the *associativity* of *and* and *or* operations. The third and four identities represent the *distributivity* of *and* over *or*, and vice versa.
4. By constructing appropriate truth tables, show that:

   (iii) ¬(B + C) = (¬B) · (¬C)
   (iv) ¬(B · C) = (¬B) + (¬C)

   These identities are known as de Morgan's rules.
5. Outline how you would construct a three-digit decimal counter, which counts from 000 to 999, by making use of three single-digit decimal counters which count from 0 to 9.
6. Outline how you would construct a single-digit decimal counter by making use of four flip-flops. Note that the count must be reset to 0 after it reaches 9.
7. Recall that Fig. 3.10 shows a register bank consisting of eight *N*-bit registers, along with its associated data and control signals. Draw a similar figure for a register bank consisting of 32 *N*-bit registers; show clearly the required data and control signals.
8. A physical memory device stores four megabytes of memory. However, the memory device is not byte addressable, since it performs *read* and *write* operations only on one word—i.e. four bytes—at a time. Show the schematic memory organisation and input/output signals specific to this memory device, by drawing diagrams similar to Figs. 3.12 and 3.13.
9. A computer system has 24 address lines, for a total memory addressability of 2^{24} = 16 megabytes. However, the system needs to be provided with only two megabytes

of physical memory, by making use of two memory devices of one megabyte each. The two megabytes of memory provided are to occupy the lowest addresses in the total addressable memory of the system.

Outline how you would decode and make use of the 24 system address lines to achieve this design objective.

10. Show the truth table of an 8-to-3 encoder, in a format similar to that of Table 3.1, keeping in mind the constraint that exactly one of the encoder inputs has value 1 at any time.

11. Consider the multiplexer shown in Fig. 3.15. Let A, B, C and D represent the four sets of input lines to the multiplexer, and let O represent the set of output lines. Outline how you would use this multiplexer in such a way that the output lines are connected, in turn, to lines A, B, C and D, and then back again to A, switching at the rate of one per second.

In other words, for one second, A lines are connected to O; then for one second, B lines are connected to O, and so on.

Hint: This can be achieved by connecting an appropriate *timer* or *counter* device to the two control signals of the multiplexer.

12. Outline how you would use a multiplexer and a demultiplexer to build a 4-line, 4 × 4 *switch*, i.e. a device which can connect any set of input lines to any set of output lines (see Fig. 3.20).

Hint: Make use of the control signals of the two devices.

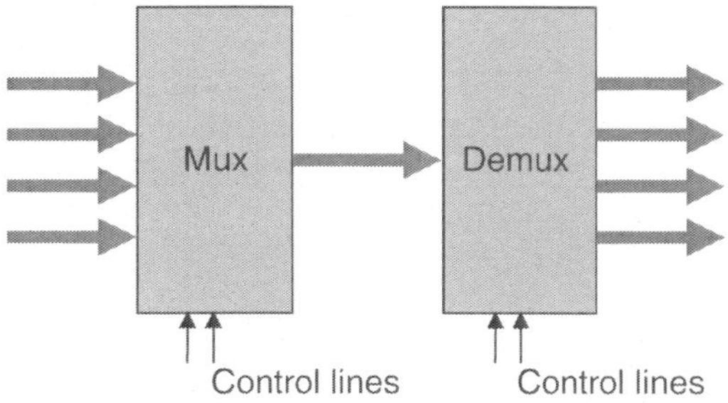

Fig. 3.20 **Combination of multiplexer and demultiplexer**

PROCESSOR INSTRUCTION SET-I

4

4.1 INTRODUCTION

In Chapter 1, we saw that the processor operates by repeatedly cycling through two steps which define the execution of a single instruction. These two steps are called the *Fetch* and *Execute* steps, respectively. This combination of *Fetch* and *Execute* steps runs as long as the processor is powered up and not explicitly halted.

The principle here is that an instruction stored in memory cannot be executed until it is first fetched—or brought—into the processor. Or, in other words, the main memory of a computer system does not have the capability to execute the instructions stored therein.

Thus, we saw that the working of a typical processor can be described using the following algorithmic notation:

```
repeat forever
{
  fetch the next instruction from main memory
  execute—i.e. carry out—the instruction fetched
}
```

For a proper understanding of the processor, it is necessary to look at two somewhat independent and complementary aspects of the working of a processor, namely:

a. how a processor is programmed, and
b. how a processor is designed so as to execute, one by one, the instructions which make up a program.

When we study (a), we look at the different ways in which instructions can operate on data. We then look at how a sequence of instructions—i.e. a *program*—can collectively perform a specified task. This is the goal of this chapter and the next. In other words, in Chapters 4 and 5 we shall take a look at how the processor can be programmed to perform specified tasks. Since a program is nothing but a sequence of instructions, we shall first study a single typical instruction, and then study how instructions can be combined together to produce functionally useful programs.

Chapters 6 and 7, on the other hand, address the point (b) above. We shall see how the processor can be organised internally, using the basic hardware building blocks we studied in Chapter 3, to carry out the *Fetch* and *Execute* steps—also known as *Fetch* and *Execute phases* (or *cycles*). While the *Fetch phase* does not vary much from instruction to instruction, the *Execute phase* clearly must vary from instruction to instruction, since different instructions operate on data in different ways.

4.2 A TYPICAL INSTRUCTION

Instructions provided on a processor are also commonly referred to as *machine instructions*. A typical such instruction may have the structure:

< opcode >

or the structure:

< opcode, operand >

or the structure:

< opcode, operand-1, operand-2 >

Here *opcode* is an abbreviation for *operation code*, indicating which operation the processor is being instructed to perform. Addition of two integers, for example, may be indicated by opcode ADD.

The processor performs operations on operands. As seen above, an instruction may have none, one or two operands. Thus *operand*, *operand-1* and *operand-2* here represent the operands of the operation indicated by *opcode*. Suffixes '*-1*' and '*-2*' distinguish the two operands of an instruction which has the *two-operand* structure shown above*.

Note 4.1

In the course of this and subsequent chapters, we shall most frequently refer to operation codes using their corresponding *mnemonics*, for example ADD above is the mnemonic which represents the operation code for addition. These mnemonics are selected so that anyone working with such instructions—a hardware or software engineer, for example—can easily associate the function carried out by an instruction with its mnemonic.

Of course, the hardware circuits inside the processor do not recognise instruction mnemonics, but only their corresponding *binary codes*. In sections of the book dealing with the byte lengths and the actual execution mechanisms of instructions, we may need to look at typical binary representation of instructions.

For initially learning how to program a processor, however, it is not necessary to learn the binary representation of instructions. But, at the same time, it is important for the student to remember that mnemonics are used only by the programmer, and that the hardware only recognises the binary language made up of '0's and '1's.

Most programmers write computer programs using *higher level* programming languages—such as C++ and JAVA—in which even mnemonics such as ADD do not have any role. Such programmers are in that sense one step further removed from the hardware of the computer for which they are writing programs. We may say that programming languages such as C++ and JAVA provide a *higher level of abstraction* than that which is provided by hardware and by individual instructions such as ADD.

In Chapter 15, we shall discuss in some more detail the important role of software in computer systems. There we shall see how a program written in a higher level language is transformed into its binary representation and then executed on the computer system.

---

*Processors have also been designed which provide *three-operand* instruction formats. In an introductory book on computer systems, however, it is not necessary to review all possible ways to define machine instructions; it is sufficient to study one machine instruction set which illustrates the basic concepts; see Section 4.3 below.

The operands for a particular instruction may be *explicit* or *implicit.* Consider as an example the *two-operand* instruction:

ADD A, B

Let us assume that A and B are two registers within the processor which contain the two operands of the addition operation.

We might guess that the instruction here is 'Add A to B', since this is similar to how we would read this command in English. But in the context of a processor, the above instruction might well be 'Add B to A', with the roles of A and B reversed. In the first case, the final sum A + B would replace the previous value stored in B, whereas in the second case, the final sum would replace the previous value stored in A. Thus, in either case, the final destination of the result A + B is *implicit* rather than *explicit.*

Now suppose a processor provides the *one-operand* instruction:

ADD A

Here only one operand is specified explicitly. Therefore, apparently even the second operand of the addition operation is implicit. Presumably, in this case, the value A will be added into the contents of a register within the processor which is implicit. The previous value stored in that register will be replaced by the sum.

Typically, instructions such as ADD find their operands, whether implicit or explicit, within so-called *general-purpose* registers—also known as *programmable* registers—provided within the processor.

Note that, unless explicitly specified otherwise, arithmetic operations such as ADD here will be assumed to operate on *integer* rather than *floating point* operands. In latter parts of the book, where necessary, the corresponding floating point operations will be referred to as FADD, for example.

4.3 THE PROCESSOR *NICE*

For learning to write programs in the binary language of a processor, naturally we need to select a specific processor on which our programs would run. For this purpose, instead of selecting a commercially available processor, we have designed a simple processor of our own which brings out the relevant technical features and principles.

The processor we have designed has been named *NICE*. This name is not an acronym, but rather it reflects the fact that the processor in question is a nice and simple one, suitable for a first course in Computer System Organisation.

Since *NICE* is not available as a hardware product, we have developed a *software simulator* for it, which is available for download on the website associated with this book. The simulator—which runs on a standard PC—enables a student to run *NICE* assembly language programs, and to examine the status of the processor before and after the execution of each instruction.

Other specific features of *NICE*—such as its various instructions, word size, and so on—will be introduced as we proceed further in this chapter and the next.

4.4 PROGRAMMABLE REGISTERS

A basic fact of present-day computer design is that operands stored in general-purpose programmable registers within the processor can be accessed much faster than those stored in main memory.

One reason for this speed mismatch is that the electronic storage elements within the processor, including all the registers, provide much faster access times than those in main memory, which are limited by its size and internal organisation. Also, data paths within the processor are shorter and faster than those between processor and main memory, and therefore access by the processor to local registers is much faster than access to main memory locations.

From the earliest days of computers, therefore, it has become standard practice to provide at least a few general-purpose programmable registers within the processor. This allows the faster arithmetic and logic operations within the processor to be carried out without being slowed down too much by frequent accesses to main memory.

Frequently used operands within a program can be *loaded* from main memory into processor registers, so that subsequent operations on them can proceed at higher speeds. If an operand is no longer to be used frequently, it can be *stored* back into main memory, so that the same register can then be used to hold another operand.

This is typically how a programmer makes use of programmable registers provided within a processor.

How many such programmable registers should a processor have?

Over the past few decades, with advances in integrated circuit (IC) technology, this number has shown a steady increase. With modern tools and techniques of processor design and manufacture, it is neither too difficult nor too expensive to provide many such registers within the processor. However, constraints on instruction formats may place a limit on the number of registers provided within the processor.

NICE processor, which serves as our running example in this book, has been provided with *sixteen* programmable registers, designated by the symbols R0 through R15.

With sixteen programmable registers, we need 4 bits within an instruction to select—or specify—one of these registers as an operand, since $2^4 = 16$. This number is much smaller than the size of a main memory address, i.e. number of bits required to select an operand in main memory. Thus the use of programmable registers allows operands—and therefore instructions—to be specified in a compact and therefore efficient manner.

We shall further assume that the programmable registers of *NICE* are functionally alike, in the sense that none of these registers has been assigned a special role which has been denied to the others*. If an instruction, say ADD, has two operands in registers, then these two operands may be in any two of the sixteen registers available.

Thus we may have an actual instruction such as, for example:

ADD R3, R4

This could mean: Add the contents of R3 to the contents of R4, and store the result in R4. But, as we saw above, this could also mean: Add the contents of R4 to the contents of R3, and store the result in R3.

Which is right? The answer is: The designers of the processor decide which is right!

Technical specifications of the processor spell out in detail the instruction formats and their correct interpretations, and programmers must follow these specifications to write programs which make use of available instructions.

---

*We shall make one exception to this rule, for reasons which will be seen in Chapter 6.

For *NICE*, we have selected the first interpretation. The above instruction then means:

Add the contents of R3 to the contents of R4, and store the result in R4.

Another way of saying this is that our two-operand instructions have the format:

< opcode, *source* operand, *destination* operand >

Here the words *source* and *destination* make clear the role of each operand.

What is the size, in number of bits, of each register?

For efficient arithmetic operations and also other processor operations, a single eight-bit byte is a very small unit of storage. Therefore programmable registers are usually made several bytes wide. We have designed each of the programmable registers R0 to R15 of *NICE* to be four bytes—or 32 bits—wide.

With such registers, a single instruction of our processor is capable of performing an arithmetic operation, logical operation, or memory operation on 32-bit quantities. We designate such a quantity as a *word*. One word is therefore made up of four bytes, and thus *NICE* has a *word size* of 32 bits.

Recall from Chapter 3 that the main memory may be assumed to be byte-addressable, i.e. each memory *address* uniquely identifies a single byte. For efficiency, however, a memory operation—a *read* or a *write*—may involve in general more than one byte.

With one *load* instruction, *NICE* can read from main memory either a single byte or a word (i.e. four bytes); similarly, with one *store* instruction, *NICE* can write to main memory either a single byte or a word. As we shall see in the next chapter, the programmer selects byte or word operation by using an appropriate *instruction modifier* with the instruction.

However, the simple programs of this chapter do not use instruction modifiers. Therefore—by default—each *load* instruction in this chapter transfers one word from memory to a register, and each *store* instruction transfers one word from a register to memory.

4.5 A SIMPLE PROGRAM

Consider the *NICE* machine language Program 4.1, consisting of a sequence of seven instructions.

The first LOAD instruction in this program loads the contents of the four-byte word at memory location 2000 into register R1. Similarly, the second and the third LOAD instructions load the contents of the next two consecutive memory words into registers R2 and R3, respectively.

Program 4.1

```
LOAD    2000, R1
LOAD    2004, R2
LOAD    2008, R3
ADD     R2, R1
ADD     R3, R1
STORE   2000, R1
HALT
```

The nett effect of the two ADD instructions is that the sum of these three 32-bit integers is found in R1. The STORE instruction stores this sum back into the memory word at address 2000, and the HALT instruction halts the execution of this program.

Thus this short program computes the sum of the three 32-bit integers stored at memory locations 2000, 2004 and 2008 respectively, and then stores the result back in place of the first of these three operands.

For the convenience of hardware and software engineers working with such programs, suitable *comments* must be included along with the program. This is important because, in the absence of such comments, engineers may misunderstand program logic and make avoidable programming errors. When such comments are added to Program 4.1, it takes the form of Program 4.2.

All program lines starting with two slashes ('//')—and the parts of all other lines to the right of two slashes—are to be treated as *comments*. Comments help a reader understand the program, but do not alter in any way the functionality of the program.

Program 4.2

```
//
// Program to add three 32-bit integers
//
    LOAD      2000, R1   // Load first operand into R1
    LOAD      2004, R2   // ... second operand into R2
    LOAD      2008, R3   // ... third operand into R3
    ADD       R2, R1     // Add second operand into the first
    ADD       R3, R1     // Add third operand into the sum
    STORE     2000, R1   // Store result back in place of
                         // the first operand
    HALT                 // Halt the program
```

Generally, except where binary representations of instructions are essential, we shall write programs for our processor in the format of Program 4.2. Programs written in such representation are known as *assembly language programs*, and the process of converting them into binary machine language is known as *assembly*. System programs which perform this conversion are known as *assemblers*.

The execution of Program 4.2, one instruction at a time, has been shown in Table 4.1. In the left-most column of the table, we see the instructions listed one by one. The next three columns show the contents of memory words at addresses 2000, 2004 and 2008 respectively. We have assumed that, before the program is executed, these words contain values 200, 300 and 500 respectively.

The last three columns of the table show the contents of registers R1, R2 and R3. Symbol '?' in a column indicates that the corresponding register contents are undefined—and also immaterial to the final result of the program.

In each row, the contents columns show the respective memory and register contents after the instruction in the first column has been executed. The figures in the contents column are shown in boldface in the row when they change value. For example, after the first LOAD instruction is executed, the contents of R1 change to 200.

Table 4.1 **Instruction-wise execution of program 4.2**

Instruction	Contents					
	m:2000	m:2004	m:2008	R1	R2	R3
(initial condition)	**200**	**300**	**500**	?	?	?
`LOAD 2000, R1`	200	300	500	**200**	?	?
`LOAD 2004, R2`	200	300	500	200	**300**	?
`LOAD 2008, R3`	200	300	500	200	300	**500**
`ADD R2, R1`	200	300	500	**500**	300	500
`ADD R3, R1`	200	300	500	**1000**	300	500
`STORE 2000, R1`	**1000**	300	500	1000	300	500
`HALT`	1000	300	500	1000	300	500

Needless to say, memory locations and registers not shown in Table 4.1 do not change their contents as a result of execution of Program 4.2. The student is encouraged to study the table carefully, and verify that the various contents are indeed changing in accordance with the instruction in the first column.

4.6 CONDITIONAL EXECUTION

Program 4.2 discussed in the previous section is nothing but a simple *sequence* of seven instructions. These instructions would be executed by the processor in exactly the order in which they are written, which in this case is also the order in which they are stored in memory.

But real-life computer programs perform computations which cannot be expressed as simple sequences. Even in the above example, suppose that we add the following additional *requirement* to the program:

If the sum of the three integers is less than 1000, then change the sum to 1000.

Clearly Program 4.2 does not do this. But if we insert three new instructions into it, the newly added requirement is satisfied—as seen in Program 4.3.

The three new instructions seen in Program 4.3 are COMP, JGE and MOV, which we shall discuss shortly.

Also seen in Program 4.3 is the hash symbol ('#') preceding a number, e.g. #1000. The meaning here is that the number 1000 is to be used as a *constant*, and not as a memory address. In other words, the symbol '#' indicates that the operand is the indicated constant itself, rather than the content of the indicated memory location.

The instruction COMP *compares*, in this case, the contents of register R1 with the specified constant 1000. The result of this comparison, we assume for the present, is in some suitable manner recorded within the processor.

The instruction JGE specifies that if the result of the last comparison is 'Greater or Equal'—i.e. R1 contains a value greater than or equal to 1000—then the next instruction to be fetched and executed is the one which has *label* DONE. Note that, in this case, the MOV instruction is not executed, since label DONE occurs after it.

Program 4.3

```
//
// Program to add three 32-bit integers
// If the sum is less than 1000, it is changed to 1000.
//
       LOAD      2000, R1   // Load first operand into R1
       LOAD      2004, R2   // ... second operand into R2
       LOAD      2008, R3   // ... third operand into R3
       ADD       R2, R1     // Add second operand into the first
       ADD       R3, R1     // Add third operand into the sum
       COMP      R1, #1000  // Compare contents of R1 to the
                            // constant 1000
       JGE       DONE       // If greater or equal, jump to DONE
       MOV       #1000, R1  // Change contents of R1 to 1000
 DONE: STORE     2000, R1   // Store result back in place of
                            // the first operand
       HALT                 // Halt the program
```

The MOV instruction is therefore executed only if, at the time of comparison, R1 contains a value smaller than 1000. In this case, MOV causes the constant 1000 to be *moved* into register R1, which is consistent with the revised program requirement.

Note that the JGE instruction, which may be read as 'Jump if Greater or Equal', causes the sequential execution of program instructions to be broken, in the sense that the next instruction to be executed—if the *jump condition* is satisfied—is the one with label DONE, rather than the one immediately following JGE.

Program 4.3 thus illustrates *conditional execution*—MOV is executed only if the result of the previous two ADD operations is less than 1000. Students familiar with a higher level programming language would know that, typically, an **if-then-else** type of statement in such languages allows us to program conditional execution.

As seen above, in assembly language, conditional execution is typically achieved by the combined effect of two separate instructions:

a. an *arithmetic*, *logic* or *comparison* instruction, followed by
b. a *conditional jump* instruction, such as JGE above.

The word *jump* indicates that the normal sequential execution of instructions is broken, and that execution continues at some other specified instruction, such as the one with label DONE in Program 4.3.

We shall study many assembly language programs in this and the remaining chapters of the book. However, as a first introduction to the important topic of how a processor is programmed, the simple Programs 4.2 and 4.3 serve our purpose for now.

4.7 INSTRUCTION CLASSES AND INSTRUCTION SET

The instructions we have seen so far may be grouped into several functional categories or classes:

- ADD is an *arithmetic* instruction,
- LOAD, STORE and MOV are *data transfer* instructions,
- COMP is a *comparison* instruction,
- JGE is a *transfer of control* instruction, and
- HALT may be considered a *processor control* instruction.

A typical processor has several more instructions in each category, as we shall see soon. Arithmetic instructions are usually grouped together with *logic* instructions—such as bit-wise AND and OR operations—to make up a class of instructions known as *arithmetic and logic* instructions.

The set of all instructions available on a processor is known as the *instruction set* of the processor. A natural question which arises in this context is: What are the factors which determine the size and complexity of the *instruction set* provided on a processor?

Suppose we have one processor which provides twenty different instructions, and another which provides a hundred different instructions. Of course, we must here assume that any function we wish to perform can be carried out on either processor—for, if this was not the case, we would not even be looking at both the processors!

This means that functions of the 'extra' eighty instructions of the second processor can be *programmed* using suitable combinations of instructions of the first. For example, we know that multiplication is defined as repeated addition; and we shall see later that floating point addition is performed using integer addition, shift and logic operations.

Which of these two processors has the 'better' instruction set? This is an important and interesting question, and we outline some of the factors which influence the answer.

Clearly any processor must have the necessary circuitry to execute all the instructions in its instruction set. Therefore the hardware technology available to build the processor would be one key factor in determining its instruction set. Modern electronic design and fabrication technology—such as *very large-scale integration* (VLSI)—indeed makes it possible to provide a fairly complex instruction set on a processor.

To an assembly language programmer, a complex instruction set may appear to be an advantage. If we think of each instruction as a kind of 'tool' available to the programmer, then having a richer 'toolbox' at one's disposal certainly seems like a good idea.

However, there are other factors which make it necessary <u>not</u> to go overboard with the complexity of the instruction set.

Different processors are built with different applications in mind. A processor in a mobile phone handset may have a simpler instruction set, compared to one which goes into a computer system meant for heavy scientific computations—such as numerical solutions of equations of fluid dynamics. On the mobile phone handset, reduction in power consumption would be a major factor, since it increases operating time between battery recharges; for a scientific application this would be a much less important factor.

In this context, another important factor influencing the choice of the instruction set is related to the way in which computer software is developed. Almost all computer applications are today developed using *higher level* programming languages, such as C++ and JAVA. Specially designed programs known as *compilers* convert higher level language programs into *machine language* programs, which are the binary equivalents of the assembly language programs we have seen above. This method of software development implies that the software developer does not program a computer using machine instructions such as ADD, MOV and JGE seen above.

Over the years, compiler writers—and therefore compilers—have become very good at generating efficient machine language programs. On the whole, compiler writers manage very well with a simple instruction set, and do not actively demand complex instructions. Therefore many processor designers have switched to providing a relatively simple—or *reduced*—instruction set with their processors, giving rise to a type of design which has come to be known as *RISC*, an acronym for *reduced instruction set computer*.

When a processor provides a relatively simple instruction set, the hardware circuitry inside it can be designed to run at higher speeds. The nett result very often is that—all other factors being equal—a processor with a simpler instruction set is able to get more work done per second than a processor with a more complex instruction set. This is broadly the philosophy behind the *RISC* approach to processor design.

Other processor designers, mainly with an aim to provide compatibility with earlier generations of commercially successful processors, have continued to provide processors with fairly complex instruction sets. Such processors have come to be known as *CISC* (pronounced 'sisk'), an acronym for *complex instruction set computer*.

Overall, it is fair to say that designers of the 'RISC school' have proven their point: A simpler instruction set makes it possible to design processors with higher nett processing rates, as we shall see in Chapters 6 and 7. With a complex instruction set, the processing rate of the processor is limited by the relatively complex instructions, even though these may be few in number and less frequently used in typical programs.

In terms of its instruction set, our processor *NICE* is a fairly simple processor, staying close to the philosophy of RISC processors. The main reason for this choice is that all the essential principles of computer system organisation can be brought out most effectively by following Einstein's famous dictum for any scientific theory: *Make it as simple as possible, but no simpler.*

Some more issues related to the complexity of an instruction set will be taken up in Section 5.7, and then once again in Chapters 6 and 7, when we look at how the processor is designed and how it carries out its functions.

4.8 ITERATION

Now consider Program 4.4, which introduces a few more instructions of the *NICE* processor.

Program 4.4

```
//
// Program to find the sum of integers from 1 to 100
//
        MOV     #0, R1      // Initialise R1 to 0
        MOV     #1, R2      // Initialise R2 to 1
//
LOOP:   ADD     R2, R1      // Add R2 into R1
        ADD     #1, R2      // Increment R2 by 1
        COMP    R2, #100    // Compare contents of R2 to 100
        JLE     LOOP        // If less than or equal, jump to
                            // instruction with label LOOP
        HALT                // Halt the program
```

The instruction appearing for the first time in this program is JLE, a transfer of control instruction. This instruction is similar to JGE seen earlier, except that the jump condition now is *less than or equal*, whereas earlier it was *greater than or equal.*

Every processor—including *NICE*—also provides for *unconditional jump*, JMP, which causes the next instruction to be fetched and executed from the indicated target address.

As against the algorithmic notation seen earlier, a *flow chart* is a graphical form of depicting program logic. The flow chart corresponding to Program 4.4 would be as shown in Fig. 4.1. Rectangular boxes in a flow chart represent operations to be performed, diamond-shaped boxes indicate decisions to be made, and arrows indicate how execution moves from one box to another.

The two circles with words BEGIN and END written inside indicate the beginning and end of the program represented.

The program seen above illustrates *iteration*—i.e. repeated execution of a set of operations. It is safe to say that, almost without exception, programs of any practical significance do employ iteration in one form or another. In the flow chart of Fig. 4.1, the thick dashed line in brown color marks out the so-called *program loop*—or simply *loop*—which is executed 100 times.

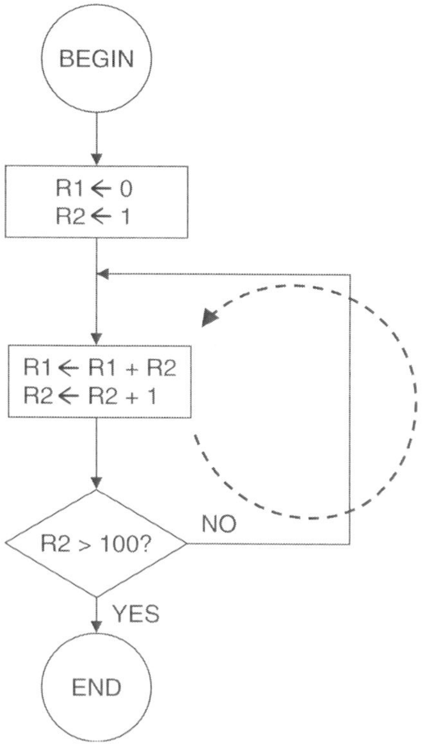

Fig. 4.1 Flow chart of program to find sum of integers 1 to 100

Note 4.2

Program 4.2 makes use of *sequential* order of execution of instructions, i.e. the instructions of the program are executed one by one strictly in the order in which they are written, which is also the order in which they are stored in memory. In Program 4.3, we studied *conditional execution* of instructions, while in Program 4.4, we saw *iterative execution* of instructions.

It turns out that any function that is to be programmed can be programmed using an appropriate combination of *sequential*, *conditional* and *iterative* 'program structures'. One could have, for example, conditional execution of instructions within a program loop, or a program loop within one *branch* of a condition, and so on.

Therefore it will prove quite useful to the student to understand at this early stage how these three basic program structures are written in assembly language.

4.9 BASIC INPUT OUTPUT INSTRUCTIONS

Now let us look at *NICE* instructions which can read data *in* from an input device and write data *out* to an output device. Note that, at this early stage, it will not be necessary for us to consider any physical details of the input or output device itself.

The input device could be a keyboard or a mouse, for example. What is relevant here is only that the *input data* from the device is available in a *device register*, and can be read into a processor register using an appropriate instruction. And similarly *output data* is written into a *device register* in the output device using an appropriate instruction.

Consider Program 4.5.

Program 4.5

```
   //
   // Program to read 100 bytes from an input device and
   // write them to an output device
   //
       MOV       #1, R2     // Initialise R2 to 1
   //
 LOOP: IN        10, R1     // Read a byte from device at
                            // address 10
       OUT       20, R1     // Write that byte out to device
                            // at address 20
       ADD       #1, R2     // Increment R2 by 1
       COMP      R2, #100   // Compare contents of R2 to 100
       JLE       LOOP       // If less or equal, jump to LOOP
                            //
       HALT                 // Halt the program
```

It can be verified easily that the iterative structure of this program is identical to that of the previous program, while the instructions within the loop are different. In this program, the two relevant instructions within the loop are:

```
IN    10, R1     // Read a byte from device at
                 // address 10
OUT   20, R1     // Write that byte out to device
                 // at address 20
```

The operation mnemonic of the first instruction is IN. This instruction reads in the contents of a *device register*, and stores these contents in processor register R1. We assume for the present that the device register in question belongs to an input device, which supplies data to the processor one byte at a time. The address 10 appearing as the first operand of IN is the *address* of the device register.

Recall that the processor register R1 is in fact of word size, which in our case is four bytes, whereas instruction IN brings in only one byte into R1. Which of the four bytes of R1 does the incoming byte occupy, and what happens to the remaining three bytes of R1?

Let us decide—since this will prove useful in programming—that the incoming byte occupies the rightmost byte (LSB) of R1, and that the remaining three bytes of R1 remain unchanged when instruction IN is executed.

Operation mnemonic of the second instruction is OUT. This instruction writes out the rightmost byte of register R1 to a byte size register associated with a device, which we assume is an output device. The address 20 appearing as the first operand of OUT is the *address* of this device register.

This program makes a crucial—but unrealistic—assumption that device registers are always *ready* to be read from, or to be written into. In practice, this is almost never the case. The fact that input and output devices are not always *ready* for input and output is what distinguishes them from memory elements.

Devices are limited in their own speeds of operation, which often involve mechanical motion. Therefore, in general, a program must first test that a device is *ready*, before the program tries to read from or write into a device. This *testing-for-device-ready* operation is omitted from the above program, but will be taken up in Chapter 10.

Figure 4.2 shows a computer system with the processor, main memory and two device controllers, which we assume are connected to an input device and an output device, respectively. From the point of view of the processor, everything to the left of the small arrow marked '1' is the input device, and everything to the left of the small arrow marked '2' is the output device. We may in fact say that, as seen from the processor, the device controller is the device.

In the program above, we have used 10 as the address of a device register in the input device, and 20 as the address of a device register in the output device. Therefore we can now say that the device register at address 10 is in the *input device controller* in Fig. 4.2, and the device register at address 20 is in the *output device controller*.

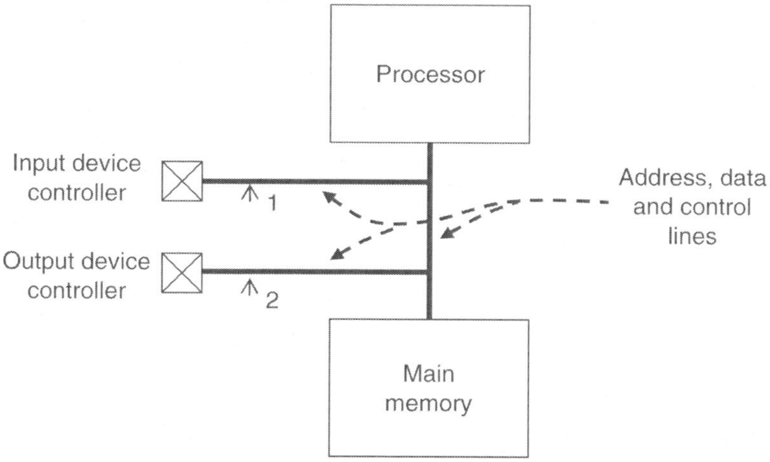

Fig. 4.2 **Computer system with processor, memory and device controllers**

Essentially the same address and data lines connect the processor, the memory, and the device controllers. How does the main memory sub-system know, for example, that the addresses 10 and 20 are not memory addresses, but the addresses of device registers? After all, we must remember that the main memory also has addresses 10 and 20—and clearly it is important that each address within the system identifies a unique location of data, either in memory, or within a device controller.

So the crucial question is this: If an address such as 10 is written out on the address lines by the processor, how do the main memory block and the various devices determine whether this is a memory address or an input/output (I/O) address?

The answer is simple. We must assume that the bus connecting the various blocks in Fig. 4.2 has one special signal line which is designated as, say, *memory-or-I/O*. When this line carries the value '1', any address on the address lines is intended for the main memory, and is decoded accordingly. Conversely, when this line carries the value '0', any address on the address lines is intended for an input or output device; decoding of this address then causes the correct I/O device to be addressed. This signal line, in other words, distinguishes memory addresses from I/O device addresses.

So we must conclude that memory instructions LOAD and STORE will cause the *memory-or-I/O* line to remain '1' during the ensuing execute cycle of the processor, and instructions IN and OUT will cause this line to remain '0' during the execute cycle. This is the essential difference between a processor instruction which addresses memory and an instruction which addresses an input or output device.

4.10 PROGRAM STATUS WORD

Consider once again Program 4.4, repeated here for convenience, and in particular the two instructions highlighted:

Program 4.4

```
 //
 // Program to find the sum of integers from 1 to 100
 //
     MOV      #0, R1     // Initialise R1 to 0
     MOV      #1, R2,    // Initialise R2 to 1
 //
LOOP:ADD      R2, R1     // Add R2 into R1
     ADD      #1, R2     // Increment R2 by 1
     COMP     R2, #100   // Compare contents of R2 to 100
     JLE      LOOP       // If less than or equal, jump to
                         // instruction with label LOOP
     HALT                // Halt the program
```

The first of the instructions highlighted is COMP, which in this case is comparing the contents of R2 with the constant 100. The second instruction JLE is then causing a *conditional* transfer of control to take place to the instruction with label LOOP—the condition in question being: *less than or equal.*

How does the second instruction 'know' the result of comparison carried out in the first instruction? Clearly, there must be a way in which the result of an instruction—such as COMP—can be somehow 'recorded' within the processor. A subsequent instruction such as JLE can then 'make a decision' based on the result.

A register is usually provided within the processor which records the relevant bits of information from the result of execution of one instruction, to the extent that these bits may be useful for conditional operations of subsequent instructions. This register is most commonly known as the *program status word* (PSW). In Fig. 4.3 we have outlined a part of the program status word of *NICE*; the names and functions of some of the so-called *flag bits* in PSW are explained in Table 4.2.

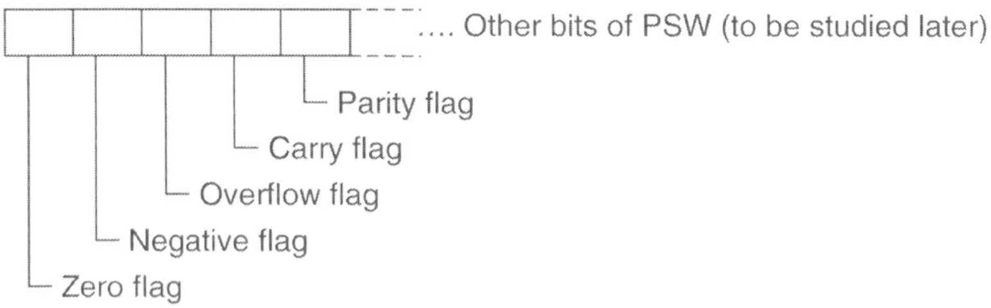

Fig. 4.3 Flag bits in program status word

Note that the condition flags listed in Table 4.2 are all *binary*—i.e. if the condition which causes a flag to be set is violated, the flag will be reset.

For the purposes of defining the 'result of previous operation', the compare instruction COMP is treated in the same way as a *subtract* instruction, the only difference being that COMP does not cause the result of the operation to be written back into the destination register. Thus the instruction:

```
COMP   R2, #100   // Compare contents of R2 to 100
```

Table 4.2 **Functions of some of the bits in program status word (PSW)**

Flag	**Abbreviation**	**Condition which causes flag to be set**
Zero	Z	Result of previous operation is zero
Negative	N	Result of previous operation is negative
Overflow	O	Previous operation causes overflow in result
Carry	C	Previous operation causes carry to be generated from leftmost bit
Parity	P	Result of previous operation has odd number of 1's

causes the constant value 100 to be subtracted from the value contained in R2, without the result being written back into any register. In other words, the result is 'thrown away', but the five flag bits of PSW shown above are set or reset accordingly.

On many processors—including *NICE*—only *arithmetic, logic, and comparison* instructions cause the flag bits to be set or reset, while *data transfer* instructions do not.

Further, on many processors, not every arithmetic or logical instruction sets or resets each of the flags listed. In general, for each instruction, the set of flag bits affected by it is separately specified. This fine distinction is made by processor designers to make it easier for programmers to write programs for, say, multiple-precision arithmetic.

For *NICE*, however, we have made the simple assumption that any arithmetic, logic, or comparison instruction causes each of the five flags shown in Table 4.1 to be set or reset, depending on the result of the operation.

Example 4.1

In Chapter 3, we have seen the binary operation *and* (see Fig. 3.5 (a)). This operation can be applied bit-wise to two operands of width n bits each, in which case the ith bit of the result is produced by applying *and* to the respective i^{th} bits of the two operands.

Now consider the following instruction of *NICE*, which causes bit-wise logical *and* operation of the content of R0 with itself:

```
AND    R0, R0
```

This instruction would reset flags C and O, since the bit-wise logical AND operation can never cause carry or overflow; and the same argument in fact applies to any logic instruction of the processor.

The instruction above would cause Z, P and N flags to be set or reset, according to the contents of R0. Note here also that an AND or OR operation of register R0 with itself does not alter its contents—and therefore this instruction is essentially a test whether the contents of R0 satisfy one or more of the three conditions Z, P and N.

In addition to the arithmetic and logic flags Z, N, O, C and P, the program status word (PSW) of a processor also contains other information related to program status, typically information related to I/O operations and memory protection, which is required when multiple programs share main memory. Such additional information recorded in PSW will be discussed later, when the corresponding processor functions are described.

SUMMARY

In this chapter, we took our first look at how a typical processor is programmed, using for this purpose our own processor *NICE*. We studied typical instruction formats, and adopted the two-address format for our arithmetic and logic instructions.

Use of the binary machine language for programming is inconvenient and also highly error-prone; therefore we used assembly language and studied a few programs involving sequential, conditional, and iterative execution of instructions; we also studied a program which performed simple input and output on hypothetical devices.

Program logic can be described as a combination of the basic sequential, conditional, and iterative control flow structures. These can be combined in various ways to design the required program logic; apart from algorithmic notation, the graphical notation of flow charts can also be used as an aid in the design of programs.

Instructions provided on a processor may be divided into various functional classes, or groups, such as *data transfer* instructions, *arithmetic and logic* instructions, *comparison* instructions, *transfer of control* instructions, and *processor control* instructions. We considered in brief the relative complexity of the instruction set provided on a processor, and some related performance issues, and discussed in brief the two main instruction set design approaches known as CISC and RISC.

Condition flags in the program status word (PSW) are used to achieve conditional transfers of control; the flags are set by arithmetic, logic, and comparison instructions, and are then used by the various conditional jump instructions.

REVIEW QUESTIONS

1. Describe in one sentence each the function performed by the processor in the fetch and execute phases of an instruction.
2. Why do we say that the fetch phase does not vary much from instruction to instruction?
3. What is the difference between an instruction mnemonic and its binary opcode?
4. Show the typical structure—i.e. format—of a processor instruction with no operands, with one operand, and with two operands.
5. What is the role of general purpose—or programmable—registers in providing operands for machine instructions?
6. Give an example each of an implicitly specified and an explicitly specified operand in a machine instruction.
7. State in brief why access by the processor to programmable registers is much faster than access to locations in main memory.
8. What is the significance of load and store operations performed by the processor for operands stored in main memory?
9. A processor under design has 64 programmable registers. How many bits must be provided within a machine instruction to specify a register operand?
10. Why is it necessary to provide for multi-byte read and write operations on main memory?
11. State in one sentence the action carried out by the following instruction:

```
LOAD  2000, R1
```

12. State in one sentence the action carried out by the following instruction:

```
ADD  R2, R1
```

13. State in one sentence the action carried out by the following instruction:

```
COMP  R6, #1000
```

14. State in one sentence the action carried out by the following instruction:

```
JGE  DONE
```

15. State in one sentence the action carried out by the following instruction:

```
JMP  DONE
```

16. State in one sentence the action carried out by the following instruction:

```
MOV  #1000, R1
```

17. Why is it important to include sufficient comments with every program we write?
18. We have seen that conditional execution is achieved typically by a combination of two instructions. Explain in brief with an example.
19. List the main classes into which machine instructions of a processor can be classified.
20. State the full forms of the two acronyms RISC and CISC.
21. What is a flow chart?
22. Define sequential, conditional, and iterative program structures in one line each.
23. State in one sentence the action carried out by the following instruction:

```
IN  10, R1
```

24. State in one sentence the action carried out by the following instruction:

```
OUT  20, R5
```

25. What is the function of the signal line *memory-or-I/O* which is associated with the address lines of a processor? What would be the value of this signal during LOAD, STORE, IN and OUT instructions?
26. What is the effect of executing the following instruction on the condition code bits?

```
OR  R4, R4
```

EXERCISES

Notes to student:

a. Include suitable comments with all the exercise programs written.
b. If necessary, you may make use of a flow chart or algorithmic notation to ensure that your program logic is right, before writing the program in assembly language.

1. Registers R1 and R2 contain two integers. Write a program which compares these two integers, and if necessary swaps them so that the larger of the two integers is brought into R1 while the smaller of the two integers is brought into R2.
2. Refer to Program 4.2, which finds the sum of three integers stored as three consecutive memory words, starting at address 2000.

Once again, you are given three integers stored as three consecutive memory words, starting at address 2000. Write a program which brings into register R1 the largest of the three integers thus stored in memory.

3. Refer once again to Program 4.2. Modify it in such a way that it finds the sum of four integers stored as consecutive memory words, starting at address 2000.
4. Refer to the program you wrote in answer to the previous exercise. Now imagine that you have to find the sum of a hundred or a thousand integers stored in memory. Would it be practical to keep modifying Program 4.2 as you modified it for the sum of four integers? Why?

   Clearly it would be advisable to make use of iteration to find the sum of N integers stored in memory, where N could be 3, 4 or 1000. Do we have the instructions needed to program such an iteration? Try it and find out.

   Note: The correct answer to this problem will emerge after we study *indirect addressing mode* in Chapter 5.
5. Refer again to Program 4.2. Note that it makes use of three programmable registers R1, R2 and R3. Modify the program in such a way as to use only two registers, say R1 and R2, but calculate the same result as Program 4.2.
6. Refer to Program 4.4. Modify the program in such a way as to calculate the sum of only the integer multiples of 3 in the range from 1 to 100, i.e. the sum of integers 3, 6, … up to 99.

   [**Hint:** Increment a register content by 3 in each iteration.]
7. Write a program to determine if the integer in R1 is divisible by 7. You may use the *subtract* instruction SUB, which has format similar to ADD. Alternatively, you may use the negative constant operand #-7 with an ADD instruction.
8. Write a program to read in twenty bytes from an input device and find their sum. Assume that the input data register of the device is located at address 30.
9. Write a program to read in positive 8-bit integer values from an input device and find their sum. 'End of data' on the input device is indicated when a zero byte is read in. Assume that the input data register of the device is located at address 30.

   Hint: Use the instruction JZ—*jump on zero*. Recall that the Zero ('Z') flag must be set/reset correctly, and that data transfer operations do not affect this flag.
10. Write a program to write to an output device the consecutive 8-bit integer values from 1 to 20. Assume that the output data register of the device is located at address 40.
11. Write a program to read in a hundred 8-bit integer values from an input device and write out to the output device only the non-zero values which are read in. Assume that the respective input and output data registers of the two devices are located at addresses 10 and 20 respectively.
12. Write a program to read in ten 8-bit integer values from an input device and write them out to the output device in reverse order. Assume that the respective input and output data registers of the two devices are located at addresses 10 and 20 respectively.
13. A program is being developed which consists of an outer loop which is similar to that of Program 4.2. Within the loop body, there is to be conditional execution of a data input operation from an input device. Sketch the flow chart of such a program.
14. A program is being developed which consists of an outer loop which is similar to that of Program 4.2. Nested within the outer loop body is an inner loop. Sketch the flow chart of such a program.

PROCESSOR INSTRUCTION SET-II

5

5.1 ADDRESSING MODES

Let us take another look at Program 4.2, which is repeated here for convenience:

Program 4.2

```
//
// Program to add three 32-bit integers
//
    LOAD      2000, R1   // Load first operand into R1
    LOAD      2004, R2   // ... second operand into R2
    LOAD      2008, R3   // ... third operand into R3
    ADD       R2, R1     // Add second operand into the first
    ADD       R3, R1     // Add third operand into the sum
    STORE     2000, R1   // Store result back in place of
                         // the first operand
    HALT                 // Halt the program
```

Notice that each of the LOAD and STORE instructions has, within it, the memory address of one operand. The specific addresses used in this program are 2000, 2004 and 2008. Recall from Chapter 3 that the number of address lines provided by a processor determines the size of its memory address space. With 24 address lines, for example, the processor has an address space of 2^{24} bytes = 16 megabytes.

We shall assume that our processor, *NICE* does in fact have 24 address lines. This means that each of the memory addresses in the LOAD and STORE instructions is a 24-bit quantity. Since memory addresses are thus included directly within the instructions, this method of addressing operands is known as *direct addressing*.

The second operand in LOAD and STORE instructions, and also both operands of the ADD instructions, are specified to be in registers such as R1, R2 and R3. This method of specifying an operand in a register is known as *register addressing*. Thus LOAD and STORE use *direct addressing* for one operand and *register addressing* for the other operand. Since *NICE* has sixteen programmable registers, each register operand in an instruction takes four bits to encode.

Now look at the following instructions, which were seen in Program 4.3:

```
    COMP      R1, #1000   // Compare contents of R1 to the
                          // constant 1000
    JGE       DONE        // If greater or equal, jump to DONE
    MOV       #1000, R1   // Change contents of R1 to 1000
```

In COMP and MOV instructions here, we see that the value of an operand—and not its location or address—is included within the instruction. The hash symbol '#' indicates that the quantity following it is the value of an operand, and not its location. In this case, we may say that the operand is available immediately within the instruction itself—and accordingly this mode of specifying an operand is known as *immediate mode.*

What about the operand of the JGE instruction? Recall that JGE causes a 'jump' in the sequence of execution of instructions if the preceding comparison resulted in condition *greater or equal.*

The label DONE here is the symbolic target of this *conditional jump* instruction. Since DONE refers to the memory address of an instruction, it must be of the same size as the memory address of an operand. This is because the memory of a computer system stores instructions as well as data using a uniform addressing mechanism. We have assumed a system with 24-bit addresses. Therefore, we conclude that the symbolic label DONE also represents a 24-bit quantity which is a memory address, in the same way as other memory addresses 2000, 2004 and 2008 are 24-bit quantities.

Thus, we can say that the instruction JGE is also making use of *direct addressing* to specify its operand, which is nothing but the address of another instruction.

In the programs of Chapter 4, we have thus seen three different ways in which instructions can specify operands:

by *direct addressing,*
by *register addressing,* and
in *immediate mode.*

The different ways in which instructions can specify their operands are known as *addressing modes.* We shall see that, to meet practical requirements which come up in programming, processors provide more than these three basic addressing modes.

Program 5.1 is a slightly modified version of Program 4.4. Instead of finding the sum of integers from 1 to 100, Program 5.1 finds the sum of a hundred integers, stored in main memory at a

Program 5.1

```
//
// Program to find the sum of a hundred integers
//
       MOV     #0, R1       // Initialise R1 to 0
       MOV     #1, R2       // Initialise R2 to 1
       MOV     #2000, R3    // Initialise R3 to 2000
//
LOOP:  LOAD    [R3], R4     // Load operand from memory to R4
       ADD     R4, R1       // Add it into R1
       ADD     #4, R3       // Add 4 to R3 so that it points
                            // to the next integer to be added
       ADD     #1, R2       // Increment R2 by 1
       COMP    R2, #100     // Compare contents of R2 to 100
       JLE     LOOP         // If less than or equal, jump to
                            // instruction with label LOOP
       HALT                 // Halt the program
```

hundred consecutive word addresses 2000, 2004, 2008, and so on. (Recall here Exercises 3 and 4 of the previous chapter).

Program 5.1 makes use of three registers. R1 is initialised to 0 and it then contains the running sum, as successive values are added into it. Therefore the final answer is also available in R1.

R2 is initialised to 1, and it then keeps track of *loop count*, ensuring—as in Program 4.4—that the loop is executed 100 times.

Register R3 has an important role to play. It is initialised to 2000, which is the memory address of the first word to be added. Each time around the loop, R3 is made to point to the next memory word to be added. The LOAD instruction here has the form:

```
LOAD        [R3], R4
```

Here we see notation [R3] in place of the first operand. What this indicates is that register R3 contains not an operand, but the memory address of an operand. In other words, the memory address of an operand is not available directly within an instruction, but is to be found in the register specified by the instruction.

R3 is initialised to 2000. Therefore, the first execution of the LOAD instruction brings into R4 the four-byte integer starting at memory location 2000. The following ADD instruction causes this integer to be added into R1, which holds the running sum. Since we are working with four-byte integers, the integer added into R1 is the one which occupies the four memory bytes at addresses 2000, 2001, 2002 and 2003.

After that, the second ADD instruction causes the content of R3 to be incremented by 4, so that, after the first iteration of the loop, R3 will point to the memory address 2004. Therefore, the second integer value to be added into R1, in the second iteration, will be the value stored in the four bytes starting at memory location 2004.

This process goes on a hundred times. In each iteration of the loop, the integer value stored at the next word address in memory is loaded into R4 and then added into R1. Therefore, after a hundred iterations of the loop, register R1 contains the required sum of the hundred integers.

Example 5.1

We have seen that Program 5.1 executes the loop 100 times, as the value of loop count R2 goes from 1 to 100. Let us calculate the memory address contained in R3 when the loop is being executed for, say, the 50th time.

The 50th iteration of the loop begins when execution branches back to label LOOP after the 49th iteration. At this time, the loop count in R2 has been incremented from 49 to 50. The address in R3, which had been initialised to 2000, has been incremented by 4 in each iteration. Therefore, its value at the end of the 49th iteration is $2000 + 4 \times 49 = 2196$; so this is the value in R3 when execution branches back to label LOOP after the 49th iteration.

The LOAD instruction at label LOOP has memory address specified in *indirect* mode as [R3]. Therefore, the memory address of the operand is 2196. Since the first 4-byte integer is loaded at address 2000, the 50th integer is loaded at the address 2196.

After the 50th integer has been loaded and added into the running sum in R1, R2 is incremented to 51 and R3 is incremented to $2196 + 4 = 2200$, in preparation for the next branch back to label LOOP for the 51st iteration.

The addressing mode denoted by [R3] is known as *indirect addressing*, since the specified register R3 contains not the operand itself, but its memory address. In accessing main memory operands whose addresses change during program execution, this mode of addressing proves to be extremely useful. On our processor *NICE*, we have physical memory addresses of 24 bits, and therefore in *indirect addressing* mode, the rightmost 24 bits of the register provide the memory address.

Suppose, we had to add not a hundred integer values stored in memory, but fifty, or a thousand, or any other number. In such a case, what will be the extent of change required in Program 5.1? The answer is: very little. In the compare instruction COMP, the second operand #100 would have to change accordingly. In such a situation, it is better to keep the second operand of COMP—which is the *final loop count*—in a register or a memory location. This allows the final loop count to be changed from 100 to any other value, without altering the COMP instruction. (See Exercise 5.1).

Therefore, to our list of addressing modes, we now add one more: *indirect addressing.*

Some processors also provide an *indexed addressing mode*, which has been used in Program 5.1a. Programs 5.1 and 5.1a compute exactly the same function, but note two key differences between Programs 5.1 and 5.1a:

(i) In Program 5.1, register R3 is initialised to 2000, whereas in Program 5.1a, this register is initialised to 0.

(ii) In Program 5.1, the first operand of the first ADD instruction is [R3], the memory location addressed by the contents of R3. In Program 5.1a, this operand is 2000[R3], the memory location addressed by 2000 + contents of R3.

Program 5.1a

```
//
// Program to find the sum of a hundred integers
// -- modified to use indexed addressing
//
      MOV       #0, R1      // Initialise R1 to 0
      MOV       #1, R2      // Initialise R2 to 1
      MOV       #0, R3      // Initialise R3 to 0
//
LOOP: LOAD      2000[R3], R4
                            // Load next operand into R4
                            // from memory location 2000+[R3]
      ADD       R4, R1      // Add it into R1
      ADD       #4, R3      // Add 4 to R3 so that it indexes
                            // the next word to be added
      ADD       #1, R2      // Increment R2 by 1
      COMP      R2, #100    // Compare contents of R2 to 100
      JLE       LOOP        // If less than or equal, jump to
                            // instruction with label LOOP

      HALT                  // Halt the program
```

We saw that in Program 5.1a, register R3 provides the *index* into an *array of word-size integers* which is stored at successive memory addresses 2000, 2004, and so on. The *starting address* or *base address* of the array is 2000; and the contents of R3—denoted by [R3]—provide the *index* or *offset* into this array.

Example 5.2

Like the previous program, Program 5.1a also executes its loop 100 times, as the value of loop count R2 goes from 1 to 100. Now let us calculate (i) the offset value in R3, and (ii) memory address of operand, when the loop is being executed for, say, the 50th time.

(i) The 50th iteration of the loop begins when execution branches back to label LOOP after the 49th iteration. At this time, the loop count in R2 has been incremented from 49 to 50. The offset value in R3, which had been initialised to 0, has been incremented by 4 in each iteration. Therefore its value at the end of the 49th iteration is $4 \times 49 = 196$, and this is the value in R3 when execution branches back to label LOOP after the 49th iteration.

(ii) The LOAD instruction at label LOOP has memory address specified in *indexed* mode as 2000[R3]. Therefore, the effective memory address of the operand is 2000 + contents of R3, which equals 2196. Since the first 4-byte integer is loaded at address 2000, the 50th integer is indeed loaded at the address 2196.

After the 50th integer has been loaded and added into the running sum in R1, register R2 is incremented to 51 and R3 is incremented to $196 + 4 = 200$, in preparation for the next branch back to label LOOP for the 51st iteration.

An advantage of Program 5.1a over Program 5.1 is that the roles of *base address* and *index* are clearly separated. Working with arrays of various kinds of data, and also with other types of aggregated data, is a frequent requirement in software development. In all such cases, clear separation between *base* and *index* helps in writing the programs.

Yet another addressing mode, which we shall see later in this chapter, is the so-called *implicit addressing mode*. In this addressing mode, the operand is <u>not</u> specified explicitly within the instruction. Depending on the instruction, the operand is accessed in a pre-defined manner within the processor or from main memory.

Thus far we have seen five addressing modes: *register*, *direct*, *immediate*, *indirect* and *indexed*, and we shall see examples of the *implicit* mode soon. Some processors provide enhancements over the *indirect* and *indexed* modes, for example, by providing along with these modes, the options of auto-increment and auto-decrement of a register value.

Why must all such addressing modes be provided with a processor?

Basically, so that instructions can access their operands in a logical and efficient manner. Most software is not written in assembly language today, but in higher level languages such as JAVA and C++. The compilers of these languages generate instructions making use of these addressing modes, resulting in more efficient programs.

Suppose, for example, that a program is able to hold its variables in programmable registers while performing computations on them—as opposed to loading them from memory and storing them back in memory after each operation. Having operands thus available in registers has a clear two-fold advantage in program efficiency:

(i) Access to registers is much faster than that to memory locations, so instructions take less time to execute, and
(ii) With intermediate results available in programmable registers within the processor, a smaller number of instructions need to be executed for a given computation.

When dealing with aggregates of data and so-called *linked* data structures, the *indirect* and *indexed* addressing modes are indispensable. The reason is that programs operating on such data structures keep changing the memory addresses to point to various specific data items in main memory. The memory addresses in effect serve as *pointers* to data. For such types of programming, the *direct* addressing mode proves to be insufficient, but *indirect* and *indexed* addressing modes can be used very effectively.

Note 5.1

The instruction set of a processor is said to be *orthogonal* if, across all its instructions, any operand can be specified using any available addressing mode.

We have seen in Chapter 4 that instructions fall into various classes. The concept of orthogonality of an instruction set can best be applied to *arithmetic*, *logic*, *data transfer*, and *comparison* instructions. However, even then, considerations of efficient realisation in hardware limit somewhat the extent to which orthogonality can be supported. For example, if an operand of an arithmetic instruction can reside in main memory, the additional memory access required in 'execute phase' will create difficulty in pipelined implementations of the processor (which we shall study in Chapter 6).

In this sense, *NICE*—the processor which we are using as a running example in this book—has a simple but only partially orthogonal instruction set.

5.2 FUNCTIONS AND FUNCTION CALLS

The programs which we have seen so far contain only about eight to ten instructions each. Most programs which we use on our computers—word processor, mail software, spreadsheet, compiler—contain hundreds of thousands of instructions, or sometimes even millions of instructions. In higher level programming languages, such programs are made up of tens or hundreds of thousands of lines of program code.

Any program of non-trivial size—i.e. somewhat larger than what we have seen so far—needs very careful attention to the question of how it is *organised* or *structured*. It is not possible to write non-trivial programs using only the sequential, conditional, and iterative program structures that we have seen so far.

The most useful technique for structuring large programs is to break up such large programs into *functions* of manageable size. The program may be thought of as a collection of *functions*, each of which performs a clearly specified task.

Example 5.3

A program for processing examination results at a school or college may have the following structure, in terms of successive sub-tasks to be performed:

Read students' marks
Find average marks
Sort marks in descending order
Find names of top ten students
Display suitable output

As seen, the program is made up of five logical sub-tasks. In a similar way, any complex processing task is made up of smaller sub-tasks—which in computer terminology are called *functions*.

In fact, it is not possible for us to even *specify* clearly a complex processing task without breaking it up into smaller sub-tasks; and programming any task correctly is definitely not possible without a clear *specification* of the task.

The human mind can deal with a complex system only by breaking it up into smaller, less complex *sub-systems*. Naturally, the smaller, less complex sub-systems interact with each other as parts of the larger, more complex system.

In the context of computer programs, a larger program is organised as a collection of smaller processing tasks—or *functions*—which interact with each other as required. In Example 5.3 above, we saw that the program for processing examination results can be organised as a sequence of five functions.

Of course, it is quite possible that some of the functions used by the *main program* are themselves organised in terms of other 'lower level' functions, as we now illustrate with the next two examples.

Example 5.4

The following sequence of four processing steps defines a function to find and display the distance between two points in the X-Y plane:

Read coordinates x_1, y_1 of first point
Read coordinates x_2, y_2 of second point
Distance = square root of $(x_1 - x_2)^2 + (y_1 - y_2)^2$
Display distance with suitable message

We assume that this function is required as part of a larger program being developed.

For performing steps such as (i) reading the coordinate values, (ii) finding the square root, and (iii) displaying the result, a programmer would typically make use of 'lower level' functions which are provided with the programming language.

In general, today it is not possible for a programmer to write any non-trivial program without making use of many such functions which are provided with the programming language and with the operating system.

Now suppose we have available with us a function for finding the square root of a floating point number. This means that, occupying some locations in main memory are the instructions which perform the task of finding square root. The first instruction to be executed as part of this 'square root function' in main memory is called the *starting address* of the function.

At some stage in our own program, we wish to find the square root of a number, say X. How do we get the square root function, available elsewhere in memory, to get to work on finding the square root of this particular number X?

The answer is: We place the value X in a pre-designated place, say register R0, and then *invoke* or *call* the function, which will find the square root of the number placed by us in R0. When the square root is found, the answer is made available to our program once again in a pre-designated place, say register R1.

The logical relationship between our 'main program', which needs the square root of X, and the function which calculates the square root of X, can be depicted as in Fig. 5.1.

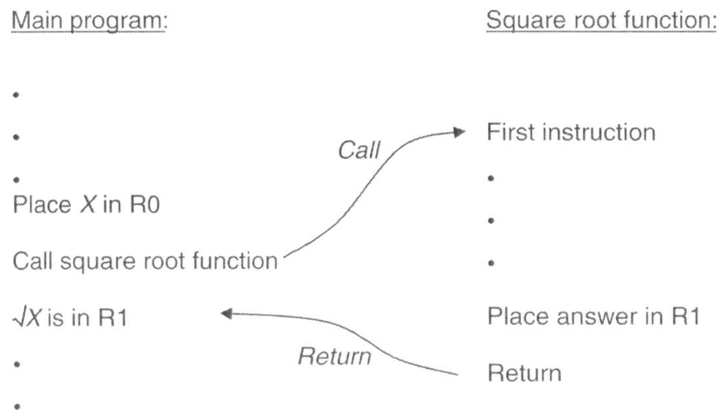

Fig. 5.1 Schematic diagram of function *call* and *return*

One point has to be noted carefully in Fig. 5.1. After the square root function completes its task, the next instruction in our 'main program' which must be executed is the one immediately after the point from which the square root function is called. This is perfectly logical. Since the required square root would be available after that function completes its task, the 'main program' must resume from its next instruction.

This is the crucial distinction between the *jump* instructions which we have used earlier and the *function call* mechanism which we are now studying. Once a *jump* in the path of execution takes place, whether conditional or unconditional, there is no associated mechanism for returning to the instruction after the *jump*.

Thus a *function call* is also a transfer of control, similar to *jump*, except that the point of return must also be remembered—i.e. saved—by the processor. This point of return is the instruction immediately after the call, and its address is known as *return address*.

But things can get a little more complicated, as seen in the next example.

Example 5.5

Consider a graphics program, which must frequently obtain from the user a pair of points. For each such pair of points obtained from the user, the program must find the distance between the pair of points.

The program is structured as (i) the main graphics program, (ii) a separate function to obtain a pair of points from the user, and (iii) another function to find square root. The square root function here is exactly as seen in Example 5.4 above. The graphics program calls the pair of points function as needed, and the latter calls the square root function.

Let 'pp' and 'sr' denote the pair of points and the square root function, respectively. Then the arrangement of function calls and returns is as shown schematically in Fig. 5.2.

At time Cpp, the graphics program calls the function 'pp'; and at a later time Csr, the function 'pp' in turn calls the function 'sr'.

At the time marked Rsr, when the function 'sr' completes its work, it returns to the function 'pp'. And at a later time Rpp, when 'pp' also completes its work, it returns to the main graphics program. On time axis, these four events are ordered as:

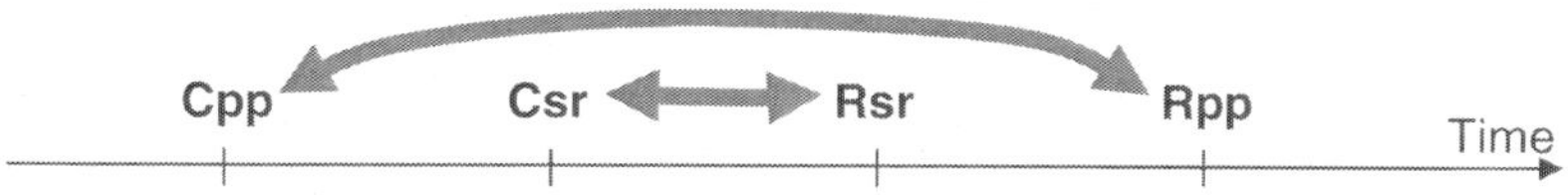

Cpp and Rpp are the call and return associated with the function 'pp' (the longer thick arrow in the diagram), while Csr and Rsr are the call and return associated with the function 'sr' (the shorter thick arrow in the diagram).

Note that 'sr' is the second function to be called, but the first one from which return is made; and 'pp' is the first function to be called, but the second one from which return is made. As the arrows in the time diagram indicate, we say that the function call to 'sr' is *nested* within the function call to 'pp'.

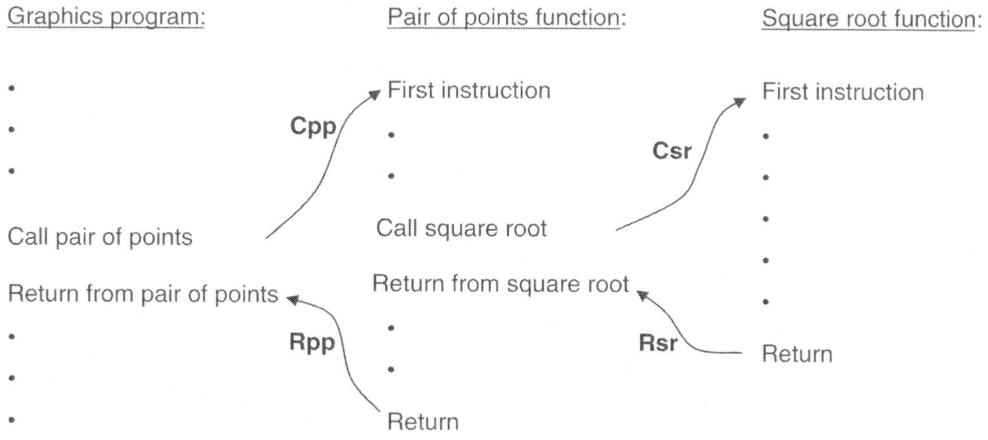

Fig. 5.2 **Schematic diagram of *nested* function call and return**

We have already noted that the appropriate return address must be saved at the time of each function call. From Example 5.5, we come to the following further conclusion:

In the case of *nested* function calls, the last function called is the first one from which return is made. In other words, the time order of returns from functions is the reverse of the time order in which functions are called. Therefore return addresses must be saved by the processor in such a way that they are utilised in a *last-in first-out* manner.*

Having studied the need to provide a function call and return mechanism, we now take a look at the two specific processor instructions which provide for this mechanism. Function call instruction has mnemonic CALL, and it works with a direct address in exactly the same way as JMP does. The difference is that CALL also causes the *return address* to be saved, as explained before. The return address is the address of the next instruction after CALL.

Function return instruction has the mnemonic RET, and it has no explicit operand. Execution of this instruction causes the program to continue execution from the last return address saved. In conjunction with the CALL instruction, this ensures that the last function called is the first one from which return is made.

Note that, in terms of addressing modes, CALL uses *direct addressing*, while RET uses *implicit addressing*.

Program 5.2 performs the same computation as Program 5.1, except that it has been written in the form of a function which may be called by any other program**.

Program 5.2

```
//
// Function to find the sum of a hundred integers.
// Input: Memory address of first integer is specified in R0.
// Output: The final sum is returned in R1.
// Registers used: R0, R1, R2, R3
//
SUM:   MOV    #0, R1      // Initialise R1 to 0
       MOV    #1, R2      // Initialise R2 to 1
//
LOOP:  LOAD   [R0], R3    // Load operand from memory to R3
       ADD    R3, R1      // Add it into R1
       ADD    #4, R0      // Add 4 to R0 so that it points
                          // to the next integer to be added
       ADD    #1, R2      // Increment R2 by 1
       COMP   R2, #100    // Compare contents of R2 to 100
       JLE    LOOP        // If less than or equal, jump to
                          // instruction with label LOOP
       RET                // Return to calling program
```

*How this important *last-in first-out* function call and return mechanism is implemented will be discussed in the next chapter.

**The question arises: What is the difference between a program and a function? In fact the two concepts are very similar, except that a program is invoked by the operating system, while a function is contained within a program, and invoked within the running program.

We can invoke—i.e. call—the function SUM (in Program 5.2) if, at any stage in programming the system, we need to find the sum of a hundred integers stored sequentially in memory. This point is illustrated in the following example.

Example 5.6

Assume that the hundred integers are stored, in one case, at memory addresses 4000, 4004, 4008 and so on. Then the relevant call to the function SUM would be:

```
      MOV      #4000, R0    // Move address of first integer in R0
      CALL     SUM          // Call function SUM
  // After the return, result is available in R1
  // Previous contents of R0, R2 and R3 are lost
```

Elsewhere in our program, suppose we wish to find the sum of a hundred integers starting at memory location 4500. We would then make the following function call to SUM:

```
      MOV      #4500, R0    // Move address of first integer in R0
      CALL     SUM          // Call function SUM
```

Thus, we see that the function SUM can be called from more than one point in our program. In each case, SUM calculates the sum of the specified hundred integers; and in each case, return is made to the instruction immediately after the call, since the correct return address is saved. This program structure is depicted schematically in Fig. 5.3.

This point brings out other important benefits of structuring programs using functions. In memory, in Example 5.6, we have only one copy of the function SUM, which is invoked from two points in the main program. In general, a single copy of a function in memory can be called from any number of other points in the program. This arrangement has two important benefits:

(i) We do not use up memory for storing multiple copies of the same piece of code.

(ii) We need to *maintain* only one copy of code. If a change or correction is to be made in a function, we need to make it only in its single copy.

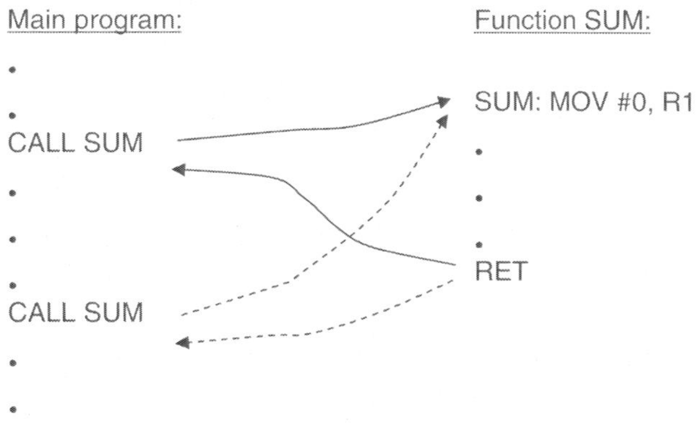

Fig. 5.3 **Function SUM called from two points in the program**

As pointed out earlier, most software today is written in higher level languages. Even in that context, however, large programs must be structured using functions, the reasons being essentially the same as those which have been discussed here.

5.3 TABLE OF INSTRUCTIONS

Our processor *NICE* has a so-called *load and store* type of instruction set, which means that:

(i) Memory operands must be loaded into programmable registers before any operation can be performed on them; similarly, the results of arithmetic and logic operations must be explicitly stored back from processor registers to memory. Instructions LOAD and STORE are provided on the processor for these two operations.
(ii) Arithmetic and logic operations can be performed on operands only after they have been brought into programmable registers, and they leave their results in programmable registers.

Some commercial processors do not have this type of an instruction set. For example, a processor may provide a form of ADD which—in one instruction—causes an operand to be brought in from memory and added into a programmable register.

On our highly 'non-commercial' processor *NICE*, this would require two instructions—a LOAD followed by an ADD. The advantage here, however, is that the instruction set of *NICE* remains simple—in keeping with the RISC approach—and therefore it can facilitate more efficient implementation. Also, for learning the essential principles of computer system organisation, a complex instruction is not really an advantage, and may in fact prove to be a distraction or even a disadvantage.

With this viewpoint, let us take a quick look at the instruction set of *NICE*, including in particular the instructions which we have not yet had an occasion to use in the programs studied so far. Table 5.1 summarises the instructions.

Table 5.1 has a column headed *Instruction Modifier*. Most instructions of *NICE* are available in more than one variant, and the *Instruction Modifier* indicates the variant being used. As can be seen, the most common entry in this column is *byte/word*, which indicates whether the operands of the instruction are one byte each or one word each. In the instruction mnemonic, we use suffix letter B to indicate *byte*, while no suffix indicates *word*. Thus, for example, LOADB is *load byte*, and LOAD is *load word*.

When a byte mode operation is carried out, only the rightmost—i.e. least significant—byte in the source operand takes part in the operation, and likewise only the least significant byte in the destination register is affected. Consider, for example, the following byte mode MOV instruction:

```
MOVB R2, R4
```

Execution of this instruction causes the rightmost byte of register R2 to be copied to the rightmost byte of register R4. The remaining three bytes of destination register R4 remain unchanged. A similar interpretation holds in the case of all arithmetic and logic instructions in byte mode.

SHIFT instruction in particular has several other variants possible—*shift left* or *shift right*, and *shift with carry* or *shift without carry*. In the table, these are indicated as instruction modifiers; their notation and operation are explained in the next section.

The two columns headed *First Operand* and *Second Operand* in the table indicate the addressing modes which can be used with the respective operand. In assembly language notation, we have already seen that symbols such as '#' and '[R2]' indicate the addressing mode used.

Table 5.1 Instruction set of our processor *NICE*

Instruction	Modifier	First Operand	Second Operand	Remark
DATA TRANSFER Instructions				
LOAD	byte/word	memory address—direct, indirect, or indexed	register	
STORE	byte/word	memory address—direct, indirect, or indexed	register	
MOV	byte/word	source–register or immediate	destination–register	
IN		port number	register	one byte input
OUT		port number	register	one byte output
ARITHMETIC and LOGIC Instructions				
ADD	byte/word	source–register or immediate	destination–register	
SUB	byte/word	source–register or immediate	destination–register	
AND	byte/word	source–register or immediate	destination–register	
OR	byte/word	source–register or immediate	destination–register	
XOR	byte/word	source–register or immediate	destination–register	
NOT	byte/word	register		unary operation
SHIFT	byte/word, left/right, with/without carry	register	number of bits	unary operation
COMPARISON Instruction				
COMP	byte/word	source–register or immediate	destination–register	
TRANFER OF CONTROL Instructions				
JMP		destination address—direct		
J*flag*		destination address—direct		*flag*: Z, N, O, C or P
JN*flag*		destination address—direct		*flag*: Z, N, O, C or P
J*condition*		destination address—direct		*condition*: GT, GE, LT, LE, EQ or NE
CALL		destination address—direct		
RET				
MISCELLANEOUS Instruction				
HALT				

The first group of instructions in the table is *Data Transfer Instructions*. This group includes LOAD and STORE, IN and OUT, and MOV instructions*. All these instructions have already been used in the programs studied so far, and their operation has been discussed. From the addressing modes

*Some authors group IN and OUT instructions separately as *Input and Output Instructions*. No particular advantage seems to be gained thereby, while such a grouping does give an erroneous impression to the student that input and output operations involve something other than data transfer, which of course they do not.

listed in the table, it may be noted that MOV performs data transfers between registers, while LOAD and STORE perform data transfers between main memory and a register.

Sections 5.4 and 5.5 below discuss the other main groups of instructions in Table 5.1.

5.4 ARITHMETIC AND LOGIC INSTRUCTIONS

We have seen many examples of the instruction ADD being used in word mode. The subtract instruction SUB works in a similar way. When the result of addition cannot be accommodated in 32 bits (in word mode) or 8 bits (in byte mode), a *carry* condition is generated and recorded in the C flag of the program status word.

The corresponding condition after a subtract instruction SUB is known as *borrow*, which arises when the operation of subtraction cannot be restricted within 32 bits (in word mode) or 8 bits (in byte mode). After a subtract operation, the same C flag in the program status word indicates *borrow* condition.

Example 5.7

(i) Suppose we subtract the 8-bit integer 00001111 from the 8-bit integer 00010011, as indicated below:

```
0 0 0 1 0 0 1 1
0 0 0 0 1 1 1 1
---------------
0 0 0 0 0 1 0 0
```

The student can verify that, in decimal, this subtraction is 19 − 15 = 4. When we number the eight-bit positions from right to left as 0 to 7, then we see borrow taking place from bit position 4 to the preceding two bit positions (as indicated by the arrows).

(ii) Now suppose we subtract 11110000 from 0011000. Note that the two left half-bytes (i.e. left nibbles) of these quantities are identical to the right half-bytes of part (i). When the subtraction is carried out, therefore, a borrow will take place <u>into</u> the leftmost bit position—as shown below—and this will get recorded in the processor as the C flag.

```
C 0 0 1 1 0 0 0 0
  1 1 1 1 0 0 0 0
  ---------------
  0 1 0 0 0 0 0 0
```

The comparison instruction COMP works in exactly the same way as SUB, except that the result of subtraction is <u>not</u> stored back in the destination register. This changes the subtraction into a comparison, and all the flags—Z, N, O, C and P—are set according to the result of the comparison.

Note 5.2

Strictly for the sake of readability, we make one difference between the ways in which SUB and COMP instructions are written in assembly language. We assume that a subtract instruction with an immediate operand is written in the form, for example:

```
SUB        #10, R0     // Subtract 10 from R0
```

whereas a similar comparison instruction is written in the form:

```
COMP       R0, #10     // Compare R0 with 10
```

AND, OR and XOR are bit-wise logical instructions, which correspond respectively to bit-wise *and*, *or* and *exclusive or* operations in the registers specified. Each of the 8 or 32 bits of the destination register is operated bit-wise with the corresponding bit of the source operand, and the result stored in the destination register.

We have seen in Chapter 3 the definitions of binary functions *and* and *or*. The *exclusive or* function proves to be useful in many contexts, and is defined as shown in Fig. 5.4.

Value of input X_1	Value of input X_2	Value of output Y
0	0	0
0	1	1
1	0	1
1	1	0

Fig. 5.4 **Table of *exclusive or* function**

NOT is a bit-wise logical instruction with only one operand, corresponding to the *not* operation seen in Chapter 3. Each of 8 or 32 bits of the operand is complemented and the result is stored back in the same register.

In its various flavors, the *shift* operation on register contents proves to be useful in many different contexts—for example in programming floating point operations. The first operand of the SHIFT instruction is the register whose contents are to be shifted, and the second operand is the number of bits to be shifted.

SHIFT instruction on our processor *NICE* has three modifiers: *byte/word*, *left/right* and *with/without carry*. The first of these has the interpretation which is common to several other instructions, and has been discussed in the previous section.

The second modifier, *left/right*, indicates whether the register bits are shifted towards the left or towards the right. In part (1) of Fig. 5.5, we have shown the 32-bit contents of a register before and after a *left* shift by 3 bits, without carry. In case of such a left or right shift without carry, an equal number of '0' bits are inserted from the other end.

The third modifier of SHIFT instruction is *with carry/without carry*. Of these, a shift *without carry* has already been explained above, and illustrated in part (1) of Fig. 5.5. We saw that, in this case, carry flag C takes no part in the operation.

When SHIFT *with carry* is carried out, carry flag C is logically placed to the left of the operand, and the resulting 1 + 8 or 1 + 32 bits are shifted left or right by the number of bits specified. Shifts with carry are shown in parts (2) and (3) of Fig. 5.5.

In part (2) of the figure, we see that a left shift with carry causes '0' bits to be inserted from the right.

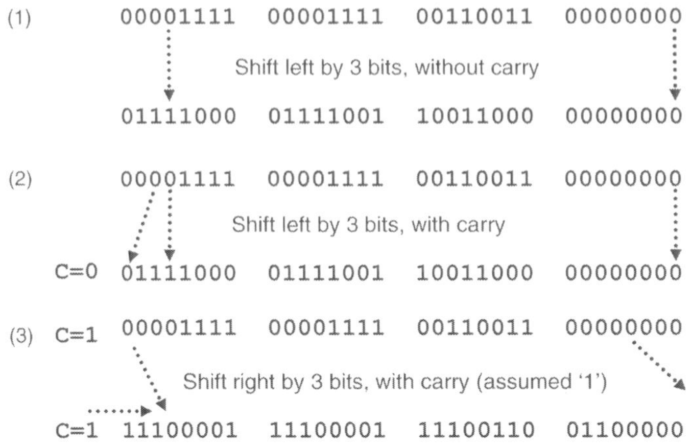

Fig. 5.5 **Three variants of 3-bit shift on a 32-bit quantity**

In part (3) of the figure, we see that a right shift with carry causes the C bit value to be inserted from the left, without any change in the C bit value.

The asymmetry between left and right shift with carry proves to be useful in the programming of operations such as multiplication.

5.5 TRANSFER OF CONTROL INSTRUCTIONS

Transfer of control instructions as seen in Table 5.1 form a group by themselves. Of these, the pair CALL and RET has been discussed in detail in Section 5.2, while the unconditional jump JMP was discussed in Chapter 4. In this section, therefore, we shall concentrate on the various types of conditional jump instructions.

When an arithmetic, logical, or comparison instruction is executed, the processor records in its status word (PSW) the resulting condition by setting or resetting the five basic condition codes—also known as 'flags'—Z, N, O, C and P (see Table 4.1). Based on these, three types of conditional jump instructions are possible:

(i) Jump on one of the flag bits being set, i.e. '1',
(ii) Jump on one of the flag bits being reset, i.e. '0', or
(iii) Jump on a useful combination of flag bits being set and/or reset.

The row in Table 5.1 showing **J*flag*** in the 'Instruction' column corresponds to (i) above. A jump takes place if the indicated *flag* bit is set. Mnemonics for the corresponding instructions are, respectively, JZ, JN, JO, JC and JP, which may be read as 'jump on zero', 'jump on negative', and so on.

The row in Table 5.1 showing **JN*flag*** in the 'Instruction' column corresponds to (ii) above. A jump takes place if the indicated *flag* bit is reset. Mnemonics for the corresponding instructions are, respectively, JNZ, JNN, JNO, JNC and JNP, which may be read as 'jump on non-zero', 'jump on non-negative', and so on.

The next row of the table has the entry **J***condition* in the 'Instruction' column. In the last column, we see that possible values of *condition*—in mnemonic form—are GT, GE, LT, LE, EQ and NE. These stand for, respectively, the six *arithmetic* conditions: *greater than*, *greater than or equal*, *less than*, *less than or equal*, *equal*, and *not equal*.

Of these, the last two can be tested either after an arithmetic operation or after a logical operation, since they correspond simply to flag bit Z being set or reset, respectively. Thus the pair of mnemonics JEQ and JNE generate the same machine instructions as the pair of mnemonics JZ and JNZ, respectively. We can say that the alternative mnemonics may in some cases give better readability to assembly language programs.

The first four conditions—GT, GE, LT, LE—would normally be tested after a subtraction or comparison operation (SUB or COMP), and in that sense they refer to arithmetic rather than purely logical conditions. Within the processor circuits, these conditions are in fact generated as appropriate combinations of the flag bits Z, N, O and C.

The student may wonder why so many variants of the conditional jump instruction are required. The answer can be related to the concept of *flow of control* within a program, which is the nett result of conditional and unconditional jumps, as well as nested function calls and returns. With a generous choice of conditional jump instructions, processor designers enable compiler writers and/or assembly language programmers to generate relatively efficient machine language code for the required flow of control.

Example 5.8

Suppose that a particular processor provides the instruction JC (jump on carry), but not JNC (jump on no carry). Equivalent effect of JNC can be obtained by a combination of JC and unconditional jump JMP, as shown below—but only at the cost of using two instructions in place of one.

```
      .                            .
      .                            .
      JNC destination              JC HERE
      .                            JMP destination
      .                  HERE:
      .                            .
                                   .
```

(a) Using instruction JNC   (b) Using instructions JC and JMP

Transfer of control instructions usually make up a fair proportion of all the machine instructions of a program, and this fact has a crucial bearing on the choice of conditional jump instructions provided on a processor.

5.6 CHARACTER AND STRING OPERATIONS

The programs which we have seen so far, in this and the previous chapter, involve either (a) 32-bit integer operands in main memory, or (b) input or output of a number of bytes of data. In practice, a large part of information processing involves processing of sequences of characters, also known as *character strings*.

As seen in Chapter 2, all forms of text are stored in computer systems as sequences of characters. Word processors operate on text, and search engines on the *world wide web* operate on the text stored in millions of web pages around the world.

In this section, we shall study a simple assembly language program which copies a string of characters from one location to another location in memory. We shall assume that each character occupies one byte, which means that this program will not work correctly with two-byte Unicode characters. Also, we assume that the length of the original sequence of characters is known to us.

To simplify program design, we also assume that memory locations of the source and destination strings are non-overlapping. In practice, if this assumption does not hold, the programmer has to take a little extra care not to lose data (see Exercises 5.9 and 5.10).

So as to create another simple example of a function, Program 5.3 has been written as a function, with its *arguments* (or *parameters*) being passed to it in registers.

Note in particular the use of LOADB and STOREB instructions in Program 5.3, using (i) indirect addressing, and (ii) 'byte mode' operations—i.e. loading from memory and storing into memory one byte at a time.

Also, note that the *loop count* in Program 5.3 is operating in 'down counting' mode, from its initial value in register R2 down to zero.

Program 5.3

```
//
// Function to copy a string of characters.
// Input: R0—Memory address of source string
//        R1—Memory address of destination string
//        R2—Length of source string
//
// Assumes non-overlapping source and destination locations.
//
// Registers used: R0, R1, R2, R3
//
COPY:  LOADB    [R0], R3   // Load source byte into R3
       STOREB   [R1], R3   // Store it at destination address
       ADD      #1, R0     // Add 1 to source address
       ADD      #1, R1     // Add 1 to destination address
       SUB      #1, R2     // Decrement count by 1
       JNZ      COPY       // If not zero, iterate
       RET                 // Return to calling program
```

Other useful operations on character data which are needed commonly in information processing applications are:

Searching within data for a specified string,
Lexicographic comparison of two strings,
Concatenating two strings,
Finding the length of a variable length string,
Changing the attributes of a character string, and so on.

While working with character strings, we may not always have strings of constant length. 'Null termination' is a common method of defining variable length character strings. Of course, the starting location of the character string in memory must be known; the string is then assumed to stretch out towards higher memory addresses until the first '*null* byte'—i.e. all '0' byte, see Table 2.1—is encountered.

5.7 ROLE OF INSTRUCTION SET

In the previous chapter, we discussed in brief the issue of whether the instruction set of a processor should be relatively complex, or relatively simple (i.e. *reduced*). The argument in either case has to be based on *processor performance*, since a computer system must be judged on its performance.

The point to note is that there is nothing final or sacrosanct about an instruction set—either the instruction set which we have been using, or the instruction set of any other processor. An instruction set is nothing more than a convenient way of packaging the operations which we commonly perform on a processor. Finally, all instructions are executed in hardware using primitive operations such as *and*, *or* and *not*.

Consider Fig. 5.6, which shows the stages of (i) writing a program in a higher level language, (ii) compiling the program, and (iii) executing (or running) the machine language program on the processor*.

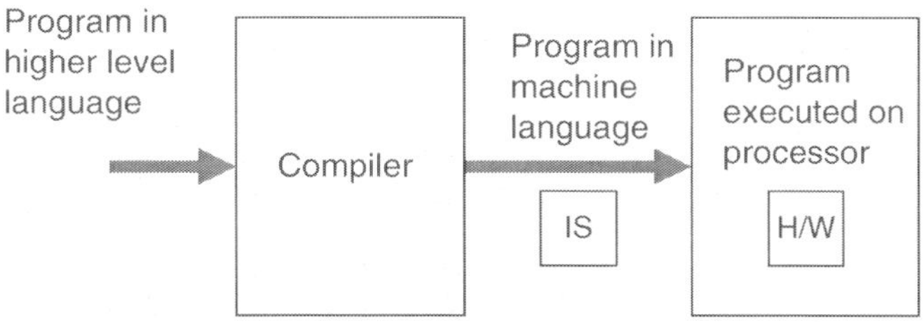

Fig. 5.6 Stages in writing, compiling and executing a program

The instruction set of the processor plays the key role in the intermediate stage, which is marked 'IS' in the figure. But increased complexity of the instruction set ('IS') does not necessarily lead to greater processor performance—since such increased complexity can slow down the last stage (marked 'H/W', for 'hardware'), which must cope with the complexity of the instruction set.

On *NICE*, we have so far provided a fairly simple instruction set. For example, we have not provided on *NICE*: (a) integer multiply and divide instructions, (b) floating point instructions, and (c) instructions which operate on blocks of data.

Of course, such operations can be programmed using the machine instructions which we have at our disposal. But any such operation implemented in software will be slower—i.e. it will take many more processor clock cycles—than the same operation implemented in hardware. Therefore,

---

*For simplicity, a stage known as *linking* has not been shown. See Chapter 15.

for an application making heavy use of floating point operations, for example, the user must select a processor which provides floating point operations in hardware. Similarly, for an application which makes heavy use of graphics, the user may select a system which has hardware for enhanced graphics performance.

In practice, what sometimes happens is that a low-cost or low-power version of a processor may not have such extra capability, while a 'higher end' processor in the same *processor family* may have it. Based on requirements of the application, a user can choose the right processor from within a processor family. Of course, all members of the processor family provide the same 'core' instruction set.

Such factors become especially important today because of the rapid advances which are taking place in IC technology. Typically, a processor family has a life which spans more than one generation of IC technology; therefore, over its long life, it spans several processor models from the lower to the higher end.

Example 5.9

Suppose one processor of a processor family has a floating point addition instruction FADD which has a format similar to integer ADD. Thus we write in a program, say:

```
LOAD        X1, R0      // First operand in R0
LOAD        X2, R1      // Second operand in R1
FADD        R0, R1      // The sum in R1
```

Now, if another processor in the same family does not have this instruction, we need to write a function for floating point addition. Let us say this function is called FADDS, where the last 'S' distinguishes this function from the instruction mnemonic. In place of the above instruction, we then need to write the equivalent code:

```
LOAD        X1, R0
LOAD        X2, R1
CALL        FADDS       // Performs the operation of
                        // the third instruction above
```

Since the assembly language programmer as well as compiler writer know which model of processor they are writing for, they can choose the right instruction.

5.8 SAMPLE PROGRAMS

We now study a couple of other simple programs, so that the student can gain a further level of comfort in working with machine instructions.

Program 5.4 finds the largest of a set of a hundred integers. The program is written in the form of function MAX. Address of the first integer is supplied to MAX in register R0; the function finds the largest integer and returns its value in R1.

Program 5.4

```
//
// Function MAX finds the largest of a hundred integers.
//
// Input: Memory address of first integer is in R0.
// Output: The largest integer is returned in R1.
//
// Registers used: R0, R1, R2, R3
//
MAX:    LOAD [R0], R1         // Load first integer into R1
        ADD #4, R0            // Make R0 point to second integer
        MOV #1, R2            // Initialise count R2 to 1
                              //
LOOP:   LOAD [R0], R3         // Load integer from memory to R3
        COMP R3, R1           // Compare it with R1
        JLE NEXT              // If smaller/equal, do not change
                              // value in R1
        MOV R3, R1            // Move larger integer into R1
                              //
NEXT:   ADD #4, R0            // Add 4 to R0 so that it points
                              // to the next integer to compare
        ADD #1, R2            // Increment count R2 by 1
                              //
        COMP R2, #100         // Compare contents of R2 to 100
        JLE LOOP              // If less than or equal, jump to
                              // start of loop
                              //
        RET                   // Return to calling program
```

Program 5.5 is written in the form of a function LOWER which converts a set of a hundred upper case letters of the English alphabet to lower case. Address of the first character is supplied to the function in register R0.

Program 5.5

```
//
// Function LOWER converts a hundred characters of English
// alphabet from upper to lower case.
//
// Input: Memory address of first character is in R0.
//
// Registers used: R0, R1, R2
//
LOWER: MOV #1, R2             // Initialise loop count
                              //
```

```
LOOP:    LOADB  [R0], R1       // Load first character into R1
         ORB     #32, R1       // Convert it to lower case
         STOREB [R0], R1       // Store it in same location
                               //
         ADD #1, R0            // Increment R0 so that it points
                               // to the next character
         ADD #1, R2            // Increment count R2 by 1
                               //
         COMP R2, #100         // Compare contents of R2 to 100
         JLE LOOP              // If less than or equal, jump to
                               // start of loop
                               //
         RET                   // Return to calling program
```

Note in particular the use of byte mode operations in Program 5.5.

From Table 3.1, we can verify that the ASCII code for upper case letter 'A' is hexadecimal 41, i.e. binary 01000001, while the ASCII code for lower case letter 'a' is hexadecimal 61, i.e. binary 01100001. Counting the bits from right to left as $b_7b_6b_5b_4b_3b_2b_1b_0$, as usual, we see that the difference in lower case 'a' is that bit b_5 is set to '1'. This pattern is in fact repeated in all the letters of the alphabet.

Therefore, in Program 5.5, we must turn b_5 to '1' to convert any letter from upper case to lower case. This is being done by using the OR instruction in byte mode. The decimal constant 32 equals 2^5. Therefore, when it is written in 8-bit binary, it has only the bit b_5 set, while all its other bits are reset.

SUMMARY

In this chapter, we completed the study which began with the previous chapter—namely, study of the instruction set of a typical processor.

We first looked at the various *addressing modes* provided in the instruction set to address operands. The basic reason for providing a variety of addressing modes on a processor is to enable access to required data in main memory which can be organised—or structured—in a number of different ways.

Functions are the crucial building blocks for the design and development of software. We studied the way in which function call and return are associated, and also the *last in, first out* mechanism of nested function calls and returns.

According to the operations performed, processor instructions fall into a few different groups. We studied in some depth the main such groups—*data transfer* instructions, *arithmetic, logic, and comparison* instructions, and *transfer of control* instructions. Table 5.1 summarised the instruction set which we have been using.

Operations on blocks of data—either bytes or words—are not provided in hardware on *NICE*. With a simple example, we saw how one can program the string copy function for a character string of known length. Towards the end, in Section 5.7, as a follow up on Section 4.6, we discussed in brief some issues related to the machine instruction set provided on a processor.

REVIEW QUESTIONS

1. Why does the instruction set of a processor provide a variety of addressing modes?
2. Define the following addressing modes, and give one example of each:

   Direct addressing,
   Register addressing,
   Immediate addressing,
   Indirect addressing, and
   Indexed addressing.

3. When are indirect and indexed addressing modes especially useful in writing programs?
4. State the basic reasons why program efficiency and speed-up are achieved by holding operands in programmable registers.
5. When is the instruction set of a processor said to be orthogonal?
6. What is the role of a *function* in providing well-defined structure to a program?
7. Why is it necessary to save the return address when a function is called?
8. What is the meaning of 'nested' function calls? In the case of nested function calls, why is it necessary to make use of return addresses in 'last-in, first out' manner?
9. When do we say that a processor has a *load and store* type of instruction set?
10. What is the role of the instruction modifier in the instruction set of the processor which we are using?
11. What is the difference between the subtraction instruction SUB and the comparison instruction COMP?
12. What are the three modifiers of the SHIFT instruction?
13. In the instruction set of Table 5.1, what is the difference between instructions JN and JNN?
14. A processor provides 'jump on zero' instruction JZ, but not 'jump on non-zero' instruction JNZ. Show how you would achieve the effect of JNZ by using a combination of JZ and unconditional jump.
15. Show how you would call the function COPY of Program 5.3 to copy 200 bytes from source memory address 4000 to destination memory address 6000.
16. Define a possible 'calling interface' for a function which finds the length of a null-terminated character string. Recall that such a string starts from a specified memory address and extends towards higher addresses until the first 'null' byte.
17. Consider function LOWER of Section 5.8. What does this function do if the original hundred characters in memory contain some characters which are already in lower case?
18. Consider again function LOWER of Section 5.8. What does this function do if the original hundred characters in memory contain some characters which are not letters of the English alphabet?

EXERCISES

Notes to student:

a. Include suitable comments with all the exercise programs written.

b. If necessary, you may make use of a flow chart or algorithmic notation to ensure that your program logic is right, before writing the program in assembly language.

1. Recall that Example 5.1 shows the working of Program 5.1 during its 50th iteration. Repeat the work of Example 5.1 for the (i) 80th iteration, and (ii) 100th i.e. last iteration of Program 5.1.

2. Program 5.1 finds the sum of a hundred integers, with the final loop count being included within the instruction COMP. This means that the loop count can be changed only by altering this instruction, which is usually not a good practice. Rewrite Program 5.1 so that the final loop count is in a memory location which has label N.

3. Recall that Program 4.3 finds the sum of three integers stored in memory locations 2000, 2004 and 2008. Convert this program to a function ADD3 which finds the sum of three integers stored in memory. The memory address of the first integer is provided in register R0; the other two integers occupy successive memory words. Upon return from the function, the answer should be available in register R1.

4. Write a function MAX3 which finds the largest of three integers stored in memory. The memory address of the first integer is provided in register R0; the other two integers occupy successive memory words. Upon return from the function, the answer should be available in register R1.

5. Recall that Program 4.4 finds the sum of the hundred integers from 1 to 100. Convert this program to a function SUMN which finds the sum of integers from 1 to N. The argument N is provided to the function in register R0, and upon return from the function, the answer should be available in register R1.

6. Write a function SWAP which swaps the contents of the two memory words, of which the two addresses are contained in registers R0 and R1 respectively.

7. Write a function UNPK which 'unpacks' the two halves of a four-byte word. When UNPK is called, register R0 contains the word to be unpacked. The function moves the leftmost two bytes of R0 into the rightmost two bytes of R1, and then sets the leftmost two bytes of both the registers to all zeros. See Fig. 5.7.

Fig. 5.7 **Unpacking the two halves of a four-byte word**

8. Multiplication of integers can be viewed as repeated, addition, for example, 3 × 7 is nothing but 7 + 7 + 7. Using algorithmic notation, show how you would perform the multiplication of two 8-bit unsigned integers using this property.
9. Convert the algorithm of Exercise 8 into a function MPY8. The two 8-bit arguments to the function are provided in registers R0 and R1, and the answer should be available in register R2.
10. Recall Program 5.3, which is a function for copying a string of one-byte characters. Registers R0, R1 and R2 contain, respectively, source address, destination address and string length. A crucial assumption made is that the destination memory addresses have no overlap with source addresses.

    Now assume that this assumption does not necessarily hold—i.e. there may be an overlap between source and destination memory addresses. Show in algorithmic notation how the program should take into account this possibility.

    Hint: In one case, you will need to copy bytes in the order of decreasing memory addresses.
11. Convert the algorithm of Exercise 9 into a function COPY, which has arguments similar to those seen in Program 5.3.
12. Write a function which locates the terminating null byte in a character string. The starting address of the string is provided to the function in register R0. Upon return, R0 contains the address of the null byte which terminates the string, and register R1 contains the length of the string, excluding the null byte.
13. Similar to function MAX in Section 5.8, write a function MIN which finds the minimum of a set of a hundred integers.
14. Similar to function LOWER in Section 5.8, write a function UPPER which converts a hundred lower case letters of the English alphabet to upper case.
15. Improve the function UPPER of Exercise 15 in the following way: If a character occurs within the hundred which does not belong to the English alphabet, then it should be left unchanged. Punctuation marks are examples of such characters.

PROCESSOR DESIGN

6

6.1 INTRODUCTION

The processor of a computer system may be thought of as the 'brain' of the system. Apart from performing actual operations on data such as addition and subtraction, the processor controls the operations of all other hardware elements of the computer system, including its input and output devices. The processing of data, as well as control of other hardware elements, takes place according to the program running on the processor.

Note 6.1

Every computer system must have at least one *main processor*, also known as the *central processing unit* (CPU). A modern system, however, may be provided with more than one processor. Firstly, there are the multiprocessor systems and multi-core processor chips which contain a symmetric set of multiple processors. Secondly, even on systems with a single main processor, there may be other processors to handle input/output or graphics, or processors embedded within a disk controller or a network controller.

The principles of processor design discussed in this and the next chapter apply to any processor, whether or not it is the main processor—the CPU—of a computer system. That is the reason, we feel, that the title Processor Design is appropriate for this chapter, although some authors may prefer to use the term *CPU Design*.

In this chapter, we shall study how the processor can be organised internally—using the hardware building blocks described in Chapter 3—to carry out repeatedly the *fetch* and *execute* phases of machine instructions. The fetch phase does not vary much from one instruction to the next, since any instruction must first be brought into the processor before it can be executed. During the execute phase, however, actions carried out by the processor do depend on the instruction, its modifier(s), the addressing mode used, and the program status word.

To carry out operations on data, the processor contains *programmable registers*, *functional units* such as adder and shifter, and *data paths* connecting all of these in an appropriate manner. We shall see that, apart from programmable registers, the processor also contains several other registers which are not directly accessible to the programmer, but which are important to processor operations.

We shall also see that actions are carried out in the processor when the correct *control signals* are applied to the registers, functional units and data paths.

Thus the internal design of the processor gets separated into two parts:

(i) registers, functional units, and data paths, and
(ii) the mechanism for generating the right control signals at the right time instants, for the operations required to be performed by the processor.

Processor architecture is defined by the various elements of (i), while *control unit* is the name given to the mechanism mentioned in (ii).

6.2 PROCESSOR ARCHITECTURE

We have seen that a processor contains a set of programmable registers. On our own processor *NICE*, for example, these are the sixteen 32-bit registers R0 to R15.

For carrying out arithmetic and logic operations on data, the processor has a functional unit commonly called *arithmetic and logic unit*, or ALU. Typically, the ALU performs integer addition and subtraction, bit-wise logical operations, and shift operations. On our processor *NICE*, for example, operations corresponding to machine instructions ADD, SUB, AND, OR, XOR, NOT, SHIFT and COMP would be performed by the ALU.

For floating point operations, a processor may also have a separate *floating point unit*, or FPU. As pointed out in the last section of the previous chapter, however, the FPU may be thought of as an optional element within a processor. The current 'low-cost' version of the processor we are using—*NICE*—has not been provided with an FPU.

For storing the instruction currently under execution, the processor has a register known as *instruction register*, or IR.

For storing the memory address of the next instruction which would be fetched—after the current instruction is executed—the processor has another register known as the *program counter*, or PC.

Note that IR and PC are not programmable registers. Each of them has a very specific function assigned to it, which is central to running a program on the processor, and which cannot be changed by a running program. In this sense, this role of IR and PC can be contrasted with the role of programmable registers such as R0 to R15.

Another special purpose register in the processor is the *program status word* (PSW), which contains the flag bits Z, N, O, C and P; and some other useful information about the running program which we shall see later. The flag bits are set by ALU operations, and the C flag in particular also participates in some of the ALU operations.

For interacting with main memory and input/output device controllers, the processor has two other special purpose registers: *address* and *data.*

We have seen that, when the processor performs a data transfer operation with main memory or a device controller, the operation involves both address and data. The specified data is transferred to or from the specified address—which is a memory address in case of LOAD/STORE, and a device address in case of IN/OUT. The role of special purpose registers *address* and *data* in the processor is to hold the required address and data involved in these data transfer operations.

Connecting these various elements within the processor are internal *data paths*—or *data busses*—equal in width to the word size of the processor. In addition, the processor also has an *external bus* on which other elements of the system are connected. The *address* and *data* registers mentioned before are connected respectively to *address* and *data lines* of the external bus, which also has *control signals* that govern bus data transfers.

Figure 6.1 shows in schematic form the hardware architecture of a simple processor, on which the instruction set of Table 5.1 can be implemented.

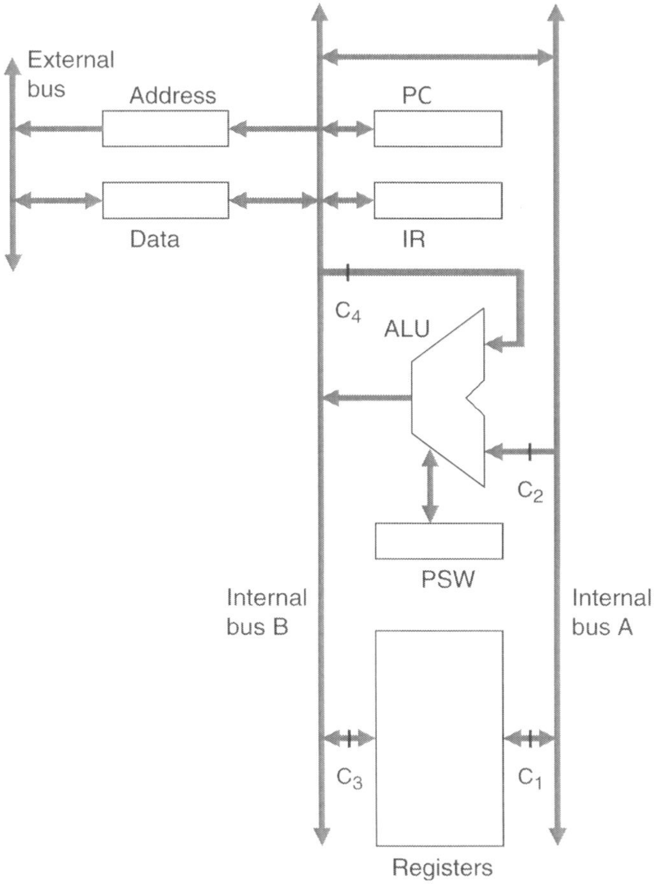

Fig. 6.1 **Hardware architecture of a simple processor**

The student should note that we have now seen two very different views of the processor:

a. In one view, the machine instruction set of Table 5.1 defines the processor. This is the view taken by the programmer, and this view makes no reference to *how* the processor hardware is organised internally. This view—known as the *instruction set architecture* (ISA) of the processor—has been the subject matter of Chapters 4 and 5.
b. In the other view, it is the hardware architecture of Fig. 6.1 which defines the processor. This is the view of the hardware designer, who may be interested in a more efficient design of the processor hardware, rather than in programming the processor.

6.3 CONTROL SIGNALS AND CONTROL UNIT

Elements within the processor—such as data busses and functional units—do not operate on their own. For any required operations within the processor, the correct *control signals* must be applied to its various elements.

In Fig. 6.1, we have labeled four illustrative points within the processor where control signals must be applied to carry out specific operations—their respective labels being C_1, C_2, C_3 and C_4. In fact, there would be many other such points within the processor where, depending on the operation required, appropriate control signals must be applied. For the present, however, it is not necessary for us to enumerate all of these points.

Control signals at C_1 cause data from a selected register to be placed on internal bus A; similarly a control signal at C_2 causes data on internal bus A to be supplied as one of the two inputs to ALU. Therefore, if appropriate control signals are applied at both C_1 and C_2, data from a selected register is supplied as one of the two inputs to the ALU.

In an exactly similar manner, if appropriate control signals are applied to both C_3 and C_4, data from another selected register is supplied—via the other internal bus B—as the second input to the ALU.

These two data transfers from registers to ALU can take place *in parallel* if the required hardware elements along the two respective paths of data transfer are independent of each other, as indeed they are in Fig. 6.1. Achieving such parallelism within the processor is often an important design goal, and this is the main reason for providing two internal busses—A and B—with the architecture shown.

With such an architecture, it becomes possible to transfer within one clock cycle, say, the contents of register R1 as one operand of ALU, and the contents of register R2 as the other operand of ALU. Such considerations become important when designers try to extract the maximum possible performance from a processor.

Let us now consider a few specific examples of control signals required for typical operations performed by the processor. In each of the three examples below, the student is urged to trace out in Fig. 6.1, the elements of the processor architecture which are taking part in the operation.

Example 6.1

Consider the memory element shown in Fig. 3.11, with *enable* and *read/write* control signals connected to it. When *enable* has value '0', the memory element performs neither a *read* nor a *write* operation. When *enable* has value '1', the memory element performs a *read* or a *write* operation, depending on the state of the other control signal *read/write*. In addition, the address lines specify the memory location and data lines carry the data which is being read or written.

Thus the operation of the memory element is governed by address lines, data lines, and the two control signals. The required control signals are provided by the processor along the external bus, shown on the top left of Fig. 6.1. In this way, the external bus allows memory elements and input/output devices to be connected to the processor.

Example 6.2

During the *fetch* phase, the instruction stored in main memory at the address given by PC must be brought into IR. For this, the contents of PC must be transferred to the *address* register along internal bus B, and *read* control signal must be applied to main memory.

The instruction read from main memory is transferred on the external bus into *data* register, and then it is transferred into IR along internal bus B. At this time, the contents of PC are also incremented, so that it points to the next instruction in memory.

Example 6.3

Consider the execute phase of an instruction such as ADD R1, R2. The contents of R1 and R2 must be transferred to the two inputs of ALU, along the two internal busses, as described before. In the next clock cycle, the output of ALU must be transferred to destination register R2 along bus B.

Now consider the execute phase of the instruction JMP *target*. Since the target address of the jump is available in IR, it must be transferred to PC along bus B, so that the next fetch phase will correctly bring in the instruction from address *target* in main memory.

Even for a simple processor architecture such as that of Fig. 6.1, there would be many points where control signals must be applied to carry out appropriate operations.

The ALU, in particular, is capable of performing several different operations. These include:

integer arithmetic operations,
logic operations, and
shift operations in the various modes provided.

On *NICE*, each of these operations may be specified in byte mode or word mode. In a given clock cycle, which operation the ALU performs depends on the control signals applied to it. If, for example, the total number of ALU operations is 16, then a 4-bit control signal can be used to specify an operation. Of course, for a shift operation, the shift count would have to be specified separately.

In all, therefore, even a relatively simple architecture such as that of Fig. 6.1 typically requires a few dozen control signals for its proper operation. In each clock cycle of the processor, the control unit must generate appropriate control signals for the required operations to be performed.

The important question here is: What is it that determines the control signals which must be generated in a given processor clock cycle?

The answer to this question may be given in two parts:

(i) The *fetch* phase of the processor does not vary from instruction to instruction. Therefore, we may say that the control signals required during the *fetch* phase should—in some appropriate sense—be 'pre-wired' into the processor.

(ii) During the *execute* phase, the control signals required depend on the instruction being executed, its modifier(s), the addressing mode, and also the program status word (PSW).

As mentioned before, the *control unit* of the processor has the specific function of generating the correct control signals in each processor clock cycle; a typical such control unit is shown schematically in Fig. 6.2.

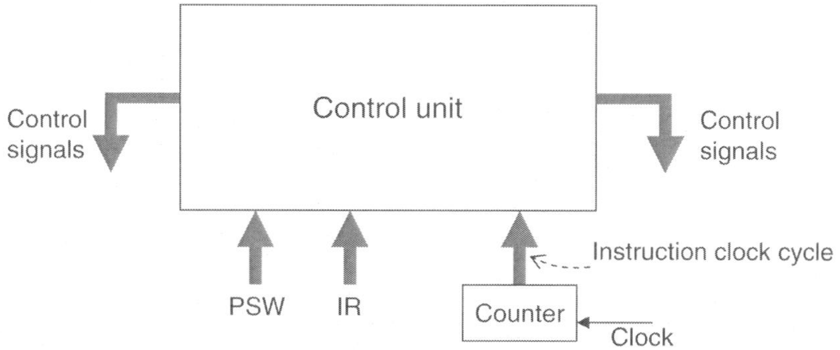

Fig. 6.2 **Control unit of the processor**

It is best to visualise the control unit of the processor in a plane which is located above the processor architecture shown in Fig. 6.1. From the latter, the control unit takes as inputs the instruction register IR (which also contains the modifiers and the addressing modes), and the program status word PSW.

The control signals generated by the control unit are applied at the appropriate points within the 'lower' plane of the processor architecture. As an aid in understanding, this has been depicted in Fig. 6.2 by drawing arrow-heads such that (i) inputs to the control unit point upward, and (ii) the control signal outputs point downward.

There is one other crucial input to the control unit which has not been discussed so far. This is the *counter* shown on the lower right in Fig. 6.2, with a clock signal connected to it. The reason why such a counter is needed is the following:

Over its *fetch* and *execute* phases, an instruction needs several clock cycles to complete. This number depends on several factors, such as the relative speeds of the processor and memory, the operation performed, and the addressing modes being used. In practice, this number may vary from two to more than half a dozen.

Say a particular machine instruction needs a total of n processor clock cycles to fetch and execute.

Clearly then the control signals required will vary with clock cycle i, for $0 \leq i \leq n - 1$, where, as usual, we have numbered the clock cycles from 0 to $n - 1$. Thus, the control signals generated depend not only on the machine instruction and the program status word, but also the clock cycle i, $0 \leq i \leq n - 1$, with n as defined above*.

The instruction cycle counter shown in Fig. 6.2 keeps track of the processor clock cycle within the combined fetch and execute phases of each machine instruction—i.e. it counts up from 0 to $n - 1$, with the value of n depending on the instruction. We shall refer to this counter output as the *instruction clock cycle*.

When the next instruction is to be fetched, this counter is reset to zero, and then it starts counting all over again for the next instruction. Thus the counter is reset to zero when a new fetch phase starts, i.e. in the last clock cycle of the previous instruction.

*The instruction cycle counter shown in Fig. 6.2 is often identified as a *sequencer*, which only means a counter being made to work in this particular context.

We have seen the typical inputs of the control unit, and a few typical control signals it must generate (in Examples 6.1, 6.2 and 6.3).

The question now is: Is the control unit a *combinational* circuit or a *sequential* circuit?

The answer is: Because the instruction cycle counter has been made external to it, the control unit itself is nothing but a *combinational* circuit, with the inputs and outputs as shown in Fig. 6.2. In other words, the control signals generated depend only on the current instruction in IR, program status word, and counter output which has the instruction clock cycle.

Therefore, in theory, any standard technique for combinational circuit design should serve to design the circuit for the control unit. The circuit itself may be quite complex, because of the large number of inputs and outputs it has—but in principle it is nothing but a combinational circuit.

When a control unit is designed and built in this manner—as one complex combinational circuit—it is known as *hardwired* control unit. In such a control unit, the logic required to generate control signals is wired into the combinational circuit. As a result, once it is built, such a circuit cannot be easily changed. This will become clearer when we study in the next chapter some further aspects of such hardwired control, as well as an alternative technique for building the control unit known as *microprogrammed* control.

Before we can do that, however, it is necessary to pay some attention to how instruction opcodes, modifiers, etc. may be coded in binary.

6.4 INSTRUCTION FORMATS AND CODES

In Chapter 2, we saw how integers, floating point numbers and characters can be coded into their binary representation. Needless to say, processor instructions, instruction modifiers, and addressing modes must also be suitably coded into binary, so that the processor circuits can correctly interpret them.

As we have seen in Table 5.1, the instructions of a processor do not have a uniform format. They vary in terms of their operation codes (*opcodes*), modifiers, addressing modes, and the number of operands. Compared to the various types of data we have seen, instructions have a very different role to play in the system. Naturally, therefore, the issues involved in the coding of instructions are also quite different.

In the previous section we have seen that, regardless of how instructions are encoded in binary, a suitable digital circuit can always be designed for the control unit. This is in principle no more than a standard combinational circuit design problem: Given a table of its inputs and outputs, design a circuit which maps each possible pattern of input signals to its corresponding pattern of output signals. The circuit in question in this instance is the control unit, shown as the central box in Fig. 6.2.

But this is only a theoretical point. It certainly does not imply that the instructions can be coded into binary using just any random scheme. Since there is plenty of choice available in the coding of instructions, the designer's *dharma* is to look for the particular coding scheme that yields maximum advantage in terms of final system performance.

So the key question here is: What are the performance advantages which we may look for in coding our instruction set into binary?

We can easily list at least three possible answers to this question:

a. Code the instructions such that the resulting binary—i.e. *machine language*—program is made as compact as possible, so as to minimise the total time spent by the processor in fetching instructions from main memory.
b. Code the instructions such that the maximum gate delay between inputs and outputs in the control unit of Fig. 6.2 is minimised—so that the processor can be driven at as high a clock rate as possible.
c. Code the instructions such that the control circuit is made as compact as possible, i.e. it is built using the minimum number of gates possible. This will be the right option if—in some sense—the cost of building the control unit is high, and it depends critically on this gate count.

Clearly each of these three would count as an advantage in a system. While (a) and (b) may result in higher processing speeds, (c) may yield a circuit which occupies relatively less space and consumes less power. In practice, however, as the student can imagine, it is not possible to achieve all these goals simultaneously. But, at the same time, it is also not possible to ignore completely any one of these objectives while aiming for another.

In practice, processor designers try to ensure that each of the three objectives listed above is satisfied to the extent possible, without paying a prohibitive penalty in terms of any one of them. Achieving this requires as much art and ingenuity as science, and sometimes prior experience may provide only blinkers.

Consider *NICE*—the processor which we have been using as a running example. Subject to certain restrictions, it is possible to encode its instructions in such a way that any machine instruction is 1 byte, 2 bytes, or 4 bytes in length. An instruction such as RET—return from a function—can be encoded in one byte, while a LOAD instruction in our case needs 4 bytes, since it includes a 24-bit address.

Appendix A presents one possible way of coding the instruction set of *NICE*. To ensure that instruction lengths remain 1 byte, 2 bytes, or 4 bytes, some restrictions had to be placed on (i) the size of immediate operands, and (ii) the number of bits which can be shifted in one SHIFT instruction. This means that when a larger immediate operand or shift is needed, an additional instruction must be used.

RISC processors, in particular, have machine instructions of uniform length, with relatively simple formats. As has been mentioned before, the idea behind such instruction formats is to speed up instruction decoding and generation of control signals. Since RISC processors make use of instruction pipelines operating at high clock rates (see Section 6.10 ahead), issues of RISC instruction formats and codes receive special attention.

6.5 ARITHMETIC AND LOGIC UNIT (ALU)

The arithmetic and logic unit (ALU) of the processor performs integer addition and subtraction operations, logic operations, and shift operations. Inputs to the ALU come from selected programmable register(s)—one register for unary operations such as SHIFT and NOT, and two registers for binary operations such as ADD and OR.

In the processor architecture of Fig. 6.1, the two ALU input registers are connected to internal busses A and B, respectively, and the ALU output register is connected to internal bus B. Data on an internal bus is *gated* into an ALU input register when the appropriate control signal is applied*; and similarly data in the ALU output register is placed on the output bus when the appropriate control signal is applied.

All the operations carried out by the ALU can be described as combinational functions of its one or two inputs. Thus the ALU is basically a combinational circuit—but one which must be designed with special care to reduce the total gate delay in its addition and subtraction circuits, a topic which we shall discuss further in Chapter 8.

Figure 6.3 shows a more detailed diagram of the ALU than the one seen in Fig. 6.1. The ALU is shown with two word-size registers at its input for its operands, and one word-size register at the output for the result of the operation carried out by the ALU.

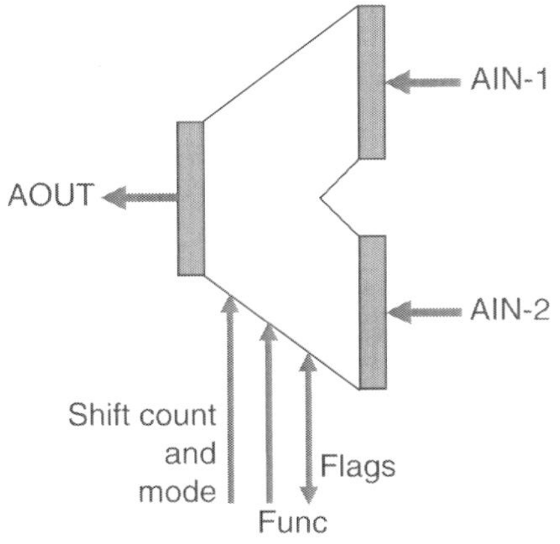

Fig. 6.3 **Arithmetic and logic unit (ALU)**

The function carried out by the ALU is determined by the machine instruction being executed. If an ALU is capable of performing, say, 16 different arithmetic, logic and shift operations, then a 4-bit function code is needed to select the right ALU function for the machine instruction being executed. In the figure, the function code supplied to the ALU is shown as an incoming arrow at the bottom, with label 'Func'.

The ALU can shift left or right the contents of its input by a specified number of bits, in accordance with the SHIFT machine instruction and its modifiers (recall Table 5.1). In Fig. 6.3, the relevant control input to the *shifter* part of the ALU is shown as an incoming arrow at the bottom, with the label 'Shift count and mode'.

As we have seen, ALU operations set or reset the condition flags maintained by the processor in PSW. Also, some operations of the ALU take into account the status of some of the condition flags. This relationship of the conditional flags to ALU operations is shown in the figure using a bi-directional arrow with the label 'Flags'.

The ALU performs basically a combinational function on its inputs, and therefore it is designed with a total gate delay which is only a fraction of the processor clock cycle time. The ALU can be connected to the internal busses even without the input and output registers shown in Fig. 6.3, thus avoiding the delays involved in writing data into these registers. However, we have included these registers in Fig. 6.3 specifically because modern processors are often provided with multiple ALUs and/or FPUs, so as to allow parallel operation between them**. In such cases, each such functional unit certainly does need its own input and output registers.

---

*This means that a control signal applied to a logic *gate* causes data on the bus to be written into the ALU input register. In this context of digital electronics, the noun *gate* can be used as a verb.

**Technical issues related to the provision of parallelism in computer systems have been discussed in Chapters 13 and 14.

6.6 DATA TRANSFER AND MANIPULATION

As we have discussed, the control unit of the processor generates the control signals required in each clock cycle to carry out the task specified in a machine instruction. Say a machine instruction requires a total of n clock cycles in its fetch and execute phases. The counter shown in Fig. 6.2 keeps track of the clock cycle within the instruction, which goes from 0 to $n - 1$; recall that this counter output is the *instruction clock cycle.*

In each of the n clock cycles required to fetch and execute a given instruction, the right combination of control signals is generated by the control unit. What does a typical control signal accomplish within the various hardware elements in a processor?

Basically, control signals perform individual *micro-operations* within the processor, of which the following are typical examples:

- Selection of a register from a register bank,
- Transfer of data from one register to another within the processor, along an internal bus,
- Selection and initiation of an operation within a functional unit such as the ALU,
- Initiation of a memory read or write operation, and
- Initiation of an input or output operation.

The function specified by the given machine instruction is carried out through the right combination of such *micro-operations* in each instruction clock cycle from 0 to $n - 1$. Before studying the next example, a quick review of the examples of Section 6.3 will prove to be helpful to the student.

Example 6.4

Figure 6.4 shows how the contents of one register may be transferred to another register over a data bus connecting them. In the Figure, the two registers have been named X and Y, but in general they may be any two registers within the processor.

To place its contents on the bus, register X is provided with control signal X_{out}; and to gate the data in from the bus, register Y is provided with control signal Y_{in}. In one clock cycle, if both the control signals X_{out} and Y_{in} are asserted, the nett result will be that the contents of register X will get copied into register Y over the bus connecting them.

Fig. 6.4 Data transfer from register X to register Y

Recall from Section 3.6 that the rising edge and the falling edge of a clock pulse can both be used within a digital circuit. For the transfer shown in Fig. 6.4, for example, the rising edge of a clock pulse can activate data transfer from X to the bus, and the falling edge of the same clock pulse can activate data transfer from the bus to Y. The time delay between the rising and the falling edges allows the electronic signals to propagate and settle, and thus the required data transfer can be completed in one clock cycle.

If the contents of X need to be transferred to two registers Y and Z in the same clock cycle, then naturally the required control signals would be X_{out}, Y_{in} and Z_{in}.

Any type of data *manipulation*—i.e. addition, subtraction, shift, logic operations, and so on—occurs only in a *functional unit* within the processor, when the required control signals are applied to the unit. In the previous section, we have studied such a functional unit—namely, an ALU with its inputs, outputs, and the required control signals.

A *floating point unit* (FPU) is another example of such a functional unit, although of course, the processor of Fig. 6.1 has not been provided with an FPU.

In Chapter 8, we shall discuss the basic concepts related to arithmetic operations on integer and floating point data. We shall see that, as compared to integer operations, floating point operations require several additional sub-steps—and this is the reason why integer and floating point operations are provided in separate functional units.

6.7 PROGRAM COUNTER

We have seen that the program counter (PC) is a special register in the processor which contains the memory address of the next instruction which is to be fetched and executed. We have seen that, at the end of execution of one instruction, the processor goes on to execute the next instruction which is one of the following:

a. the immediate next instruction stored in memory,
b. after a jump or a function call, the instruction stored at the target address, or
c. after a return instruction, the instruction after the last function call.

Therefore—after the current instruction is fetched, and during its execution—the PC must be made to point to the next instruction to be fetched, in accordance with (a), (b) or (c). Usually this is done through two steps carried out in the following order:

(i) After the current instruction is fetched, PC is incremented by an amount equal to the length in bytes of the current instruction. This causes PC to point to the next sequential instruction stored in memory, which would be fetched if no jump, function call, or return takes place during the execute phase of the current instruction.
(ii) If a jump, function call, or return—i.e. a transfer of control—does take place during the execute phase of the current instruction, the correct address according to (b) or (c) is transferred to PC, overwriting the value which was incremented in step (i).

With reference to step (i), note that the length of the current instruction is known only after it has been *decoded*—which may be thought of as the preparatory step prior to instruction execution. Therefore, step (i) must be carried out after the current instruction is decoded, but before it is executed. However, if all the instructions have uniform length, then step (i) can be carried out even before the current instruction is decoded.

On *NICE*, machine instructions have length of one, two or four bytes. Therefore, we provide a 2-bit wide control signal PC_{inc} associated with the PC. The three possible non-zero values of PC_{inc}—which are 01, 10 and 11—cause PC to be incremented by 1, 2 or 4, respectively. The required circuit for incrementing PC is provided with it, so that the ALU is not used for this purpose. Figure 6.5 shows the arrangement schematically.

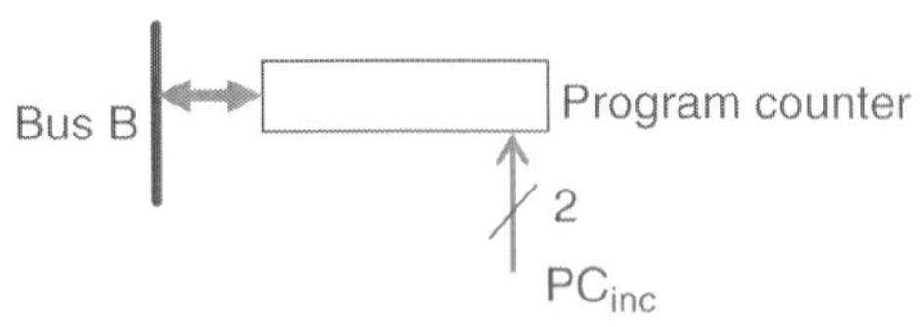

Fig. 6.5 Program counter and control signal PC_{inc}

6.8 NESTED FUNCTION CALLS AND THE STACK

For most of the instructions of *NICE*—in fact all the instructions in Table 5.1 except CALL and RET—it is a fairly simple matter to outline the micro-operations which must be performed within the processor in the *fetch* and *execute* phases. The examples in Section 6.3 and the discussion in Section 6.6 illustrate the actions required in the form of micro-operations and the control signals which activate these micro-operations.

However, when we consider the function call and return instructions CALL and RET, a little extra complexity creeps in, because of the need to store return addresses of *nested* function calls. The need for providing CALL and RET instructions was explained in Section 5.2, based on the way in which computer software is designed. Now we must study how exactly the processor manages to keep track of return addresses.

Example 6.5

Suppose a 'main' program P calls function F_1, which in turn calls function F_2, and F_2 again in turn calls function F_3. Clearly this is an instance of *nested* function calls, and we say that the *depth of nesting* in this case is three.

At this stage, somewhere in the system, we must have with us three return addresses—for the function returns, respectively, from F_3 to F_2, from F_2 to F_1, and from F_1 to the 'main' program. Let us denote these three return addresses as R_{32}, R_{21} and R_{1mp} respectively. As was also explained in Section 5.2, these return addresses will be used in *last-in, first-out* order: first R_{32}, then R_{21} and finally R_{1mp}.

Before looking at the mechanism for storing return addresses, we must note two key requirements that this mechanism must satisfy:

(i) We must not place an arbitrary limit on the maximum depth of nesting of function calls which may occur in a running program. In fact, when a function is called, the depth of its nesting is not even known within the function. Also, in so-called *recursive* function calls, the maximum depth of nesting depends on the input supplied to the program.

This means that we must not place an arbitrary limit on the maximum number of return addresses which need to be stored at one time.

(ii) As discussed, the return addresses stored must be used in *last-in, first-out* order.

A moment's reflection will convince the student that the processor architecture seen in Fig. 6.1 cannot satisfy the first requirement. The reason for this negative assessment is quite simple: The number of registers in the processor available to store return addresses must remain limited; and therefore, any arrangement based on these registers will violate condition (i) above.

Therefore, we need to provide space in main memory to store return addresses in *last-in, first-out* order, with virtually no upper limit on the number of addresses thus stored. Fortunately, this can be achieved using a simple mechanism known as a *stack*. For an understanding of how the stack operates, we may refer to Fig. 6.6.

In Example 6.5, the three return addresses we were dealing with were denoted by R_{1mp}, R_{21} and R_{32}, which is the order in which we store them as the 'main' program calls F_1, F_1 calls F_2, and F_2 calls F_3. This notation has been carried forward to Fig. 6.6.

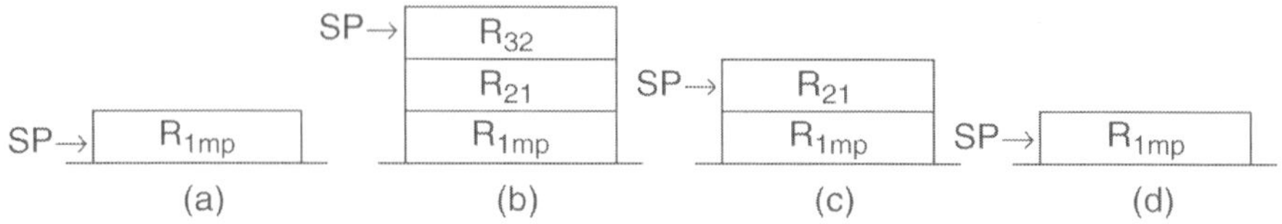

Fig. 6.6 **Principle of operation of a *stack***

We also see in Fig. 6.6, the notation 'SP→', which indicates here that a register named SP in the processor holds the address of the last element added to the *stack*. The letters SP stand for *stack pointer*, which is the special register in the processor.

In part (a) of the figure, we see only the return address R_{1mp} on the stack. This happens after the 'main' program calls function *F*1. In part (b), we see two more addresses on the stack—first R_{21} gets on to the stack when *F*1 calls *F*2, and later R_{32} gets on to the stack when *F*2 calls *F*3. Therefore, part (b) shows the state of the stack after *F*3 has been called, but before it returns to *F*2.

Part (c) of the figure shows the stack after execution returns from *F*3 to *F*2. Note that return address R_{32} has been removed from the stack. In fact, it is removed from the stack precisely to fulfill its role—when this saved return address R_{32} gets back into PC, execution resumes in *F*2 from the point just after the call to *F*3, as required.

Thus we conclude that: (a) a CALL instruction causes the return address to be added on top of stack in main memory, and (b) a RET instruction causes the return address to be removed from the stack and copied into PC, so that execution returns to the instruction after the function call.

Part (d) of the figure depicts the stack after the return from *F*2 to *F*1. Note that, at this point, the stack has the same appearance as in part (a).

We see that the stack grows and shrinks only from the top. This is the reason why, no matter how many elements are added to the stack, only one *stack pointer* register SP is needed to hold the address of the *top of stack**; this point has been shown using notation 'SP→' in Fig. 6.6.

When an element is added to the stack, with its consequent change in SP, the operation is known as a PUSH operation. And when an element is removed from the stack, with the opposite change in SP, that operation is known as a POP operation. Thus, the two main operations on a stack are PUSH and POP.

Execution of CALL instruction causes the return address to be pushed on to the stack. Execution of RET instruction causes the address pushed on the stack previously to be popped and moved into PC. This solution fully meets the requirements (i) and (ii) listed before for the function call and return mechanism.

Some processors provide PUSH and POP as machine language instructions available to the programmer. This is not the case with *NICE*, however. Instead, we have assigned to register R15 the role of *stack pointer* SP. Thus, in the assembly language of *NICE*, R15 and SP signify the same register. This is also the reason why SP is not seen as a separate register in Fig. 6.1.

---

*During normal stack operations, the so-called *bottom of stack* does not get affected, because a programmer would not normally remove something from the stack which has not been added to it earlier. If such an error does occur in a running program, it is called *stack underflow*. A *stack overflow* occurs when a stack outgrows the space allocated to it in main memory. Details of how these errors are handled are not needed at present, since we are not attempting complete processor design; for a brief discussion, see Section 8.8. In Fig. 6.6, *bottom of stack* may be imagined to be at the horizontal line drawn under the stack—or at any point lower down.

6.9 CACHE MEMORY

As has been mentioned before, in general, processor circuits operate at a much faster speed than *read* or *write* accesses to main memory. The reasons for this speed mismatch may be listed as: (a) the way in which main memory circuits are built and operate, and (b) the larger effective distance from processor to main memory that signals have to travel.

This speed mismatch between processor and main memory is a fact of life that, with present-day technology, we have to accept as inevitable. Over the past few decades, both processors and memories have become faster by some orders of magnitude, but the ratio of processor speed and main memory speed has in fact increased.

Processor designers understood long ago that such a speed mismatch proves to be a major 'brake' on system performance. For example, suppose that the processor clock runs twenty times faster than *read* or *write* accesses to main memory. This means that, every time the processor accesses main memory, it would waste twenty of its own clock cycles doing nothing! Naturally, in an effort to derive more mileage out of the processor, processor designers had to find ways to overcome this speed mismatch.

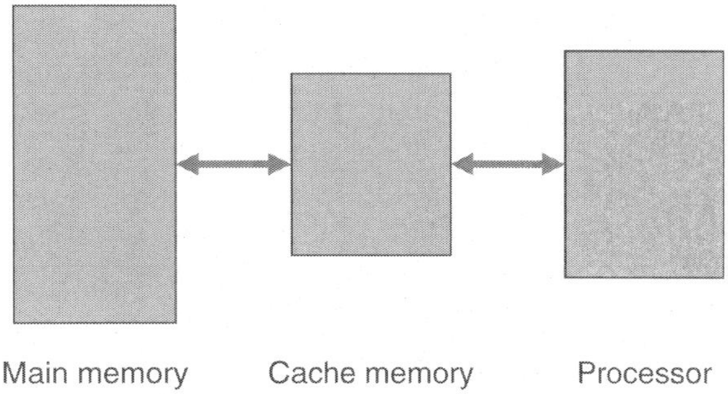

Fig. 6.7 Cache memory

One standard technique developed in response to this major performance challenge is to provide a so-called *cache memory** between the processor and main memory, as shown schematically in Fig. 6.7.

The speed of cache memory is much closer to that of the processor. This means that access by the processor to a byte or word from cache memory is much faster than access to a byte or word from main memory. The capacity of cache memory provided in the system is, however, much smaller than that of main memory. The simple reason for this is that, on a bit-wise comparison with main memory, cache memory occupies more space, consumes more power, and is also more expensive.

Since cache memory is much smaller in capacity than main memory, it can contain only a small fraction of the programs and data which reside in main memory. The key question therefore is: Which part of main memory contents must be brought to the cache?

The answer is: The cache memory must be designed in such a way that, with a high probability, the main memory content most recently used by the processor is brought into cache memory and is available there.

In general, programs make memory accesses in such a way that the memory content accessed in the <u>recent past</u> is also more likely to be accessed in the <u>recent future</u>. Assume that such 'currently in use' memory content is made available in the cache. Then, most of the references made by the processor to main memory are satisfied by the copy of memory content maintained in the cache—thereby yielding faster and effective access by the processor to main memory content.

---

*The word *cache* is pronounced in the same way as 'cash'. Its meaning is related to a *hoard*, as in—'A cache of gold and jewellery was discovered in the house'. In the context of computer systems, the word *cache* is also used frequently as a verb, as in—'These web pages are cached in the local server'.

The property of running programs mentioned above is known as *temporal locality of memory references*. Running programs also exhibit a dual property known as *spatial locality of memory references*—i.e. content is more likely to be accessed from memory addresses which are close to addresses recently referenced. Running programs almost invariably exhibit both these types of locality of references, and therefore memory sub-systems are designed to take advantage of this property.

When the processor finds a required memory byte or word in cache, the event is known as a *cache hit*. Occasionally the processor will access a memory byte or word not present in the cache. The cache sub-system will detect this event as a *cache miss*, and initiate access to main memory to transfer the required byte or word from main memory to cache. To make room for incoming content, some other cache content may need to be written back from cache to main memory—although even this is not necessary, if the copy of the content in cache has not been modified since it was brought in from main memory.

To take advantage of spatial locality of references in cache memory design, it is necessary that data transfers between main memory and cache take place in a uniform size which is larger than a word. This transfer size is defined by the so-called *cache block size*—which may be of the order of sixteen bytes, i.e. four 32-bit words.

Naturally, not every read or write access by the processor to main memory will be satisfied from cache memory. Memory references will result in mix of cache hits and cache misses. In general, of course, we would expect that cache hits would be much more frequent that cache misses. The following example illustrates how we can calculate the effective memory access time in a system provided with cache memory.

Example 6.6

On a computer system, assume that cache access takes 4 nanoseconds, while main memory access takes 50 nanoseconds. It is found empirically that about 90% of all memory accesses are satisfied from the cache, and the rest from main memory.

The effective memory access time in this system can then be calculated as the following weighted average of the two access times:

$$T_{eff} = 0.9 \times T_{cache} + 0.1 \times T_{main}$$

With the values as given, this yields $T_{eff} = 0.9 \times 4 + 0.1 \times 50 = 8.6$ nanoseconds.

We may say that, with the cache mechanism in place, the processor in effect 'sees' a memory system which is as large as the main memory provided—but has access time closer to that of cache. This is an instance of how processor designers always try to achieve 'the best of both the worlds'.

Note that the presence or absence of cache memory is completely transparent to the program running on the processor. When the program makes access to main memory—for an instruction or data—the required byte or word becomes available in the processor regardless of whether cache memory is in place, and regardless of its size and speed. But clearly the program will run faster on the processor with larger cache—since, on average, memory access will be faster on this processor.

On some systems nowadays, two or sometimes even three levels of cache memory are provided. In Fig. 6.7, these may be imagined as so many cache memory blocks placed in series—between the processor shown on the right and main memory shown on the left. Starting from the processor side, these are usually named as Level 1 or 'L1' cache, Level 2 or 'L2' cache, and so on.

L1 cache—the one closest to the processor—is placed on the same VLSI chip as the processor. The cache closest to main memory may be on a separate chip, or it may even be integrated with main memory.

If three levels of cache are provided, then L1 would be smaller but faster than L2, and L2 would be smaller but faster than L3.

The processor tries to access a byte or word from L1 and L2 in parallel; if a *cache miss* occurs in L1, the required byte or word is accessed from L2. If the byte or word is not found in any cache, naturally it is accessed from main memory—and in the process, it also becomes cached along the path from main memory to the processor.

Note 6.2

The principle of caching is generally applicable whenever a solution is sought to the problem of speed mismatch in accessing data. Between secondary storage and main memory, for example, there is a huge speed mismatch. Therefore operating system designers try to cache the 'in-use' blocks of secondary storage on main memory, so that they can be accessed faster by the running program. In this context, see also Section 9.1 on Memory Hierarchy.

The student may also know about web pages from a distant web server being cached on the local server, for faster access to them by local web browsers.

In Chapter 9, we shall discuss the broad topic of Memory Organisation, of which the cache memory sub-system makes up one part. In that context, in Section 9.9, we shall take a somewhat more detailed look at the various ways in which the cache memory sub-system can be organised.

6.10 PIPELINED IMPLEMENTATION

We saw that cache memory is introduced in the system to squeeze more performance out of the processor. With this same objective, another important technique is also commonly implemented in processors which are designed for high performance.

Unlike cache memory, however, this particular technique is not a distinct hardware element added to the system. It is rather a technique for designing the processor, paying careful attention to the various stages in the fetch and execute phases of an instruction. To understand the concept, we first study a simple example of how a factory may operate.

Example 6.7

Consider a factory which produces bicycles. Each bicycle produced goes through five consecutive *stages* of production—such as adding the front wheel, adding the handle-bar, and so on. We assume that each such bicycle part is available in stock.

Assume that each of the five stages of production takes 6 minutes. Then it is simple arithmetic to conclude that—from the first stage to the last—it takes a total of 30 minutes to fully assemble a bicycle. But it should also be equally simple to conclude that the factory produces one bicycle every 6 minutes!

Such a production *pipeline* has been illustrated in Fig. 6.8. As soon as the last stage—on the extreme

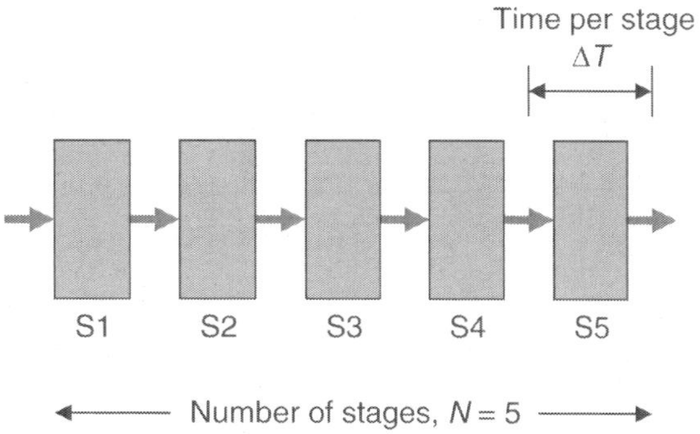

Fig. 6.8 **A pipeline of five processing stages**

right in the figure—puts out one finished bicycle, its preceding stage passes on the next bicycle to it, to be finished in the next 6 minutes.

In fact every stage finishes its share of the work on one bicycle in 6 minutes, passes that bicycle on to the next stage, and receives the next bicycle from the preceding stage. For 'clog-free' working of such a pipeline, it is necessary that each stage finishes its share of the work in exactly 6 minutes—i.e. that the stages remain *synchronised.*

To ensure that no stage of production remains idle, we must ensure that the first stage of production begins work on a new bicycle once every six minutes. Suppose that—for some reason—the first stage remains idle for one time slot of 6 minutes. Clearly then, in the subsequent consecutive time slots, this idle time of 6 minutes—which we may call a 'bubble'—will pass through each of the remaining four stages of the pipeline.

Now consider the stages of processing that an instruction goes through during its *fetch* and *execute* phases. These stages for processing a typical instruction—such as the ones we have been using in earlier chapters—have been listed below:

1. Instruction fetch (IF)	the instruction is fetched from cache memory
2. Instruction decode (ID)	fields making up the instruction in IR are decoded (but see also Note 6.3 on page 135).
3. ALU operation (OP)	specified arithmetic/logic operation takes place in ALU
4. Memory access (MA)	access is made to cache memory for read/write
5. Result stored (RS)	result is stored in destination register

In a pipelined implementation, the basic idea is that each of these stages should take one clock cycle of the processor. Thus, instead of the 6 minute 'clock' of bicycle production, we have here the processor clock cycle, which may be measured in nanoseconds.

In every processor clock cycle, the instruction moves forward one stage in the pipeline. Thus one instruction completes its execution in every clock cycle, while each instruction still does take five clock cycles to complete. If an instruction does not require any operation in a particular stage—for example, if it does not require a memory access in stage 4—then it simply passes through that stage as a 'no operation'.

Access to slow main memory would starve a pipelined processor of instructions and data. Therefore pipelined processors must also be provided with cache memories. Further, to avoid having two pipeline stages contend for cache access, separate *instruction cache* and *data cache* are usually provided with pipelined processors.

It is also important to note here that, with a *load and store* type of instruction set, there is at most one memory access for data in each instruction, in stage 4.

Example 6.8

Assume that a processor is designed with five pipeline stages, and that the clock driving this pipeline is running at 500 megahertz.

In terms of the notation used in Fig. 6.8, we now have $N = 5$ and $\Delta T = 2$ nanoseconds. Thus, this processor can finish executing one instruction in every 2 nanoseconds, while each instruction takes a total of $5 \times 2 = 10$ nanoseconds in its five execution stages.

The total time taken by an instruction—through all the pipeline stages—is known as the *instruction latency* of the processor, while the rate of execution of instructions is known as its processing *throughput.*

The processor of this example can sustain a maximum processing throughput of $1/(2 \times 10^{-9}) = 500$ million instructions per second (i.e. 500 MIPS). The actual throughput achieved cannot exceed this figure., but it will in general be less than this figure. In other words, there is a potential 'fly in the ointment', which we shall uncover now.

In a pipelined processor with N stages, at any time instant a maximum of N instructions would occupy these stages. The instruction in the last stage, shown on the right in Fig. 6.8, would be in its last clock cycle of execution; and the instruction in the first stage, shown on the left, would be in its first clock cycle of execution. In general, the instruction in the kth stage would be in its kth clock cycle of execution, for $1 \leq k \leq N$.

Consider a full pipeline, i.e. one in which all N stages are occupied by instructions. The first of these N instructions to enter the pipeline would, after $N - 1$ clock cycles, be in the last stage of the pipeline. The remaining $N - 1$ instructions in the pipeline would have entered it, one by one, after the first instruction.

Figure 6.9 illustrates how a five stage instruction pipeline—i.e. with $N = 5$—executes a sequence of instructions, which are denoted here as i_1, i_2, i_3, and so on. For simplicity, we have assumed here that the pipeline is empty before instruction i_1 enters the first stage of instruction fetch (IF). The five rows in this figure represent the pipeline in five consecutive clock cycles, as indicated on the left.

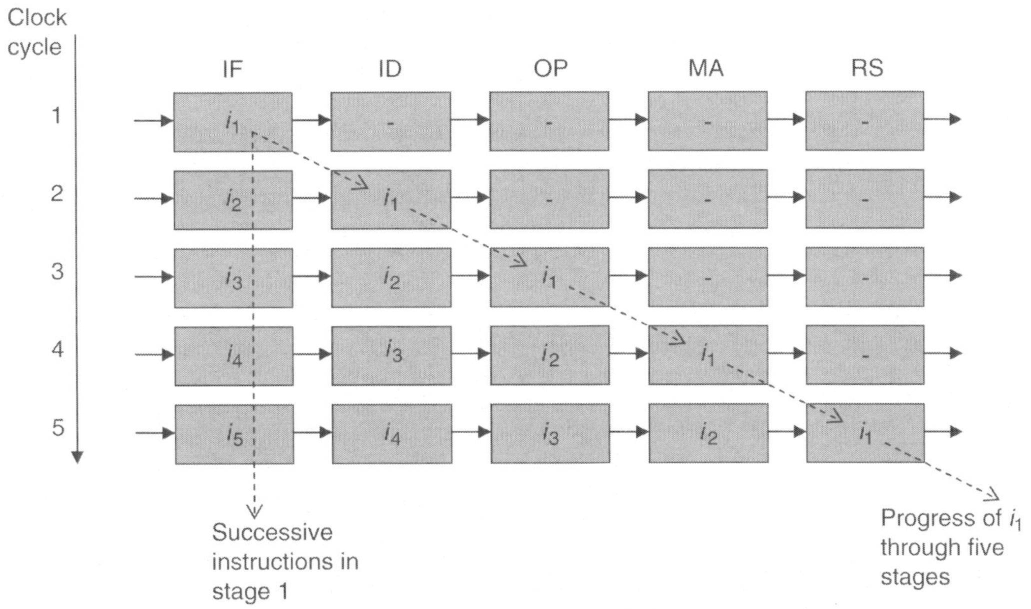

Fig. 6.9 Instruction pipeline filling up in five clock cycles

It is seen clearly in this figure that instruction i_2 follows i_1 in the pipeline—i.e. it is behind i_1 by exactly one clock cycle. Similarly, i_3 follows i_2, i_4 follows i_3, and so on. The two dashed arrows drawn in the figure indicate, respectively: (a) the successive occupants of stage 1 (IF), and (b) the progress of i_1 through the five stages.

In the last clock cycle shown—which is clock cycle 5—the pipeline is seen to be full. We see that the five instructions i_5, i_4, i_3, i_2 and i_1 are occupying pipeline stages 1, 2, 3, 4 and 5, respectively (note the reverse order!). Instructions complete the last stage—i.e. RS—one per clock cycle, even though each instruction takes five clock cycles to execute.

Now consider what happens if the first instruction i_1 causes a branch—i.e. transfer of control—to an entirely different target instruction, of which there is no trace in the pipeline at that time instant. Clearly, this means that the instructions behind i_1 in the pipeline are wrongly occupying the pipeline—and therefore they must be *flushed* from it. But note that this fact becomes known only when the transfer of control instruction is executed. If k pipeline stages are occupied behind i_1, they must be cleared out, which mean that k processor clock cycles are wasted.

Unfortunately, in general there is no known technique which can eliminate completely such time-wasting pipeline *flushes* during regular operations of a pipelined processor. However, by using techniques such as *branch prediction*, processor designers try to reduce the occurrence and/or performance impact of such pipeline flushes.

We have seen that the processor of Example 6.7 is capable of maximum sustained throughput of 500 MIPS. Clearly this is on the unrealistic assumption that no pipeline flushes occur while we measure its performance. For real life programs, this is never a valid assumption—and that is one key reason why the actual processor performance measured on real life programs is in general less than its theoretical maximum.

As the following example makes clear, however, there are also other reasons which cause the actual performance of a pipelined processor to be less than its theoretical maximum.

Example 6.9

A condition can arise within a pipelined processor which makes it necessary to 'skip' one clock cycle in introducing an instruction into the first stage. This is illustrated in Fig. 6.10, where we see that no instruction enters the first IF stage of the pipeline in clock cycle 3. This stage therefore remains empty in clock cycle 3.

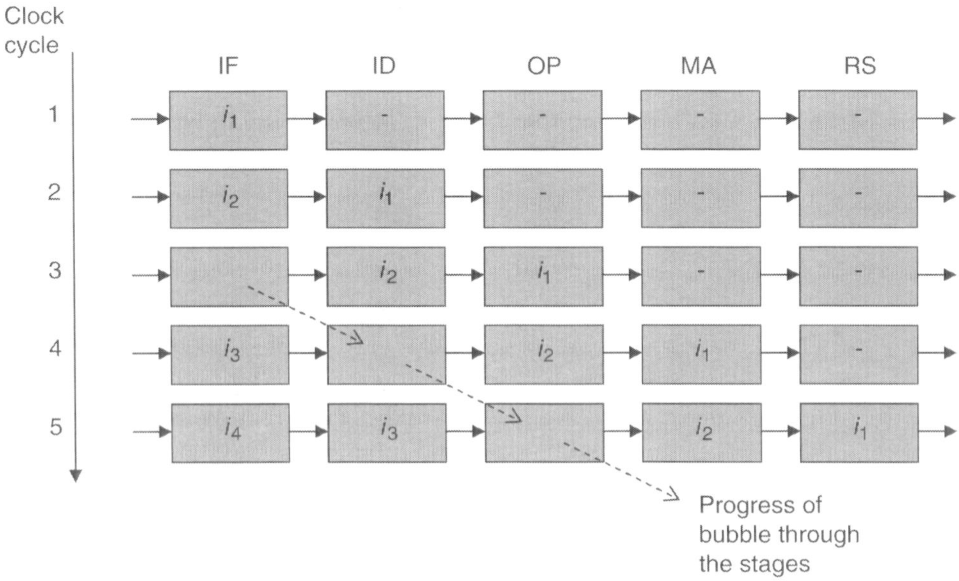

Fig. 6.10 **A 'bubble' in instruction pipeline**

When instruction i_3 enters the pipeline in clock cycle 4, the second stage of the pipeline becomes empty, because the instruction i_2 which was in it has moved forward. In this way, in every clock cycle, the 'bubble' in the pipeline—i.e. a stage which is doing nothing for one clock cycle—moved forward, as shown in Fig. 6.10.

Conditions which can cause such a 'bubble' to enter the pipeline include (i) a cache miss and (ii) a dependency between instructions, i.e. when the result of one instruction is not available in time for the subsequent instruction to execute. The occurrence of an empty stage in the pipeline is known in technical terms as a pipeline *stall*, while the conditions which cause stalls are known collectively as *hazards*.

We should think of 'one instruction per processor clock cycle' as the target which processor designers can aim for. To achieve this target, designers try to reduce the occurrence and/or performance impact of pipeline flushes and stalls.

But the design objectives scale up, if the processor has been provided with multiple functional units—for example, an ALU such as the one in Fig. 6.1, and also a separate *floating point unit* (FPU) which can operate independently, in parallel with the ALU. On processors with multiple functional units, the designers aim to achieve a maximum performance which exceeds 'one instruction per processor clock cycle'.

Note 6.3

Stage 2 of the five stages shown above is *instruction decode*. The name of this stage is somewhat inaccurate, in the sense that the instruction is never fully decoded. If a 16-bit instruction is fully decoded, for example, the decoder will have 65,536 outputs—but all of these will never be used during the execute phase. For example, an immediate constant is never decoded, and a memory or I/O address is decoded outside the processor.

What happens in instruction decode stage is that some of the key fields of the instruction in IR are decoded. For example, the addressing mode bits must be decoded to determine the micro-operations required for the selected mode.

Register select bits in the instruction will be decoded when they are used by the register bank to select the correct register for a read or a write operation. Similarly, the ALU function bits (see Section 6.4) may be decoded within the ALU.

6.11 DESIGN OF A RISC PROCESSOR

In Chapters 4 and 5, we studied the instruction set of a simple processor. We saw that the instruction set defines the programmer's view of a processor, and we discussed in brief the question of whether the instruction set should be made relatively simple or relatively complex. In the present chapter, we have studied the various elements which go into the hardware design of a processor.

Proponents of the RISC approach to processor design showed that a *reduced* instruction set can yield greater processor performance*. This happens because RISC makes possible processor hardware design which achieves higher instruction execution rates. Over the last couple of decades, this approach has had a significant influence on instruction set and processor design.

---

*The word 'reduced' can be understood in this context as relatively simple and uniform. The names of David Patterson and John Hennessy are most closely associated with the original RISC approach to processor design. See, for example, their book *Computer Architecture: A Quantitative Approach*, published by Morgan Kaufmann.

In this section, we shall discuss very briefly some specific ways in which a reduced instruction set allows the processor to be designed for higher execution instruction rates. Towards this end, we shall see in brief how the various hardware elements discussed in the earlier sections of this chapter can be combined in a RISC processor.

Every machine instruction—even on a RISC processor—takes multiple clock cycles to fetch and execute. Therefore, to achieve a processing rate of one instruction per clock cycle or greater, the RISC processor must be provided with an instruction pipeline. Let us see briefly how the basic processor architecture of Fig. 6.1 must be modified to include the required pipeline stages. Stages of the five-stage instruction pipeline seen in the previous section are repeated here for convenience:

1. Instruction fetch (IF)
2. Instruction decode (ID)
3. ALU operation (OP)
4. Memory access (MA)
5. Result stored (RS)

The pipelined RISC processor has internal architecture which resembles in essence the pipeline stages shown in Fig. 6.8, and the time per stage is one processor clock cycle. *Pipeline registers* are required between stages, so that the relevant output from one stage is passed to the next stage in the pipeline register between the two stages.

Figure 6.11 shows the structure of a pipelined processor with the five stages discussed above; note that pipeline registers have been shown between two successive stages. Also shown in the figure is the bank of programmable registers of the processor, such as the registers R0 to R15 which we have been using. The registers may be accessed by two or more stages of the pipeline, as illustrated in the figure and in the next example.

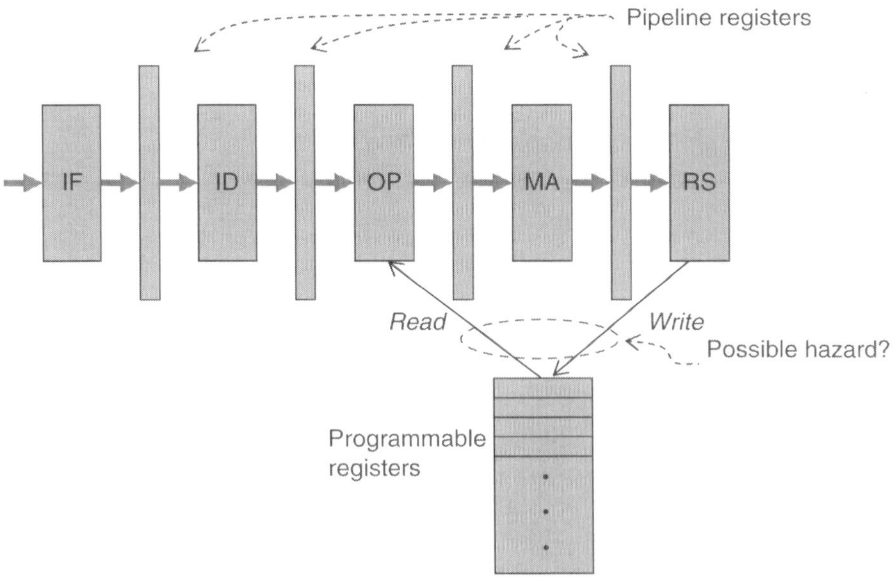

Fig. 6.11 **Processor pipeline showing a possible hazard**

Example 6.10

Consider the following sequence of two instructions, labeled i_k and i_{k+1} for reference:

i_k	**LOAD**	`2000, R3`
i_{k+1}	**ADD**	`R3, R4`

In a pipelined processor, these two instructions would occupy two successive stages. But note that i_{k+1} has one operand R3 whose value is only obtained when i_k completes its memory read operation. This value of R3 would be written in stage 5 (RS) of the pipeline—which means that, if a cache miss occurs in the memory read operation of i_k, instruction i_{k+1} must not move to stage OP until the required data arrives in R3. In the figure, this possibility is shown as a possible hazard, which would necessitate a pipeline stall.

Issues related to the efficient utilisation of an instruction pipeline involve so-called *instruction level parallelism*, a topic which has been discussed briefly in Section 13.2.

Note that memory access by the processor takes place in two of the pipeline stages:

(i) In stage 1, for instruction fetch, and
(ii) In stage 4—but only for instructions LOAD, STORE, CALL and RET.

We have seen that, to speed up both these types of memory access, use is made of cache memory. However, in order to perform an instruction fetch in every clock cycle in the first (IF) stage of the pipeline, PC must be incremented within the first stage itself—so that the next successive instruction fetch can take place in the very next clock cycle. But this in turn requires that:

a. All instructions must have fixed and uniform length (say four bytes)—since otherwise the instruction length is not available in stage 1, and
b. Separate cache memories must be provided for instructions and data, so that cache access in stage 4 does not contend with ongoing instruction fetches in stage 1.

An RISC processor must have a *load and store* type of instruction set, such as the one provided on our own processor. This ensures that:

(i) In execute phase, an instruction makes at most one memory reference for data, and
(ii) A memory reference instruction does not involve an ALU operation on data.

Such a load and store instruction set allows any address calculation required before the memory operation in stage 4 (MA) to be performed by the ALU in stage 3 (OP)—so as to support the various addressing modes which we discussed in Chapter 5.

We have mentioned earlier that, for *NICE*, it is possible to encode instructions in binary with lengths of 1, 2 or 4 bytes*. However, for a pipelined implementation, all the instructions must be encoded to a uniform length of 4 bytes—which means that some amount of 'padding' is unavoidable in the encoding of instructions. This implies that the possible design goal of compact encoding of instructions (see Section 6.4) must be sacrificed to some extent to achieve uniform instruction lengths in an RISC processor.

In the same way, block data instructions must not be included in the instruction set, since they cannot be accommodated in the instruction pipeline. Instructions must be encoded in binary in such a way as to facilitate more efficient decoding in stage 2 of the pipeline—in line with design goal (b) of Section 6.4.

*Appendix A shows one possible way to achieve such an encoding.

All the design goals of an RISC processor can be achieved with a *hardwired* control unit—which, as we saw, is basically a large and complex combinational circuit. A hardwired control unit can be operated at a speed consistent with the RISC design objective of 'one instruction per clock cycle' or greater. The alternative design of a control unit—known as *microprogrammed control*, which we shall discuss in the next chapter—is slower, and is therefore not viable for use in a pipelined implementation of a processor.

SUMMARY

Registers, data paths, and functional units are the basic hardware elements which define processor architecture. For the simple processor which we have been using, we designed an architecture based on two data busses, a bank of programmable registers, an ALU, and several special-purpose registers such as the PC, IR, *address* and *data*. The external bus allows the processor to communicate with main memory and I/O devices.

Micro-operations are carried out on these hardware elements in response to specific control signals; the control unit of the processor generates these signals in accordance with the machine instruction being executed. The machine instruction set and its encoding in binary play a key role in the process.

Various specific elements of the processor architecture include the arithmetic and logic unit (ALU), data busses and the typical data transfer mechanism, the program counter, and the mechanism of stack which is required to support nested function calls and returns. Return addresses associated with function calls are stored using the *last-in, first-out* storage mechanism of the stack.

Processor circuits operate at speeds which are at least one order of magnitude faster than main memory speeds. To enhance processor performance, use must be made of cache memory as well as instruction pipeline. An RISC processor utilises an instruction pipeline and a split instruction and data cache in an attempt to achieve its target processing rate of 'one instruction per clock cycle', or greater. However, in practice, pipeline flushes and stalls make it difficult to achieve this target rate.

REVIEW QUESTIONS

1. List the main elements which define the hardware architecture of a processor.
2. What is the function of the control unit in a processor?
3. List the functions performed by the arithmetic and logic unit (ALU) in a processor.
4. What are the functions of the instruction register (IR) and the program counter (PC)?
5. List the functions of the program status word (PSW), and the two registers—*address* and *data*—shown in Fig. 6.1.
6. List the main signals provided on the external bus of the processor.
7. What is meant by the instruction set architecture (ISA) of a processor?
8. What is the function of control signals generated by the control unit?

9. What determines the control signals which are generated by the control unit in a given processor clock cycle?
10. What is the role of the counter shown in Fig. 6.2? What is the relationship of this counter with the instruction clock cycle?
11. List three possible criteria which must be kept in mind in coding processor instructions into binary.
12. List the typical inputs, outputs and control signals of the ALU.
13. Explain in one sentence what is meant by 'gating data from a data bus into a register'.
14. Give a few examples of micro-operations in the course of execution of a machine instruction.
15. Recall Example 6.4, which deals with a data transfer from register X to register Y over the bus connecting them. List the control signals needed in a clock cycle to carry out a data transfer in the opposite direction, i.e. from Y to X.
16. Once again with reference to Example 6.4, list the control signals needed in a clock cycle to carry out a data transfer from register Y to registers X and Z.
17. At the end of execution of one instruction, the processor goes on to execute the next instruction which is obtained in one of three different ways. List these three different ways.
18. What is the role of control signal PC_{inc} on our processor *NICE* ?
19. Suppose a main program P calls function F_1, which in turn calls function F_2, and F_2 again in turn calls function F_3. After the return from F_3, F_2 calls another function F_4. What is the depth of nesting while function F_4 is executing?
20. What are the two key requirements which must be satisfied by the mechanism of storing return addresses?
21. What is the basic reason for the introduction of cache memory into a computer system?
22. State the main reasons why the size of cache memory provided in a system is much smaller than that of main memory.
23. State the basic criterion which a cache memory sub-system must be designed to satisfy.
24. State in one sentence each the meaning of temporal and spatial locality of program references.
25. State in one sentence each the meaning of cache hit and cache miss.
26. List the typical five stages in the processing of an instruction in a processor pipeline.
27. Why is it necessary for a pipelined processor to also be provided with cache memory? Why must this cache memory be divided between instruction and data cache?
28. What is the instruction latency and maximum possible throughput of a processor with a five-stage pipeline, driven by a clock of 1 gigahertz?
29. What is the meaning of a pipeline flush operation? When is this operation carried out?
30. What is the meaning of a pipeline stall and pipeline hazards?
31. What is the role of pipeline registers in an instruction pipeline?

EXERCISES

1. Consider the processor architecture of Fig. 6.1, but with one significant change. All the registers and the ALU are connected to a single internal bus provided for the purpose—rather than the two busses A and B as seen in the figure. Clearly, this single internal bus can carry out only one data transfer in a clock cycle. Draw the modified diagram of this so-called single-bus architecture.
2. Discuss in brief the implications of the change described in Exercise 1 on the *execute* phase of the instruction: `ADD R7,R9`.

   Note: For the next three exercises, we revert back to the processor architecture of Fig. 6.1. The machine instructions being used are from those listed in Table 5.1.
3. Consider the machine instruction: `AND R3,R7`. List the sequence of control signals which would be required in the *execute* phase of this instruction.
4. Consider the machine instruction: `JMP address`. List the sequence of control signals which would be required in the *execute* phase of this instruction.
5. Consider the machine instruction: `SHIFTL R5,8`. List the sequence of control signals which would be required in the *execute* phase of this instruction. Make suitable assumptions about the capability of the ALU.
6. A running program *P* calls function *F*, which in turn calls another function *G*. After execution returns from *G* to *F*, *F* calls another function *H*. Successive returns then take place from *H* to *F*, and then from *F* to *P*. Using appropriate symbols, show the stacked return addresses before and after each function call and return.
7. A running program *P* calls function *F*, which in turn calls another function *G*. Function *G* then successively calls three other functions *H*1, *H*2 and *H*3—i.e. calling *H*2 after the return from *H*1, and *H*3 after the return from *H*2. Successive returns then take place from *H*3 to *G*, from *G* to *F*, and from *F* to *P*. Using appropriate symbols, show the stacked return addresses before and after each function call and return.
8. On a processor, a cache memory with access time of 4 nanoseconds has been provided. The size of this cache memory is such that on average 80% of all references to main memory are satisfied from the cache. Main memory access time is 60 nanoseconds. Calculate the effective average access time for memory references.
9. On a processor, a cache memory with access time of 2 nanoseconds has been provided. Main memory access time is 50 nanoseconds. Processor designers aim to achieve effective average access time of 5 nanoseconds for memory references. What must be their target cache hit ratio to achieve this design aim?
10. A processor has a five-stage pipeline, with a processor clock cycle of 1 nanosecond. On a set of benchmark programs, it is found that the processor delivers an average performance of 400 million instructions per second (MIPS). Find (a) the theoretical maximum performance of this processor in MIPS, and (b) the average pipeline utilisation while running the benchmark programs.

CONTROL UNIT

7

7.1 INTRODUCTION

In the previous chapter, we have studied the basic concepts of processor design. Processor architecture is defined by its registers, data paths and functional units. A machine instruction is executed when micro-operations appropriate to it are performed in each processor clock cycle of the instruction. The control unit of the processor generates the control signals to activate the required micro-operations in each clock cycle.

Based on what we have learned, in this chapter we take a somewhat more detailed view of the control unit of a processor. In particular, we first study the control signals required in each clock cycle of a typical machine instruction. For this purpose, we shall specify the required control signals using a simple and precise notation.

The concept of hardwired control unit was introduced in the previous chapter. We have seen that, in essence, it is nothing but a combinational circuit with the inputs and outputs as shown in Fig. 7.1 (which is only a slightly redrawn version of Fig. 6.2). The combinational circuit realises the required functional relationship between the input signals and the output signals of the control unit.

The student should note here that one crucial input to the control unit is supplied by the counter—shown on the lower left in the figure—which tracks the instruction clock cycle. As we have seen in the previous chapter, this counter is needed because the control signals required to be generated for an instruction vary from cycle to cycle, as the instruction proceeds through from its fetch phase to execute phase.

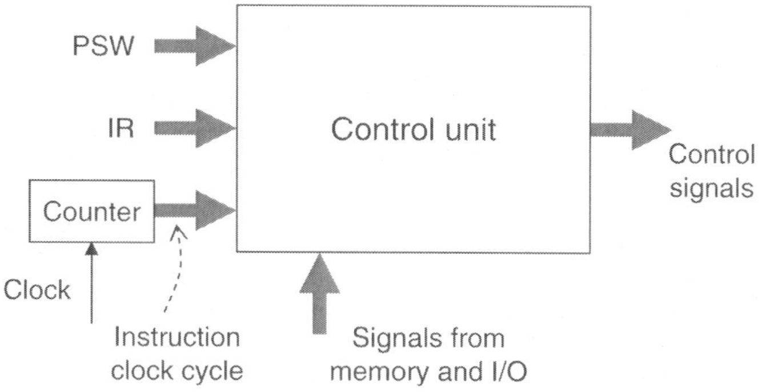

Fig. 7.1 **Control unit of a processor**

Note 7.1

There is one group of *signals* in Fig. 7.1—labeled as *signals from memory and input/output*—which, for the sake of simplicity, has not been shown earlier in Fig. 6.2. These inputs are required because the control signals generated by the control unit also depend on the status of the data paths connecting the processor to main memory and input/output devices.

Some typical functions which are performed by this group of signals are: (a) insertion of processor wait cycles for access to slower main memory, (b) processor response to completion of an input or output operation, and (c) placing the memory bus on *hold* for an I/O device to transfer data directly to or from main memory.

Points (b) and (c) will become clearer to the student in Chapter 10, when we look at the organisation of the input and output sub-system of a computer system.

It was mentioned in the previous chapter that two techniques are at present available for designing and building the control unit of a processor:

(i) hardwired control, and
(ii) microprogrammed control.

After discussing some further aspects of the hardwired control unit, we discuss in this chapter the technique of *microprogrammed control.* In essence, this technique relies on programming the required micro-operations into a special memory element in the processor. As this 'program of micro-operations'—known as *microprogram*—is executed, the control signals required for the machine instruction are generated.

In the last section of the chapter, we compare in brief the salient characteristics of hardwired and microprogrammed control units.

7.2 IMPLEMENTING A TYPICAL INSTRUCTION

We have discussed the role of control signals in carrying out the micro-operations required for a machine instruction. Let us now take a specific machine instruction as an example and examine the micro-operations and control signals it would require. The simple machine instruction we have chosen for this example is:

```
ADD R3, R4
```

We shall now see: (a) how the fetch and execute phases of this machine instruction are broken down into micro-operations, and (b) what control signals are required to carry out these micro-operations.

For this purpose, we assume that we are working with the processor architecture of Fig. 6.1, which is a non-pipelined design. For reasons which will be explained shortly, we also assume that the processor is provided with a cache memory, so that an instruction fetch takes one processor clock cycle if the instruction is found in cache—i.e. if there is a *cache hit.* For the sake of simplicity, we shall not discuss explicitly the mechanism which generates an access to main memory on a cache miss.

The required micro-operations and control signals for the instruction are shown in Table 7.1. We see that, with this design and the assumptions mentioned above, the instruction takes five clock cycles, which are numbered in the table from 0 to 4.

Table 7.1 Micro-operations and control signals required for instruction

Instruction Clock Cycle	Micro-operations Required	Control Signals Required
0	Initiate memory read for instruction	PC_{out}, ADR_{in}, READ
1	Move instruction into IR	$DATA_{out\text{-}B}$, IR_{in}
2	Move register operands to ALU, increment PC	$R3_{out\text{-}A}$, $AIN\text{-}1_{in}$, $R4_{out\text{-}B}$, $AIN\text{-}2_{in}$, PC_{inc}
3	Perform ALU operation	ALU_{ADD}
4	Move result to R3, reset control unit counter	$AOUT_{out}$, $R4_{in}$, CTR_{reset}

In naming the control signals, subscripts *in* and *out* are used to designate, respectively, control signals which gate data into and out of a register, for example PC_{out}, PC_{in}, $DATA_{out}$, $R4_{in}$, and so on. If a register is connected to both the internal busses A and B, then subscript *out-A* or *out-B* indicates the bus being used. Control signal CTR_{reset} seen in the last clock cycle of the instruction resets the instruction cycle counter (see Fig. 7.1), so that the next fetch phase starts again from instruction clock cycle 0.

We describe in brief below the operations which must be carried out in each of the five instruction clock cycles of this instruction:

CC 0: Contents of PC are moved to address register, and READ control signal is generated for the cache memory.

CC 1: Word read from cache is moved into IR, for instruction decoding.

CC 2: Contents of R3 and R4 are moved into the two ALU inputs IN-1 and IN-2 respectively. PC is incremented.

CC 3: Addition operation is performed in ALU.

CC 4: Contents of ALU output register are moved into R4. Instruction cycle counter of the control unit is reset to zero for the next instruction.

Figure 7.2 shows these operations taking place on the processor architecture of Fig. 6.1. Labels from 'CC 0' to 'CC 4' have been used to differentiate the operations taking place in the five clock cycles of the instruction. Clock cycles 'CC 0' and 'CC 1' constitute fetch and decode, and they appear in the top part of the figure. The remaining three clock cycles constitute the execute phase, and appear in the lower part.

As has been mentioned before, processor circuits operate at a much faster speed than *read* or *write* accesses to main memory. In the present design, we have assumed that the cache memory allows instruction fetch to take place in one processor clock cycle, but we have not discussed in detail how the hardware handles a cache miss.

In the case of a cache miss—and also on a low-end processor without cache—extra *memory wait* cycles are inserted in the fetch control sequence for the instruction from main memory to become available in DATA register. These extra wait cycles are inserted between cycles 'CC 0' and 'CC 1' seen before. Clearly, in such cases, memory wait cycles would also be required in the execute phases of LOAD, STORE, CALL and RET instructions, because of the memory accesses required.

On a system with cache memory, such 'wasted' wait cycles occur only on a cache miss, and thus we can understand the effect of cache memory on processor performance.

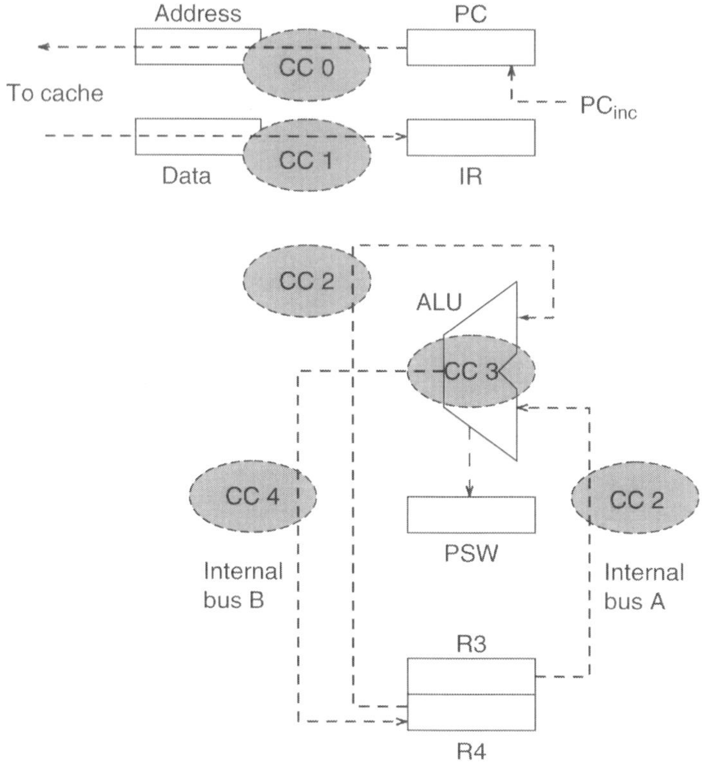

Fig. 7.2 **Operations in the five clock cycles of instruction ADD R3, R4**

On a pipelined processor, a cache miss requires access to slower L2 cache, or to even slower main memory. As we saw in Section 6.10, this delay introduces so-called *stalls* in the instruction pipeline—which are basically empty pipelines stages, implying wasted processor cycles. Techniques known as *instruction level parallelism* (ILP) have been developed in an effort to avoid such wasted processor cycles. Section 13.2 discusses in brief some of the issues related to instruction level parallelism.

7.3 HARDWIRED CONTROL UNIT

Consider once again the control unit shown in Fig. 7.1, whose outputs are the control signals such as the ones we used in the previous section. These outputs are combinational functions of the inputs, which are IR, PSW, memory and I/O status, and the instruction cycle counter. Recall that IR contains the instruction currently under execution, PSW contains the condition flags, and the instruction cycle counter sequences through from 0 to $n - 1$ for an instruction requiring a total of n processor clock cycles.

It has been mentioned earlier (see Section 3.3) that in theory any combinational circuit can be implemented with a maximum of two gate delays between its inputs and outputs. With present-day technology, combinational logic gates such as *and*, *or* and *not* can be built with gate delays in picoseconds (10^{-12} seconds), and therefore, combinational circuits are never the speed limiting elements in a computer system. (That dubious honour usually goes to memory elements!)

Therefore, a simple and direct method for building the control unit of a processor is to build a combinational circuit with the required functional relationship between its inputs and outputs. This is the basic concept of a *hardwired* control unit. Standard design techniques for such circuit design are very well developed, and automated design tools are also available which allow the circuit to be designed, fully verified, and integrated with the rest of the processor.

The basic organisation of such a hardwired control unit is shown in Fig. 7.3. Note that its inputs and outputs match exactly the ones seen above in Fig. 7.1.

The first part of the control unit, shown on the left in the figure, is the *instruction decoder*. We know that machine instructions provided on the processor are encoded in binary (recall Section 6.4). The instruction fetched into IR must be decoded, so that the appropriate control signals for it can be generated in each instruction clock cycle.

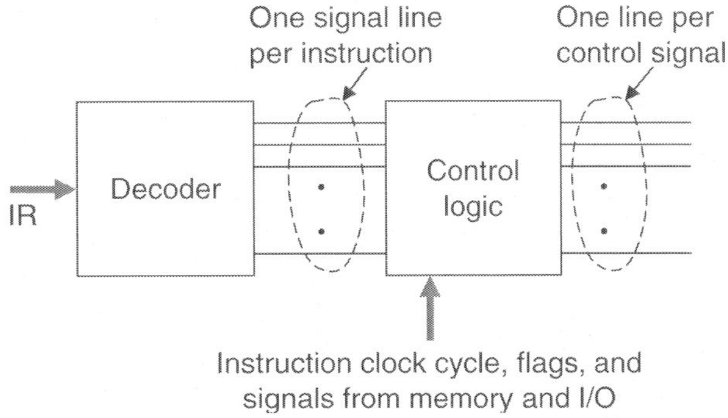

Fig. 7.3 **Basic organisation of a hardwired control unit**

In principle, the output of the instruction decoder has one separate signal line for each instruction, addressing mode, and instruction modifier. These lines, along with the other inputs to the control unit—i.e. instruction clock cycle, flags, and signals from memory and I/O—are provided as inputs to the control logic, to produce the control signals required in each instruction clock cycle. The part of the circuit containing all the control logic is shown on the right in Fig. 7.3, and the process of generation of control signals is illustrated in a simplified way in the following example.

Example 7.1

Suppose the processor designers have determined that a control signal X_{in} must be generated in clock cycle CC 2 of ADD, SUB, and a few other similar instructions involving ALU operations. Then it is easy to see that the control logic shown in Fig. 7.4 (a) satisfies this design requirement.

The output of the first *and* gate is enabled for instruction ADD in CC 2; similarly, the output of the second *and* gate is enabled for instruction SUB in CC 2. Thus, there is one *and* gate in this part of the circuit for each combination of instruction and clock cycle which must generate the signal X_{in}. The outputs of all these *and* gates are sent as inputs into the *or* gate, so that the control signal X_{in} is enabled for all the required combinations of instructions and clock cycles.

Part (b) of Fig. 7.4 shows a much simpler solution to generate the required control signals. But the key to the solution of part (b) lies in the binary encoding of instructions. Let us assume that the following property is satisfied by the binary instruction codes:

For all the instructions requiring control signal X_{in} in clock cycle CC 2—and only for these instructions—the two bits IR_k and IR_{k-1} in the instruction are set to '1'.

We have seen in the previous chapter that processor instructions fall into a few natural groups, such as arithmetic and logic instructions, transfer of control instructions, etc. For this reason, the assumption made above is not at all unrealistic—and now we shall see that it results in a much simpler logic design.

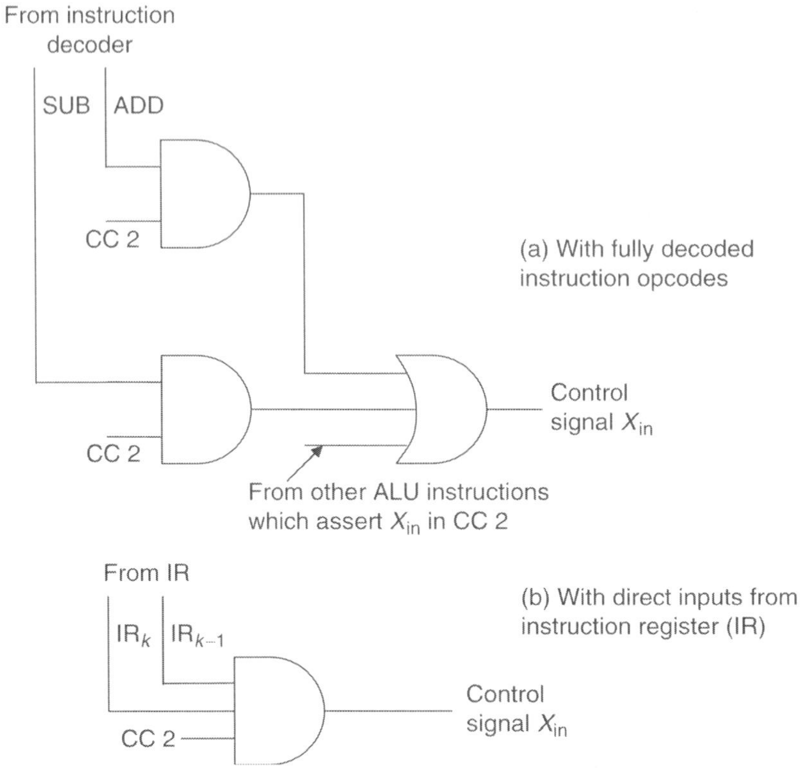

Fig. 7.4 Examples of control signal generation

In part (b) of Fig. 7.4, we see that whenever bits IR_k and IR_{k-1} of the instruction are '1', the *and* gate output is '1' in clock cycle CC 2. Thus, this single *and* gate takes care of all instructions which require X_{in} to be enabled in CC 2, and a separate decoded line for each of these instructions is not required (at least for this part of the control logic)*.

A solution of the type shown in part (b) of Fig. 7.4 requires that machine instructions should be encoded into binary with special care—so that groups of related instructions can easily be 'picked out' by examining only a few bits in IR. In general, since there are few other constraints on the binary encoding of instructions, we should assume that such encoding can always be achieved by processor designers. Recall also in this connection the design goals (b) and (c) listed in Section 6.4.

For incorporation into processors built using VLSI technology, circuits known as *programmable logic devices* can be used for hardwired control units. An example of a programmable logic device is the *programmable logic array* (PLA), of which a typical example with *n* inputs and *m* outputs is shown in schematic form in Fig. 7.5.

As seen on the left in the figure, a PLA allows any input signal x_i to be used directly, or in inverted form $\neg x_i$. The AND array shown next allows sets of inputs—either direct or inverted—to be combined using *and* gates. The outputs of the AND array are fed to the OR array, where they can be

* At this point, the student may wish to take another look at Note 6.3 in the previous chapter.

combined using *or* gates. It is a property of combinational circuits that any combinational function of *n* inputs can be realised in this manner, subject of course to the number of physical gates available in the PLA.

A basic similarity can be noted easily between the PLA structure of Fig. 7.5 and the type of control logic illustrated in parts (a) and (b) of Fig. 7.4.

A PLA has a highly regular structure, and all the required logic is 'programmed' into it in the form of connections made between row lines and column lines of the two arrays. This regular structure allows its circuit components to be made extremely small, and operating voltages to be kept low—which means that such circuits can be operated at high speeds and they consume less power. Also, sophisticated design and verification tools are available for such devices, resulting in faster design times and lower costs.

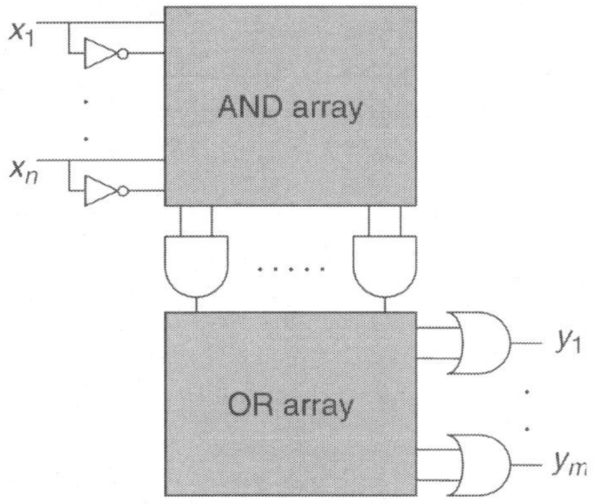

Fig. 7.5 **A programmable logic array (PLA)**

7.4 A LIMITATION OF HARDWIRED CONTROL

We have now seen that devices such as PLAs offer high speeds of operation, compact size, lower design times, and so on—everything that a circuit designer can hope for. In this way, to build a hardwired control unit, excellent design options are available.

But, in spite of this fact, an alternative design technique for the control unit of a processor has been proposed and used in the past—and is still being used for certain types of designs. With the help of a simple example, we shall now try to understand the need for this alternative design technique.

For this purpose, we must consider a machine instruction quite different from the one which we studied in Section 7.2. Consider the following *block copy* instruction (which has not been provided on the processor which we have been using):

```
BCOPY  Ri, Rj, Rk
```

The three register operands provided specify, respectively, a *source address* in main memory, a *destination address* in main memory, and a word or byte *count*. When this machine instruction is executed, the specified number of words or bytes must be copied from main memory locations starting at the source address, to main memory locations starting at the destination address.

Recall the function COPY which we studied in Section 5.6, that was written using machine instructions. The single machine instruction BCOPY here should be seen as a hardware implementation of the copy function which we saw earlier in software.

In the BCOPY machine instruction, since the word or byte count is specified by the programmer, it may vary from zero to tens of thousands. Let *C* denote the value of this count as specified by the programmer. In the execute phase of this instruction, therefore, we need to copy *C* words or bytes—one at a time—from one location to another location in main memory. This requires an iterative action to be performed C times in the execute phase, and therefore the number of processor clock cycles required in the execute phase of this instruction is given by $b \times C$, for some constant b.

Recall that, for the hardwired control unit which we have seen in Fig. 7.3, we have assumed that each machine instruction takes a fixed number of clock cycles n, which does not depend on the operands specified by the programmer. The instruction cycle counter in Fig. 7.3 keeps count from 0 to $n - 1$ as the instruction is executed.

For the BCOPY instruction, however, the number of clock cycles required in execute phase is $b \times C$—and it certainly does depend on the count C specified by the programmer. Clearly, therefore, a control unit of the type shown schematically in Fig. 7.3 will not suffice for machine instructions such as BCOPY.

In general, if a processor has such complex instructions in its instruction set, then a combinational circuit cannot suffice as the control unit. Therefore, while a hardwired control unit certainly has the many crucial advantages which we have discussed, it is not suitable for complex instructions—of which the BCOPY machine instruction above is one example. In fact, it was this limitation of hardwired control which prompted computer scientists to propose a *reduced instruction set*—since that allows the crucial advantages of hardwired control to be exploited fully for higher processor throughput.

So we must now turn our attention to this alternative technique for designing a control unit, which yields slower control units, but which can accommodate instructions of virtually any complexity.

7.5 BASIC CONCEPT OF MICROPROGRAMMED CONTROL

Consider the two input, two output combinational circuit shown in Fig. 7.6 (a). Its inputs are labeled X_1 and X_2, while the outputs are labeled Y_1 and Y_2. In Fig. 7.6 (b) we have shown one possible truth table of the circuit. For each possible combination of values of X_1 and X_2, the table gives the corresponding values of Y_1 and Y_2.

Now imagine that we have a memory element with four locations, their addresses in binary being 00, 01, 10 and 11. Each memory location stores only two bits. Location 00 stores the values of Y_1 and Y_2 from the first row of the table in Fig. 7.6 (b); location 01 stores Y_1 and Y_2 values from the second row, and so on.

(a) Block diagram

Input X_1	Input X_2	Output Y_1	Output Y_2
0	0	0	1
0	1	1	1
1	0	1	1
1	1	1	0

(b) Truth table

Fig. 7.6 **A combinational circuit with two inputs and two outputs**

So when address 00 and *read* control signal are applied to the memory element, the Y_1 and Y_2 values from the first row of Fig. 7.6 (b) appear at the output. Similarly, address 01 and *read* control signal bring out Y_1 and Y_2 values from the second row, and so on. In fact, the memory element will have the same general appearance as the 'circuit block' of Fig. 7.6 (a), except that it also has a *read* control signal coming into it.

Thus, we see that the memory element stores the values of each possible output of the combinational circuit of Fig. 7.6 (a). This means that such a memory element provides an alternative to logic gates for implementing the function of a combinational circuit. This method of implementing a combinational function is known as *table look-up*. The memory element serves as the table of values of the function, and the input values provide the *row index* into the table.

For a combinational circuit having m inputs and n outputs, the memory element would need 2^m locations, where each location stores n bits. In the example circuit of Fig. 7.6, we have $m = n = 2$.

In practice, memory elements offer far slower speeds of operation than logic gates, and therefore they are not generally used in place of logic gates. For building the control unit of a processor, however, the *flexibility* offered by memory elements can sometimes offset the speed advantage of logic gates—and then this basic concept can be used to build the control unit of the processor. For reasons which will become clear soon, such a control unit is known as a *microprogrammed* control unit.

Let us now examine this essentially simple idea in a little more detail. We shall see that, while the basic idea is workable, a microprogrammed control unit needs somewhat more complexity than a memory element providing table look-up.

Even a simple control unit—of the generic type shown in Fig. 7.1—may have, say, at least 20 inputs and 40 outputs. If we follow the table look-up method illustrated in Fig. 7.6 (b), we would need a memory element with 2^{20} locations, with each location storing 40 bits. This is quite a large size for a memory element, given that it must also be fast, so that the processor can operate at a high speed.

The bits stored at each location in the memory element specify the values of every output signal of the control unit (recall again Fig. 7.1). These bits make up a so-called *control word.* The '1' and '0' bits in a control word specify which control signals must be enabled in a particular instruction clock cycle. Recall that this is the basic function of the control unit. The memory element in which all the control words are stored is known as *control memory* or *control store.*

As control words are read out from the control memory, one after another, they enable control signals of the processor. As we have seen in Section 7.2, these control signals cause the respective micro-operations to take place in the processor—and as a result, a machine instruction is fetched and executed.

Let us define *control sequence* as a sequence of control words which are read out from the control memory, one after another.

At this point, a few difficulties must be noted with the simple-minded approach of Fig. 7.6 (b) which we have been following:

(i) A control memory in the processor with, say, 2^{20} locations is impractically large.
(ii) Even if, somehow, we can provide such a large control memory, we would have to maintain a large number of unnecessary copies of many control words.
(iii) The requirements of a complex instruction such as BCOPY of Section 7.4 are not addressed by this simple table look-up method.

Let us first consider the point (ii) in some more detail. If we use the simple table look-up method of Fig. 7.6 (b), we run into the following types of difficulty:

The *fetch* phase, as we know, is common to all instructions. The control sequence required for fetch will be repeated in control memory for each combination of instruction, instruction modifiers, addressing modes, and PSW. Thus, there will be a huge number of copies of the fetch control sequence in control memory—and likewise also for other control sequences which may be common to multiple instructions.

This is impractical and therefore unacceptable, since the number of such repeated combinations for each instruction may run into thousands or even more. This can never be considered good engineering, even if we manage somehow to deal with the issue of the extremely large size of control memory required.

We must therefore find a way to address this difficulty, and one obvious way is to aim at the following:

a. Store only a single copy of the *fetch* control sequence in control memory, to be used by all the machine instructions.
b. Store only a single control sequence for each machine instruction in control memory, and
c. If two or more machine instructions have a common part in their control sequences, then store only a single copy of the shared part of control sequence.

We can summarise these points in a simple way by saying that there should be no unnecessary duplication of control sequences in the control memory.

In the following section, we shall describe how this is achieved, and also how the requirement (iii) above is addressed. We shall see that, once we achieve (a), (b) and (c) above, the required control memory size becomes much smaller. In this way, we can address each of the difficulties mentioned—while still retaining the flexibility offered to the processor designer by the technique of microprogrammed control.

7.6 MICROINSTRUCTION SEQUENCING

The discussion of the previous section clearly implies that the control sequences stored in the control store should not form a simple table like that shown in Fig. 7.6 (b). Instead, the control sequences must have a *structure* like that of a computer program.

Figure 7.7 depicts such a possible structure of control sequences, with a common *fetch* control sequence for all machine instructions, followed by a separate control sequence for each machine instruction*. The structure of control sequences shown in this figure may be compared to the structure of a computer program shown using a *flow chart*—such as the one shown in Fig. 4.1.

*In practice, the structure formed by control sequences is more complex than the one shown in Fig. 7.7, since there is some commonality between the control sequences of different machine instructions. Also, some complex machine instructions such as BCOPY require iterative execution of microinstructions. However, for the purpose of our present discussion, the simplified control sequence structure shown in Fig. 7.7 is sufficient.

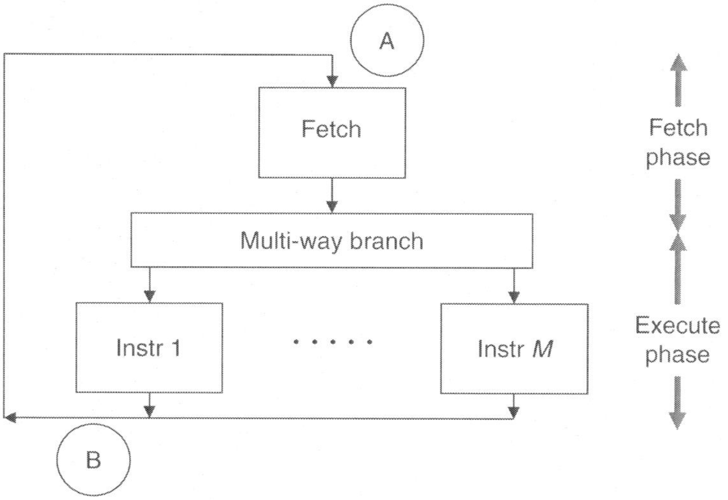

Fig. 7.7 **Broad structure of control sequences in control memory**

The full set of control sequences in the control store, shown schematically in Fig. 7.7, makes up the so-called *control program* for the processor. Because the control program governs individual micro-operations within the processor, it is more commonly known as the *microprogram*, and a single control word in a microprogram is also known as a *microinstruction*. The execution of one machine instruction requires—at a lower level—the execution of several microinstructions, in as many processor clock cycles.

The relation between a computer program, machine instructions and microinstructions has been illustrated in Fig. 7.8.

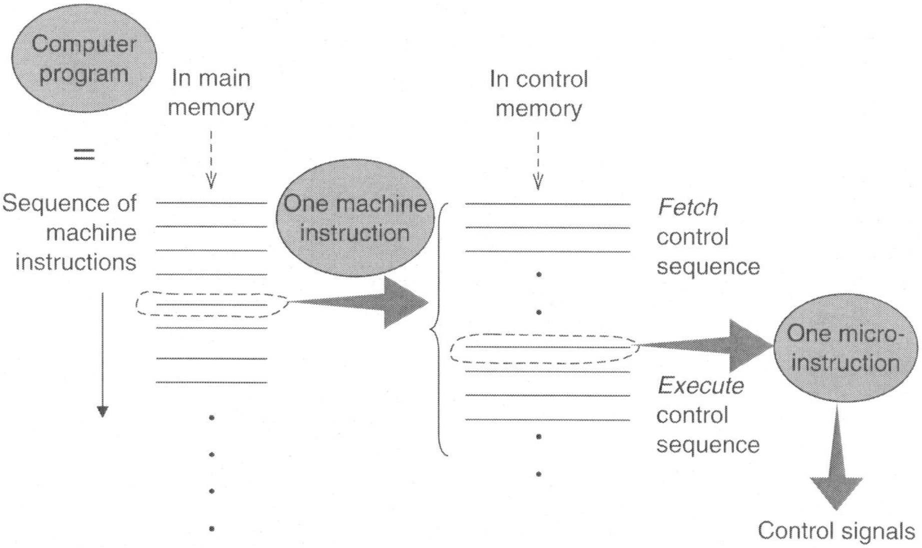

Fig. 7.8 **Relation between computer program, machine instruction and microinstruction**

As we know, a computer program is a sequence of machine instructions. The execution of a single machine instruction involves multiple microinstructions, in as many processor clock cycles. Of these, the *fetch* control sequence contains microinstructions which are common to all machine instructions, while the *execute* control sequence varies from one machine instruction to another. In each clock cycle, a microinstruction generates the processor control signals required, exactly as we saw in the example of Section 7.2.

Recall from Chapter 4 that, in a computer program, machine instructions are fetched and executed in the order in which they are stored—unless an explicit transfer of control occurs. Exactly the same technique is used with microprograms.

A microprogammed control unit reads out microinstructions from control memory in the order in which they are stored—i.e. from successive control memory locations—unless an explicit transfer occurs. One microinstruction is read out in every instruction clock cycle, and it activates the required micro-operations of that cycle. Thus, a machine instruction requiring a sequence of *n* microinstructions is executed in *n* clock cycles.

Note that the basic concept of instruction clock cycles remains the same in a hardwired and a microprogrammed control unit. In practice, however, because the control store tends to be slower than logic gates, a microprogrammed control unit is likely to operate with a much slower processor clock than a hardwired control unit.

The common *fetch* control sequence of Fig. 7.7 results in a machine instruction being fetched into IR. Once the machine instruction is available in IR, a conditional *jump* takes place in the microprogram to the control sequence of the machine instruction in IR. In Fig. 7.7, this conditional *jump* is labeled as 'multi-way branch'—since, on a processor with *M* machine instructions, exactly one of *M* control sequences is selected, depending on the machine instruction in IR.

The control sequence specific to that machine instruction then causes the processor to go through the *execute* phase. In the last microinstruction of the *execute* phase, an unconditional 'backward' *jump* takes place to the common *fetch* sequence for the next machine instruction to be fetched. At this time, the instruction clock cycle is also reset.

Thus, we see that each microinstruction in the control store operates at the level of micro-operations. The combined effect of a sequence of microinstructions is the execution of a machine instruction. In Fig. 7.7, suppose we trace out exactly one of *M* possible paths from the point marked 'A' to the point marked 'B'. Then, the sequence of microinstructions on this path will correspond to the *fetch* and *execute* phases of exactly one machine instruction.

7.7 MICROPROGRAMMED CONTROL UNIT

We have studied the basic functional requirements of a microprogrammed control unit, and also the kind of microinstruction sequencing which is required in the control program. Now we come to the question of physical organisation—i.e. how a microprogrammed control unit can be built using the hardware building blocks of Chapter 3.

A typical internal arrangement of this type of control unit has been shown in Fig. 7.9.

The central component in Fig. 7.9 is seen to be the control store, which holds the control program. To its left is the so-called *control address register* (CAR), which holds the address of the current microinstruction—just as, at the level of machine instructions, the program counter (PC) holds the address of the machine instruction.

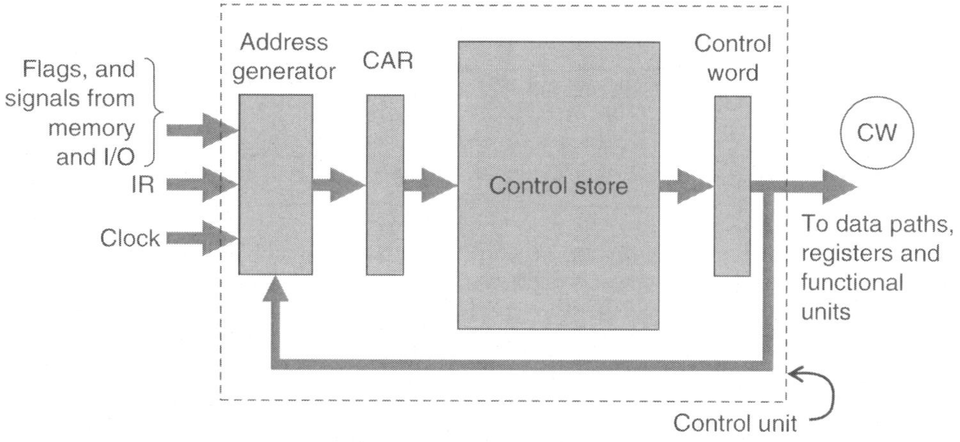

Fig. 7.9 **A microprogrammed control unit**

The clock input on the left of Fig. 7.9 ensures that one microinstruction is read out from the control store in every instruction clock cycle, from the location specified in CAR. Control signals of the microinstruction then act upon the data paths, registers and functional units within the processor, as shown at the point marked 'CW' in the figure.

Thus, if a given machine instruction takes, say, *n* processor cycles to fetch and execute, it will have a corresponding sequence of *n* microinstructions in the control store. Of these *n* microinstructions, some will make up the common fetch control sequence, and the rest will make up the control sequence specific to the machine instruction.

In Fig. 7.9, a separate *address generator* is seen to the left of CAR. The function of this unit is to provide the next control address to CAR, to match the requirements of the control program structure shown in logic of 7.7. Based on the discussion in the previous section, we may list four different ways in which the next control address may be calculated:

(i) CAR is incremented by 1, to generate the sequentially next control address.
(ii) The next control address is taken unconditionally from the control word (CW), along the backward arrow shown in Fig. 7.9. This creates an unconditional branch in the control program.
(iii) The next control address is taken conditionally from the control word (CW). This creates a conditional branch in the control program, depending on a condition flag in PSW, a processor condition, or a memory or I/O status.
(iv) The next control address is computed from the instruction opcode in IR, so as to generate the multi-way branch shown in Fig. 7.7. One way to do this, for example, is to shift the opcode left by four bits—i.e. multiply it by 16—to generate the next control address.

Such address generation logic transforms the control store from a static table to a microprogrammed control unit—and in this sense, the address generator may be viewed as the key element in the microprogrammed control unit.

The outer rectangle in the figure, shown in broken lines, has been labeled as *control unit.* This rectangle has the same inputs and outputs as the generic unit shown in Fig. 7.1. This should not come as a surprise, since the generic block diagram of Fig. 7.1 is applicable to both hardwired and microprogrammed control units.

Control Memory

We have seen that the control memory or control store is the central component which holds the entire microprogram—also known as *microcode*—for the machine instruction set provided on the processor.

As we have seen earlier, access times of memory elements are invariably much longer than the gate delays of combinational circuits and the access times of individual processor registers. Therefore, we must conclude that, in a microprogrammed control unit, the control memory will be slower than everything else around it—and hence it will become the speed-limiting element in the processor.

This implies that the processor cycle time will be determined by the access time of control memory. The speed of access of control memory therefore becomes a key parameter in the design of a microprogrammed control unit.

However, the size requirement of control memory is not really prohibitive, as the following simple example shows.

Example 7.2

Suppose that a processor has about fifty different machine instructions, and that a machine instruction needs an average of eight processor clock cycles—i.e. eight microinstructions—to execute. Thus, the number of microinstructions needed for the machine instructions is about $50 \times 8 = 400$.

Even allowing for addressing modes, instruction modifiers, and so on, we may need a control memory having less than a thousand control words. Control word size—i.e. width—would be closely related to the number of control signals needed in the processor.

The example architecture of Fig. 6.1 requires less than forty control signals, and some more bits are required for the *next control address* and *condition* fields, as we shall see in the next section. Thus, the total number of bits per control word is under 60.

In number of bytes, the control memory size therefore is less than 8 kilobytes, which is certainly not large. Thus we may conclude that the speed of control memory is a major issue, but not its size.

The earliest microprogrammed control units made use of read-only memory (ROM). Since then, however, read-write control memory also came into use, which offers the advantage that microcode can be upgraded on an existing system.

7.8 MICROINSTRUCTION FORMATS

Horizontal Format

The simplest and most obvious format we can imagine for a microinstruction is the following:

Suppose there are a total of S control signals being used within the processor. As we saw, typically S is of the order of forty for a processor such as the one shown in Fig. 6.1. The control signals include those which we have used in the example of Section 7.2, but also many others which we have not enumerated.

Corresponding to each such control signal, there is a single bit in the microinstruction. A '1' in this bit means that the control signal is enabled—or asserted—in an instruction clock cycle, and a '0' means that the control signal is not enabled. With this simple arrangement, every control signal in the processor can be independently enabled in any clock cycle, and a total of *S* bits in the microinstruction provide for this one-to-one mapping with the control signals in the processor.

In addition to these *S* bits, there is a *next control address* field in each microinstruction, so that transfers of control—such as those seen in Fig. 7.7—can be provided in the structure of the microprogram, as discussed above. Note that providing a next control address field in each microinstruction is better than providing separate 'jump' microinstructions, because the latter would consume one extra processor clock cycle.

The size of the next control address field in each microinstruction depends on the maximum required size of control memory. For example, if control memory size will not exceed 16K = 2^{14} control words, then this field is 14 bits. In addition, *condition bits* in each microinstruction determine whether a jump takes place in the microprogram after the current microinstruction, or whether the sequentially next microinstruction stored in control memory is accessed in the next clock cycle.

Thus the simplest microinstruction format provides for: individual *control bits* for the control signals, a *next control address* field, and some *condition bits*. A typical such microinstruction format is illustrated in Fig. 7.10 (a). Such a format is known as *horizontal* microinstruction format or structure.

Now consider the multi-way branch in the microprogram structure shown in Fig. 7.7. This multi-way branch occurs at the end of the *fetch* phase, and it causes a transfer of control to the control sequence for the *execute* phase of the current instruction.

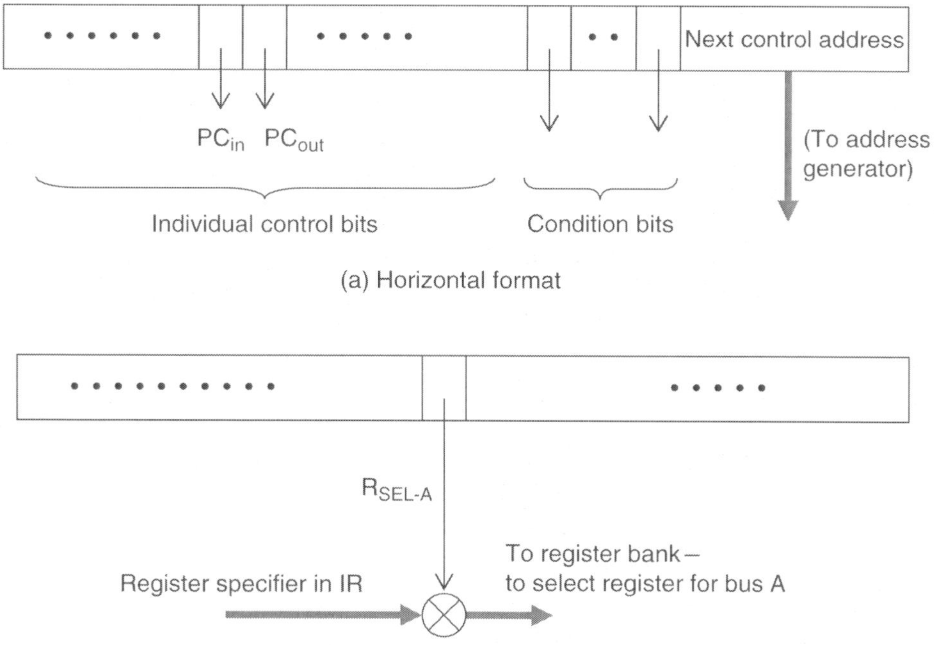

(a) Horizontal format

(b) Selection of IR field

Fig. 7.10 Microinstruction formats

The microinstruction format of Fig. 7.10 (a) does not provide for this multi-way branch, which therefore must be provided separately. In fact, the work of this multi-way branch is done by the address generator block shown in Fig. 7.9. Since the instruction in IR is available to the address generator, it only needs to generate a control address based on the instruction opcode. As we have seen, a simple calculation such as 16 times the numerical value of opcode may suffice to generate the target control address.

Vertical Format

Sometimes, to limit the width of microinstructions, it is necessary to deviate from the horizontal format shown in Fig. 7.10 (a). Suppose, for instance, that there are eight control signals in the processor, named a_0 to a_7—of which it is known that *exactly one* is active in any processor clock cycle. Then the required control signal can be *encoded* in a field of three bits, reducing the required field width from 8 bits to 3 bits.

Of course, these three bits in the microinstruction must be decoded outside the control unit, at the point marked 'CW' in Fig. 7.9. Since such decoding is a combinational function with small total gate delay, the saving achieved in microinstruction width may be justified, depending on specific design goals. A microinstruction format which uses mostly such encoded fields is known as *vertical* microinstruction format.

Direct Use of IR Bits

We must also consider yet another way in which a control signal operates, using once again a simple instruction as an example:

```
ADD R1, R3
```

When this instruction is in IR, different fields of the instruction will specify the opcode, the source register, and the destination register. In Section 7.2, we have used a control signal named $R1_{out\text{-}A}$ to have the contents of R1 placed on internal bus A. But, taking our own processor *NICE* as an example, R1 is one of sixteen registers in the bank of programmable registers, and so there is a 4-bit field in the instruction to specify the source register.

Since this 4-bit field in the instruction specifies R1, all that we need to do is to *gate*—i.e. pass on—this field from IR directly to the register bank, which will then select R1 and place its contents on bus A, as required. This is illustrated in Fig. 7.10 (b), where a control signal named $R_{SEL\text{-}A}$ has been shown which enables the required gating.

Thus the effect of control signal $R1_{out\text{-}A}$ seen in Section 7.2 is really achieved through the control signal $R_{SEL\text{-}A}$ shown in Fig. 7.10 (b). Similarly, the effect of $R3_{out\text{-}B}$ of Section 7.2 would be achieved through control signal $R_{SEL\text{-}B}$, and the effect of ALU_{ADD} would be achieved by gating to ALU the relevant opcode bits of the instruction; let us name the control signal which gates relevant opcode bits from IR to ALU as ALU_{SEL}.

Thus, with this arrangement, register specifier bits of IR will be decoded in the register bank, and ALU function specifier bits of IR will be decoded in the ALU (see Note 6.3).

Three microinstruction formats have been discussed above: horizontal, vertical, and with gating of appropriate IR fields to register banks and functional units. The question arises: Of these three formats, which particular format must a processor designer choose?

There is only one logical answer to this question: He or she must choose the best option—or combination of options—for the specific design in hand.

In practice, there will be little need to use the vertical—i.e. encoded—format when the third option is used, i.e. direct gating of IR fields to register banks and functional units. The reason is simple—IR fields such as opcode, source register, and destination register are already encoded. They only need to be decoded at the point of use.

Therefore we may conclude that, in practice, a microinstruction would contain mainly un-encoded—i.e. horizontal—control signals, with some of them being used to directly gate appropriate IR fields to register banks and functional units.

7.9 COMPARISON OF HARDWIRED AND MICROPROGRAMMED CONTROL UNITS

Now we come to a more important question: Which technique does a processor designer use in a given instance—*hardwired* control or *microprogrammed* control?

As we have seen, hardwired control offers the advantages of much higher speed of operation and a more compact implementation. It is also the only technique suitable for a pipelined processor.

Microprogrammed control offers the advantages of flexibility and extensibility—i.e. the machine instruction set of a processor can be enhanced by adding microinstructions to the control store. This proves useful in designing enhanced versions of an existing processor, and also sometimes in allowing the user to add machine instructions to the processor which are specific to an application. But slower speed of operation and unsuitability for pipelined processors are two major drawbacks of microprogrammed control.

We may therefore say that the choice between the two techniques is governed by:

a. the relative complexity or simplicity of instruction set of the processor, and
b. the relative importance of speed versus flexibility and extensibility in the design objectives of the processor.

Recall the discussion initiated in Section 4.5 about the *RISC* and *CISC* approaches to instruction set design. For complex machine instructions, microprogrammed control may be the only available choice— as we saw using the example of a *block copy* instruction. And for pipelined processors, hardwired control is the only feasible choice. Therefore some CISC processors today combine hardwired control logic for simpler instructions, with microprogrammed control for complex instructions.

Field upgradability used to be cited as a major advantage of microprogrammed control. On a computer system already in operation 'in the field', it would be possible to upgrade the microprogram to a newer version, which would provide useful extensions to the machine instruction set—including possibly user-defined extensions. However, in the present age of low-cost but powerful single-chip processors, this advantage of microprogrammed contol has lost its earlier value—it would be less expensive today to simply replace the entire processor, if required, rather than to change the microcode in it.

Microprogrammed control was proposed originally to cope with the complexity of implementing machine instruction sets. Over the last couple of decades, however, the trend in instruction set design has been towards simplicity. In addition, today excellent tools are available for circuit design, and very high clock rates are achievable in VLSI circuits. But memory speeds have not increased to the same extent as processor speeds—and therefore the relatively slow control store would today have a major adverse impact on processor performance. In view of all these factors, processor designers today rely less on microprogramming, except for specialised designs.

SUMMARY

Building upon the basic concepts which were introduced in the previous chapter, we studied in this chapter the basic function and design of the control unit of a processor. A specific example was considered of the control signals required in the various clock cycles of a typical machine instruction. Inputs to the control unit are: the instruction in IR, instruction clock cycle, flag bits, and relevant signals from memory and I/O.

A hardwired control unit can be viewed as a combinational circuit which generates the required control signals in each instruction clock cycle. A hardwired control unit can be designed and built using a programmable logic device, which offers the advantages of higher clock speed, compact size, and low power consumption.

In a microprogrammed control unit, the required control sequences are programmed into control memory in the form of microinstructions. These microinstructions are read out from control memory, one in every processor clock cycle, and thereby the corresponding control signals are generated. Microinstruction sequencing is achieved through the address generator, which supplies the control address to control memory. A microinstruction may have a horizontal or a vertical format, though in practice bits from IR may also be directly applied to a functional unit or register bank.

Hardwired control units offer the important advantage of allowing faster clock speeds. For pipelined processors, this is in fact the only viable option. Microprogrammed control units offer flexibility, extensibility, and support for complex instructions.

REVIEW QUESTIONS

1. What is the function of the control unit of a processor?
2. Which are the two main techniques available today for building the control unit of a processor?
3. What is the role of memory wait cycles in designing read and write access by the processor to main memory?
4. A processor clock runs at 2 gigahertz, and an average processor instruction takes 10 clock cycles to fetch and execute. What is the total time taken by an average instruction to fetch and execute?

5. Based on the data given in the previous question, what can we say about processor throughput?
6. List the inputs—or groups of inputs—to the control unit of a typical processor.
7. A control signal Y is required in clock cycle CC 2 of machine instruction α, and in clock cycle CC 3 of machine instruction β. In the manner of Fig. 7.4 (a), draw the control logic required to generate Y.
8. Which are the two main arrays of gates in a programmable logic array (PLA)?
9. Explain in brief why hardwired control unit does not suffice to generate control signals for complex machine instructions.
10. A combinational function with 4 input signals and 6 output signals is to be implemented using table look-up. What is the size of memory element needed?
11. Explain very briefly the terms: control memory, control word, and control sequence.
12. Consider a processor with instruction length 16 bits, PSW 4 bits, ICC 4 bits, and memory and I/O status 4 bits. How many 'rows' i.e. words are needed in the control store if we use table look-up? Is this practical?
13. Why is a microprogrammed control unit slower in operation than a hardwired control unit?
14. What is the function of the control address register (CAR) in a microprogrammed control unit?
15. What is the function of the address generator in a microprogrammed control unit?
16. List the four different ways in which the next control address may be calculated in a microprogrammed control unit.
17. With a microprogrammed control unit, the processor cycle time is determined by the access time of control memory. Justify this statement in brief.
18. In a microprogrammed control unit, one-to-one mapping is provided between control signals needed in the processor and bits in the microinstruction. Does the microinstruction have horizontal or vertical format?
19. A high-performance processor is being designed with an instruction pipeline. Which type of control unit is suitable for this processor?
20. A processor is being designed for an application where it is essential to allow users to define machine instructions to meet their specific requirements. Which type of control unit is suitable for this processor?

EXERCISES

1. Using a tabular format similar to Table 7.1, list the micro-operations required for the following two machine instructions:

   LOAD 2000, R1

   and

   STORE 2000, R1

   Make a suitable assumption for transferring the address field of IR to the address register of the processor.

2. Using a tabular format similar to Table 7.1, list the micro-operations required for the following two machine instructions:

   JMP 2000

   and

   JMPZ 2000

   Make a suitable assumption for transferring the address field of IR to PC.
3. Make a list of all the control signals which you think would be required to implement the instruction set of Table 5.1 on the processor architecture of Fig. 6.1, along with a brief description of their functions. Make use of the concept of selection of IR field illustrated in Fig. 7.10 (b).
4. Consider the general control program structure shown graphically in Fig. 7.7. Show this same control program structure using algorithmic notation.
5. Recall that the address generator block shown in Fig. 7.9 provides for the multi-way branch at the end of *fetch* phase of each instruction. Using algorithmic notation, describe the function which must be performed by the address generator block, consistent with its inputs and outputs shown in Fig. 7.9.
6. Recall the micro-operations shown in Table 7.1 for the instruction:

   ADD R3, R4

   Control signals $R3_{out\text{-}A}$ and $R4_{out\text{-}B}$ have been used in Table 7.1, which imply that selection of register using an IR field—as illustrated in Fig. 7.6 (b)—has not been used. Re-write the control signal sequence of Table 7.1 to make use of $R_{SEL\text{-}A}$ and $R_{SEL\text{-}B}$, which enable the gating of source and destination register fields in IR to the register bank.

   Hint: Use also the control signals $R_{READ\text{-}A}$, $R_{WRITE\text{-}A}$, $R_{READ\text{-}B}$ and $R_{WRITE\text{-}B}$, which determine whether a read or a write operation takes place on the register bank, in a given processor clock cycle, from the two internal busses.
7. The control signal sequence of Table 7.1 includes the signal ALU_{ADD}, which means that the opcode field of IR is not being directly used for the selection of ALU operation to be performed. Re-write the solution to Exercise 5 using the control signal ALU_{SEL} to gate the opcode field of IR to ALU for the selection of ALU operation.
8. Repeat Exercise 1, making use of $R_{SEL\text{-}A}$ or $R_{SEL\text{-}B}$, as needed, to enable the gating of source or destination register select fields in IR to the register bank. Use the signals $R_{READ\text{-}A}$, $R_{WRITE\text{-}A}$, $R_{READ\text{-}B}$ and $R_{WRITE\text{-}B}$, defined in Exercise 6, as required.
9. A processor has to be provided with a machine instruction to find the square root of a floating point number. The algorithm to be used involves *iteration*, such that in each iteration we get closer to the final answer. Iteration stops when two successive calculated values are equal to within an acceptably small margin.

   Can hardwired control be used for implementing this instruction? Justify your answer in brief.

COMPUTER ARITHMETIC

8

8.1 INTRODUCTION

In this chapter, we shall see that—to a great extent—arithmetic as implemented in computer circuits follows the same rules as the familiar decimal arithmetic we learn at school. The differences we see arise mainly from the two facts that:

a. Computer circuits work on binary rather than decimal data, and
b. Higher operating speed is normally a major objective of circuit designers, whereas as human beings we are happy to just get the result right, even if it takes a little longer!

To review some background and notation, we first consider a simple example of addition of three digit decimal numbers:

It is easily verified that if A = 359 and B = 927, then their sum S = A + B has the value 1286. Now let us consider digit by digit—from right to left—how we get this result.

First of all, let us number the digits of A, B and S as $a_2a_1a_0$, $b_2b_1b_0$ and $s_3s_2s_1s_0$ respectively. This numbering of digits—which we also used in Chapter 2—has the great advantage that the applicable power of ten in the kth position is simply 10^k. This is the reason why the rightmost digit of the number is known as the *least significant digit*, and the leftmost digit as the *most significant digit*.

Now let us look closely at the above-mentioned addition operation:

```
 1   1    0
   3 5 9
  +9 2 7
  -------
 1 2 8 6
```

In the rightmost digit position, we see that 9 + 7 yields 16. Since this is a two-digit number, we leave 6 as the value of s_0—the rightmost digit of the sum—and take 10 forward as *carry* into the next digit position on the left. In its new home, this 10 actually appears as 1, since a digit on the left has place value which is ten times larger.

Here we say that there is a *carry out* from digit position 0, and *carry in* at position 1. *Carry out* is thus an 'overflow' from a particular digit position to the next higher digit position on its left. In decimal arithmetic, its numerical value in position k is 10^k—i.e. the same as the value of digit '1' in that particular digit position.

Next, for finding the value of s_1, we calculate 1 + 5 + 2 and get the result 8. Since this is a single digit, there is no *carry out* from digit position 1 into position 2 on its left.

Next, while adding a_2 and b_2, we get the sum 12, which means $s_2 = 2$, and there is a *carry out* from digit position 2 into the non-existent digit position 3 to its left. We can say that $s_3 = 1$, which means that the result has four digits, even though the two operands A and B were both three-digit numbers. This final *carry out* from the leftmost digit position of A and B appears as the leftmost digit '1' of the sum S, which in our notation is s_3.

When a digit position does not have *carry in* coming into it—such as position 2 above—we can also say that its incoming carry is 0. Similarly, since the rightmost digit position does not have an incoming *carry*, we may say that its incoming carry is 0.

We are adding only two decimal numbers, which means that the largest sum we can have in any digit position is $1 + 9 + 9 = 19$, including a possible *carry in*. This means that the *carry out* from any digit position can only be 0 or 1.

With this quick review of background and notation, let us study how computer circuits can be designed for arithmetic operations on binary data.

8.2 INTEGER ADDITION AND SUBTRACTION

Let us say that we are adding two n digit positive integers, and consider the single digit addition as it takes place in the ith digit position, for any i in the range $0 \le i \le n - 1$. Let c_{i-1} and c_i denote, respectively, the *carry in* and *carry out* at position i, as shown below.

```
ci <-   <-  ci-1
       ai
     + bi
     -------
       si
```

The above notation is general, in the sense that it applies to any chosen radix. In decimal addition, a_i, b_i and s_i will be decimal digits, while c_{i-1} and c_i can only be 0 or 1.

Exactly the same arrangement also applies to addition in binary, with the only change being that a_i, b_i and s_i may only be binary digits, or bits—i.e. either '0' or '1'. Naturally, the basic concepts of integer addition remain the same, whether we use decimal radix 10, or binary radix 2. But we shall see that things are in fact much simpler in binary.

In binary, we continue to use the notation a_i, b_i, c_{i-1}, s_i and c_i that has been introduced above for the ith digit position. Of these five bits, we now think of a_i, b_i and c_{i-1} as inputs to a digital circuit, and s_i and c_i as outputs of the circuit, as depicted in Fig. 8.1. For historic reasons, this circuit is known as a *full adder**.

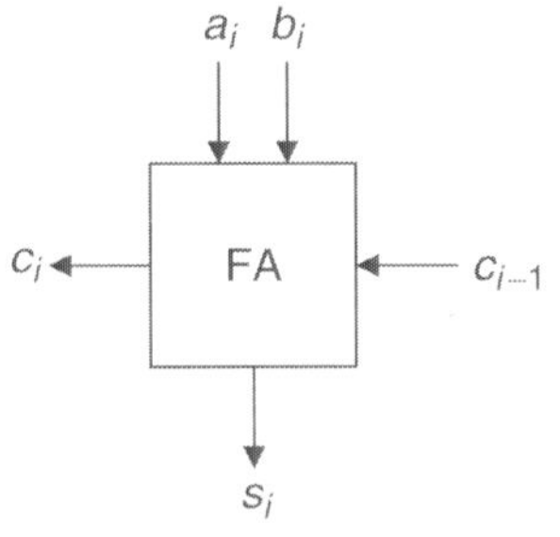

Fig. 8.1 One stage of integer addition in binary using a *full adder*

Each of the circuit inputs a_i, b_i and c_{i-1} will be either '0' or '1', and the circuit will add up their values. Note here that, between the three input bits, there is no relative place value—i.e. a '1' has numerical value one, whether

*A simpler circuit, which can do half the work of a full adder, is known as a *half adder*. Two half adders can be connected together to yield a full adder. For our purposes, it is not necessary at present to follow that approach to binary addition. However, see Exercise 2.

it occurs as the value of a_i, or b_i, or c_{i-1}. Therefore, we need to simply count how many of these input bits are '1'.

This count of '1' bits on the three inputs is necessarily in the range from 0 to 3. We encode this count into two bits, which are the output bits c_i and s_i. Note that there is certainly now relative place value between the output bits. Since carry out c_i is taken into the next position on the left, its place value is twice that of s_i.

Table 8.1 is the complete truth table of the *full adder*. Since the circuit has three inputs, the table has $2^3 = 8$ rows. The first row corresponds to all inputs being '0', i.e. the total count of '1' bits is zero. This naturally means that both c_i and s_i remain '0'.

The next three rows of the table correspond to any one input to the circuit being '1'. No *carry out* is generated in these three cases, and we get outputs c_i = '0' and s_i = '1'.

Table 8.1 Truth table of full adder

Inputs			Outputs	
a_i	b_i	c_{i-1}	c_i	s_i
0	0	0	0	0
0	0	1	0	1
0	1	0		
1	0	0		
1	1	0	1	0
1	0	1		
0	1	1		
1	1	1	1	1

The next three rows of the table correspond to any two inputs to the circuit being '1'. A *carry out* is generated in these three cases, and we get outputs c_i = '1' and s_i = '0'.

The last row of the table corresponds to all three inputs to the circuit being '1'. A *carry out* is generated in this case, and the sum bit s_i also becomes '1'. We therefore get outputs c_i = '1' and s_i = '1'.

In Table. 8.1, we thus have the complete behavioral specification of the full adder. The circuit in question is clearly a *combinational circuit*—the output at any time is a function only of the input at that time. The circuit has no memory of prior inputs or outputs.

As has been mentioned in Chapter 3, standard design techniques exist for translating the truth table specification of a combinational circuit into an appropriate realisation of the circuit, using basic logic gates. Furthermore, these design techniques can ensure that the gate delay between any input and any output is limited to a maximum of 2.

So we now have the useful *full adder* circuit with us, with a limit on maximum gate delay, which can perform the required work of binary addition at one bit position, when both the operands A and B are assumed to be n-bit integers. Recall that subscript i in our notation stands for the ith bit position, for any i in the range $0 \leq i \leq n - 1$.

Now we must see whether n of these full adders can be connected together to provide us with a circuit for full n-bit addition. In theory, this is a very simple matter, since the only 'cause-and-effect' relationship between the stages is this: *Carry out* c_i from bit position i becomes *carry in* c_{j-1} at bit position $j = i + 1$ to its left.

To ensure that the above relationship between *carry out* and *carry in* bits is correctly reflected in our n-bit addition circuit, we simply need to 'string together' n instances of the full adder, as shown in Fig. 8.2. Note how the *carry out* bit of one stage becomes the *carry in* bit of the next stage to its left.

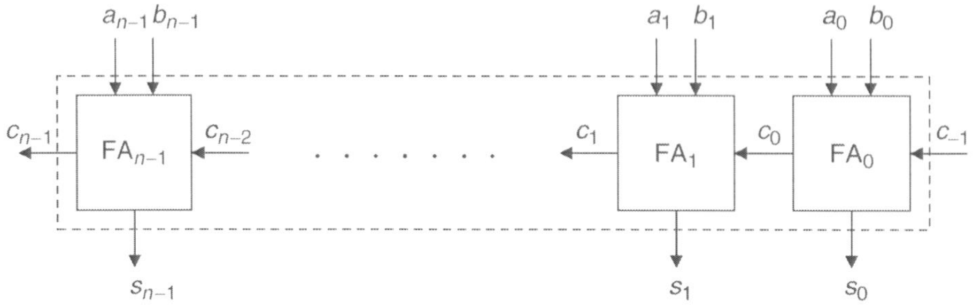

Fig. 8.2 Circuit for n-bit addition, using n full adders

For consistency of numbering, the *carry in* bit of the rightmost stage—i.e. bit position 0—has been numbered as c_{-1}. The *carry out* bit of the leftmost stage $n - 1$ becomes the final *carry out* of the n-bit adder. At the end of addition, this bit is made available to the programmer as the *carry* condition flag C described in Chapter 4.

In Fig. 8.2, the outer rectangle in dashed lines encloses the n full adders connected together as described above. This complete circuit has as its inputs the two n-bit integers A and B, and the *carry in* c_{-1} shown on the right. Outputs of the circuit are the n-bit sum S, and *carry out* c_{n-1} shown on the left.

The circuit of Fig. 8.2 is the n-bit adder we need. The circuit meets our functional requirements—but unfortunately it also has a shortcoming that needs to be addressed.

Example 8.1

Consider for simplicity the case of $n = 8$, and the two unsigned binary inputs A = 11111111 and B = 00000001. In decimal, these two numbers are 255 and 1, respectively. Their sum S = 256 cannot be accommodated in eight bits, and in our notation, the outputs of the circuit will be S = 00000000 and final *carry out* c_7 = '1'.

The point to note here is that, if the circuit of Fig. 8.2 is used, then each of the eight stages of addition generates *carry out.* The student should verify this fact by hand-performing this binary addition, from the rightmost to the leftmost bit.

Since each of the eight stages of addition generates *carry out,* we have c_i = '1' for all i, $0 \leq i \leq 7$. Each *carry out* except c_7 becomes *carry in* input for the next stage to its left.

In any physical digital circuit, there is a certain *time delay* between the time T_{in} when inputs are applied to the circuit, and the time T_{out} when circuit outputs attain their functionally correct value. For a combinational circuit such as the adder shown, this time delay is related to the maximum number of logic gates on the circuit path between inputs and outputs, and is approximately equal to the total *gate delay*.

In the circuit of Fig. 8.2, the maximum number of logic gates is encountered in the paths between the inputs a_0, b_0 and c_{-1} on the right, and the outputs s_{n-1} and c_{n-1} on the left. These circuit paths pass through each of the n full adders in the circuit, from right to left. Each full adder on the path contributes 2 gate delays, and therefore the total gate delay of the circuit is $2n$*.

In Example 8.1, we may say that the carry bit is being *propagated* from the rightmost stage to the leftmost stage, encountering in its path the 2 gate delays of the full adder at every stage. This propagation resembles a ripple, and therefore the n-bit adder of the type shown in Fig. 8.2 is known as *ripple carry adder.*

With larger processor word size, say $n = 32$, the total gate delay of the ripple carry adder is proportionately longer. Such an n-bit adder is a key part of the arithmetic and logic unit (ALU) we saw in Chapter 6. For performance reasons, therefore, a gate delay of $2n$ is unacceptable, and in the next section, we shall discuss ways to reduce it.

Recall the discussion in Section 2.2 on signed integer representation using 2's complement, and recall in particular Fig. 2.3 which shows 4-bit signed integers in this representation. In the light of that discussion, we can now conclude that the adder we have designed will work correctly with signed integers in 2's complement form, subject of course to the range of integers which can thus be represented. This is one of the natural advantages of 2's complement representation—the same adder circuit works correctly with unsigned integers and with signed integers in 2's complement representation.

We have not yet discussed separately the *subtraction* operation on unsigned or signed integers. Fortunately, this topic does not require a lengthy discussion of its own. We need to recall only that $A-B$ is equal to $A + (-B)$. In our context, this means that, in order to calculate $A-B$, we first find the arithmetic negative of B, and then make use of the adder circuit we already have, to calculate the sum of A and $(-B)$.

For finding the arithmetic negative of B, a simple technique was shown in Section 2.2, which consists of two steps: (i) find the bit-wise complement of B, and (ii) add 1 to the result. Finding the bit-wise complement of B is a simple operation, requiring one inverter gate at each bit b_i of B, for $0 \leq i \leq n - 1$. For adding 1 to the result, we already have a device in place—the *carry in* bit c_{-1} in Figs. 7.2 and 7.3. For addition, this bit is set to '0'; for subtraction, c_{-1} is set to '1', to take care of step (ii) above.

Example 8.2

Let us illustrate the above method with a simple example. Suppose we wish to subtract the 8-bit binary number 00001111 from the 8-bit binary number 01100000.

(a) We first carry out this subtraction in the usual way, one bit at a time, from right to left, generating *borrow* bits as needed:

```
0 1 1 0 0 0 0 0
0 0 0 0 1 1 1 1
---------------
0 1 0 1 0 0 0 1
```

The small arrows above indicate *borrow* bits generated.

*Note that the total circuit delay is being stated here in terms of *gate delays*, rather than by using a specific unit of time. The reason is that the gate delay of a logic gate depends on the electronic technology employed to build the gate. Such electronic technology is not under discussion here, but rather the manner of interconnection of logic gates. Therefore, it makes sense to talk about circuit delay in terms of gate delays. With present day VLSI technology, the actual gate delays of logic gates are in *picoseconds*—i.e. thousandths of nanoseconds.

(b) Now let us carry out the same subtraction by taking bit-wise complement of the second number and then adding 1 as *carry in* to the addition process:

```
0 1 1 0 0 0 0 0 1 (Carry in)
1 1 1 1 0 0 0 0
-----------------
0 1 0 1 0 0 0 1
```

Naturally, we obtain the same answer. However, we see that in (b) there is *carry out* from the leftmost bit position, whereas in (a) there was no *borrow* in that position. Thus, when we use this method of subtraction, the *borrow* bit in the leftmost position is the complement of the *carry* bit of the addition step.

Needless to say, the method is also applicable to 16-bit or 32-bit subtraction.

Incidentally, note that an n-bit adder can also take care of the operation *increment by 1*. For this, we simply set all the b_i inputs to '0', $0 \leq i \leq n - 1$, and set c_{-1} to '1'.

8.3 CARRY LOOK-AHEAD

As we saw, the total gate delay of the n-bit ripple carry adder of Fig. 8.2 is unacceptably high. Fortunately, a way to reduce the total gate delay of an n-bit adder suggests itself without too much difficulty. Recall that the so-called *full adder* is basically a 1-bit adder which provides for *carry in* and *carry out*. We connected n of these full adders together to obtain the ripple carry n-bit adder. In this sense, the 1-bit full adder served as our basic building block for the circuit of Fig. 8.2.

Instead, suppose we use as our building block a 2-bit adder which also provides for *carry in* and *carry out*. Then we could connect $n/2$ of these new building blocks together, and allow the carry to ripple through these $n/2$ stages, to obtain the required n-bit adder. Each 2-bit adder is a combinational circuit, and therefore it can be designed with 2 gate delays. The complete n-bit adder will now have $n/2 \times 2 = n$ gate delays, rather than the $2n$ gate delays seen earlier—and will thus be faster by a factor of 2.

This argument can be taken further. Suppose our combinational building block is a 4-bit adder which provides for *carry in* and *carry out*. We connect $n/4$ of these 4-bit adders together, to obtain an n-bit adder with a total gate delay of $n/4 \times 2 = n/2$.

Figure 8.3 shows the inputs and outputs that such a 4-bit adder will have. Its two 4-bit inputs are $A = a_3a_2a_1a_0$ and $B = b_3b_2b_1b_0$; the 4-bit sum is $S = s_3s_2s_1s_0$. *Carry in* is c_{-1} as before, and *carry out* is c_3. Recall from Chapter 2 that when we group 4 bits together, we generate a single hexadecimal digit. Therefore, we may also think of this 4-bit adder as a single digit hexadecimal adder.

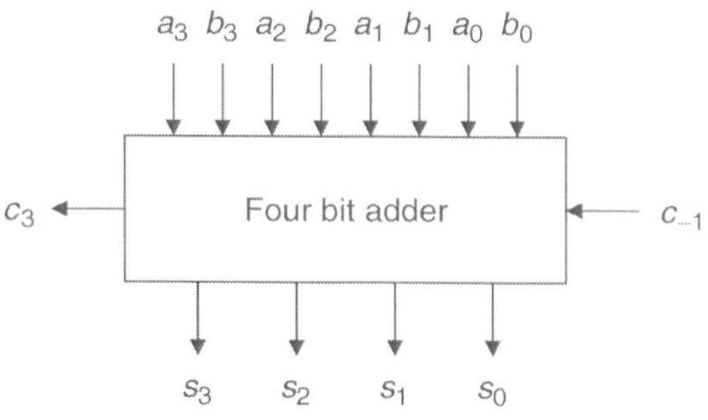

Fig. 8.3 A 4-bit adder as a combinational building block

Carry look-ahead is the name given to a technique for designing such multiple bit adders in a systematic manner. To understand this technique, however, we need to consider once again the 1-bit full adder discussed in the previous section. In the ith stage of an n-bit adder, we define the following two functions of input bits a_i and b_i:

Generate function $g_i = a_i \cdot b_i$
Propagate function $p_i = a_i + b_i$

It can be verified easily, with reference to Table 8.1, that the carry out bit c_i is given by:

$$c_{i+1} = g_i + p_i \cdot c_{i-1}$$

The generate bit g_i indicates that the ith stage *generates* carry out, regardless of whether there is carry coming into this stage. The propagate bit p_i indicates that the ith stage *propagates* the incoming carry, regardless of whether there is carry generated in this stage. The expression for c_i above can be read as:

There is *carry out* from stage i if: (a) stage i generates a carry, and/or (b) stage i receives incoming carry c_{i-1}, which it propagates to the stage on its left.

For the left-most stage of a 4-bit adder, we can now write:

$$c_3 = g_3 + p_3 \cdot c_2$$

Substituting in this the corresponding expression for c_2, we get:

$$c_3 = g_3 + p_3 \cdot (g_2 + p_2 \cdot c_1)$$

By substituting for c_1, and then for c_0 in the resulting expression, we can finally obtain an expression for c_3 in terms of *carry in* c_{-1} and the input bits a_i and b_i, for $i = 0$ to 3. This can serve as a basis for designing the 4-bit adder shown in Fig. 8.3.

Note that the sum bit s_i of each stage is a function of a_i, b_i and c_{i-1}, and therefore it must still be determined as before in the 1-bit full adder of the ith stage, after the *carry look-ahead* bit c_{i-1} is available. The key point here is that the determination of carry bits c_i, for $i = 0$ to 3, does not require a carry to ripple forward stage by stage from right to left. Thus, carry out c_3 is calculated in the same time period as the sum bits s_i, for $i = 0$ to 3; i.e. the slow 'ripple carry' from right to left has been eliminated.

Now, to build a 16-bit adder, for example, one obvious method available to us is to connect together four of the 4-bit adders built using carry look-ahead. However, if we do this, a carry still has to ripple through from right to left, from one 4-bit adder to its left neighbor. This is because, while each 4-bit adder internally makes use of carry look-ahead, there is no carry look-ahead between stages.

Fortunately, the principle of carry look-ahead which we applied within a 4-bit adder—in the form of the *generate* and *propagate* functions seen above—also applies to a set of 4-bit adders connected together. *Generate* and *propagate* functions must be calculated for each 4-bit adder, and utilised to avoid having the carry ripple through from one 4-bit adder to its left neighbor. This scheme is illustrated in Fig. 8.4.

Notation 'g' and 'p' in the figure indicates *generate* and *propagate* functions, respectively, from the single 4-bit adder shown. Carry look-ahead logic is shown above it, as a separate sub-circuit, to which four such 4-bit adders are connected.

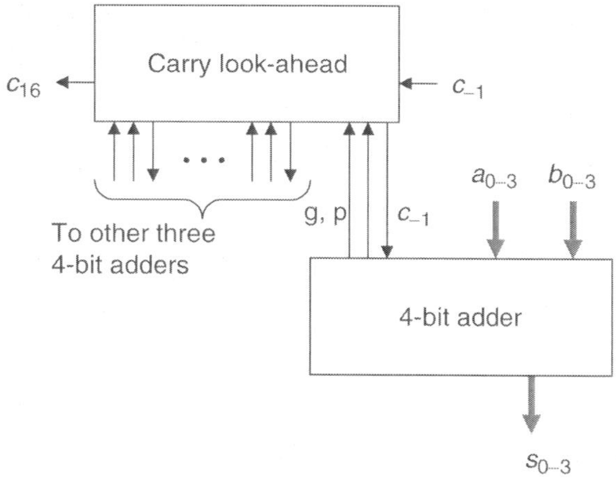

Fig. 8.4 Carry look-ahead applied to set of four 4-bit adders

8.4 UNSIGNED INTEGER MULTIPLICATION

The idea of integer multiplication is first introduced as *repeated addition*. When we read 5 × 7 as 'five times seven', the words mean that 'seven' is to be repeated 'five times', i.e. the expression is equivalent to 7 + 7 + 7 + 7 + 7. (See Exercises 7 and 8 of Chapter 5.)

For larger integers, however, this proves to be a very inefficient method. For example, to calculate 379 × 213, we do not wish to perform 379 additions. So we make use of *place value* of digits in the multiplier, and adopt the faster so-called *multiply-shift-and-add* method, which involves multiplication by one multiplier digit at a time. This familiar method has been illustrated below:

```
      2 1 3
    x 3 7 9
  ---------
    1 9 1 7   ⎫ Partial
  1 4 9 1 0   ⎬
  6 3 9 0 0   ⎭ products
  ---------
  8 0 7 2 7
```

In the second partial product here, we see that the product 7 × 213 = 1491 has been shifted one position to the left. This is because this shift multiplies the product 7 × 213 by 10, to give us the product 70 × 213. Similarly, the third partial product involves a left shift by two digits. We may say that the multiplier 379 is broken up as 9 + 70 + 300, and each partial product represents the product of one of these terms with the multiplicand 213.

It should be noted that multiplication of two n digit integers will in general produce a product which has $2n$ digits. Doubters may calculate 99 × 99 and verify.

In *multiply-shift-and-add*, we have a much more efficient method of multiplication, since any multiplication of two n digit numbers will require the addition of n partial products, regardless of the magnitude of the multiplier. We shall soon see that—apart from the fact of working with binary rather than decimal digits—this is exactly the method employed in computer systems to carry out integer multiplication.

So let us turn first to unsigned binary integers and apply the same *multiply-shift-and-add* method of multiplication. Say we wish to calculate the binary product 1011 × 1100 (which in decimal would read 11 × 12, giving answer 132). Working of this method on the given pair of unsigned 4-bit integers is shown below:

```
          1 1 0 0
        x 1 0 1 1
        -------
          1 1 0 0     ⎫
        1 1 0 0 0     ⎪ Partial
      0 0 0 0 0 0     ⎬
    1 1 0 0 0 0 0     ⎭ products
  ---------------
  1 0 0 0 0 1 0 0
```

Naturally the method has yielded the correct answer in binary. And we may observe a clear and simple pattern in the way that the partial products are generated. Let the four bits of the multiplier 1011 be denoted by $b_3b_2b_1b_0$ respectively.

We then observe that:

a. When a multiplier bit b_i is '0', the corresponding partial product is zero, and
b. When multiplier bit b_i is '1', the corresponding partial product is simply a shifted version of the multiplicand 1100. Since multiplier bit b_i is '1', no actual multiplication is needed, and we can even describe the method as simply *shift-and-add.*

In the multiplication above, underlined zeros in partial products show the number of positions that the multiplicand has been shifted to the left. To implement this method on a computer, we need to make some further observations:

(i) For the final product, we must reserve a register of size $2n$ bits, if the two operands are each of size n bits. For its 'double size', let us name this register W2.

(ii) To keep the multiplicand unchanged through the multiplication process, we can shift W2 to the right at each step, instead of shifting the multiplicand to the left. We see below that while the effect is somewhat unfamiliar, the final answer is of course unchanged.

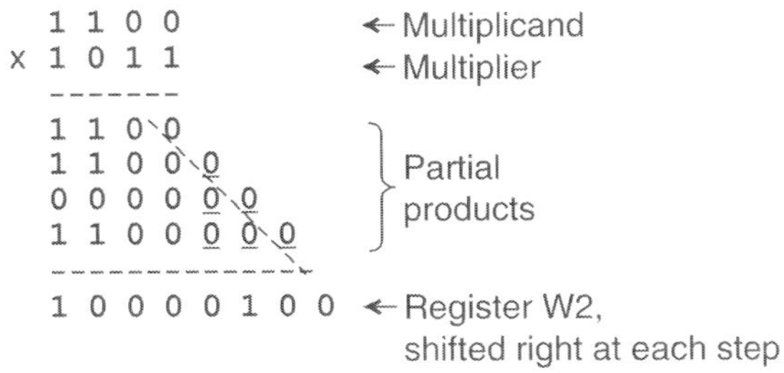

The dashed inclined line above corresponds to the rightmost vertical line of '0' bits which we had earlier. Note that, if the addition of partial products above is to be verified by hand, additions must be performed in the direction of this line.

At this point, we make a few more pertinent observations:

(iii) We need not store all the partial products corresponding to multiplier bits which are '1'. As soon as a partial product is generated through an appropriate shift of the multiplicand, it can be added into W2—and it is not needed again. Therefore, we certainly do not need separate registers for the n partial products.

If we implement the technique as outlined so far, we need two separate n-bit registers for the multiplicand and multiplier, and another $2n$-bit register W2 into which the partial products get added, and which therefore finally stores the result. Recall that an adder and a shifter are already available to us within the ALU.

But computer designers are always on the lookout for any possible saving in hardware required. With that aim in mind, it should be observed here that:

(iv) W2 must be initially zero, and only n of its $2n$ bits are utilised in the first *shift-and-add* step that is carried out. The reason is that, in the first step, we will only add the n-bit multiplicand once into W2, if the rightmost bit of the multiplier is '1'. After that, we shift W2 to the right by one bit, which means that we then utilise $n + 1$ bits of W2. Thus, after each of the n shifts, we utilise one more bit of W2.

(v) Once a bit b_i of the multiplier has been examined—to determine whether or not the multiplicand must be added into W2—then that bit is not required again during the rest of the multiplication process. Therefore multiplier bits can be shifted out one by one.

The implication of (iv) and (v) is that the right half of W2—which we denote as W2(R)—can be used to initially hold the multiplier. As a bit of the multiplier gets shifted out on the right, one more bit of W2 is available to store the accumulating product.

(vi) When the multiplicand is added into W2, a carry may be generated. This carry is a part of the accumulating product, and must be shifted in from the left during the next right shift, into the most leftmost bit position of W2.

Taking into account (iv), (v) and (vi), we may now illustrate the method as follows:

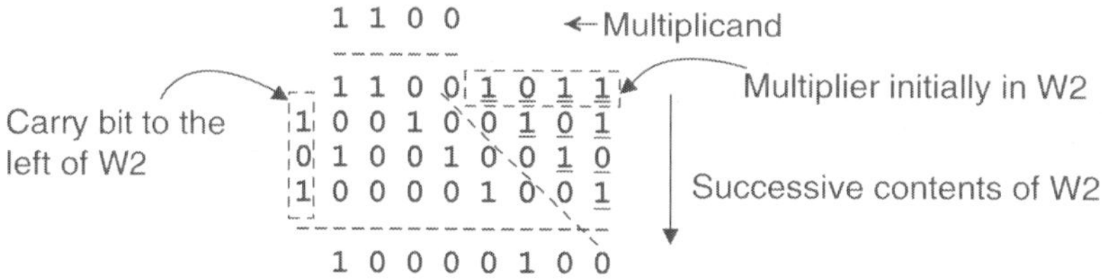

Note that the bits which are underlined on the right above are successive bits of the multiplier. One by one they get shifted out. At any step, the multiplicand is added into W2 only if the particular multiplier bit is '1'.

The inclined dashed line above shows how the rightmost '0' bit of the multiplicand gets shifted right one bit position at a time, and finally it becomes the rightmost bit of W2. Recall that if the multiplicand is even, the final product must also be even.

Figure 8.5 shows in algorithmic notation this standard technique for unsigned integer multiplication. Note that the inner loop is repeated n times, for n-bit multiplication.

Let us briefly address the question of how this algorithm can be implemented in a computer system. Note that, in a typical processor, the $2n$-bit register W2 will in fact be a pair of n bit general purpose registers, e.g. R3 and R4, and M will be a third such register.

a. If the processor does not provide an integer multiply instruction, we can program the algorithm in assembly language, using ADD and SHIFT machine instructions within the loop, to provide the multiply function in software.

```
initialise W2(L) to zero, and
           W2(R) to multiplier
multiplicand is in register M
repeat n times
{
   if rightmost bit of W2 is '1' then
      add M to W2(L), saving carry
   shift carry & W2 one bit to right
}
final product is in W2
```

Fig. 8.5 **Algorithm for unsigned integer multiplication**

b. If the processor needs to be provided with a hardware integer multiplier, then the algorithm above must be translated into an appropriate *sequential* digital circuit, and provided as a functional unit within the processor. Integer multiply will then be a machine instruction, similar to ADD and SUB. Naturally, such an instruction will have much faster execution time than a similar function written in software.

c. If the processor does not provide an integer multiply instruction, but does have a *microprogrammed* control unit (recall Chapter 7), then it is possible to implement the multiply algorithm in *microcode*—i.e. by microprogramming the steps of Fig. 8.5, including the iteration. Multiply instruction is thereby added to the instruction set. Other factors being equal, such microcoded implementation will provide execution time which is much faster than that of software, but slower than that of a hardware multiplier.

8.5 BOOTH'S ALGORITHM AND INTEGER DIVISION

The algorithm seen in the previous section cannot be used directly for multiplying signed integers. Of course, what can always be done is: (a) Convert both operands to positive integers before multiplying them, and (b) Find the arithmetic negative of the final product if the two original operands had differing signs.

An alternative multiplication algorithm—known as *Booth's algorithm*—is not only potentially faster, but it also takes care of signed multiplication in a natural way, if negative integers are represented using 2's complement.

Suppose we need to calculate by hand the product 73 × 999. It is fair to say that most persons will simply find the answer as 73000 − 73 = 72927. Note that no multiplication has been carried out, but simply shift and subtract. When multiplier 999 is written as 1000 − 1, the logic behind this multiplication becomes clear.

This logic can also be applied when integers are in their binary representation. For simplicity, we consider the 8-bit multiplier 00111111, which equals decimal 63. This can be written as 64 − 1, which in binary is 01000000 − 00000001. The first term represents a left shift of the multiplicand by 6 bit positions, whereby it is multiplied by 64. The second term represents a subtraction of the multiplicand.

Now let us consider the multiplier 00111100, which has decimal value 60. This can be written in binary as 01000000 − 00000100, i.e. 64 − 4. The first term is the same as above, while the second term represents left shift by two positions and a subtraction.

What we have observed in these examples may be summarised as follows:

Let us say that the multiplier contains a sequence of k consecutive '1' bits, within its total size of n bits. When we focus our attention on these k bits, the relevant part of the multiplier has the form:

```
.. 0 1 1 1 1 1 1 0 ..
     <---------->
       k '1' bits
```

Let the rightmost of these k '1' bits be b_j. Then, the leftmost of these k bits is b_{j+k-1}. The numerical value of these k bits is, therefore, given by:

$$\sum_{i=j}^{j+k-1} 2^i$$

This is a summation of k different powers of 2, which would need k steps of *shift-and-add*. But it is easy to verify that the summation equals $2^{j+k} - 2^j$, which would involve only one addition and one subtraction. Therefore, if $k > 2$, then instead of k additions, we can get by with one addition and one subtraction, for a total of 2 operations—keeping in mind the fact that, in clock cycles, a subtraction is no 'costlier' than an addition.

This is the essence of the so-called Booth's algorithm for multiplication. This algorithm has the additional benefit that in a perfectly natural manner it also takes care of signed operands in 2's complement form. To see that, consider the following multiplier:

```
1 1 .. 1 1 1 1 1 1 0 ..
```

$\longleftarrow$ k '1' bits $\longrightarrow$

Compared with the previous example, the difference now is that the k '1' bits are now the leftmost k bits in the n-bit multiplier, i.e. $j + k - 1 = n - 1$. Summation of powers of 2, as seen above, is still applicable, so we get the equivalent value of the multiplier as:

$$2^{j+k} - 2^j = 2^n - 2^j$$

The value 2^n would correspond to bit b_n—which however is not within the n bits $b_{n-1}..b_0$ of the multiplier. This bit has in effect 'spilled over' on the left. If we drop this bit, then the value of the summation reduces to -2^j, which is nothing but the numerical value of the leftmost k bits of the multiplier in 2's complement!

Thus Booth's algorithm gives us the two-fold advantage that (a) long sequences of '1' bits in the multiplier are handled more efficiently, and (b) signed operands are handled in a natural manner, assuming of course that 2's complement representation is used. Note however that this algorithm proves 'costlier' if the multiplier consists of alternating '1' and '0' bits, and this point must be correctly addressed in any practical design.

To consider integer division, we must recall that (i) integer division can be viewed as repeated subtraction, and (ii) in binary, the usual 'long-hand' method of division amounts essentially to a sequence of *shift-and-subtract* operations.

Just as the *shift-and-add* steps of multiplication gave us the algorithm of Fig. 8.5, the *shift-and-subtract* steps of division can generate the integer division algorithm. As in the case of multiplication, it is possible to implement the division algorithm in software, hardware, or microcode.

8.6 FLOATING POINT OPERATIONS

While studying floating point operations such as addition and multiplication, the key differences between floating point and integer number representation must be kept in mind (recall Sections 2.5 and 2.6). These differences may be listed in brief as:

a. A floating point number has separate sign, exponent and mantissa, and
b. The number is *normalised*, such that the most significant bit of the mantissa (which is implicit), is '1'.

While adding two floating point numbers, it is necessary to make their exponents equal, before the mantissas can be added. To appreciate this point, let us calculate (in decimal) the sum $3 \times 10^4 + 2 \times 10^2$. Naturally, we first re-write the second number as 0.02×10^4 and then readily get the answer 3.02×10^4.

In the simple example of the previous paragraph, the number 2×10^2 is unchanged in value when it is re-written as 0.02×10^4. In exactly the same way, a floating point number in binary remains unchanged in value if its mantissa is shifted right by *k* bit positions and the exponent is increased by *k*. Because of the finite number of bits available to represent a number, some lower order bits of the mantissa may be lost in the shift operation—but this is inevitable when we add numbers with vastly different magnitudes.

By applying this transformation to the operand with the smaller exponent, we can make the two exponents equal. The number thus transformed becomes *un-normalised*—but it has to be accepted as inevitable that floating point operations may generate *intermediate values* which are un-normalised. Example 8.3 below will make this point clear.

Once the two exponents are made equal, the two mantissas can be added. The sum will, in general, be un-normalised, and must be normalised as the final step of the operation.

Example 8.3

Let us add the two floating point numbers 32 and −15.5, using the basic method outlined above. We have the representation of the second number from Example 2.7, and the first number from the simple observation that $32 = 1 \times 2^5$, giving stored mantissa of all zeros (remember the implicit '1' bit), and stored exponent $127 + 5 = 132$. Thus our two floating point numbers in standard representation are:

```
0    10000100    00000000000000000000000    = +32
1    10000010    11110000000000000000000    = −15.5
↑    \___ ___/   \__________ __________/
Sign 8-bit exponent  23-bit stored mantissa
bit
```

For addition, we need to make the two exponents equal. Therefore, we un-normalise the second number—we shift its mantissa to the right by 2 bits, and increase its exponent by 2, giving us the following un-normalised number:

```
1    10000100    0111110000000000000000000    = −15.5
↑    \___ ___/   \___________ ___________/      Un-normalised
Sign 8-bit exponent  25-bit mantissa of
bit                  intermediate value
```

Note that the number is now un-normalised, and there is no longer any hidden '1' bit, since the former hidden bit is now included in the $23 + 2 = 25$ bits of mantissa in this intermediate value. The two extra bits in the mantissa have been shown underlined.

Now that the two exponents are equal, we can add the numbers. Since the first number is negative, we need to perform subtraction of the two mantissas, keeping in mind that one mantissa has the implicit '1' bit with it. The subtraction is shown below:

```
                1. 000000 (zeros)     Implicit '1' bit of first mantissa
                                      Implicit binary points
     (minus)    0. 011111 (zeros)
                -----------------
            =   0. 100001 (zeros)  <- Result mantissa, to be re-normalised
```

Now we must again normalise the result. The most significant '1' in the result has been shown underlined. This must be shifted left by one position, made implicit, and the exponent must be reduced by one. When the result is thus normalised, its full form is:

```
0     10000011    00001000000000000000000     = 16.5
↑
Sign  8-bit exponent    23-bit stored mantissa
bit
```

The student should verify that this is indeed the standard representation of the result 16.5.

As we know, in floating point representation, the sign of the number is stored separately. Therefore, addition and subtraction of floating point numbers go through the same series of steps outlined above. The sign bits of the two operands must of course be properly taken into account during the process. Subtraction of a negative number, for example, amounts to addition of the corresponding positive number.

For multiplication and division, the two respective exponents need not be equal. In multiplication, exponents of the two operands are added; in division, exponent of the divisor is subtracted from that of the dividend. As we know, the exponents are stored in excess 127 form in single precision and in excess 1023 form in double precision. The sum or difference of exponents must therefore be corrected after the multiplication or division of mantissas, and the result normalised. Multiplication, as we know, involves repeated shift and addition, while division involves repeated shift and subtraction.

Thus, we see that arithmetic operations on floating point numbers involve basic steps which are very similar to those which we studied earlier for integer operations. Some extra work needs to be done, of course, for the reasons outlined above—but this extra work also makes use of familiar steps such as shift, addition and subtraction.

Therefore, for implementing floating point operations on a processor, once again we have the same three options which we discussed earlier: *software*, *dedicated hardware*, or *microcode*. Possible trade-offs involved between these options—in terms of cost versus performance—are basically the same as those discussed in Section 8.4.

When floating point operations are provided using dedicated hardware, what we have within the processor is typically a separate functional unit, usually named *floating point unit* (FPU). With reference to the diagram of Fig. 6.1, the FPU may be thought of as having function and location similar to—and parallel to—that of the ALU.

In such cases, the two functional units ALU and FPU are usually capable of operating *in parallel*—for example, the FPU could be performing a multiply operation while the ALU is performing an independent ADD operation. Such parallelism in operations is a major potential source of performance enhancement—provided of course that the hardware and software are designed to find and exploit such parallelism. In Chapters 13 and 14, we shall examine some basic issues related to parallelism in computer systems.

8.7 BINARY CODED DECIMAL (BCD) ARITHMETIC

In earlier days of computer technology, use was frequently made of so-called *binary-coded decimal* (BCD) number representation for integers, and also for fixed-point numbers such as those used for keeping financial accounts. The commonly used *packed* BCD format used a nibble—i.e. half-a-byte, 4 bits—for each decimal digit. For example, the eight digit number 31052008 would be packed into four bytes as:

0011 0001	0000 0101	0010 0000	0000 1000

The student should verify that the eight nibbles within these four bytes contain the binary encoding of the eight decimal digits in the number. The word *packed* here indicates that two decimal digits are being 'packed' into one byte.

Special machine instructions were usually provided to operate on numbers in packed BCD representation. To see the need for such instructions, consider the addition of two decimal digits '5' and '7'. Clearly the sum digit is '2', and a carry '1' has to be passed to the digit position on the left. But, if the addition is performed on binary representations of the two digits '5' and '7', then the answer 12—which is 1100 in binary—gets stored in just one nibble, and no carry is generated.

Assume that the left nibble contains decimal '0'—i.e. binary 0000—before the addition. Then, to convert the binary sum 1100 into two decimal digits '1' and '2' stored in two nibbles, the following *decimal adjustment* must be made to the binary value:

> If binary value in a nibble exceeds 9, add 6 to it. This generates a carry out from the nibble, which must be added into the nibble immediately to its left.

Some older processors provided a *decimal adjust* instruction to make this correction on packed BCD bytes which have been added as binary integers. However, with the newer generation of powerful processors, integers are represented only in 2's complement, and any re-formatting between binary and decimal is performed entirely in software.

Some programming languages used in earlier years provided a packed BCD type of number representation. With present-day programming languages such as JAVA and C++, the *integer* data type takes care of all such requirements; input and output data is formatted in software using any preferred style of decimal representation.

8.8 CONDITIONS, EXCEPTIONS AND FAULTS

In Chapter 4 we saw that, as a result of an integer arithmetic instruction, comparison, or a logic instruction, one or more of the conditions *zero*, *negative*, *overflow*, *carry* and *parity* may occur. The ALU detects these conditions—and accordingly each of the flags Z, N, O, C and P in the program status word (PSW) is either set or reset.

These condition flags can be utilised to provide required conditional jumps within a program. An instruction such as *jump on zero* (JZ) involves only the Z flag, while an instruction such as *jump on greater or equal* (JGE) involves a combination of flags. These flags are made available to the programmer for precisely the purpose of allowing conditional jumps, which are normal ingredients of any machine language program.

If floating point operations are implemented in hardware or in microcode, it is possible to give a well-defined meaning to *zero* (Z) and *negative* (N) conditions—but not to the other three conditions. Of course it is perfectly legitimate to have jump instructions such as JGE, JLE or JNZ which depend on results of floating point operations.

We do not associate any of the condition flags with *errors*. Rather, these conditions are expected to occur in any running program, and the programmer is expected to respond to them as appropriate to program requirements. Branch decisions made on the basis of these conditions make up the *flow of control* within a program.

But there are other conditions which may arise as a result of floating point operations which need to be handled in a different manner. For example, floating point *overflow* or *underflow* may occur if the result of an operation cannot be represented as a normalised single- or double-precision number. Also, if integer or floating point division is provided on a processor, the condition *divide by zero* may occur.

Typically, conditions such as floating point *overflow* and *underflow*, and integer or floating point *divide by zero*, do not cause any condition flags to be set in PSW. Instead, these conditions are treated as 'run-time' errors which are known as *exceptions*. Through a mechanism which we shall see in Chapter 10, such exceptions force the running program to execute instructions which result in either corrective action, or—*by default*, i.e. if no such corrective is specified—termination of the running program.

Yet another type of condition which can arise within a processor is termed as a *fault*. In such a condition, it is not possible that the program itself can be made to take corrective action. Such a *fault* forces the processor to execute so-called *fault handler* instructions which are included with the operating system.

A *memory access violation*, for example, is a *fault* caused by a program attempting to access a part of memory which is not present in the system, or to which the program does not have access right. Usually this fault results in the termination of the faulting program. A *page fault*, on the other hand, is a condition for which the operating system does take corrective action, by arranging to bring in the required *page* from disk to main memory. We shall study such memory management mechanisms in the next chapter.

Exceptions and faults are handled by the generic mechanism of *interrupts*—which means that the normal program flow of the running program is interrupted, and forced to transfer to another location which is determined by the condition which caused the interrupt. The source of an interrupt may be:

a. an external input or output device, such as keyboard or disk,
b. a condition occurring within the processor, such as floating point overflow or memory violation, or
c. a so-called *software interrupt*, which is a machine instruction executed by the running program, usually to invoke a function provided by the operating system.

The topic of interrupts and interrupt handling will be discussed in Chapter 10.

SUMMARY

In earlier chapters, we have used arithmetic instructions such as ADD without addressing the question of how such operations are implemented within the ALU. In this chapter, we have studied the basic principles underlying the design of digital circuits to perform arithmetic operations on integer and floating point operands.

For integer addition, the first step is to understand the working of a full adder. After looking at the simple but slow ripple carry method, we have seen how carry look-ahead can speed up the operation. Subtraction, as we have seen, is nothing but arithmetic negation followed by addition.

Integer multiplication can be performed using the *shift-and-add* technique. The product of two n-bit integers will, in general, be a $2n$-bit integer. Booth's algorithm runs faster, by handling efficiently sequences of consecutive '1' bits in the multiplier, and this algorithm also treats signed multiplication in a natural way.

Floating point addition requires making the two exponents equal, by shifting one mantissa and thereby making an intermediate value *un-normalised.* In general, floating point operations involve more work than integer operations. If provided in hardware, they are usually implemented in a separate floating point unit.

In the last section of this chapter, we have discussed in brief the various conditions, exceptions, and faults which can arise as a result of processor operations—arithmetic or otherwise—and the ways in which the processor handles such events.

REVIEW QUESTIONS

1. List two differences between computer methods and human methods for performing arithmetic.
2. In a computer system, arithmetic is being performed in hexadecimal. Consider the right-most, i.e. least significant digit of an n-digit hexadecimal number. What are the numerical values of *carry in* and *carry out* from this digit position?
3. Consider once again the computer system of the previous question. What are the numerical values of *carry in* and *carry out* from the digit position which is next to the rightmost digit position?
4. List the binary inputs and outputs of a full adder circuit.
5. The maximum total gate delay of a full adder circuit is 10 picoseconds. What is the maximum possible gate delay of a 32-bit ripple carry adder?
6. Write logical expressions for the *generate* and *propagate* functions g_i and p_i of the ith bit stage of an n-bit adder.
7. *Multiply-shift-and-add* method of decimal multiplication becomes simply *shift-and-add* when carried out in binary. Justify this statement in brief.
8. Give an example of two 4-bit unsigned binary integers whose product is an 8-bit binary integer.
9. List the number and size of registers required for implementing *shift-and-add* multiplication in a processor.
10. List, in order of decreasing speed, the relative speeds of software, hardware and micro-coded implementations of *shift-and-add* multiplication.
11. List the advantages of Booth's multiplication algorithm over *shift-and-add* multiplication algorithm.
12. Verify that the summation $\sum_{i=j}^{j+k-1} 2^i$ equals $2^{j+k} - 2^j$.

13. Consider Booth's algorithm applied to 16-bit operands, i.e. $n = 16$. Suppose in one instance the multiplier bits are 1111110000000000. In terms of the notation used in Section 8.5, what is the value of j? Verify that the above multiplier has value -2^j in 2's complement representation.
14. List the main steps in the addition or subtraction of two floating point numbers.
15. List the main steps in the multiplication or division of two floating point numbers.
16. List the options available for implementing floating point operations in a computer system.
17. What is the function of a Floating Point Unit (FPU) in a processor?
18. Determine the minimum number of bytes needed to store a ten-digit decimal number using packed BCD.
19. Show that the decimal adjustment mentioned in Section 8.7 works correctly for the BCD addition of digits '7' and '9'.
20. What is the meaning of an *exception* occurring in a running program? Give one example.
21. What is the meaning of a *fault* occurring in a running program? Give one example.
22. Name the mechanism by which exceptions and faults are handled in a computer system.

EXERCISES

1. Four pairs of 8-bit binary quantities are shown below. Treating each of them as an 8-bit unsigned integer, carry out pair-wise binary addition as it would take place on a ripple carry adder built using eight full adders. Determine in each case the status of condition flags Z, N, O and C.

(a)		(b)		(c)		(d)	
	01101111		11111111		11111111		11110000
	00100101		00000001		11111111		00001111

2. A *half adder* can be defined as a circuit which adds two bits, say a_i and b_i, and produces the sum bit s_i and carry out bit c_i. Develop the truth table of a half adder. Show how two half adders can be connected together to produce a full adder, remembering that

$$a_i + b_i + c_{i-1} = (a_i + b_i) + c_{i-1}$$

3. Verify, with reference to Table 8.1, that *carry out* bit c_i from stage i is given by:

$$c_{i+1} = g_i + p_i \cdot c_{i-1}$$

where the *generate* and *propagate* functions g_i and p_i are as defined in the text.

4. Recall that Table 8.1 is the truth table of a full adder, which finds the sum of two single bit operands a_0 and b_0, with carry in c_{-1}. Table 8.2 is an <u>incomplete</u> truth table of a 2-bit adder, in which the two operands are 2-bit quantities $A = a_1a_0$ and $B = b_1b_0$, with carry in c_{-1}. Outputs are the 2-bit sum $S = s_1s_0$ and carry out c_1. In order to avoid drawing $2^5 = 32$ rows, however, Table 8.2 has been grouped according to the $2^3 = 8$ possible combinations of <u>outputs</u>.

   Complete the entries in Table 8.2 which show '?'.

   Hint: Think of b_1 and a_1 as forming one group of inputs, and b_0, a_0 and c_{-1} as forming another group of inputs.

Table 8.2 Truth table of 2-bit adder (incomplete)

Inputs	Outputs		
$a_1, a_0, b_1, b_0, c_{i-1}$	c_1	s_1	s_0
All inputs are '0'	0	0	0
Only one of a_0, b_0, and c_{i-1} is '1', all others are '0'	0	0	1
?	0	1	0
?	0	1	1
?	1	0	0
?	1	0	1
Only one of a_0, b_0, and c_{i-1} is '0', all others are '1'	1	1	0
All inputs are '1'	1	1	1

5. Simulate the addition of pairs of unsigned 8-bit integers listed in Exercise 1, making use of four of the 2-bit adders designed in the previous exercise. As before, carry out from one adder is connected to carry in of the next adder on the left.
6. Interpret all the 8-bit quantities listed in Exercise 1 as signed integers in 2's complement form; for example, **11111111** will have value −1. Verify that the additions performed on them generate correct results as signed integers, even though there is no change in the addition steps performed. Recall that this was described as the main advantage of using 2's complement form to represent signed integers.
7. Consider once again the pairs of 8-bit quantities of Exercise 1 as signed integers in 2's complement form. For each pair, subtract the second integer from the first, using the method outlined in the text, and verify the result. Determine in each case the status of condition flags Z, N, O and C.
8. Consider the following two pairs of unsigned 8-bit integers. Treating the first number as multiplicand and the second as multiplier, carry out multiplication in each case using the *shift-and-add* method.

   (a) **01101111** (b) **00111111**
   00100101 **00011110**

9. For pair (b) of unsigned integers of the previous exercise, carry out multiplication using Booth's algorithm.
10. Recall that, in Example 2.7, we saw that the following 32-bit quantity represents the decimal value −15.5 in single-precision floating point number representation:

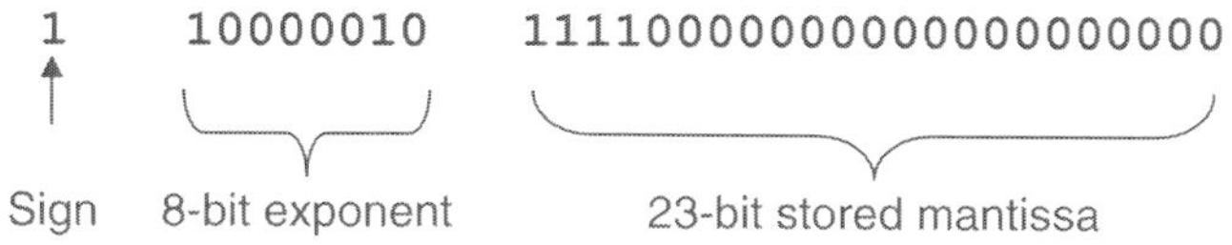

a. Find the single-precision floating point representation of the decimal value 65536.75.

b Add the two quantities −15.5 and 65536.75 as single-precision floating point numbers, using the steps outlined in Section 8.6.

11. Describe the steps required for floating point addition, either by drawing a flow chart or in algorithmic notation. Note that this answer requires some elaboration of the steps listed in answer to Review Question 14.

12. Describe the steps required for floating point multiplication, either by drawing a flow chart or in algorithmic notation. Note that this answer requires some elaboration of the steps listed in answer to Review Question 15.

MEMORY ORGANISATION

9

9.1 MEMORY HIERARCHY

In the computer system, we have seen the use of four distinct types of memory:

a. Registers in the processor, such as R0–R15, IR, PC, and so on,
b. Cache memory, which speeds up access by the processor to main memory,
c. Main memory, which holds the programs and data under execution, and
d. Secondary storage—usually magnetic disk, but can be flash RAM—to meet the long-term storage requirements of programs and data.

Of these, the operation of cache memory is transparent to the running program. The programs which we studied in Chapters 4 and 5 would run correctly regardless of whether cache memory is available on the system—the only difference being that they would run faster on a system with cache memory. We also saw in those chapters that operands in general purpose registers are operated upon by instructions such as ADD and SUB, while memory operands are accessed by instructions LOAD and STORE. In Chapter 6, we saw the function of other processor registers such as IR and PC.

Each of the types of memory listed above has a very specific and important role in the working of a computer system. We should observe that, as we go down the above list from 'a' to 'd', the memory in question becomes (i) slower, and (ii) less expensive per bit. The fourth type of memory listed, secondary storage, is also *non-volatile*, since it must preserve programs and data even when electric power is switched off.

In terms of memory speed and capacity, note that processor registers may have access time which is in picoseconds, and combined capacity which may be of the order of a hundred bytes. At the other end, secondary storage devices may have access times measured in milliseconds, and capacity of a few hundred gigabytes. Several orders of magnitude thus separate processor registers and secondary storage devices.

Figure 9.1 depicts these four types of memory as making up four levels of a *memory hierarchy*. At each level of this hierarchy, a rectangle has been drawn. The width of the rectangles becomes bigger as we go from top to bottom, reflecting larger memory capacity as we go down the hierarchy. Conversely, the height of the rectangle becomes bigger as we go from bottom to top, reflecting faster memory speeds.

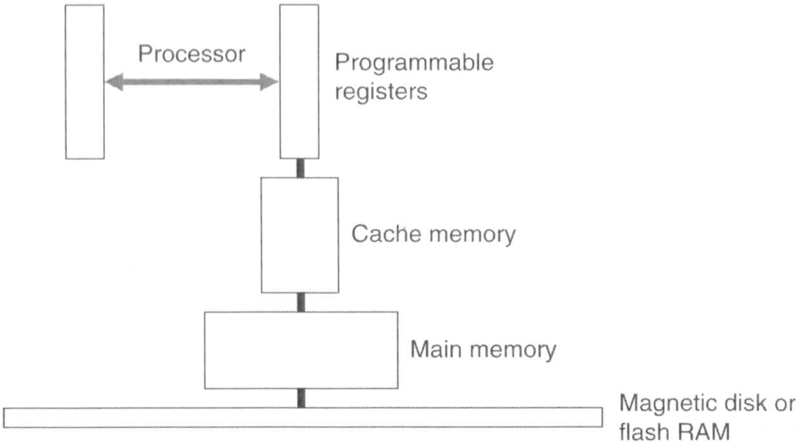

Fig. 9.1 **Memory hierarchy in a computer system**

The processor has been shown as a separate rectangle on the left, interacting with processor registers. The heights of these two rectangles are shown to be equal, since the processor registers, functional units and busses operate at comparable speeds. One aim of computer system design is that the processor should execute instructions at its maximum rate possible—without being slowed down by having to fetch instructions and data from slower memories which are lower down in the memory hierarchy.

An ideal but imaginary computer system would therefore have a single type of memory, which is as fast as processor registers, has as much capacity as magnetic disk, and is non-volatile! Unfortunately—due to cost, power consumption, packaging, and other practical constraints—it is not possible to provide such memory in a real computer system.

Therefore system designers aim for the following practical goal:

As far as possible, make instructions and data available to running programs at the speed of faster memory, fetching these from slower memory when required. The attempt is to make available in faster memory, the instructions and data which are *currently in use*. Recall that this strategy was discussed in Section 6.9 in connection with the operation of cache memory. When applied across the memory hierarchy, this strategy reduces the impact on program execution speed of accesses to slower memories.

In this context, two important techniques which can be used to extract the maximum performance from a computer system are *multiprogramming* and *virtual memory*. In the remaining part of this chapter, we discuss these and some other related techniques.

Before starting on those topics, however, it is necessary to make an important general point about system performance and system design.

Computer systems today span a vast range in terms of size, cost and applications. Every system within this vast range is designed with a specific set of objectives and constraints. A system to control the operations of a microwave oven, for example, is very different from one which is meant for intensive scientific computations. A specific performance enhancement technique—such as *cache memory*, *pipelined processor*, *multiprogramming*, or *virtual memory*—is included in a system only if it is consistent with the basic objectives and constraints of system design.

Memory management techniques are discussed in this chapter in the order of increasing sophistication. Depending on the specific application—and constraints such as cost and power consumption—the appropriate technique would be selected for a system.

This point about computer systems is in fact applicable to a much broader range of systems. One model of a passenger car, for example, may cost an amount C and be meant for one type of customer; another model may cost $10 \times C$ and be meant for another type of customer. For each model, the technology built into the car will be determined by its basic design objectives and constraints.

9.2 MULTIPROGRAMMING

We saw above that the multiple types of memory which must be provided within a computer system vary widely in speed and capacity—and that the system designer aims to minimise the adverse effect on performance of memory speed mismatches.

But there is yet another major speed mismatch in a computer system with which the system designer must also cope—namely, the speed mismatch between the *processor* and *input/output (I/O) devices*. Most I/O devices operate at speeds which are comparable to those of secondary storage devices, and are therefore several orders of magnitude slower than the processor.

We must first understand why this speed mismatch is a performance issue. Consider the typical behavior of a running program, in terms of the time it spends in:

a. *Compute phase*, i.e. executing processor instructions, and
b. *I/O phase*, i.e. performing an input or output operation on a device.

Clearly any real life program will spend time in each of these two phases*. Also, any action performed by a running program necessarily belongs to either compute or I/O phase. This means that, over time, the behavior of a running program can be visualised as an alternating sequence of compute and I/O phases, as shown in Fig. 9.2.

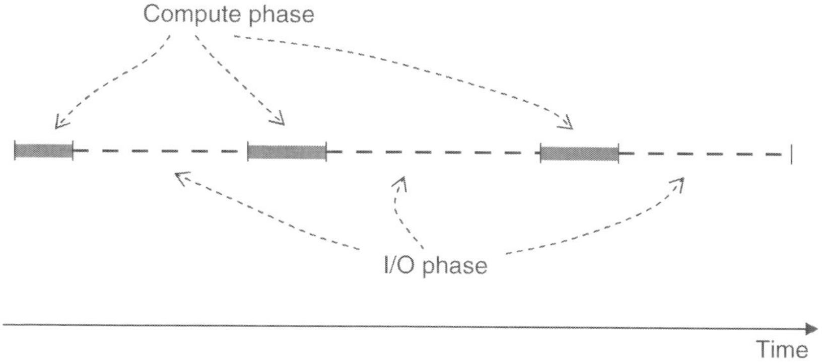

Fig. 9.2 Compute and I/O phases of a running program

*A program is known as *compute intensive* or *I/O intensive* depending on whether it spends the major portion of its time in one or the other phase.

We have assumed here that we are working with a *sequential* program—i.e. a program which alternates over time between compute and I/O phases, rather than performing them *in parallel*. This is a perfectly valid assumption for two important reasons:

(i) Most computer programs are in fact written as sequential programs, and
(ii) A standard model of parallelism is that of sequential programs which are running in parallel*—and therefore we must study sequential programs before studying the effects of their parallel operation.

In Fig. 9.2, we must also factor in the huge speed mismatch between processor and I/O devices. When that is done, we see that a program may spend a very large fraction of its time in performing I/O operations. In terms of Fig. 9.2, this means that the dashed lines of *I/O phase* may be much longer than the thick lines of *compute phase*.

Now, if the program in question is the only program running on the system, what work can the processor do while an I/O operation is in progress? The answer is: nothing! In a sequential program, the next compute phase cannot begin until the ongoing I/O operation is over. And therefore, the processor must remain *idle* for a large fraction of its running time. In practice, this means that the processor executes an *idle loop* of the type,

```
IDLE:    JMP    IDLE    // Idle loop
```

until it is 'yanked out' of the loop when the I/O operation completes—like a drunk being pulled up by his shirt-collar by a policeman.

With a single, typical sequential program running on a computer system, such processor idling is unavoidable**. At the same time, the resulting low *processor utilisation* is also unacceptable. So what is the solution?

Conceptually, the solution is simple: Hold multiple programs in memory—which we assume are independent of each other—such that if one program is in I/O phase, another program in *its* compute phase would be running on the processor. Thus, if the processor is not executing the instructions of one program, it is executing those of another program. The nett effect of multiprogramming is that processor utilisation remains high, and the system completes more work per unit time—i.e. it has higher total *throughput*.

The number of programs *n* which the system holds in memory is known as its *degree of multiprogramming*. Note that, since we have been looking at systems with only one processor—i.e. so-called *uniprocessor systems*—at most one of these *n* programs can run on the processor at any given time.

---

*In a so-called *multi-threaded* program, pieces of a single running program run in parallel as so many sequential *threads*. In this case also, the system performance issues discussed here remain valid, and in fact provide the main justification for multi-threaded programs.

**Unless, of course, the single program running is very highly compute intensive. The argument made in the text applies to typical computer programs, which alternate though compute and I/O phases as shown in Fig. 9.2.

Example 9.1

Assume that a typical program spends 10% of its time on the processor, and the remaining 90% of its time in I/O operations. We can thus say that the probability p that such a program is performing an I/O operation at a given time is 0.9.

If only one such program is running on the system, then the processor utilisation of the system will clearly be 10%.

Now suppose we run eight such programs on the system in multiprogramming mode—i.e. the degree of multiprogramming is 8. In such a system, the processor will be idle only if all eight programs are performing I/O operations at a given time.

Since the programs are assumed to be independent of each other, the probability that all eight are performing I/O operations at a given time is $(0.9)^8 = 0.43$. This is the probability that the processor is idle—and therefore the processor utilisation is now $(1 - 0.43) \times 100 = 57\%$. Thus processor utilisation has increased from 10% to 57%, with degree of multiprogramming $n = 8$.

Example 9.1 brings out the performance gain achieved through multiprogramming in terms of increased processor utilisation. But in fact even the utilisation of I/O devices improves in the process—since multiple running programs are performing I/O in parallel on the set of devices available. And thus we can see that the overall system *resource utilisation* certainly improves as a result of multiprogramming.

What about the running time of any one of the n programs which are now sharing the system? Does it improve or degrade as a result of multiprogramming?

Alas, the running time of a single program cannot improve as a result of multiprogramming. Due to contention between the n programs for processor and I/O devices, the running time of any one program may in general increase as we increase n.

Therefore, in operating a computer system under multiprogramming, a performance *trade-off* is involved between (a) utilising system resources to the full, and (b) providing acceptable running time to each program running on the system.

In the remaining sections of this chapter, we shall study some details of the techniques and issues involved in equipping a system for multiprogramming.

9.3 PARTITIONED MEMORY

If multiple programs are to reside in main memory and run independently, then arrangements must be made for the sharing of main memory between these running programs in such a way that:

a. Each running program is allocated the amount of memory required for its instructions and data, and
b. No running program can make references to instructions or data outside of the main memory allocated to it.

Requirement (b) above can be termed as a *protection* requirement, in the sense that every program residing in main memory must be protected from invalid accesses by any other running program.

In general—in any computer system—the requirement of *sharing* resources between running programs invariably gives rise to the converse requirement of *protecting* resources from invalid access.

The simplest way to share main memory between *n* user programs is to divide it into an appropriate number of *partitions*. This means that the main memory is divided into *contiguous* chunks for the *n* programs—plus of course one other chunk for the operating system. Each such contiguous chunk of main memory is known as a *partition*, and the main memory is said to be *partitioned*.

Figure 9.3 depicts such a partitioned main memory, shared between two programs and the operating system. In this case, the degree of multiprogramming *n* is 2.

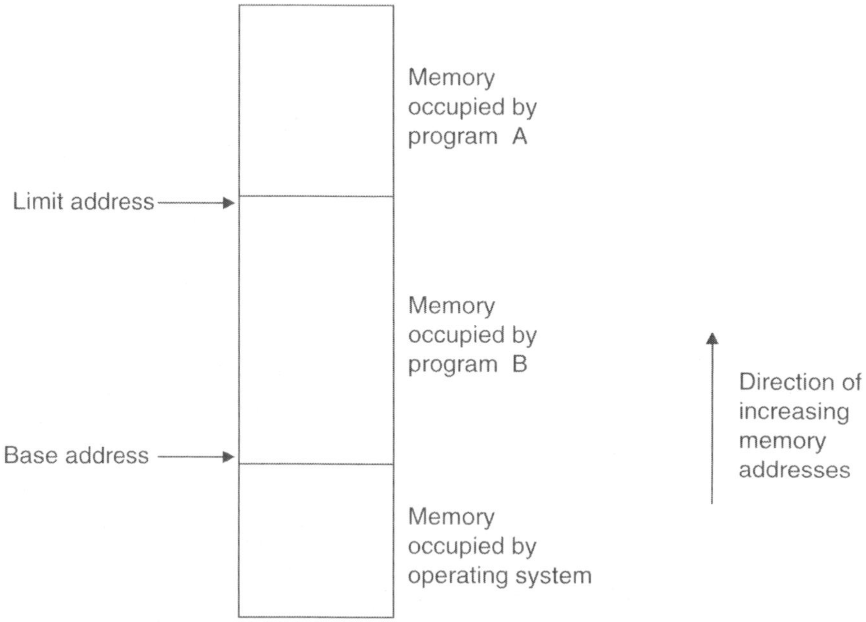

Fig. 9.3 Sharing of main memory by two programs and the operating system

Each memory partition has a *start address* and an *end address* in *physical* memory. The term *physical* here signifies that we are referring to the actual memory sub-system with its address lines, data lines, decoding circuits, and so on.

When main memory is thus shared between *n* independently running programs, naturally we do not expect the computations performed by any one program to be affected by what the other $n - 1$ programs are doing. This is in fact implied by the requirement (b) above, and must be seen as a critical requirement for multiprogramming to succeed.

Fortunately there is a simple and clean solution to satisfy this critical requirement. The idea is to provide each running program with its own *logical memory space*, which is completely independent of the logical memory spaces of other programs. In other words, while the *n* programs—and the operating system—share physical memory space, each operates within its own independent logical memory space.

The logical memory space 'seen' by a running program is more commonly called its *logical address space*; in a similar way, the memory space spanned by physical memory addresses is called the *physical address space* of a system.

The logical address space of a program comprises all the memory addresses which a program can use, for instructions as well as data. Each such address used within a program is known as a *logical address*. Suppose, for example, a program includes the following machine instruction:

```
LOAD  2000,  R1
```

Memory address 2000 here is a *logical* address, referring to a specific location within the logical address space of the program. Of course, the LOAD instruction itself is stored at some other logical address within the logical address space of the program.

Now suppose this program occupies physical memory starting at *physical* memory address 40000. Then the location 2000 in the instruction above must be seen as *relative* to the physical starting address of the program. Therefore, the reference to *logical* address 2000 will be *mapped* to physical address 40000 + 2000 = 42000.

The following example will help make this idea clear.

Example 9.2

Suppose we have a twenty volume encyclopedia, with its volumes numbered from 1 to 20. To arrange these twenty volumes in a bookcase, we have a few different options.

a. If these twenty volumes are the only occupants of the bookcase, and are arranged serially, then the kth volume will be found at position k in the bookcase. In our current terminology, we can say that, in this case, logical volume k in the set is found at physical location k in the bookcase.
b. Now suppose the bookcase is being shared with two hundred other books, and that the twenty volumes of the encyclopedia occupy contiguous locations numbered 51 to 70 in the bookcase. In this case, we shall find logical volume k of the encyclopedia at physical location $50 + k$ in the bookcase.
c. Going further, let us suppose that the twenty volumes of the encyclopedia do not even occupy contiguous locations in the bookcase—i.e. they are not arranged serially, next to each other. In this case, for each of the twenty volumes, we must separately record its physical location. Encyclopedia volume k will now be found at location $f(k)$, where f is the function mapping the *logical* volume number to its *physical* location.

We see that in case (a) above, there is no distinction between logical volume number and the physical location of the volume in the bookcase. In case (b), the logical to physical mapping involves a simple addition, while in case (c), a table-lookup is required to implement the mapping denoted by function $f(k)$ above.

In Fig. 9.3, we see that each partition of physical memory is a contiguous block, and thus it corresponds to case (b) of Example 9.2—where we allocated contiguous space in the bookcase to all the encyclopedia volumes. Each memory partition in Fig. 9.3 has a unique *start* address and *end* address in physical memory. However, as seen in the figure, we have termed these two addresses as *base address* and *limit address*, respectively, because this is the terminology in more common use.

Now the important question arises: If the system designer opts for partitioned main memory as described above, what implications does that have for processor design? Or, in other words, how should the processor architecture of Fig. 6.1 be modified—or enhanced—to support multiprogramming with partitioned main memory?

Consider again the following reference to address 2000 made by a running program:

```
LOAD   2000,  R1
```

As we saw in Chapter 7, during *fetch* phase, the *logical* address 2000 will be copied from IR to the *address* register, so that it can be made available to main memory via the address bus of the system. The address 2000 in the program is a *logical* address, while the address actually placed on the address lines is a *physical* address.

Now we see that, with partitioned memory, logical address 2000 will correspond to physical address 42000, if the base address of the memory partition is 40000. In other words, now we have the mapping:

$$\textit{physical address} = \textit{base address} + \textit{logical address}$$

For protecting other partitions from invalid access, we also need to ensure that:

$$\textit{physical address} \leq \textit{limit address}$$

We thus see that the mapping from logical address to physical address involves basically one addition—and an extra comparison thrown in for memory protection. The hardware required for implementing this mapping is fairly simple, as shown in Fig. 9.4. With reference to the processor architecture of Fig. 6.1, we may now note that:

(i) The *address* register shown on the top left in Fig. 6.1 provides the logical address shown in Fig. 9.4, and
(ii) The physical address shown in Fig. 9.4 is carried via address lines to the memory sub-system.

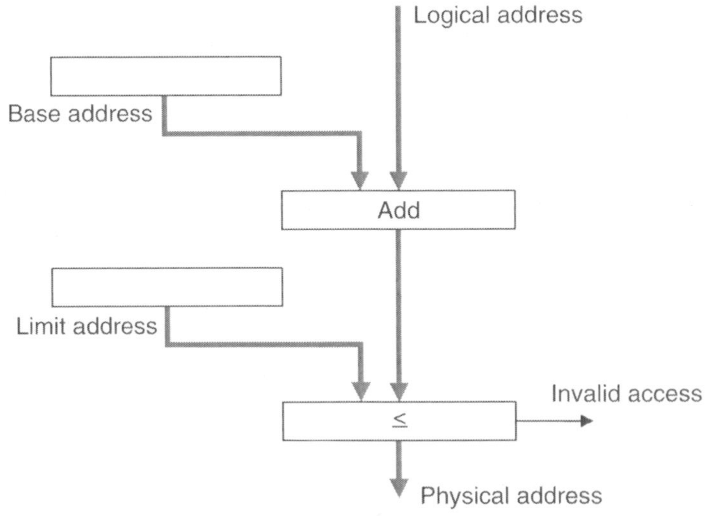

Fig. 9.4 Mapping from logical to physical address, for partitioned memory

Thus, for partitioned memory, the so-called *memory management* hardware shown in Fig. 9.4 is added on to the processor of Fig. 6.1. This hardware raises *invalid access* exception—see Section 8.8—if a running program attempts to access a physical memory address outside its partition defined by the base and limit registers.

When a program runs on the processor, the operating system ensures that the *base* and *limit* registers in the processor are loaded with the correct values for the memory partition allocated to the program. However, the alert student will note that—at this point—no instruction listed in Table 5.1 is capable of thus loading these two registers!

Such instructions should in fact be considered *privileged instructions*, in the sense that only the operating system can execute them. Any processor capable of supporting multiprogramming must provide such instructions, for operating system functions which must not be entrusted to user programs. For this purpose, it is also necessary that the program status word (PSW) has *mode* bit(s) indicating whether the processor is running in *privileged mode* (also known as *supervisor mode*) or *user mode.*

9.4 NON-CONTIGUOUS MEMORY ALLOCATION

With n partitions in memory for user programs, and one partition for the operating system, the degree of multiprogramming achieved will be n. But there are still some technical difficulties in this arrangement which cause poor memory utilisation:

In a general purpose system with multiprogramming, the mix of user programs running on the system varies with time—i.e. it is *dynamic.* This means that the number of programs running on the system changes continually with time, as do the partition sizes required by these programs.

As one program terminates, the memory partition occupied by it becomes available to be used by another program. Let us say the size of the partition thus freed up is S. Now the next program to be run on the system may need a partition which is larger or smaller than S. If the next program needs a partition larger than S, it simply cannot be loaded into the available partition of main memory; if it needs a partition smaller than S, it can be loaded into the partition, but a part of memory allocated to it remains unutilised.

After such a multiprogramming system runs for some time, the partitioned main memory of the system becomes *fragmented.* We can think of a *fragment* as an unused block of memory which cannot be utilised for running a program, either because (a) the fragment is too small for a running program, or because (b) the fragment is inside a larger memory partition already allocated to a program. These two types of fragmentation are known as *external fragmentation* and *internal fragmentation*, respectively—and both lead to poor memory utilisation*.

When the root cause of such fragmentation is analysed, it is found that it lies in one basic assumption that we have made all along, which is this: A program requiring amount of memory P must be loaded in a *contiguous* partition of memory of size $S \geq P$. As long as we hold on to this assumption, memory fragmentation is unavoidable in a *dynamic* multiprogramming environment.

But then how do we get out of this assumption, which seems so natural to our basic understanding that a program must be 'loaded into a block of memory'? For an answer, we must look once again into

*See Exercise 9.4 at the end of this chapter for a simple numerical example of how external and internal fragmentation occurs.

case (c) of Example 9.2, where we decided that it was not necessary to store the twenty volumes of the encyclopedia into twenty *contiguous* locations within the bookcase.

Applying this concept to programs and main memory, we can try the following:

(i) Allocate main memory to programs in multiple units of fixed size, making the unit size much smaller than typical programs, and also independent of program size.

(ii) Allocate to any running program as many of these memory units as it requires—but not necessarily in a single contiguous block.

The fixed size unit of allocation of memory referred to in (i) and (ii) above is known as a *page*. Typical *page size* in computer systems may be in the range from 1 kilobyte (= 2^{10} bytes) to 4 kilobytes (= 2^{12} bytes). On systems with large physical memory, the page size may be made larger—but it is still much smaller than the size of a typical program.

When memory is thus allocated to programs in integer number of pages, a memory address—whether *logical* or *physical*—gets divided in a natural manner between a *page number* and an *offset* within page, as the following example should make clear.

Example 9.3

Recall that the processor which we have used in Chapters 4 and 5 has a 24-bit logical address, for a total logical address space of 16 megabytes. On a system using this processor, let us assume that the page size is 4 kilobytes = 2^{12} bytes. This means that any byte within a page can be specified by means of a 12-bit *offset* within the page.

a. Let us say that the following 24-bit address refers to some location within the logical address space of a program running on this system*:

```
0000 1111 0000 1000 0000 0011
```

Logical page number (first twelve bits: 0000 1111 0000) — Offset within page (last twelve bits: 1000 0000 0011)

Since the memory is organised in terms of pages, we can say that, as shown:

(i) the higher order twelve bits of this address point to the logical memory page within which this address lies, and

(ii) the lower order twelve bits of the address provide the offset within that page of the memory location.

In our case, as shown above, the page number is 000011110000 (binary) = 240 (decimal), while the offset within the page is 100000000011 (binary) = 2051 (decimal). We say that the memory address lies in *logical* page number 240, at offset 2051. The word *logical* is being used here since the address in question is that used by the running program.

b. Now assume that the system has been provided with 256 megabytes = 2^{28} bytes of physical memory, requiring 28 bits of physical address. Further, let us assume that the logical page number 240 of (a) above has been loaded into physical page number 8400 in physical memory.

---

*For convenience, we have separated the address into 4-bit 'nibbles'.

Since the page size is fixed, any offset within the logical page is necessarily also the offset within the corresponding physical page. In this case, therefore, the offset of 2051 within logical page number 240 is also applied to physical page number 8400, to find the required memory location in physical memory. Thus, the required physical memory address is given by physical page number 8400 and offset 2051. In binary, this is:

```
0010 0000 1101 0000   1000 0000 0011
```

Physical page number (first 16 bits); Offset within page (last 12 bits)

Thus, in this case, we can say that logical page number 240 (decimal) occupies physical page number 8400 (decimal) in main memory.

The logical to physical address translation described in Example 9.3 is illustrated in Fig. 9.5. It is seen that the logical page number gets mapped to the corresponding physical page number, while the offset within page is carried forward unchanged. The required mapping from logical to physical page number is implemented in hardware using a fast memory element in the form of a *page map table.*

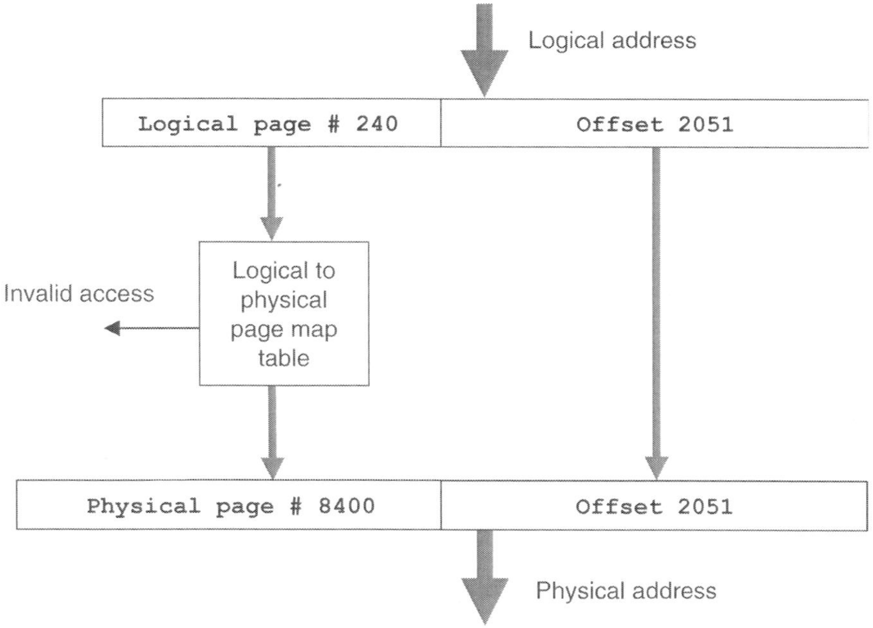

Fig. 9.5 **Logical to physical address translation with fixed size pages**

The logical page number serves as the *index* into the page map table—i.e. it provides directly the location in the table where the corresponding physical page number is stored. For logical page number i, say, the ith entry in the table stores the corresponding physical page number p_i. The page map table entry also stores memory protection bits for logical page i—according to which *read*, *write,* or *execute* access can be granted to the running program for this page.

If a running program makes reference to a page outside its own logical address space, or makes reference to a page which violates its protection bits, the hardware associated with the page map table raises *invalid access* exception (see Section 8.8).

With the type of mapping illustrated in Fig. 9.5, it is not necessary that consecutive logical pages of a running program get mapped into consecutive physical pages in main memory. Physical pages—which are also known as *page frames*—can be allocated to a program wherever unused pages happen to be in physical memory. Thus, the physical memory allocated to a running program is *non-contiguous*. This solves to a great extent the problem of fragmentation mentioned above, since an 'empty'—i.e. unallocated—page frame anywhere in memory can be allocated to any program that needs a page.

It is important to note that—in terms of their inputs and outputs—the *memory management* mechanisms of Figs. 9.4 and 9.5 are identical. Both take as input the logical address, provide as output the corresponding physical address, and raise invalid access exception if the input logical address is illegal. The difference between the two mechanisms is that one implements partitioned memory using contiguous blocks, while the other implements non-contiguous allocation using fixed size pages. Thus the two mechanisms support multiprogramming in two different ways.

Recall that, in the case of base and limit registers of Fig. 9.4, it is necessary to re-initialise these two hardware registers when the processor switches, say, from running program A to running program B. In other words, the base and limit address values of each running program must be maintained, and loaded into base and limit registers when the program begins—or resumes—execution on the processor. As we saw, this work is done by the operating system using privileged instructions of the processor.

In an exactly analogous manner, and for exactly the same reasons, the page map information for each running program must be maintained, and loaded into the hardware page map table shown in Fig. 9.5 when the program begins—or resumes—execution on the processor. As mentioned above, this work can only be done by the operating system using privileged instructions.

9.5 PRINCIPLE OF VIRTUAL MEMORY

As a challenge to their ingenuity—and also to gain an edge in market competition—computer system designers are always seeking ways to squeeze more performance out of a system. Whenever some resource in a system is seen to be underutilised, system designers immediately start asking themselves how to better utilise the resource, and thereby perhaps obtain better performance out of the system.

The techniques of *multiprogramming* and *non-contiguous memory allocation* provide better utilisation of main memory, and thereby also better utilisation of the processor and I/O resources. This is typical in a complex system: better resource utilisation in one sub-system may also lead to better resource utilisation in another sub-system.

But designers saw that more is possible. As early as in the 1970s, computer system designers saw that there is yet another important way in which main memory utilisation can be improved. The technique they developed is based on the following observations:

1. Instruction execution times in a processor are of the order of nanoseconds, while typical program execution times may run into seconds, minutes, or much longer time intervals. Somewhere between these two vastly different time-scales lie the access times of secondary storage devices, which are in the range of about ten milliseconds*.
2. Say a program runs on a computer system for a few seconds, a few minutes, or even longer. When we consider the behavior of such a program over a time-scale which is of the order of tens or even hundreds of milliseconds, we find that the program does not make references to its entire logical address space. Rather, over such time intervals, the program makes references only to some *localised* portions of memory locations in its logical address space.

   This property of running programs is known as *locality of program references*. It can be considered a 'natural' property of real-life programs, since it seems to be related closely to the way in which we design and write programs to solve computational problems.
3. In view of the previous two observations, a memory management technique can be developed with the following aim:

   > Over time periods which are of the order of tens of milliseconds, or preferably even longer, we hold in main memory only the portions of the logical address space of a running program which are actually being referenced by it.

Note that, if this strategy is adopted, then the main memory does not hold the entire logical address space of a running program—but only the portions of it being referenced by the program over a period of time. When reference is made by the running program to a logical address which is not available in main memory, the portion containing it must be brought in from secondary storage. The entire logical address space of a running program is maintained only in secondary storage—and portions brought in and out of main memory as required.

The strategy outlined in (3) is said to provide a computer system with *virtual memory*, since it allows the total extent of logical address space of all running programs to exceed the amount of main memory available on the system.

As a simple example, assume that ten programs are running on a system, with a total logical address space of about two hundred megabytes. With virtual memory, these ten programs can run on the system in multiprogramming mode even if the main memory available is less than two hundred megabytes—provided of course that this amount of space is reserved on secondary storage for the purpose. In this sense, therefore, space on secondary storage is providing 'virtual' memory on the system—while the real, physical main memory available is smaller in size.

Of course, the system performs additional work in transferring portions of running programs between virtual memory and main memory. However, since main memory is thereby better utilised, a higher degree of multiprogramming is made possible. The nett result is that—if the right balance is struck between these factors—overall system utilisation, and in particular processor utilisation, improves significantly.

An additional benefit of virtual memory comes into play when programs become very large, and consist of many commands, options and operating modes—not all of which are used by every user.

---

*Instruction execution times and storage access times are much faster today than they were in the 1970s. However, the basic argument made here was also valid back then.

For example, a word processor program may have a total size of, say, fifty megabytes. If the entire program is to be loaded into main memory, the loading process itself may take a few seconds—which may be unacceptable if the system is to provide quick responses to user commands.

With a virtual memory system, only that portion of the word processor program is first loaded into main memory which shows the initial screen and command menu; the word processor can begin execution with only these portions in main memory. Other parts of the program are loaded into main memory only when they are required, thus reducing the demand on main memory, and at the same time making the system more responsive.

At this stage, the student should understand clearly the distinction between:

a. an executable program—such as a word processor or a web browser program, and
b. the virtual memory image of the logical address space of a running program.

An executable program resides in the *file system* created in secondary storage, and thus has a name and other attributes of a file. The image of a running program, on the other hand, remains in virtual memory only as long as the program runs, and is not visible to the user as part of the file system. If a user opens a web browser thrice, for example, each running instance of the browser creates its own image in virtual memory, but there is only one copy of its program file in the file system.

9.6 VIRTUAL MEMORY WITH PAGING

As we saw in the previous section, the concept of virtual memory requires that only the portions of a running program 'currently in use' need to be loaded into main memory. It may be recalled from Section 6.9 that a similar idea is also exploited in the design of cache memory. Of course, the similarity should not be carried too far, because the two techniques apply to different levels in the memory hierarchy.

To implement the idea of virtual memory, the following questions must be addressed:

1. How do we define 'portions of a running program'?
2. How does the system determine which portions are 'currently in use'?
3. What are the implications of this design on the logical to physical address translation scheme, such as the one illustrated in Fig. 9.5?

Recall from Section 9.4 the technique of non-contiguous memory allocation based on fixed size memory pages. We shall see that answers to the above questions can be developed in a logical and fairly simple manner if the virtual memory system is also based on the use of fixed size pages and non-contiguous allocation.

If such a system is designed, 'portions of a running program' currently in use become simply the set of *logical* pages currently in use. Recall from Example 9.3 and Fig. 9.5 that the logical page number referenced by a running program is obtained simply as the higher order bits of the referenced logical memory address.

The set of logical pages of a running program currently in use is known as the *working set* of the program. As long as the working set of a running program is available in main memory, the program can run on the processor. But the working set of a program changes with time, and therefore occasionally—but we hope not too frequently!—the running program does reference a logical page which is not available in main memory.

In the mechanism of Fig. 9.5, such a 'missing page' event generates a hardware exception known as a *page fault*. At this stage, the running program is 'suspended' by the operating system, while it arranges to fetch the required page from secondary storage. When the required page is available in main memory, the suspended program is once again ready to resume execution on the processor.

Example 9.4

Let the hundred logical pages being used by a particular running program be numbered 0, 1, 2 ... up to 99. Over a period of time, the program makes the following twenty references to its logical pages, in the order shown:

0, 1, 2, 21, 22, 1, 2, 21, 52, 53, 1, 61, 53, 1, 2, 61, 1, 71, 61, 72

Suppose that the program has been allocated six page frames in main memory to hold its logical pages 'currently in use'. At the end of the twenty references shown, the six most recently used logical pages of the program are: 53, 1, 2, 61, 71 and 72*. Thus only these six pages would be in main memory at the end the twenty references shown.

Now suppose the twenty first reference made by the program is to logical page number 81. Since this page is not available in main memory, the attempted reference to it will generate a page fault. In response, one of the six logical pages in main memory must be replaced by the required page coming in from secondary storage, which is page 81.

We see that the logical pages required by a program are brought in 'on demand'—i.e. when the program generates a page fault on a required page. This mechanism of bringing in required pages from secondary storage is therefore known as *demand paging*.

Conversely, a mechanism is also required to free up physical pages in memory—i.e. page frames—to make room for incoming pages demanded by a running program. Naturally, the aim should be to remove from main memory those pages which are not likely to be used by a running program. But the difficult question here is:

How does the system know which pages of a running program are not likely to be used? This question is the converse of question (2) listed above—and it needs to be answered as well, since we have only a finite number of page frames to load incoming pages.

The system designers must rely on a 'rule of thumb' to answer this question. Broadly, this so-called *page replacement algorithm* is based on removing from main memory either (a) a page which is not among the recently used pages, or (b) a page which has not been frequently used in the recent past. In either case, the technique must be carefully designed so as to minimise its overhead on the system.

The concepts of *working set* and *demand paging*, with a suitable *page replacement algorithm*, address the questions (1) and (2) listed above. Question (3) pertains to the translation required from logical address to physical address. For this, the page map table mechanism shown in Fig. 9.5 can once again be used, with some enhancement.

If a logical page is available in main memory, the page map table provides its physical address, exactly as shown. However, if a logical page is not available in main memory—i.e. a *page fault* occurs—the page map table provides its address in secondary storage. The operating system then arranges

*In each such instance, the student is encouraged to verify the statement made in the text, using one or two steps of simple reasoning.

to bring the required page into main memory, after freeing up a page frame for it by using the page replacement algorithm.

Thus we see that the basic page map table mechanism of Fig. 9.5—designed to support page-based non-contiguous memory allocation—can be adapted to support a page-based virtual memory system. Certainly the servicing of page faults places an additional overhead on the system; but as long as the frequency of page faults is not too high, the overall system throughput improves.

In a computer system with multiprogramming, it is necessary also to provide for two or more running programs to *share* a part of their logical address space. If three running programs, for example, are just different 'instances' of the same web browser, then they can share the program code part of their address space, while of course maintaining their distinct data spaces. Some applications may also require that two or more running programs share some part of their data spaces.

In a scheme based on fixed size pages—with or without virtual memory—such sharing can be provided in units of pages. Whenever a page is to be shared between multiple programs, the corresponding physical page appears in the page map table of each of the programs, as illustrated in Fig. 9.6. If such a page is to be made *read-only*, or *execute-only*, that can also be achieved by setting the appropriate flags in the page map table.

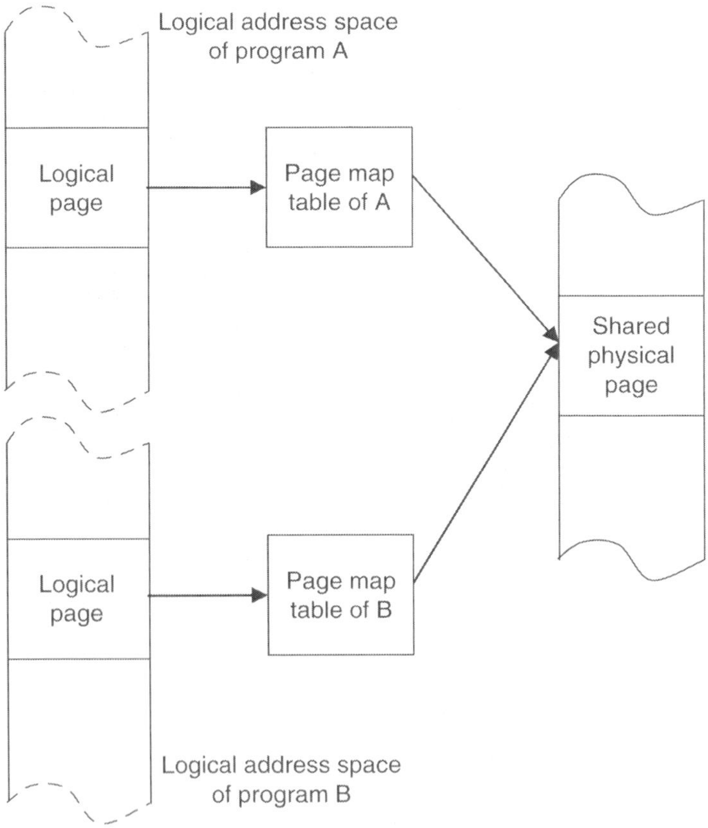

Fig. 9.6 **Sharing of a physical page between two running programs**

Thus we see that the general mechanism of paging can support virtual memory, sharing of pages between running programs, and also page-wise access protection, i.e. *read*, *write* and/or *execute* access per page. A page fault or any form of access violation is detected in hardware, for appropriate action to be taken by the operating system. The hardware making up these functions is very closely associated with the processor, and is known as the *memory management unit*. One possible way to place this unit in relation to the processor and main memory—or cache memory—is illustrated in Fig. 9.7.

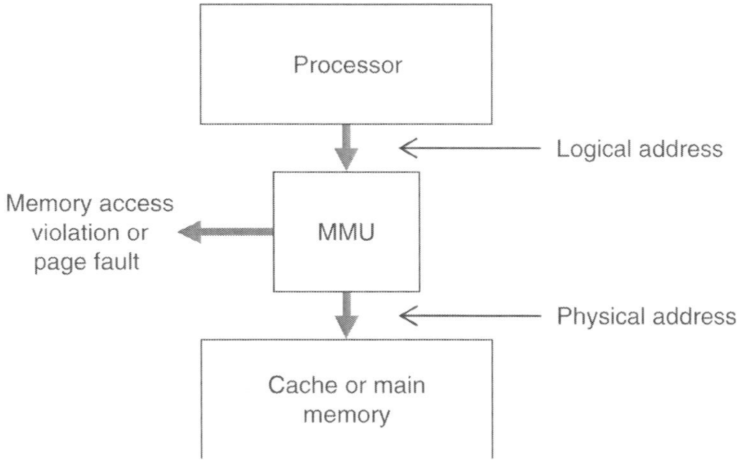

Fig. 9.7 **Role of memory management unit**

9.7 SEGMENTED LOGICAL ADDRESS SPACE

Relatively large and complex applications—such as, for example, financial accounting for a large corporation—are developed not in the form of one program, but as several independently running programs interacting with each other and with the users. The running programs interact with each other either by (a) sharing code and data, or by (b) sending and receiving *messages* to and from each other.

When such applications are to be designed and developed, it becomes immensely helpful to be able to provide the logical address space of a running program not as a single, linear sequence of N bytes, addressed from 0 to $N - 1$, but as several independent *segments*, each of which is a linear sequence of bytes.

This concept is depicted schematically in Fig. 9.8, which shows the logical address space of a program as being made up of three segments, numbered 0, 1 and 2. Each segment is a linear sequence of bytes, from 0 to $N_k - 1$, where we are using subscript k as segment number, so that here $k = 0, 1, 2$, and the size of segment number k is N_k.

Clearly, to refer to any memory location within the logical address space of a running program, we must now specify (i) the segment to which the memory location belongs, and (ii) the offset of the memory location within the segment, considering as usual that each segment starts from its own offset 0.

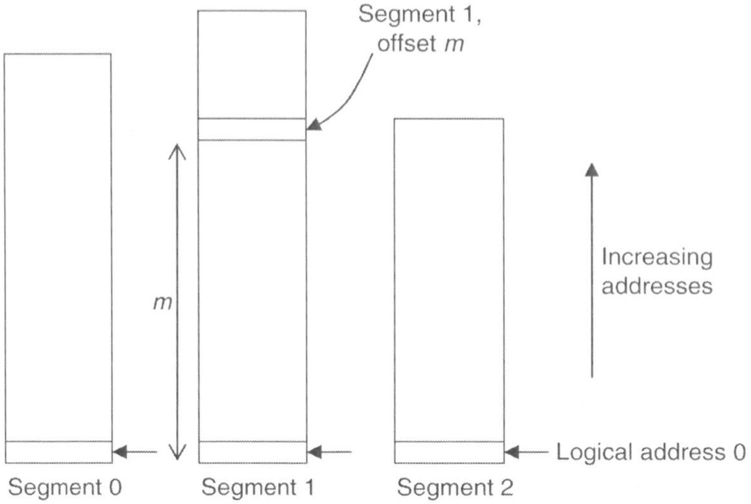

Fig. 9.8 **Segmented logical address space of a single program**

In other words, the logical address of any memory location is now split into two parts, in the form:

```
segment number : offset within segment
```

This is depicted in Fig. 9.8 for a memory location at offset *m* within segment 1.

Of course, the concept of segmented logical address space cannot be implemented without appropriate hardware support in the processor and the memory management unit. A simple and hypothetical implementation of segmented logical address space is described in Example 9.5.

Example 9.5

Assume that a processor provides for segmented memory, in which every logical address is made up of an 8-bit segment number and a 24-bit offset within segment. Thus, the size of the two-part logical address is 32 bits. The maximum number of segments a running program can address is $2^8 = 256$, with each segment limited to $2^{24} = 16$ megabytes.

Each memory reference in the program—for load/store, conditional or unconditional jump, or function call—should in theory specify the 32-bit address.

Usually, however, for ease of programming, provision is made in the machine instruction set for common types of memory references which do not require a separate segment number. This is achieved by providing within the processor special *segment registers* to hold the starting addresses of commonly used segments.

Suppose, for example, that a *code segment register* holds the starting address of the segment which has program code. Then so-called *intra*-segment jumps and function calls within this segment do not need to specify separately the 8-bit segment number, since the target addresses are already implied to be the current code segment.

Similar arrangement can be made for references to the *data* segment and the *stack* segment. Such an enhancement can be designed for the processor *NICE* which we are using in Chapters 4 and 5, without making any changes in the basic instruction set shown in Table 5.1.

Often, the techniques of paging and virtual memory are combined with the concept of segmented logical address space. In this case, each segment must be provided with its own page map table, and the memory management unit designed accordingly.

As was mentioned at the beginning of this section, there are applications in which two or more programs may need to *share* a segment, which must therefore be included in the logical address space of each sharing program. Now we can easily see how this may be achieved—basically, each such program sharing the segment must use the page map table of that segment. And memory protection can be provided on segment-wise basis, by providing appropriate *read*, *write* and *execute* flags per segment.

9.8 ASSOCIATIVE MEMORY

In Section 3.8, we discussed the most commonly used random access organisation of a memory element, employing separate address lines and data lines. Main memory today is almost invariably made byte addressable—which means that at every address in main memory we read or write one byte; of course main memory is usually designed so that multiple bytes can be read or written in one cycle. The twin concepts of (i) *memory address*, and (ii) *data* stored at the address are central to main memory organisation.

For certain specialised functions within a computer system, a fundamentally different type of memory element is required, which is *content addressable* or *associative**. Data in such a memory element is located not by its address, but by a part of the content stored in the memory element itself. The principle of such a memory element is illustrated schematically in Fig. 9.9.

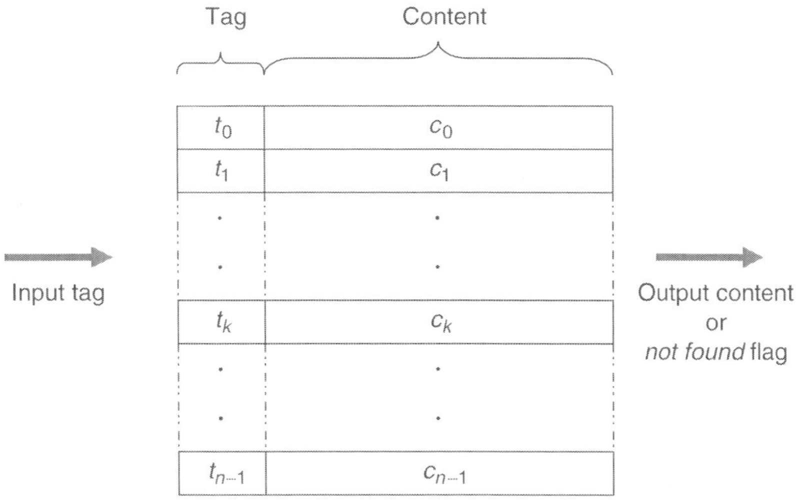

Fig. 9.9 Principle of associative memory

*In the human mind, recall of information or knowledge or memories happens on the basis of *associations* made by the mind between such items. The ability to make such associations is a key aspect of human intelligence.

In the figure, we have shown an associative memory having n locations. The data stored in each location is made up of two parts: *tag* and *content*. For convenience, in the figure we have identified these two parts as t_k and c_k, for $0 \leq k \leq n - 1$.

To locate a particular item in such an associative memory, it is supplied with the *tag value* being sought. This tag value is 'matched in parallel'—i.e. in one clock cycle—with all the tag values stored. If a match is found, the corresponding content is read out and placed on memory output; otherwise, a hardware flag *not found* is raised.

Note that, with the commonly used random access memory, the search for a matching tag would require looking *sequentially* at the n tag values stored—which requires on average $n/2$ accesses to memory and comparisons. With associative memory, this work is being done in a single clock cycle, since the comparisons are being made in parallel.

Within the processor, the management of cache memory requires such a fast search and access—so that cache content can be made available to the processor in one or two clock cycles. As we shall see below, certain types of cache memories employ an associative memory for fast access to cache content. For essentially similar reasons, associative memory is also used for access to page map tables in a virtual memory system.

9.9 CACHE MEMORY ORGANISATION

In Section 6.9 we saw that, for faster access by the processor to main memory content, it is necessary to provide the system with a faster but smaller cache memory. We saw that cache memory serves to bridge the relatively large speed mismatch between processor and main memory. In this section, we shall take a slightly more detailed look at how the cache memory sub-system is organised.

Recall from Section 6.9 that any running program exhibits both *temporal locality* and *spatial locality* in the memory references it makes. To take advantage of spatial locality, the cache block size is taken as a multiple of word size, so that when a byte or word is brought into cache, its neighboring bytes and words also become available.

When the processor makes an access to a byte or word in main memory, the required byte or word must first be sought in the cache. This implies that the memory address of the accessed byte or word must be *mapped* to a location in cache memory. The simplest way to map a memory address to a location in cache is known as *direct mapping*.

The following example shows how a cache memory can be organised using such *direct mapping*.

Example 9.6

Let us assume that a processor with 24-bit logical address is provided with cache memory of size 4 kilobytes, with a cache block size of 16 bytes.

With a cache block size of 16 bytes and a cache size of 4 kilobytes, there are a total of $4096/16 = 256$ blocks in the cache. Since $16 = 2^4$ and $256 = 2^8$, the lowest order 4 bits of logical memory address are used to select a byte within a cache block, and the next higher order 8 bits are used to select a cache block, as seen in part (a) of Fig. 9.10.

The remaining higher order $24 - 8 - 4 = 12$ bits of the memory address are used as a *tag*. The use of this 12-bit tag can be understood as follows.

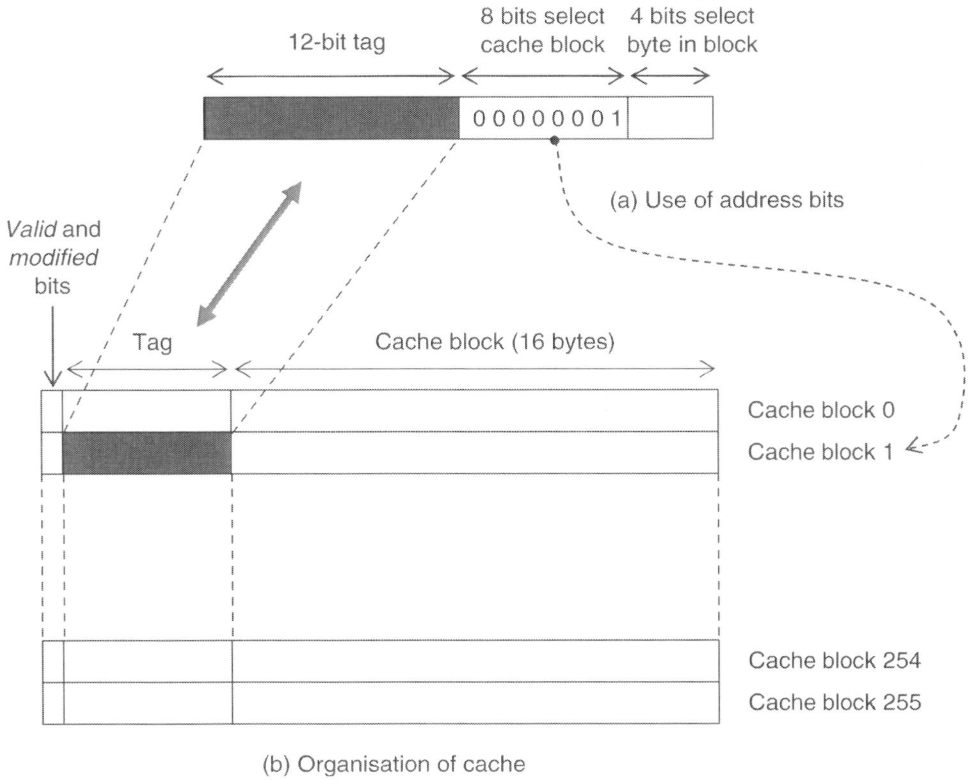

Fig. 9.10 **Direct-mapped cache of Example 9.6**

The logical address space of 2^{24} = 16 megabytes of this processor consists of $2^{24}/2^4 = 2^{20}$ blocks, each of size 16 bytes. When one of these blocks is brought in from main memory to cache, which one of the 256 blocks does it occupy in the cache?

The answer is: Under *direct mapping*, the cache block occupied by an incoming memory block is specified uniquely by the 8 bits which select cache block, as seen in part (a) of the figure. If we label the 24 bits of the address as a_{23}, a_{22}, ... a_2, a_1, a_0 in the usual way, then part (a) of the figure shows that:

4 bits $a_3..a_0$ select a byte within a cache block,
8 bits $a_{11}..a_4$ select a cache block, and
12 bits $a_{23}..a_{12}$ serve as tag.

In our case, the logical address space consists of 2^{20} blocks, each of 16 bytes. Therefore, with 2^8 = 256 blocks in the cache, the ratio of memory blocks to cache blocks is $2^{20}/2^8 = 2^{12}$. In other words, there is a *many-to-one mapping* between memory blocks and cache blocks. Therefore the 12-bit tag in each cache block is used to indicate which particular memory block—if any—resides in the cache block at a given time.

Accordingly, when a memory block is brought into cache, the tag part of its address is also stored in the cache—as indicated in part (b) of Fig. 9.10.

When a required memory byte or word is sought in cache, the tag part of its logical address is matched against the tag part stored in cache. This has been indicated in Fig. 9.10 (b) by means of the thick arrow between the tag part of the logical address and the stored tag value in block 1 of the cache memory. The two 12-bit quantities being matched are shown using lightly shaded rectangles.

We have assumed here that the 8 bits of cache block number of part (a) point to block 1 of the cache—as indicated by the curved, dashed arrow on the right going from part (a) to part (b), pointing to cache block 1. Accordingly, these 8 bits of the address are shown to have binary value 00000001.

If the referenced tag in the logical address and the stored tag match, it means that the memory block containing the referenced byte or word is indeed present in that cache block. Therefore such a match of tag values indicates a *cache hit.*

If these two tag values do not match, it means that the memory block containing the referenced byte or word is not present in the cache—since this is the only possible cache block it can occupy. In this case, therefore, we have a *cache miss.*

When a system is first powered up, or after a hardware reset, the cache will not contain any blocks from main memory. Therefore, in such a state, all the cache blocks should be judged to be *invalid*, regardless of their stored tag values. A single bit flag known as *valid bit* is therefore provided with each cache block, as indicated in part (b) of the figure. These bits are initialised to all '0's—i.e. initially all cache blocks are set to be invalid. When a cache block is invalid, any reference to it generates a cache miss.

Also present with each cache block is a *modified bit*, indicating whether the block content has been modified since it was brought into cache from main memory. Clearly, if the block content has not been modified, then the block can be freed up when required without writing the content back to main memory.

The above example illustrates the working of a simple *direct-mapped* cache. Recall that, in this example, 2^{12} memory blocks were mapped to the same cache block. With a larger address size, this number would be even larger. When a program makes references to two or more memory blocks mapping to the same cache block, repeated cache misses are generated—since, at one time, only one of these memory blocks can be in cache.

So-called *set-associative mapping* of cache blocks is designed to overcome this weakness of direct mapped cache memories—but at the expense of a more complex design. In a set-associative cache, typically two or four candidate cache blocks are provided—any one of which a memory block can occupy. Example 9.7 below illustrates this concept for the same cache memory that we studied in the previous example.

Example 9.7

Consider the cache memory of the previous example, but now re-designed with *two-way set associative mapping.* Basically, this means that there are two candidate blocks in cache for each 16-byte block in memory to be brought in.

This arrangement is illustrated in Fig. 9.11. The cache memory in this figure is arranged as 128 *lines*, each of which contains two cache blocks. Each block is accompanied by its valid bit, modified bit, and a tag, as was done in the direct-mapped cache of the previous example.

With this arrangement, line 0 of the cache contains blocks 0 and 1; line 1 of the cache contains blocks 2 and 3, and so on. The total number of cache blocks is still 256, and the total cache size is still 4096 bytes, exactly as in the previous example.

With a 24-bit logical address, we must now determine which line in the cache would a given memory block occupy. Since there are 128 lines, a 7-bit field in the logical address will select a cache line. Therefore, instead of the eight bits which selected a block in the previous example, we now have seven bits which select a cache line.

This means that the 24-bit logical address now gets divided up as: 13-bit tag, 7 bits to select a cache line, and (as before) 4 bits to locate a byte within a block.

To determine whether a referenced memory byte or word is available in cache, we must now match the higher order 13 bits of the logical address with both the tags stored in a cache line. In Fig. 9.11, the two tag fields of cache line 1 are shown in a light shade.

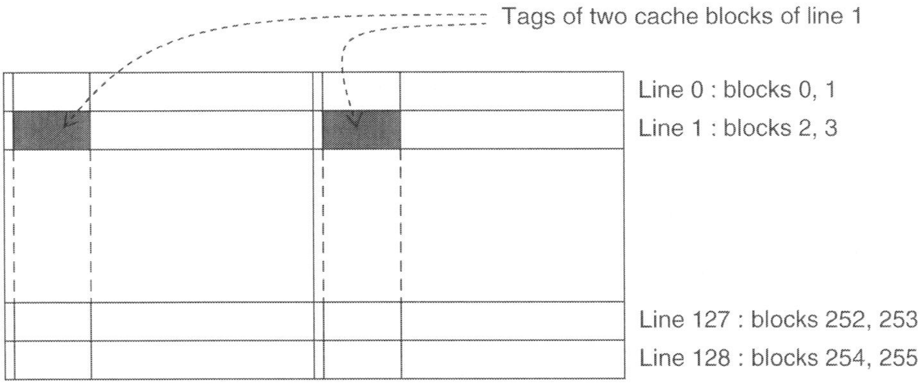

Fig. 9.11 **Two-way set-associative cache of Example 9.7**

During this operation, at most one match can occur, because we do not create two copies in the cache of any memory block. If a match does occur, the referenced memory block is available in that location; if none of the two tags match with the high order 13 bits of the memory address referenced, we have a *cache miss*.

The cache memory sub-system must necessarily be designed for fast operation. Therefore matching of the referenced address with the two stored tags must occur in parallel—rather than sequentially, one after the other. This means that *associative memory*, of the type discussed in the previous section, must be used in this type of cache design.

A *four-way set associative* cache is designed with a similar principle, except that there are four candidate cache blocks in every cache line, any one of which may be occupied by a memory block which maps to the line. In the above design, this would imply 64 cache lines, 6 bits of logical address to select a line, and the higher order 14 logical address bits serving as tag.

Another choice which cache memory designers must make is this: When a write operation takes place to a byte or word in cache, when does the main memory copy of the byte or word get written? Clearly, one option is to initiate the main memory write at the same time when the cache byte or word is written. A second option is to write the entire cache block back to main memory only when the block is removed from cache.

The first type of design is known as *write-through* cache, while the second type of design is known as *write-back* cache (or *deferred write*) cache.

For faster access to instructions and data, pipelined processors are usually provided with separate instruction and data caches at L1 level – i.e. on the same VLSI chip as the processor. This allows the so-called *I-cache* and *D-cache* to be operated in parallel, resulting in a smaller number of pipeline stalls caused by accesses to main memory. Also, since the processor does not modify the machine instructions executed, I-cache content does not need to be written back to main memory.

Figure 9.12 illustrates schematically the use of such a *split* L1 cache.

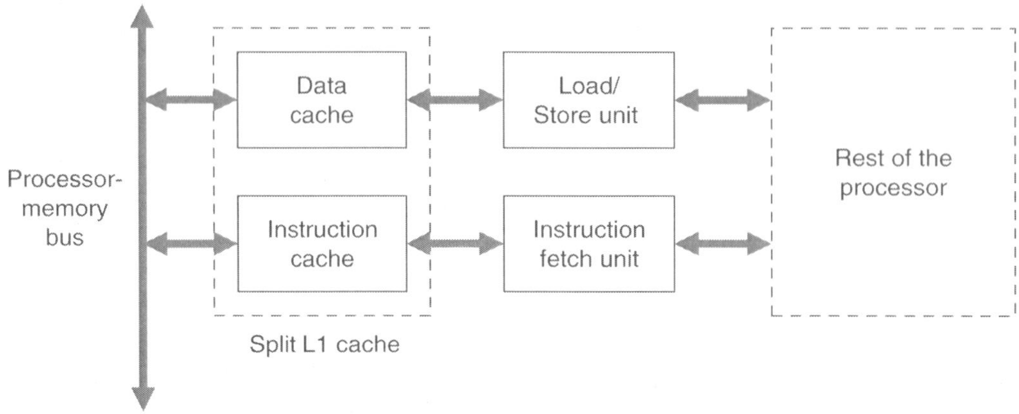

Fig. 9.12 **Use of split L1 cache**

SUMMARY

Several factors—speed of access, size, cost, power dissipation, and volatility of data—make it necessary to arrange the memory in computer system in the form of a hierarchy. Programmable registers, one or more levels of cache memory, main memory, and secondary storage make up the different layers of this hierarchy.

Most programs spend a considerable fraction of their time in performing I/O operations. For increased processor utilisation, the technique of multiprogramming is employed, which allows multiple running programs to reside in main memory and share processor time and other system resources.

For multiprogramming, the simplest memory management technique is that of creating contiguous partitions in main memory for the running programs and the operating system. Better memory utilisation—i.e. reduced fragmentation—is possible with non-contiguous allocation, using fixed size pages.

A virtual memory system makes it possible to bring only those portions of programs and data from secondary storage into main memory which are currently in use. The property of locality of references and the technique of demand paging is utilised to implement a virtual memory system. A segmented logical address space makes it possible for running programs to share memory segments, with different levels of protection for memory segments, as required for the application.

The role of memory management hardware, which is associated closely with the processor, is to provide mapping between logical and physical memory addresses, and to provide the required level of protection to memory segments or pages.

An associative memory element provides efficient content-based search for matching data. Such memory elements are used for providing fast access to data stored in cache memory and the page map tables in a virtual memory system.

The cache memory sub-system needs a mapping mechanism between memory blocks and cache blocks. Direct mapping is simpler to implement, but set-associative mapping gives better performance. Pipelined processors make use of split L1 cache for instructions and data, so as to reduce the occurrence of stalls on memory access.

REVIEW QUESTIONS

1. List the four types of memory which may be provided in a computer system. In one line each, list their functions.
2. Explain in brief why it is true to say that the operation of cache memory is transparent to the running program.
3. Speed, size and cost per bit are important characteristics of memory. How do these characteristics change as we go from the top level of memory hierarchy to its bottom level?
4. What are the typical memory speeds and sizes seen today at the top and at the bottom of memory hierarchy?
5. What is the characteristic of the 'ideal' memory for a computer system? Why is it not possible to build such a memory for a real system?
6. Given that the 'ideal' memory system is not possible, what is the design goal which must be followed for a practical memory system?
7. Over time, the behavior of a typical running program can be visualised as an alternating sequence of two types of activity, or phases. Which are these two phases?
8. In which typical situation is a processor likely to get into an idle loop? Which event would typically bring a processor out of the idle loop?
9. What is meant by 'the degree of multiprogramming' in a computer system?
10. Which is the basic performance trade-off the designers face in a computer system with multiprogramming?
11. What is meant by partitioned main memory? Which are the two parameters which specify each partition?
12. In a partitioned memory system, one particular partition starts at physical address 60000. An instruction is stored at logical address 4000 in the partition. What is the physical memory address of this instruction?
13. Using a block diagram, show the mapping from logical address to physical address in the case of partitioned memory. Include in the diagram some basic provisions for memory protection.
14. What is a privileged instruction? Why are such instructions needed on a processor?
15. What is meant by 'fragmentation of main memory'?
16. What is the meaning of a *page* in physical memory? What is the difference between a logical page and a physical page?
17. Using a block diagram, show the role of the page map table in memory management.
18. Which part of a processor implements the logical to physical translation of memory addresses?

19. What is the property of running programs known as 'locality of program references'?
20. What is the basic principle of a virtual memory system?
21. Define in one line each the terms: working set, page fault, demand paging, and page replacement strategy.
22. List the three types of access that a running program may make to a logical page.
23. What is meant by a segmented logical address space? What is the form of a logical memory address in such an address space?
24. What is the role of segment registers in a processor?
25. State the basic principle of operation of associative memory.
26. List the use of valid bit and modified bit provided with each cache block.
27. What is the advantage of set-associative mapping over direct mapping? State the difference between a cache line and a cache block.
28. State the basic difference between write-through cache and write-back cache.

EXERCISES

1. Consider once again the computer system of Example 9.1, which yields processor utilisation of 57% with degree of multiprogramming: 10. Calculate the degree of multiprogramming required if we wish to increase processor utilisation to 80%.
2. In a multiprogramming system, there are two types of programs running. Some programs are compute-bound, doing negligible input/output; it is decided to reserve 50% of processor time for these programs. Other programs are I/O-bound, spending 90% of their time doing I/O. How many of the I/O-bound programs must run on the system to ensure overall processor utilisation of 90%?
3. Recall that, in Example 9.1 and the previous two exercises, processor utilisation is calculated under the assumption that I/O-bound programs are independent of each other. In practice, to what extent is this assumption justified?

   Hint: The I/O-bound programs must contend for I/O devices and data-paths.

4. A multiprogramming system is designed with partitioned memory of the type described in Section 9.3. The total amount of memory available for user programs is 20 megabytes, divided into five partitions of size 2, 2, 4, 4 and 8 megabytes respectively. At a given time, it is required to run on the system five user programs with the following memory requirements (in megabytes): 0.75, 6.25, 4.5, 2.5 and 1.5. Would this be possible? Justify your answer in brief.
5. A multiprogramming system is designed for not-contiguous memory allocation with fixed size pages of $2^{12} = 4096$ byes, without virtual memory. The processor provides 24-bit logical memory address and 32-bit physical memory address. A program running on such a system uses 16 megabytes of memory. Calculate the size of the page map table required for this program, assuming that each entry in the table includes <u>four bits</u> for memory protection flags.

6. In a multiprogramming system, describe in brief the action that can be taken by the operating system if a running program makes an invalid memory reference.
7. In a computer system with virtual memory, memory access time is 50 nanoseconds if the page being referenced is in main memory. If a page fault occurs and the required page is to be brought in from secondary storage, the time taken is 10 milliseconds. If one page fault is generated on average for every one million (10^6) memory accesses, what is the average memory access time of this program?
8. Under a virtual memory system, a running program uses a logical address space extending to ten pages, which are numbered from 0 to 9. Over a period of time, it is found that the program makes references to six pages, in the following order:

   1, 2, 3, 4, 5, 3, 5, 4, 1, 5, 4, 3, 6, 3, 5

   ↑ Time T

   As indicated above, time T refers to a time instant immediately after the last page reference shown. At time T, order the page numbers by the criterion of recent use—i.e. from the most recently used page to the least recently used page.
9. Consider once again the 'page trace' of the previous exercise. Assume that four physical pages—i.e. page frames—are being used by the program. Since the number of pages being referenced exceeds the number of page frames available, it is clear that page faults will occur. Assuming that pages 1 to 4 are initially available in the four page frames, count the number of page faults which occur until time T. Identify any additional assumptions which you had to make to obtain this answer.
10. In a virtual memory system, to make room for an incoming page on the occurrence of a page fault, it is decided to remove a certain page P from main memory. From the page map table, it is determined that the copy of P in main memory has <u>not</u> been modified since it was brought in from secondary storage. Is it necessary to write page P back from main memory to secondary storage? Justify in brief.
11. A computer system has 32-bit logical address, with cache block size of 16 bytes and cache size 64 kilobytes. Under a direct mapping design, show how the 32 bits of logical address are used to determine the cache block number, the addressed byte within the cache block, and the tag.
12. Consider once again the computer system of the previous exercise. Assume that the cache memory has to be provided with four-way set associative mapping. Show how the 32 bits of logical address are used to determine the cache block number, the addressed byte within the cache block, and the tag.

INPUT AND OUTPUT ORGANISATION

10

10.1 INTRODUCTION

We have not had an opportunity so far to look at an essential and integral part of any computer system—its input and output facilities. A variety of input/output devices may be connected to a computer system—keyboard, mouse, display, magnetic disk, network adaptor, and so on. Clearly, no computer system can carry out a real-world task, however simple it may be, without making use of appropriate input/output (I/O) facilities.

Example 10.1

Let us consider a mobile phone handset, which has embedded within it a relatively small computer system. In fact, one may even say that the input and output facilities on this computer, combined with the right software, give it the characteristics of a mobile phone handset. How so?—a surprised student may well ask.

The keypad on the handset is an input device, while the liquid crystal display (LCD) is an output device. The microphone and the speaker are also, respectively, an input and an output device. There is also the antenna (usually not visible) through which the handset sends and receives data from the nearest 'tower', technically known as *base station.*

If the phone is equipped with a camera, then that is an input device, while a data-port for connection with a PC would have input as well as output capability.

In fact, if the battery is removed from such a handset, then most of its remaining weight would be made up of its input and output devices and the packaging. The processor and memory would be extremely small components, and the software of course would be the vital but invisible 'zero weight' element.

Even such a simple example shows that input and output devices may differ widely in terms of function, size, mode of operation, data transfer speed, power consumption, and other such characteristics. However, all devices must be connected to the processor and memory using the basic architecture outlined in Fig. 1.4.

Over the years, a few different mechanisms have been developed for connecting I/O devices to the system, and for programming input and output data transfers over the resulting connections. In this chapter, we shall discuss in some detail the basic organisation and operation of the input/output subsystem of a computer system.

10.2 INPUT/OUTPUT DEVICES AND CONTROLLERS

As we have seen in Chapter 1, an I/O device is connected to the computer system by using a *device controller*. On one side of the device controller are the address, data, and control lines of the processor, over which the processor communicates with the controller. On the other side of the device controller is the device itself, with an interconnection between the two which allows data to be transferred and control information to be passed between the controller and the device.

As we shall see in the next two chapters, I/O devices today cover a very wide range of characteristics. In particular, I/O devices may vary in terms of some or all of the following characteristics:

- Representation of data in terms of voltage, current, magnetic field, etc.,
- Speed of operation and data transfer,
- Timing and control requirement,
- Need to detect physical events—e.g. mouse clicks or key presses, and
- Need for error detection and correction.

Given such a wide range of variation, one device may need a fairly simple controller, while another may require a sophisticated controller with an embedded processor of its own. For example, a mouse is a fairly simple device, while a magnetic disk is quite a complex device. Depending on the speed of data transfer, usually a *data buffer* of appropriate size is also provided on the device controller.

On the processor side, a device controller is connected to the address, data, and control lines of the external bus (see Fig. 6.1). In addition, there is an important signal on this bus which may be sent by the device controller to the processor. This signal allows a device to *interrupt* the program running on the processor and receive service. In Section 10.4, we shall discuss the need for such a mechanism, and the way to utilise it.

For ease of understanding, we may say that: *A device controller is the device as seen by the programmer*. This is because a program running on the processor can carry out input or output on a device only through the agency of the controller—i.e. the controller 'handles' the device on behalf of the program running on the processor*.

Depending on the device, an input or output operation on it can get quite complex, especially since timing constraints must also be taken into account. For our purposes, however, we consider at first a very simple example of input operation on a device.

10.3 ACCESSING DEVICES

Recall from Section 4.8 that IN and OUT instructions can be used, respectively, to *read data in* from a selected input device, or to *write data out* to a selected output device. At the other end of the data transfer—in each of these two cases—is a processor register. The *I/O address* specified with the IN and OUT instruction selects a device.

In this way, the basic access mechanism for I/O devices was introduced in Chapter 4, along with many other issues related to programming a processor. However, a crucial point related to I/O operations was not introduced at that stage—and therefore it needs to be discussed in some detail now.

---

*Software operations specific to a device and its controller are packaged together in the form of functions in a software module usually called a *device driver* for the device.

This crucial point is that, in general, while writing a program for an input or output device, we cannot assume that the device is always *ready* for the input or output operation. A program must in general test whether a device is *ready* for input or output, before performing the required operation using an IN or OUT instruction.

This crucial feature was missing from Program 4.5, which was in fact a highly simplified version of how input and output operations are carried out.

Program 10.1 is somewhat more realistic. It reads in 100 bytes from an input device and stores them in 100 successive memory locations. But this program executes its IN instruction for data only after testing that the input device is *ready* for input.

Program 10.1

```
//
// Program to read 100 bytes from an input device and
// store them in successive memory locations starting at
// location BASE.
//
        LOAD    #0, R0      // Initialise counter R0 to 0
//
LOOP:   IN      11, R1      // Read device status from address 11
        AND     #1, R1      // Extract rightmost bit
        JZ      LOOP        // Loop if device not ready
//
        IN      10, R1      // Read data byte from device at
                            // address 10
        STOREB  BASE[R0], R1
                            // Store byte in memory location
        ADD     #1, R0      // Increment counter R0
        COMP    R0, #99     // Compare counter to 99
        JLT     LOOP        // If less, jump to Loop
//
DONE:  HALT                 // Halt the program
```

How does Program 10.1 test for *device ready*?—By checking the contents of the *device status register*. Here, we have assumed that the rightmost bit in this device status register informs us whether the device is ready for input.

We have assumed that the status register of the input device of Program 10.1 is available at address 11, while—just as in the simpler Program 4.5 seen earlier—the data register of the device is available at address 10. This means that the I/O addresses on this system are being decoded in the following manner:

When an input instruction IN specifies address 11, the processor places this address on the address lines of the external bus. Using the signal *memory-or-I/O*, the processor also indicates that an I/O operation is in progress, as opposed to a main memory operation (recall Section 4.8). Assume that, in general, several input and output device controllers are connected to the system, at different I/O addresses.

The address decoders on all the device controllers receive these address bits in parallel. However, the input device of Program 10.1 is the only one which is selected by the decoder output corresponding to address 11—and specifically it is the *status register* of the device which is selected by this decoder output. In this sense, we can say that this status register is *located* at I/O address 11.

Similarly, when an input instruction specifies address 10, the processor puts out this address on the address lines. In this case, it is the *data register* of the same device which is selected by the decoder output corresponding to address 10—and we can say that the data register of this device is located at I/O address 10.

Thus the input device of Program 10.1 occupies two locations in the I/O address map of the processor—address 10 for its data register, and address 11 for its status register. This situation is depicted schematically in Fig. 10.1.

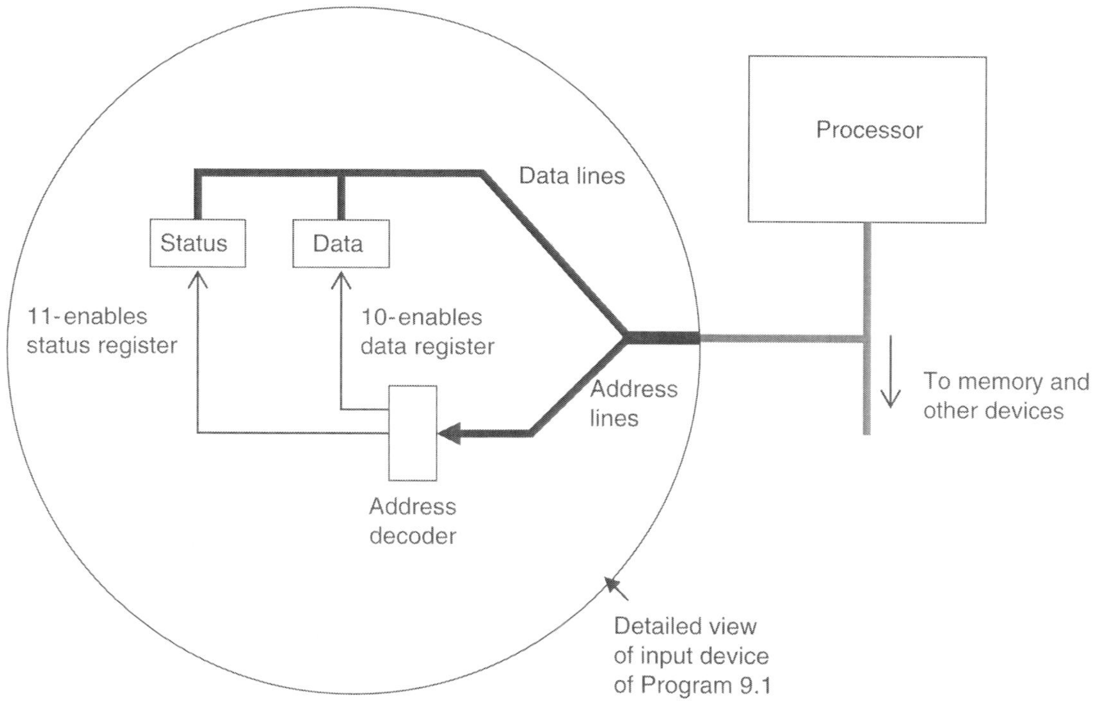

Fig. 10.1 **Input device with data register and status register**

Of course it needs to be appreciated that the physical input device—which may be a keypad or a mouse, for example—is not in fact seen in Fig. 10.1. What is seen instead is 'the programmer's view' of the device—which in this particular case consists only of (i) the two registers at the indicated addresses, and (ii) the way in which these register contents are to be interpreted by the program.

Note 10.1

We see here that a programmer's view of an input device—or any other device, for that matter—is usually very different from a user's view of the device. This difference of perception may be called an *abstraction*, in the sense that the programmer really sees only an abstract version of the device, which in Program 10.1 consists of two specific registers located at two I/O addresses.

The actual physical design of a keyboard or a mouse, for example, will involve many issues such as ease of use, properties of materials, durability, and so on. None of these important issues are relevant to the programmer—just as it is not necessary for the device designer to know which processor instructions and I/O addresses the programmer will use to access the data or status registers.

The device designer specifies the *I/O interface* for the device, and the programmer makes use of this interface to correctly program operations on the device.

In general, when a system is partitioned into two subsystems, each subsystem makes use of the functionality provided by the other—without becoming aware of how the other subsystem is in fact designed and built. The *interface specification* between the two subsystems allows them to work together. This point was also discussed briefly in Section 1.5, since it plays a key role in the design of any computer system.

We can even say that the *interface specification* brings two subsystems together—but only after separating them by defining the boundary between them. This is a fundamental principle in managing the enormous complexity of modern computer systems, and the reason why interface standards play a crucial role in such systems.

Figure 10.2 is the flow chart corresponding to Program 10.1. In this flow chart, we see an *inner loop* within the outer *main loop* of the program. The outer loop is executed once for every byte read in. The inner loop has the function of forcing the processor to *do nothing*—i.e. simply *wait*—until the input device is ready for a byte to be read in. For this reason, a loop such as the inner loop of this program is usually called a *wait loop* or *idle loop*.

Of course there is something not quite right here. Why must the processor *do nothing* until the input device is ready? What happens if the input device fails—or if the user operating that device is enjoying a cup of tea? Isn't there something else the processor can do while the device is taking its time to be *ready*?

In general, in a computer system we would not prefer to let the processor remain idle for any length of time. This would mean that we are not making full use of the processor, or perhaps that we have selected a processor which is more powerful—and therefore more expensive—than what is required for the application.

Therefore we must conclude that a mechanism is needed for a device to 'take the initiative' and inform the processor that it is *ready* for a data transfer or another operation. This would free the processor from having to constantly check device status in a *wait loop*, as in Program 10.1. Such a mechanism, which is in fact crucial to the working of any computer system, is indeed provided on all processors, and is known as the *interrupt mechanism*. We shall discuss this mechanism in Section 10.4.

How would Program 10.1 change if we were writing out 100 bytes to an output device, rather than reading in 100 bytes from an input device?

The answer is: Not much at all! The device would still have status and data registers, which should be assumed to be at different I/O addresses than those used in Program 10.1. The outer loop and the inner wait loop of the program would not change. Within the outer loop, we would first load a memory byte into a register, and then send it out to the device using OUT instruction, with the appropriate address.

Thus we may say in fact that there is no fundamental difference between programming an input device and programming an output device. The following is an example of the use of *ready* bit in the case of two familiar devices.

Example 10.2

a. The keyboard—or keypad in a mobile handset—is an input device. The *ready* bit within the keyboard controller would signify that the user has pressed the next key since data from the previous key pressed was read in by the program. In the absence of such a mechanism, the program may make mistakes such as: (i) reading in the same data multiple times, even if the user presses a key only once, or (ii) failing to read data from keys pressed, if the user presses keys in rapid succession.
b. The *dot matrix printer* (see Section 12.6) is an output device which can be used, for example, to print railway tickets, cinema tickets, and bank passbook entries. The *ready* bit in such a printer would signify that the previous line of output has been printed, so that the next line of output can be sent by the program to the printer.

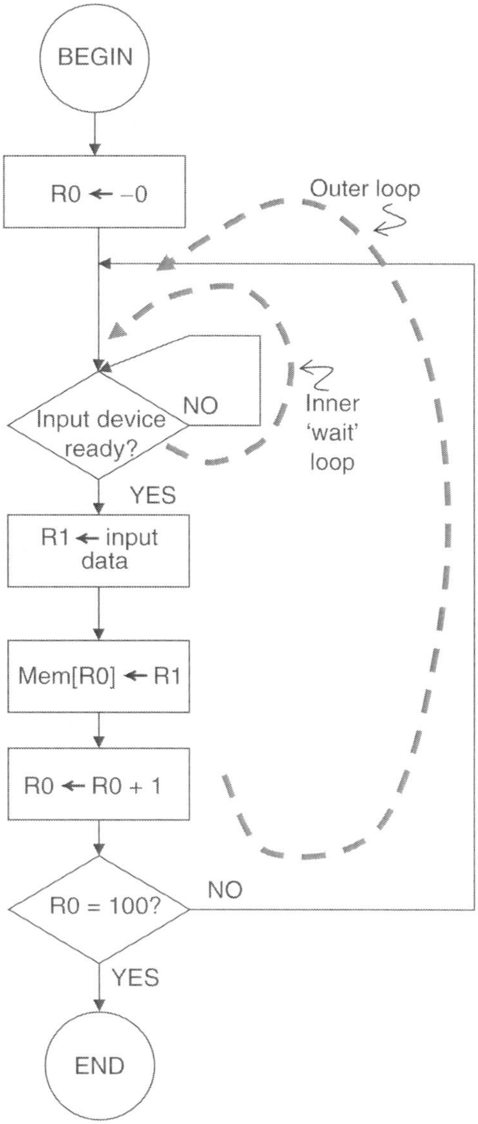

Fig. 10.2 **Flow chart of program to input data from device**

10.4 DEVICE STATUS AND CONTROL

Let us consider carefully any one of the two devices of Example 10.2. Suppose that the keyboard is *ready* with the next byte of data for the program. As we saw, after testing for *device status*, the program reads in the next byte. What effect should this action by the program have on the *ready* bit in the keyboard controller?

Or, in other words, which is the event that must cause the *ready* bit to be reset?

The answer is: When the program reads in a byte from the device controller, the *ready* bit should be reset by the controller—so that the cycle can be repeated for the next byte transfer from the keyboard to the program.

Thus the *ready* bit which we have introduced in the device controller should be seen as making up a part of—or all of—*device status*. In the keyboard controller, when the user presses a key, the *ready* bit is set; when the program reads in the byte corresponding to the key pressed, the *ready* bit is reset.

More generally, *device status* in a controller will also include information about any errors or fault conditions which might have occurred in device operation. When a user tries to write to a write-protected storage device, for example, the controller must record this as an error condition, which must be reported to the user.

In addition to *device status*, many input and output devices have functions or modes of operation which need to be controlled or selected—i.e. 'set'—by the programmer. The few examples below may help to make this point clear.

Example 10.3

a. On a PC keyboard, if a user keeps the key '*n*' pressed, for example, without releasing it, the controller generates the character '*n*' repeatedly until the key is released. In an editor program, one then sees '*nnnnnn* ...'. This is known as the *auto repeat* feature of the keyboard, and it is quite convenient at times, as when we wish to enter a long string of hyphens. But there are times when a user may wish to turn this feature off. So the *keyboard controller* provides a way for a program to turn *auto repeat* OFF or ON.
b. Most device controllers have *data buffers* in the data path from the device to the processor and memory (see Fig. 1.4). Such a *data buffer* is provided to allow for mismatch in speed, timing, or another characteristic between the source and destination of data. A program to operate a buffered device controller sometimes needs to *clear the buffer* before performing another operation. Here *clear buffer* would be a command which the program issues to the device controller using an OUT instruction.
c. For sending data out on a communication link, or receiving data from such a link, the programmer has to set parameters such as (i) *speed* of data transfer, and (ii) *parity*, which is used to detect errors. These parameters are set by issuing appropriate commands to the communication device controller, using OUT instructions.
d. The controller for a magnetic disk provides commands for operating the disk—e.g. the *seek* command to move the *read/write head* to a specified radial position over the rotating magnetic medium (see Section 12.2). The command is issued by the program running on the processor, using one or more OUT instructions. Control electronics within the device then move the read/write head to the specified radial position.

These examples have one feature in common: At times, the program must send operating parameters and/or commands to a device controller, to achieve desired operation from the device. This is done by sending relevant parameters or commands to the so-called *device control register(s)* in the controller, using appropriate OUT instructions.

We have already seen that, in general, an input or output device would be provided with registers for *input data*, *output data* and *device status*. Now we see that we would also need another register—or registers—for *device control*.

We may therefore summarise by saying that, depending on its functions and complexity, a device controller would in general have some or all of the following registers and data buffers associated with it:

Input data register or buffer,
Output data register or buffer,
Status register(s), and
Control register(s).

These registers and buffers take up an appropriate number of I/O addresses—just as we saw that the input device of Program 10.1 (shown in Fig. 10.1) takes up I/O addresses 10 and 11 for its data and status registers, respectively.

10.5 INTERRUPT MECHANISM AND HANDLING

In Program 10.1, we take care not to read the data in from the device until repeated checks on device status indicate that the device is *ready*. These repeated checks on device status are performed in the *wait loop*, which is repeated below for convenience:

```
LOOP:  IN     11, R1    // Read status of input device
       AND    #1, R1    // Extract rightmost bit
       JZ     LOOP      // Loop if device not ready
```

A processor in a *wait loop* (or *idle loop*) is in effect doing nothing. Therefore—to avoid having to thus waste processor cycles—a mechanism is required for an input or output device to *signal* the processor that it is *ready*, or that the previous operation it was performing is completed.

Such a mechanism is indeed provided on all processors, and it is known as the *interrupt mechanism*.

An *interrupt* is basically a signal which a device controller sends to the processor. At a minimum, what is needed for this signal is a single-bit input line from the device controller to the processor, as depicted in Fig. 10.3. Value '0' on this line would indicate that the device is not signaling an interrupt to the processor, while value '1' would indicate that it is signaling an interrupt.

The important question now is: What does the processor do if a device is signaling an interrupt?

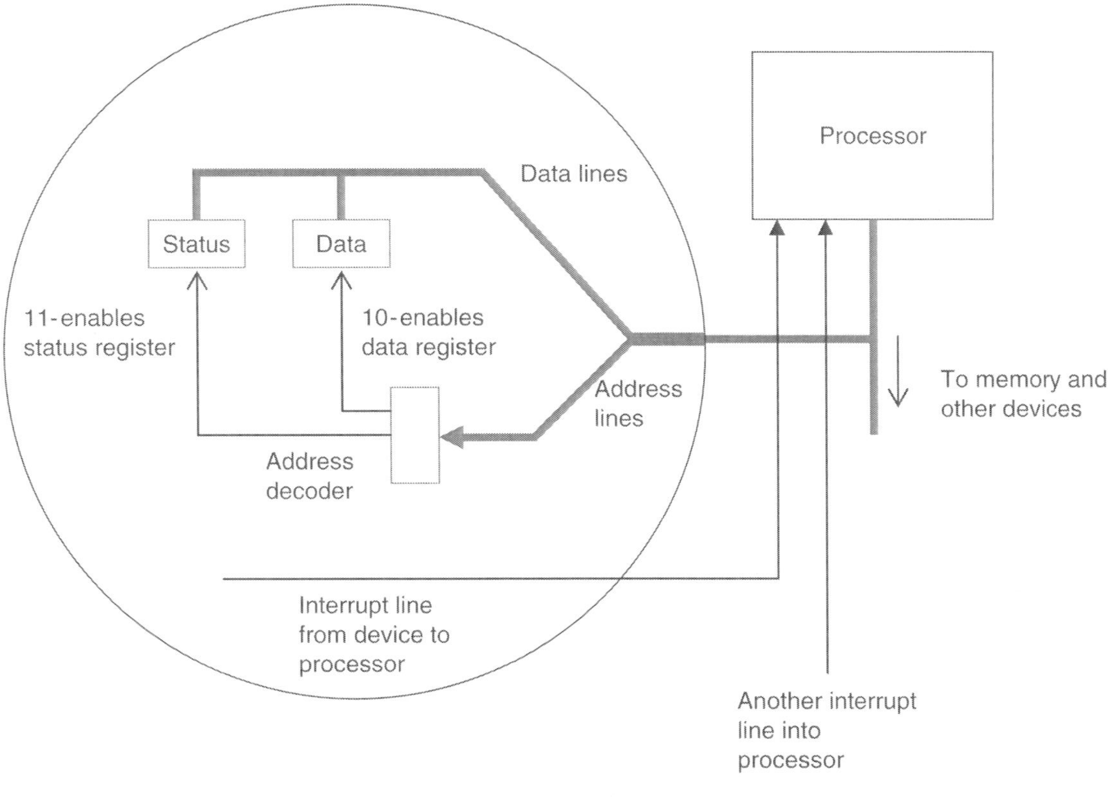

Fig. 10.3 **Input device which can signal an interrupt to the processor**

Let us assume that the processor is running a program P when a device D signals an interrupt. The meaning of the interrupt is that device D needs attention, and that therefore the running of program P must be temporarily interrupted, with the understanding that it should be resumed after device D receives its due attention—or, in other words, when the interrupt from device D has been *serviced*.

Somewhere in memory lies another program, let us call it ISRD—i.e. *interrupt service routine* for device D—which is capable of responding correctly to the interrupt signaled by device D. What is needed therefore is this:

The running of P should be interrupted in favour of ISRD, but P should resume after ISRD has done its work. This is indicated schematically in Fig. 10.4.

Note that Fig. 10.4 is somewhat similar to Fig. 5.1, which depicts a program calling a *function subprogram*. But there is one crucial difference here—P does not call ISRD. ISRD is invoked because the device D signaled an interrupt to the processor, and ISRD is the *service routine* for this particular interrupt.

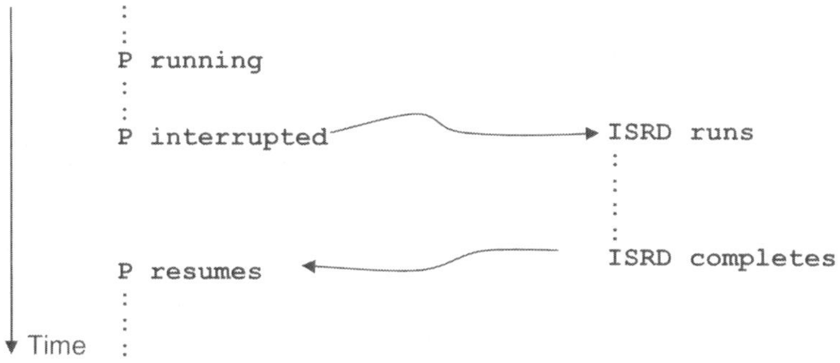

Fig. 10.4 **Interrupt service routine invoked upon an interrupt**

Thus we see that an interrupt from an input or output device must have associated with it an *interrupt service routine*, or ISR—which is basically the function (also known as 'subroutine' or 'subprogram') which correctly responds to the interrupt.

How does the processor know the memory address of the service routine of an interrupt? For this purpose, certain memory locations are pre-determined within the processor to store the required ISR addresses. When the processor detects an interrupt signal, it finds the address of the correct ISR from these pre-determined locations, which are often at the lower-most addresses in main memory.

How does the processor detect that a device has signaled an interrupt? Recall the instruction *fetch and execute* cycle which the processor performs repeatedly. This cycle, first seen in Chapter 1, is repeated in Fig. 10.5—but with a crucial extra test within the loop for any pending interrupt.

As seen in Fig. 10.5, the ISR is invoked by the interrupt signal. The ISR ends with a RETURN instruction, just as a function does. This causes the saved return address to be retrieved from the stack, which means that the interrupted program—such as P in Fig. 10.4, resumes execution exactly at the point where it was interrupted.

Of course, a computer system has a multiplicity of devices of different characteristics. Therefore, in general, a processor provides for several different interrupt signals, to which different device controllers can be connected. Usually these various interrupts available on a processor are *prioritized*—i.e. a lower priority ISR can itself be interrupted by a higher priority one, but not the other way around. Figure 10.3 shows the processor providing for two different interrupt signals (also known as *interrupt lines*).

```
repeat forever
{
     test interrupt lines for any device interrupt
     if an interrupt is signaled
          save return address on stack and jump to ISR
     else
     {
          fetch the next instruction from main memory
          execute the instruction fetched
     }
}
```

Fig. 10.5 **Processor tests for interrupt during its *fetch-execute* cycle**

When a processor provides multiple interrupt lines, it must also provide for these lines to be selectively *disabled* or *enabled* under program control. While servicing an interrupt from a high speed device, the processor may simply disable interrupts from slower speed devices. Within the processor, a register—or part of a register—contains the so-called *interrupt mask*, i.e. bits which indicate the interrupts which are enabled at a given time. Often the interrupt mask is a part of the *program status word* (PSW, see Section 4.9).

Together with interrupt priorities, the ability to selectively disable/enable interrupts allows the programmer full flexibility in deciding whether, how, and in what order the various interrupting devices in a system will receive service.

There are also techniques available for multiple devices to share a single interrupt line. When the processor detects an interrupt on such a shared line, the corresponding ISR first *polls* the status registers of the concerned devices to determine which device had signaled the interrupt. Once that is done, the correct device is then serviced by the ISR.

Other Types of Interrupts

In Chapters 8 and 9, we have seen that certain conditions within the processor—for example, *divide by zero* or *illegal memory access*—generate an internal signal which must be handled in a way that is similar to handling an external interrupt. In fact, the interrupt signals to which a processor may respond are usually classified into *external* and *internal* interrupts, the latter also being known as *traps.*

A third category of interrupts are the *software interrupts*, which allow a running user program to invoke operating system functions. A software interrupt is nothing but a machine instruction with a mnemonic such as SWI—and with a single operand which identifies the specific interrupt type. Service routine for such a software interrupt causes the processor to switch from *user mode* to *system mode* (also known as *supervisor* or *privileged* mode), and to execute the appropriate operating system function.

10.6 A SIMPLE APPLICATION

Consider the following simple application of a computer system:

A guinea pig enclosure in a laboratory is provided with four sets of lights in its four corners, with one green light and one red light in each set. Two large switches are provided in the center of the enclosure, each of which may easily be turned ON or OFF by the guinea pig using its paw.

The switches control the lights in the following way:

Switch ON	Light Pattern
None	all sets of lights blink*
Any one	only two sets of lights blink*
Both	all lights turn off

*Here 'blink' means alternately turning the red and the green light ON for one second each, and repeating the process.

The aim of the experiment is to study if a guinea pig can associate specific switches with specific patterns of lights, and thereby learn to control its environment to some extent.

Figure 10.6 shows a schematic diagram of this experimental setup. The double dashed line running through the center of the diagram separates the enclosure, on the left, from the computer and the required *interface electronics*, on the right. The required number of lines running from the switches to the interface electronics, and from the electronics to the lights, are shown using thick arrows in a lighter shade*.

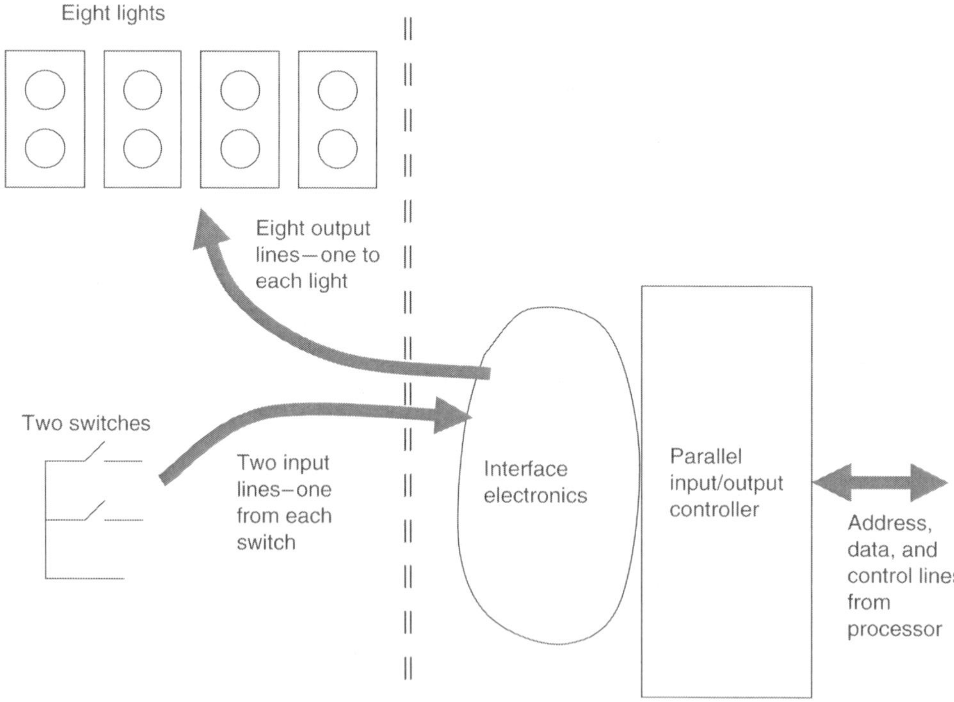

Fig. 10.6 **Experimental system of sample application**

* In reality, these lines would include a common *ground* line and also a voltage supply line, for example +5 volts. However, such details are not essential for the discussion here about how a processor carries out simple input and output operations. For the same reason, we have not shown here any details of the interface electronics.

Now we take a look at how the hardware and software of this system can be designed to satisfy the requirements of this experiment.

Note 10.2

As discussed in Section 1.2, the earliest programmable electronic computers were developed in mid-twentieth century. They were extremely clumsy to use, occupied enormous amount of space, and consumed enormous amount of power. The earliest computers were far from being commercial products, being more like one-of-a-kind laboratory prototypes.

We have seen that the two names most closely associated with the earliest development of computers are those of Alan Turing and John von Neumann. Turing developed a general mathematical model of the process of computation—known as the *Turing machine*—and von Neumann is credited with the design of the earliest programmable electronic computer.

Even in those very early days, Turing, von Neumann and other scientists wondered whether the concept of a programmable computer would throw light on the working of human intelligence. Since then, the field of *Artificial Intelligence* has developed in an attempt to create computers which can mimic at least some aspects of human intelligence. At the same time, biologists and neuroscientists have tried to understand natural intelligence, sometimes trying out ideas generated by computer scientists; their broad field of study has come to be known as *Cognitive Science*.

It has by now been established that several animals, including chimpanzees and dolphins, exhibit clear signs of intelligence somewhat similar to that of humans. Thus intelligence is not a gift that nature has bestowed solely on human beings—and scientists do carry out simple experiments on small animals of the kind described in this section.

To control each of the eight lights in the closure, we can provide an eight-bit output data register in the device controller. By writing a '0' or a '1' in each of these eight bits, we can independently turn the respective light OFF or ON.

To read in the status of the two switches, we really need only a two-bit input data register in the device controller. However, many standard device controllers available for such simple applications provide input data registers which are eight bits wide. Therefore, here we shall also assume that our device controller has an eight-bit wide input data register, even though we shall use only two of these eight bits.

The 'blink rate' specifies that each light must be alternately turned ON and OFF once every second. From this we can conclude that software running on the micro-computer must sense the status of the switches once every second, and then turn the various lights ON or OFF as specified in the table above.

We can outline the required program in algorithmic notation as shown in Fig. 10.7.

All the steps in Fig. 10.7 which are inside the outer loop can be programmed using techniques discussed in Chapter 4, Chapter 5, and the first two sections of this chapter. Basically these steps involve *iteration*, *conditional execution* and the appropriate use of IN and OUT instructions.

At this stage, however, the question remains: How does one arrange for these actions to take place precisely once in every second? So far, we have not seen any mechanism to achieve regularly timed actions such as these.

```
once every second, do
{
      for each of the four sets of lights, do
      {
            if the set is in blink mode,
                  the light which is ON is turned OFF,
                  and vice versa
      }
      read the status of the two switches
      if no switch is ON
            change all sets of lights to blink mode
      if any one switch is ON
            change two sets of lights to blink mode
      if both switches are ON
            turn off all lights
}
```

Fig. 10.7 Program needed for sample application

The answer is this: We need a timer-like device which signals an interrupt to the processor precisely once every second. Some processors—including all microcontrollers—have *programmable timer-cum-counter* devices built into them. These devices can be programmed to generate interrupts at regular intervals, for example once every second. On other systems, such a timer device would have to be connected externally, but the basic principle remains the same.

If an internal or external timer device is used in this manner, then all the actions within the outer loop in the program of Fig. 10.7 simply make up the *service routine* for timer interrupts. Once every second, the service routine is invoked and the required operations on the switches and the lights take place accordingly.

What if, for some reason, the system designer is not in a position to make use of a timer device to generate the required interrupt once every second? Does it mean that we simply cannot equip the guinea pig enclosure as we wished to?

Well, we can still build the system, but without a timer device the required program must take the form outlined in Fig. 10.8.

Notice the following differences between the two versions of the program:

(i) The outer loop in Fig. 10.7 is headed **`once every second`**, while in Fig. 10.8 it is headed **`repeat forever`**. A timer device provides outer loop timing in Fig. 10.7, while in Fig. 10.8, the timing is achieved by a *wait loop*.

(ii) In Fig. 10.8, there is a newly inserted last action within the outer loop:

`execute` ***`wait loop`*** **`of one second`**

In fact, all the prior actions within the outer loop take up only a fraction of a millisecond of time, and so the processor has to idle for almost exactly one second before taking another look at the lights and the switches.

Thus, if the system has to be built without a timer device, then the processor has to enter a *wait loop* for the required time. To program such a loop, the programmer has to take into account the time of execution of each instruction in the *wait loop*, and then select the *loop count* such that the required total delay is achieved.

```
repeat forever
{
      for each of the four sets of lights, do
      {
            if the set is in blink mode,
                  the light which is ON is turned OFF,
                  and vice versa
      }
      read the status of the two switches
      if no switch is ON
            change all sets of lights to blink mode
      if any one switch is ON
            change two sets of lights to blink mode
      if both switches are ON
            turn off all lights
      execute wait loop of one second
}
```

Fig. 10.8 **Program for sample application, without timer device**

We have assumed that the processor in this system is doing only this single task of monitoring the switches and controlling the lights. Therefore, in this case, nothing is lost by 'doing nothing' between successive rounds of the outer loop. In effect, the processor is doing useful work only once every second, and that too for a fraction of a millisecond. In a dedicated, low-cost, and simple application, this may often be acceptable.

Note 10.3

Semiconductor manufacturers have developed I/O controllers to address almost all common requirements of system designers. Such I/O controllers are interfaced with the processor over its address and data lines, and with the device by means of appropriate interface electronics. In Fig. 10.6, the rectangular box marked 'Parallel Input/Output Controller' is such a controller. *Microcontrollers* have some useful I/O controllers embedded in the same package which houses the processor and memory.

Such I/O controllers are available for parallel I/O, timing/counting functions, keyboard control, display control, serial communication, and so on. Most such controllers are made to be *configurable*, and to meet the specific needs of different applications. All such controllers make use of the basic mechanisms described in this chapter, but naturally the details vary from one controller to another. Data sheets and application notes are made available by manufacturers to help the system designer put together a system.

Sometimes a standard PC—which is a complete system in itself—has to be used to control some equipment, such as we saw in the simple application above. Such a PC provides industry standard I/O connectors, into which an 'add-on' circuit board can be plugged in for additional functionality. Such 'add-on' circuit boards are sold with matching software which makes it easier to employ a standard PC for such applications; the required application program can then be written in a higher level language.

10.7 MODES OF DATA TRANSFER

We have seen above that, in the absence of an interrupt mechanism, the processor must repeatedly check for device status, so as to determine when an input or output operation can take place. This type of repeated checking of device status is known as *polling*. Thus the system designer has the options of either polling for device status, or providing the device controller with an interrupt line to the processor.

This and other design options available for I/O can be arranged in the form of a set of choices which must be made—depending on device characteristics and also the overall system requirements. Table 10.1 summarises broadly the set of such choices available to the system designer. The first column of the table lists the I/O function or characteristic, against which the option listed in either the second column or the third column may be selected, as appropriate to the device and the system requirements.

For checking device status, we have already seen that the options available are (a) polling for device status, as seen in Program 10.1, or (b) using an interrupt mechanism.

When multiple I/O devices of one kind are connected to the system, it is often not possible to provide each device with a separate interrupt line to the processor. In such cases, an interrupt line can be shared between devices. When an interrupt is received on such a shared line, the processor must poll the devices to determine which device needs attention. This technique is listed as Option I in the second row of the table.

The unit of data transfer between an I/O device and the processor or main memory can either be a byte (or word), or an entire block of bytes. Naturally this unit of data transfer depends on the type of device—a mouse and a magnetic disk, for example, will have different units of data transfer. In the next section, we shall discuss in brief these two types of devices, usually known as *character devices* and *block devices*.

Table 10.1 Modes of data transfer

Function or Characteristic	Option I	Option II
Check for device status	Polling	Interrupt driven
Device identification	Polling—possibly with shared interrupt line	Each device has its own separate interrupt line
Unit of data transfer	Character	Block
Path of data transfer	Between device controller and programmable register	Between device controller and main memory
Width of data transfer	Single bit—serial transfer	Multiple bits—parallel transfer
Timing	Synchronous	Asynchronous

During input or output, data may be transferred between the device and the system in one of two different ways:

(i) between the device controller and a register in the processor, using IN and OUT instructions, or
(ii) directly between the device controller and main memory.

These two options are known respectively as *Programmed I/O* and *Direct Memory Access* (DMA). Program 10.1 is an example of programmed I/O, and later in this chapter, we shall discuss briefly the technique of DMA. Usually character devices are operated using programmed I/O, while block devices are operated in DMA mode.

The width of the data path between the processor and device controller depends on the width of the external bus of the processor (recall Fig. 6.1). On smaller systems, this width may be eight bits, while on larger systems it may be thirty two bits.

As against this, the width of the data path between the device controller and the device may be a single bit—allowing only *serial* data transfers—or multiple bits, allowing data transfers in *parallel**. A serial device interface offers several advantages, for example, ease of use, compact size, and lower cost. In earlier days of technology, serial interfaces offered slower data transfer speeds, but today that is no longer the case. USB is a serial device interface, while a PCMCIA slot on a PC provides a parallel interface.

The last row of Table 10.1 lists another important characteristic of a data transfer.

As seen in Chapter 3, the clock signal plays a crucial role in timing data transfers along a data path. Data transfers in which both the sending and the receiving end share a common clock signal are known as *synchronous* data transfers. So far, all the examples of data transfer which we have studied have been of this type, including implicitly the examples seen so far. The external bus between the processor and the device controller carries the clock signal required for synchronous data transfers.

Sometimes it is not possible for the sending and the receiving ends of a data transfer to share a clock signal. A common example of this is the connection between a telephone modem and a PC, which has no provision for a clock signal. In such cases, the receiving end relies on transitions in signal voltage or current to synchronise itself with the signal received. For obvious reasons, such data transfer mechanisms are called *asynchronous*.

Figure 10.9 depicts these possible modes of data transfer in a schematic manner. The options listed in Table 10.1 are shown in the figure as questions which must be answered, since these questions represent the design choices available to the designer.

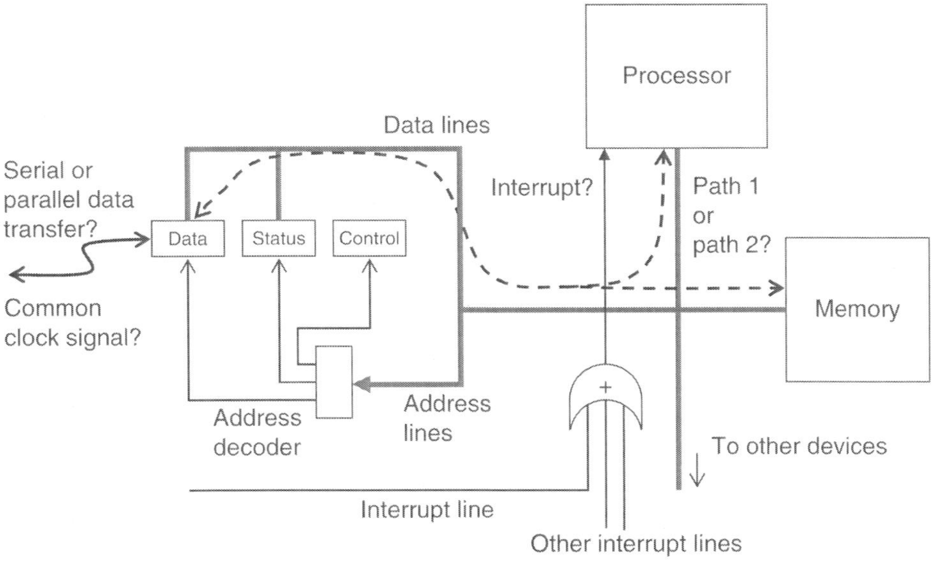

Fig. 10.9 Modes of data transfer

*At this point, it may prove helpful to the student to refer to Fig. 3.11 and the related discussion in Section 3.8.

In the lower part of this figure, we see interrupt lines from three different devices being combined using an *or* gate, and supplied as a single interrupt line to the processor. If such a shared interrupt line is available, then the processor is interrupted when one or more of the concerned devices need service. To identify the interrupting device(s), the service routine must poll the devices which share the interrupt line.

If each device in the system has its own interrupt line, then naturally a signal on that line immediately identifies the device, and there is no need for any polling. On the other hand, if no interrupt line is available—shared or otherwise—then the software must poll the devices periodically to check whether any of them needs service.

For transferring data to and from the device controller, we see two possible paths in the figure 'Path 1' is between the device controller and the processor; this path corresponds to programmed I/O, as we have used in Program 10.1 and in Chapters 4 and 5. Each byte or word is transferred to a processor register using an IN or OUT instruction.

As against this, 'Path 2' in the figure is between the device controller and main memory. Data transfers carried out along this path are said to be in Direct Memory Access (DMA) mode. Under DMA, separate IN or OUT instructions are not required for each byte or word which is transferred, and therefore this mode of data transfer is much faster than programmed I/O. Section 10.9 discusses DMA operations in some more detail.

On the left of the figure—where the physical device would be connected to the device controller—we see two other design choices: *serial* versus *parallel* data transfers, and *synchronous* versus *asynchronous* data transfers.

When only two lines are available for a data path, one of them serves as *signal ground*, and data transfers can only take place in serial mode. When multiple bits are transferred at a time over a data path—say m bits at a time—then the transfer is said to be in m-bit *parallel* mode. For such data transfers, the data path must consist of at least $m + 1$ lines, with one of them serving as signal ground.

As discussed above, the presence or absence of a shared clock signal between the sending and receiving ends of a data transfer distinguishes synchronous and asynchronous modes of data transfer. This is also indicated schematically to the left of Fig. 10.9.

Figure 10.10 shows a simplified view of the polling algorithm. The order in which devices are polled may be determined by (i) device address, or (ii) device *priority*, as assigned by the system designer. Whichever may be the polling order, the respective device status register is read into the processor, and the relevant bits examined. If the polled device needs service at the time, the appropriate *service routine* is called, and then polling resumes from the next device in polling order.

```
in priority order
(or in the order specified by the designer)
{
    read status of device k

    if device k needs service
        call service routine of device k

    select next device
}
```

Fig. 10.10 **Algorithm for polling of devices**

10.8 CHARACTER DEVICES AND BLOCK DEVICES

Input and output devices can be classified broadly into *character* and *block* types of devices. A character input or output device transfers one 'character' at a time, while a block input or output device transfers an entire block of bytes at a time—where a block may be of fixed or variable number of bytes.

The best example of a character type of input device is a keyboard. A magnetic disk is an example of a block type of device, since it can perform read and write operations only one *sector* at a time, or multiples thereof, as we shall see in Chapter 12.

In case of the keyboard—or its sister device, the mouse—the speed at which data is entered into the computer is limited by the user's ability to operate the device. The user is usually interacting with an application program through his or her key-presses and mouse-clicks. Therefore, it is necessary that the device sends in data to the processor—i.e. to the application program—as soon as the user generates it, which means one character or one mouse-click at a time.

For the magnetic disk, given the nature and speed of its operation, the smallest unit of data which it can read or write is a *sector*, which may be in the range of 512 bytes to 4096 bytes. The *disk controller* must therefore provide for sufficient buffer memory within itself to smoothen the movement of blocks of data between the magnetic storage medium and the main memory of the system.

Input, output and storage devices connected to the system would thus fall into either *character* or *block* category. Generally speaking, slower devices and those involving user interaction would be in the former category, while mass storage devices and higher speed devices would be in the latter category.

Device controllers for block devices usually tend to be fairly complex—they may have their own memory buffers, complex logic and timing circuits, and usually an *embedded* processor whose sole function is to monitor and control the operations of the controller. Such device controllers make use of DMA mode of data transfer, and usually provide a fairly sophisticated set of commands. The processor issues these commands to the device controller using programmed I/O, in order to coordinate correctly the operations of the device controller as well as the device itself.

While all this may seem a bit complicated, it does give an outline of how a program running on the main processor of the system coordinates its activities with a complex device—such as a disk or a network adaptor—using the input/output mechanisms available with the processor.

10.9 DIRECT MEMORY ACCESS

In Program 10.1, we see that every byte is read from the input device using IN instruction into a specified processor register, which is R1 in this case. Use of OUT instruction is similar—every byte or word is transferred from a processor register to a device register in response to an OUT instruction. This method of data transfer between the processor and an I/O device—known as *Programmed I/O*—works fine for simpler and slower devices, when the requirements of the application are not too demanding.

Block devices operate in a mode in which an entire block of data is transferred *from the device to main memory*—or the other way around—without the data passing through the processor. The processor is only interrupted at the end of the block transfer of data. This mode of I/O is more efficient than programmed I/O, because data does not make a slow and unnecessary detour through the processor on every byte or word. The processor can continue to run another, possibly unrelated program while such a data transfer is in progress between a device and main memory.

Such a mode of data transfer between a device and main memory is known as *Direct Memory Access* (DMA). Of course, processor intervention is needed to set up and initiate a DMA operation, and also at its completion—but the data transfer itself takes place without any processor intervention. The additional hardware which must be provided on the system to achieve such DMA transfers is known as *DMA controller*.

From this, it should be clear that while a DMA operation is in progress, both the main processor and the DMA controller would need to access main memory—since the processor as ever would be going through its own fetch and execute cycles, even while a DMA operation is in progress to or from main memory.

Figure 10.11 depicts such a data transfer taking place between an input device and main memory. The path of data is shown in the figure using a dashed, thick arrow in grey, between the device on the left, via the DMA controller, to main memory.

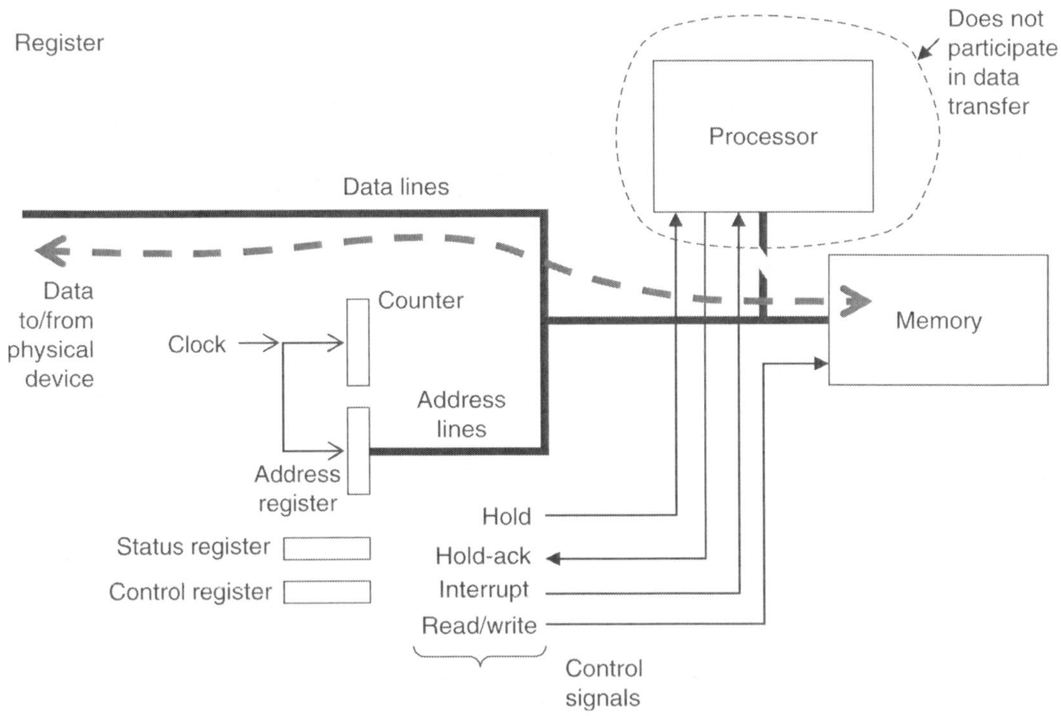

Fig. 10.11 **DMA data transfer between device and main memory**

Within the DMA controller, an *address register* contains successive memory addresses for read or write DMA operations, and a *counter* keeps track of the number of bytes transferred. The counter and address register are driven by a clock signal which maintains the required rates of data transfer.

Clearly, a mechanism must also be provided to ensure that in any one memory cycle, either the processor or the DMA controller gets access to main memory—but not both. An input signal to the processor—which we shall name as *hold*—is provided for this purpose. Using this signal, the DMA controller signals the processor to 'hold' its memory accesses, while the controller itself accesses memory to read or write data.

But the DMA controller cannot start accessing memory until confirmation is received from the processor that its memory accesses are 'on hold'. Therefore a signal with the function of *hold acknowledgement* is also provided, which is sent by the processor to the DMA controller; upon that signal, the controller can proceed with DMA. The controller makes use of *read/write* signal to main memory, to determine read or write access.

In addition to the hardware elements described, and like any other device controller, a DMA controller also has its own *status* and *control* registers. To signal completion of DMA operation, the controller may make use of an interrupt line to the processor.

To summarise, we may say that a complete DMA I/O operation has three phases:

(i) In the first phase, using programmed I/O, the program running on the processor supplies the memory address, byte count, and read or write command to the DMA controller. This is the DMA setup and initiation phase.

(ii) Based on the parameters and command supplied, the DMA controller transfers data to or from main memory, using the mechanism outlined above. On the device side, the respective device controller performs the required functions. This is the main data transfer phase, illustrated in Fig. 10.11.

(iii) At the end of data transfer, the controller sends an interrupt to the processor. The interrupt service routine completes any remaining verification and signaling required in connection with the completed data transfer.

Example 10.4

Suppose a block of 4096 bytes is transferred from a device to main memory using DMA. If one word of four bytes is written to memory in one memory cycle, the number of memory accesses required for this DMA transfer is 1024.

This number of memory accesses should be compared with a program such as Program 10.1 transferring 1024 words from a device to memory using programmed I/O. Many machine instructions are executed in the main outer loop of Program 10.1, each requiring its own fetch cycle from main memory. In addition, memory write takes place 1024 times in the execute phase of STORE instruction in the main loop. Overall, therefore, the programmed mode of data transfer will be much slower than DMA.

It should also be noted that, under programmed I/O, the processor is itself occupied in the I/O operation. Under DMA, after the processor initiates the operation, all the work is done by the DMA controller, freeing up the processor. Overall, therefore, the DMA mode of operation results in a much more efficient utilisation of system resources.

In practice, to accommodate a variety of DMA devices, functionalities of the device controller—e.g. a disk controller—and the DMA controller are clearly separated. For the most part, the discussion in this section refers to the DMA controller; the student will note that no mention has been made here of functions specific to an I/O device.

10.10 I/O INTERFACES

The crucial need for standardised interfaces to a computer system was mentioned earlier, in Section 1.9. To take an obvious example: A system as complex as a modern PC—with its vast range of *add-on* options and I/O devices which can be attached—cannot be designed, built, marketed, or serviced without such standardised interfaces.

From the very early years of computer technology, therefore, industry associations have developed interface standards which manufacturers follow. The common *serial port* and *parallel port* on the early models of the PC are two examples. Common examples used today include—USB ports, PCMCIA slot, RJ-11 jack to connect the built-in modem to a phone, jacks for external speakers, and the 15-pin connector for video output.

Any such interface standard has several important parts to it, of which we shall take only a brief overview here.

The most visible part of an interface standard is its *mechanical specification*—which includes the precise mechanical shape and dimensions of the two opposite sides of a connection, type of fit between the two sides, number and layout of pins, and so on. A poor mechanical contact results in a poor or broken electrical connection, which is a common cause of faults in electronic systems. Therefore this part of the specification is also as important as the functional characteristics which are listed in Table 10.1.

Example 10.5

Importance of the mechanical specification of an interface can be understood by the following simple exercise:

Consider a common 'memory stick' with the USB interface. Insert and remove the stick a couple of times from the USB port on a PC—and <u>observe closely the process</u>.

(i) Try to insert the memory stick into the port 'the wrong way around'—it will not go in. Observe closely the mechanical design technique used to prevent wrong insertion.

(ii) Now imagine that the USB end of the memory stick was larger or smaller by 0.25 mm—one fourth of a millimeter—and think about the consequences. If the memory stick end is larger, it will not go into the USB port on the PC. If it is smaller, it will go in very easily—but dangle loose, giving an unreliable electrical connection.

Clearly, the mechanical specification of the USB interface must be very precise—for us to be able to insert and remove a memory stick thousands of times from its port, and have a reliable connection with the PC each and every time.

After the mechanical specification of the interface comes its *electrical specification*—which may include voltage, current or power levels, speed and timing constraints, as well as other relevant electrical characteristics such as contact resistance and 'line impedance' which may have a crucial bearing on data transfers.

The *functional specification* of the interface can be viewed as being at the next higher level. Under this specification, the functional role of the electrical signal on each of the pins is defined. As we have seen, these signal lines can be grouped into data lines and control lines; on external device interfaces, separate address lines are not present. Issues such as those listed in Table 10.1 are also addressed in the functional specification.

Based on the functional specification, a programmer can write a *device driver* for a device which is connected to the system using this I/O interface. The device driver enables a user program to send data to the device, or receive data from it. In this sense, therefore, we may think of the device driver as providing a *software specification* of the device. Since this part of the specification is necessarily device-dependent, however, it is usually not included as a part of the interface standard.

10.11 I/O PROCESSORS

On the internal system bus, some computer systems provide—along with one or more main processors—a so-called *I/O Processor*. Broadly, the role of such an I/O processor is to free the main processor(s) from almost all work related to input and output of data.

In particular, an I/O processor can perform functions such as the following:

- Interface to external bus or busses
- Direct memory access
- Interaction with device controllers
- Interaction with relevant parts of the operating system
- Servicing of interrupts according to priorities
- Buffering of data

With advances in electronic technology over the last couple of decades, devices and device controllers have become faster—and also smarter, in the sense that software running in them on embedded processors provides higher levels of functionality. At the same time, standard interfaces between devices and device controllers, as also the speeds of internal system busses, have also become much faster.

Today, high performance systems make use of multiple processors for highly compute-intensive applications. As we shall study in Chapter 14, multiple processors are connected into massive clusters using fast interfaces or LANs, and operated in some form of load-sharing mode.

As a result of these advances, the typical functions for which an I/O processor may be considered—such as those listed above—may no longer be the performance limiting functions in a system. And therefore a general purpose I/O processor may no longer be an essential requirement for achieving high aggregate data rates on input and output.

For certain specialised I/O requirements, however, a separate processor may be required in order to achieve desired performance.

One obvious example of such a specialised requirement is *computer graphics*. Rendering of animated 3-dimensional objects requires the processing of a large number of 'vectors' through a common sequence of operations. The stages of such processing make up a so-called *rendering pipeline*. When these functions are implemented on a special processor, the speed and quality of computer generated graphics is greatly improved. With the use of VLSI technology, such *graphic processors* are available even on low-cost personal computers—something which was not possible in the early days of the PC.

High performance supercomputers, which are designed for highly compute-intensive applications, may also make use of a dedicated I/O processor to relieve the main processor(s) of all work related to input/output operations.

It should of course be noted that, like any other processor, an I/O processor executes its own machine instructions to perform its functions. The internal architecture of an I/O processor is in principle similar to that shown in Fig. 6.1—though it may be specially designed to reflect its functions. A graphics processor, for example, would have pipeline stages corresponding to the stages of a graphics rendering pipeline. The instruction set of an I/O processor may not necessarily be the same as that of main processor(s).

In any case, the I/O processor and the main processor(s) would share main memory, and several of the issues discussed in Chapters 13 and 14 would apply to a system which thus consists of two or more processors.

SUMMARY

The input and output sub-system of a computer system allows the system to exchange data with a wide range of I/O devices, and also with other computers. The important role of device controllers was discussed, and the concepts of programmed I/O and polling were brought out using an example program.

The mechanism of interrupts frees the processor from repeatedly checking for device status, thereby leading to much higher system utilisation. When an interrupt is received from a device controller, the appropriate interrupt service routine is invoked, and it takes care of the actual data transfer, device control, and so on. An interrupt can be external, internal, or software-generated.

A simple application was described to illustrate the use of basic input and output, taking the example of a typical laboratory experiment. Such an application can be designed in two possible ways—one with a timer device to generate interrupts, and another without such a timer device, in which case the timing must be maintained by software.

The various possible modes of I/O data transfers possible in a computer system were discussed, and summarised in the form of Table 10.1. Direct memory access—in which data passes directly between device controller and main memory—is required for block devices such as magnetic disks. The typical DMA controller has address and byte count registers, in addition to status and control. Signals such as hold and hold acknowledgement allow the DMA controller to make use of the internal processor-memory bus, while the processor itself suspends its accesses to main memory.

Standardised I/O interfaces play a very important role in the design and operation of a modern computer system. An interface standard typically includes mechanical, electrical, and functional specifications. I/O processors are provided on some systems to relieve the main processor(s) of overhead related to input and output. Special graphics processors, in particular, are very commonly used with modern computer systems.

REVIEW QUESTIONS

1. List three input and three output devices which must be provided on a typical mobile phone.
2. List five different characteristics which may distinguish one I/O device from another.
3. 'A device controller is the device as seen by the programmer'—justify this statement in brief.
4. Give two examples of the function of the device status register.
5. Why is it sometimes necessary to include a wait loop in a program which reads data in from a device, or writes data out to a device?
6. In a keyboard with a ready bit, which are the two events that will cause the ready bit to be set and reset, respectively?
7. Give two examples of the function of the device control register.
8. A device on a system is capable of data input as well as output operations. List the typical set of registers that the device controller would have.
9. State in brief the function of an interrupt signal, and the advantage of using an interrupt signal in a device interface.
10. When is the interrupt service routine for a device invoked? If a program P was running on the processor at the time, what is the status of P during and after interrupt service?
11. How does the processor detect the occurrence of an interrupt?
12. Upon the occurrence of an interrupt, how does the processor determine the memory address of the correct service routine?
13. Why does a processor provide multiple interrupt lines? Why are priorities assigned to the multiple interrupt lines? What is the function of an interrupt mask?
14. In which type of system does an interrupt service routine need to poll the status registers of multiple devices?
15. List the three main categories of interrupts.
16. In the context of input or output of data, what is the meaning of 'polling'?
17. In a computer system, multiple devices share an interrupt line on which an interrupt signal is received. Explain in brief how the interrupting device will be identified by the interrupt service routine.
18. State in brief the difference between programmed I/O and direct memory access (DMA).
19. List the advantages of a serial link between a device and the computer system, as compared to a parallel link.
20. State in brief the difference between synchronous and asynchronous modes of data transfer.
21. State in brief the difference between a character device and a block device.
22. Explain in brief the basic concept of direct memory access.
23. What is the typical set of registers available within DMA controller?
24. What is the function of signals 'hold' and 'hold acknowledgement' provided with a DMA controller?

25. Why are standardised I/O interfaces important in the design and operation of a modern computer system?
26. Give three examples of standardised I/O interfaces used in a modern computer system.
27. If a computer system has been provided with an I/O processor, what are its typical functions?
28. List one specialised I/O processor which is commonly used on modern PCs.

EXERCISES

Note to student:

A few of the exercises below involve some aspect of system design. In practice, such design is followed by its implementation using a combination of hardware and software. In order to get an experience of the complete design and implementation cycle, at least one of these exercises should be implemented during laboratory sessions.

In some cases, it might appear to the student that the exercise fails to specify fully some aspect of the system which is to be designed. This is deliberate—in practice, we are very often given incomplete requirements, and must make *justifiable* additional assumptions to complete the work of system design.

1. Refer to Program 10.1. The program performs a *wait loop* until the input device is *ready*, i.e. input data is available in its data register.

   Modify Program 10.1 in such a way that a hundred bytes are written out from memory to an output device, taking care that output is performed only after the output device is *ready*. Make suitable assumptions about the I/O addresses occupied by the output device.
2. Modify Program 10.1 in such a way that a hundred bytes are read from the input device and written to the output device, taking care in both cases that input or output is performed only after each respective device is *ready*. Make suitable assumptions about the I/O addresses occupied by the two devices.
3. Modify Program 10.1 in such a way that the modified program reads data from two input devices, checking in one *wait loop* the status of both the devices. Data is read from whichever device becomes *ready*.

   For storing the input data from the two devices, the program uses two different blocks of memory, starting at locations BASE1 and BASE2 respectively. Make suitable assumptions about the I/O addresses occupied by the two devices.
4. Recall the laboratory experiment system of Section 10.5. The system was outlined in some detail, but the description and explanation given do not really make up a complete system design. Complete the required system design, assuming that timer interrupts are available. Assume that a device control register in the timer device has to be initialised with a particular bit pattern for the device to generate one second interrupts, and make other suitable assumptions as needed.

5. A series of 32 lights is to be controlled using a computer. Given that each light can independently be turned ON or OFF, the computer operates the lights in two modes:

a. In *set mode*, a specified 32-bit word in memory is used to turn each light ON or OFF.

b. In *rotate mode*, the 32 light pattern as defined *by set mode* is rotated right at a fixed frequency, with the rightmost light getting back into rotation at the left end.

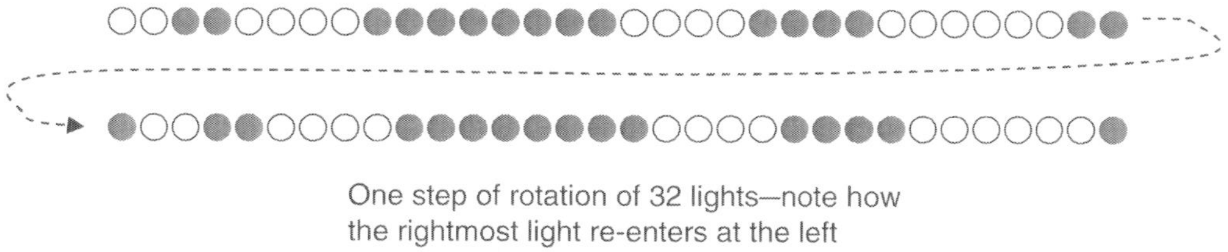

Fig. 10.12 **One step of rotation of 32 lights**

Figure 10.12 illustrates one step of such rotation of lights. Outline the hardware and software of a system which can achieve this. Note in particular that programmed I/O is performed only one byte at a time.

6. Traffic at a road junction can flow North-South (NS), Right turn from North-South (RNS), East-West (EW), and Right turn from East-West (REW). On each of these traffic flows, the lights go through the cycle: Green, Orange, and Red. Figure 10.13 illustrates NS and RNS flows; the other two—EW and REW—are analogous.

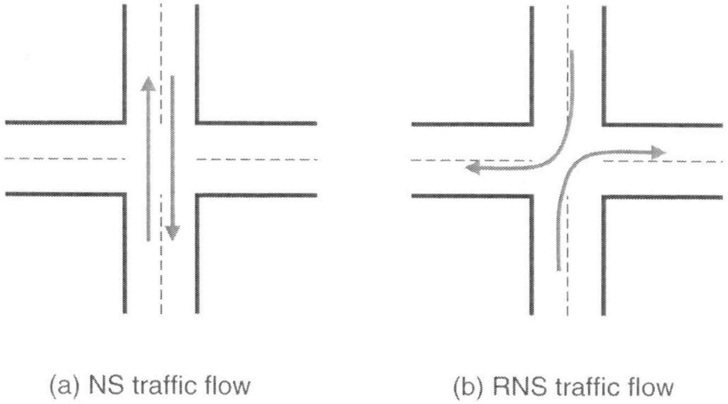

Fig. 10.13 **Traffic flows NS and RNS at a junction**

Only one traffic flow at a time is allowed through the junction. Therefore, when one flow has Green or Orange light, the three other flows must have Red light. Traffic flows are to be operated in the repeated cyclic pattern NS, RNS, EW, and REW. Green and Orange light timing on each of the four flows is equal: 30 seconds for Green and 5 seconds for Orange.

Outline the design of a computer system to control these traffic lights.

7. Modify the design of Exercise 6 in the following way:
Traffic sensors are installed at the junction. When there is no traffic in a particular flow, that particular step of the traffic cycle is skipped. For example, if there are no vehicles which will turn right from North-South, the lights will skip RNS, switching directly from NS to EW.
8. The following modification is to be made to the system of Exercise 7:
Traffic sensors at the junction are made 'smarter'. These smart sensors can supply information to the computer about whether traffic in any of the four flows is 'none', 'light', 'heavy', or 'very heavy'. The computer must allow more Green time for a traffic flow as it becomes heavier, and less time as it becomes lighter.
Note that the sensors of Exercise 7 could only give us the information that there is either 'no traffic' or 'some traffic' in each direction. The 'smarter' sensors of this exercise are able to generate four different signals for each traffic flow, and thereby able to distinguish to some extent between different traffic intensities.
The key question is: How can our system make use of this additional information from the sensors? Outline in brief how you will carry out this modification.

USER INTERACTION

11

11.1 INTRODUCTION

The earliest computers, developed in mid-twentieth century, were large in size, power hungry—and extremely difficult to program and operate. Only computer specialists worked 'hands-on' with these computer systems. Uninitiated users had to seek the help of these 'high priests' to get their work done. They submitted their program and data to the system operator and then waited patiently for their output.

Since the advent of the personal computer (PC) around the year 1980, however, a revolutionary change has come about in the way that computer systems are designed and built. Today the *end user*—who may be a manager, a doctor, or a student—operates the computer himself or herself, and therefore his or her needs are kept firmly in focus in the hardware and software design of a computer system.

Several major technological advances have contributed to computer technology over the last few decades. Amongst these, may be listed the following:

advances in VLSI, graphics display, and storage technologies;
techniques of software development and computer networking;
packaging, mass production, mass marketing, and customer support.

Of course, not all of these advances are directly related to computer system organisation, but they have certainly had a major impact on the way we use computers today.

Over this same period—and for similar reasons—the quality of interaction that a user has with a computer system has also gone through a revolutionary change. A PC or a mobile phone handset is used by millions of persons around the world. It must therefore be designed to be a versatile and *user friendly* aid at work and in daily life. If the user has to learn a specialist language to use this tool, he or she will simply not use it. This is the reason why the *graphical user interface* (GUI) has come into wide-spread use.

The quality of user interaction with a computer system depends critically on the way in which elements of the computer system interact with each other. In the design of the graphical display system, in particular, this factor is crucial—since here the speed of system response to user commands or 'mouse clicks' is very important. Applications with animated graphics make even greater demands on the ability of the system to process and display information in time.

In view of these factors, we must conclude that today *user interaction* is no longer a 'peripheral' issue but a crucial 'central' issue in the design of a computer system. The computer system as seen by a user is defined much more by the quality of user interaction it provides than by the brand of processor that lies hidden inside the packaging. Since the quality of interaction depends on the way various system elements operate together, we shall explore in this chapter some system design issues relevant to this interaction.

Figure 11.1 depicts schematically the various steps involved in the process of user-computer interaction, which may be described as:

1. user input is sensed by an input device on the system;
2. program running on the system alters display output in accordance with user input;
3. eyes perceive changes in the display;
4. user determines the next input to the system;
5. user operates the input device accordingly.

Of the five steps shown, only the steps labeled *1* and *2* are of interest to us here; steps labeled *3*, *4* and *5* are studied in other branches of science, such as *psychology* and *cognitive science*.

The step labeled *1* in Fig. 11.1 shows *input* being provided by the user to the computer system. A mouse-like input device is shown, but in fact the device could be a keyboard, a touchpad, or any other input device. Step *2* indicates graphical or textual *output* being generated and displayed by the computer system. The cycle formed by the five steps signifies the important fact that the next input given by the user to the system depends on the output seen by the user.

On almost any computer system today, a *keyboard*—either full-size, or a smaller *keypad* as in most mobile phone handsets—is a basic input device, and a *graphics display* is a basic output device. With the availability of touch-sensitive or pressure-sensitive displays on some hand-held systems, the work of a keyboard or keypad is carried out using either a pen-like pointer or simply the user's finger.

The importance of a graphics display lies in its ability to provide an attractive, functionally powerful, and yet user-friendly graphical user interface. A well-designed graphical user interface enables users to achieve higher productivity in working with computer systems. The *mouse*—table-top or button type— and the *touchpad* are *pointer* input devices, used in conjunction with graphical user interfaces.

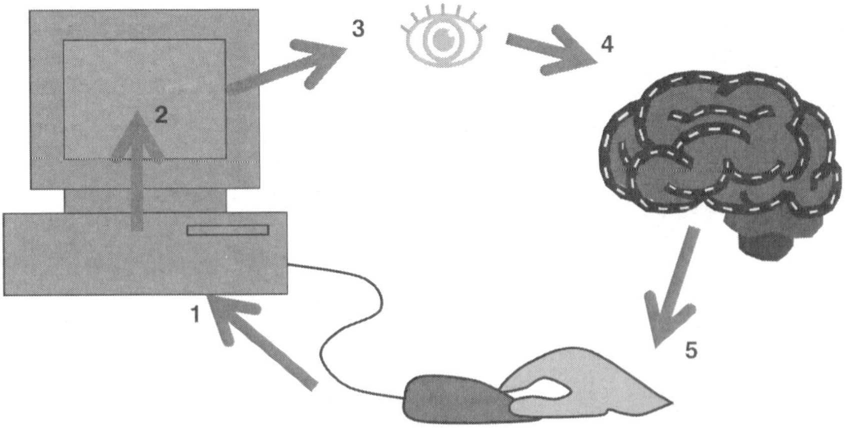

Fig. 11.1 The cycle of user-computer interaction

The keyboard, mouse, and graphics display may be considered as primary modes of input and output on a modern computer system. In Section 11.2, we study in brief the principles of operation of the keyboard and the mouse; in Section 11.3 and 11.4, we study the principles of operations of graphics displays. In Section 11.5, we then look at the kind of software that is required for effective realisation of steps *1* and *2* of the user-computer interaction, as depicted in Fig. 11.1.

11.2 KEYBOARD AND MOUSE

Keyboard

A keyboard or keypad in a computer works on the principle of electronically detecting the closing of a switch caused by a key depression. Consider Fig. 11.2, which represents in a highly simplified way the inner working of a keyboard. The figure shows six column 'wires' and three row 'wires' crisscrossing each other in a rectangular pattern. These wires lie underneath the keys that we use, and they do not normally touch each other. But one exception is shown in the figure—column wire 'c' and row wire '2' are shown connected, because the key at that position is assumed to be pressed.

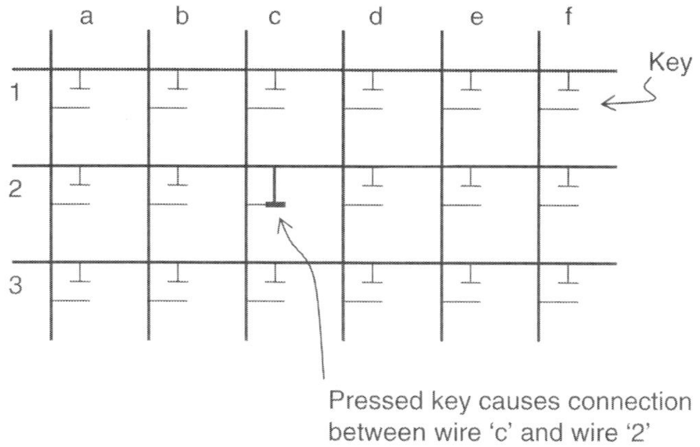

Fig. 11.2 Simplified diagram of a keyboard

Above every intersection between a column wire and a row wire, a mechanical key is provided. Pressing on a particular key causes the column and the row wires at that key position to become connected for as long as the key remains pressed. Careful mechanical design of the keys ensures this electrical connection—just as it also ensures that the keys have just the right kind of 'feel' and 'bounce' for human fingers.

Control electronics of the keyboard constantly scans column and row wires at a high speed to detect any signs of key closures. Every key closure causes a change in the voltage and/or current patterns in exactly one column and one row wire—for example, wire 'c' and wire '2' in the Fig. 11.2. Any such change is captured electronically and sent to the computer in the form of input data from the keyboard.

Every key is labeled with a character symbol, and therefore the system can easily correlate pairs of wires—such as 'c' and '2'—with the input character that the key represents. The scanning electronics can also detect whether, simultaneously with a key closure, another key such as *shift*, *control*, or *alt* is being held down. Once the correct key closure is detected, the resulting input data is transferred to the computer using the basic principles of I/O described in Chapter 10.

On many systems today, the keyboard device generates two 'input events' for each key closure—one when the key is pressed down, and one when it is released. This allows the software inside the computer to provide more user-friendly responses to key presses; in most cases, of course, when the user presses a key and then releases it, the resulting two electronic events are mapped into a single character input.

Mouse

To understand how a mouse operates, it helps first to review how a rotary volume control knob operates on an old-fashioned cassette player. As we turn the knob one way or the other, it sets the volume of the amplifier by turning a rotary electronic element inside the tape recorder. This rotary element—known as a *potentiometer*—is a part of the volume control circuit which is connected to the speakers.

A simple mechanical mouse houses a ball underneath, which rotates due to friction as we move the mouse on a flat surface. This rotation of the ball causes two potentiometers inside the mouse to rotate one way or the other. One of these potentiometers is read in by the computer as 'movement along X direction', and the other as 'movement along Y direction'. Figure 11.3 illustrates this principle—with the one difference that, for the sake of clarity, only one of the two potentiometers has been shown here.

The outputs of the two potentiometers are converted from *analog* to *digital* form (recall Chapter 3). The device interface which then sends the 'mouse input' to the processor also includes the status of the left and right mouse buttons. This device interface makes use of programmed I/O with interrupt, as described in Chapter 10. In addition to the mechanism described, today optical and laser-based versions of the mouse are also available.

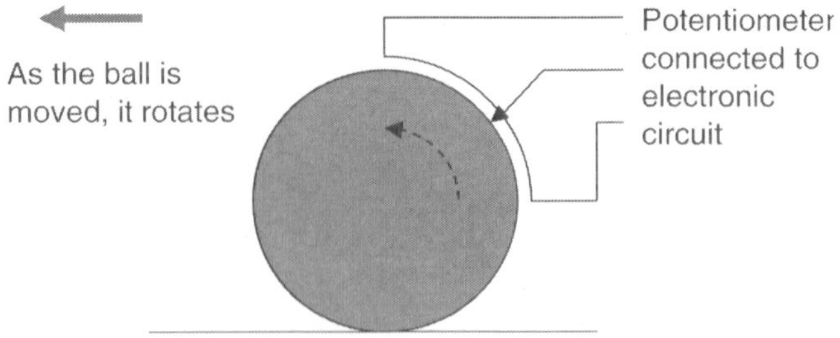

Fig. 11.3 **Principle of operation of mechanical mouse**

Touch-sensitive Input Devices

Touch-sensitive input devices make use of the basic principle illustrated in Fig. 11.4. Underneath the protective cover plate are two electrodes separated by a thin layer of insulating material (also known as *dielectric*). When a human finger touches the cover plate just above the two electrodes, the effective *capacitance* between the two electrodes changes*. This change can be sensed by an electronic circuit connected to the electrodes, which in effect means that the presence or absence of touch is sensed.

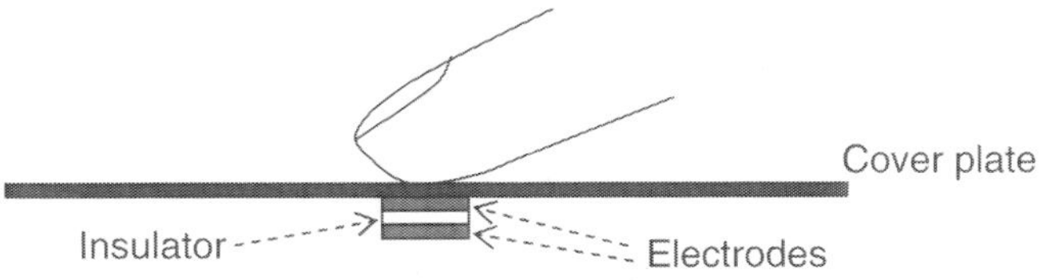

Fig. 11.4 **Technique for providing touch sensitivity**

By providing a grid of such electrodes under the cover plate—somewhat like the grid shown in Fig. 11.2—a *touchpad* is created. The grid of electrodes is made of rows and columns, and in this sense, the scanning of rows and columns is similar here to that carried out in keyboards.

11.3 GRAPHICS DISPLAY

The most common and frequently used output device on modern computer systems is the *graphics display*, which we may refer to simply as *display*. Two types of technologies are commonly used for the display device—*liquid crystal display* (LCD) technology and *cathode ray tube* (CRT) technology. In this section, we shall look at the graphics display sub-system of a computer system, while in the next section, we shall take a brief look at LCD and CRT display device technologies.

Note 11.1

Earlier generations of computers, until around the mid-1980s, often had displays which were capable of character output—typically twenty five rows of eighty characters each—but had almost no graphics capability. In those days, the phrase *graphics terminal* or *graphics display* was used to distinguish more expensive devices which could produce graphics of fairly decent quality.

Since then, however, CRT, LCD, and VLSI technologies have improved to such an extent that all the display devices produced today—even the very low cost ones—are capable of fairly good quality graphics.

Therefore today, if one says only *display device*, the term will not be mistaken for a display device which cannot also handle graphics—since they all can. The use of the word *graphics*, in other words, is no longer necessary. However, possibly because of the ubiquitous use of *graphical user interfaces* (GUI), the word *graphics* still continues to be used in connection with display devices.

*Reference was made in Chapter 3 to electric charge and voltage. The *capacitance* of an element is defined as the amount of charge which must be stored in it to produce unit voltage difference between its two terminals.

The display is usually a central and integral part of the computer system, and therefore it is not really correct to call it a 'peripheral' device. Today, the storage and processing of high quality graphics, images and animation is playing a big role in our lives. Users have therefore come to expect much from a graphics display in terms of its resolution, range of colors, and speed—i.e. the rate at which graphics can be changed.

Consider Fig. 11.5 (a), which is an image of a hand holding a pen. Although the image is *monochrome*—i.e. in shades of only one color—it does seem to give a reasonably detailed view of the hand, in which the nails of the thumb and index finger can easily be seen. In fact, compared with the high quality images which can be produced today, this particular image is only of modest quality, but it does suffice to make a point.

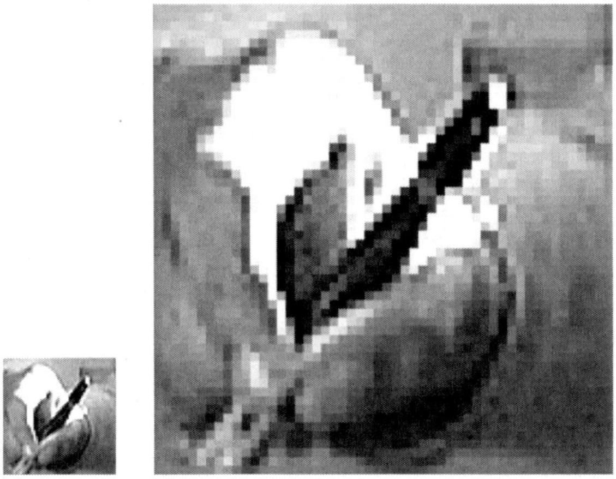

(a) (b)

Fig. 11.5 (a) Image of hand holding a pen and (b) Enlarged view of the image

That point is this: Such an image inside a computer system is made up of a large number of *picture elements*—commonly known as *pixels*—which are arranged in a regular grid of closely-spaced rows and columns. A grid of 100 rows and 100 columns, for example, would have 10,000 pixels. These pixels are arranged with a high density; therefore from normal reading distance the human eye does not see individual pixels, but only what appears to be a 'photographic' image of the object.

To bring out this characteristic of all *digital* images, Fig. 11.5 (b) shows *an enlarged view of the image* of Fig. 11.5 (a)*, in which the individual square-shaped pixels can be seen. The enlargement from Fig. 11.5 (a) to (b) is *four times along each of the two dimensions*, which means that each pixel in (b) occupies sixteen times the area it occupies in the original image (a).

Each monochromatic pixel in Fig. 11.5 (a) or (b) is white, brown, or an intermediate shade of brown—which may be thought of as a mixture of white and brown. Suppose that the designers of this particular display chose to provide a total of 256 shades of brown, including white and brown at too extremes. These shades can be numbered from 0 to 255, with 0 representing brown and 255 representing white.

*Note that this is not the same as saying '*enlarged view of the hand holding a pen*'! Figure 11.5 (b) observed from a distance of a few feet appears the same as Fig. 11.5 (a) observed at normal reading distance.

On such a system, we would need to provide 8 bits of storage per pixel to represent its possible shades of brown, since $2^8 = 256$. If the display screen was made up of, say, 200 rows and 200 columns of pixels, then the total number of pixels would be 40,000, and the amount of storage needed for one full-screen image would be 40,000 bytes.

Display memory is the name given to that memory within the computer system which stores the pixel-by-pixel binary encoding of what is displayed on the display screen. Most often, this display memory is provided within the physical memory address space of the processor, as shown schematically in Fig. 11.6.

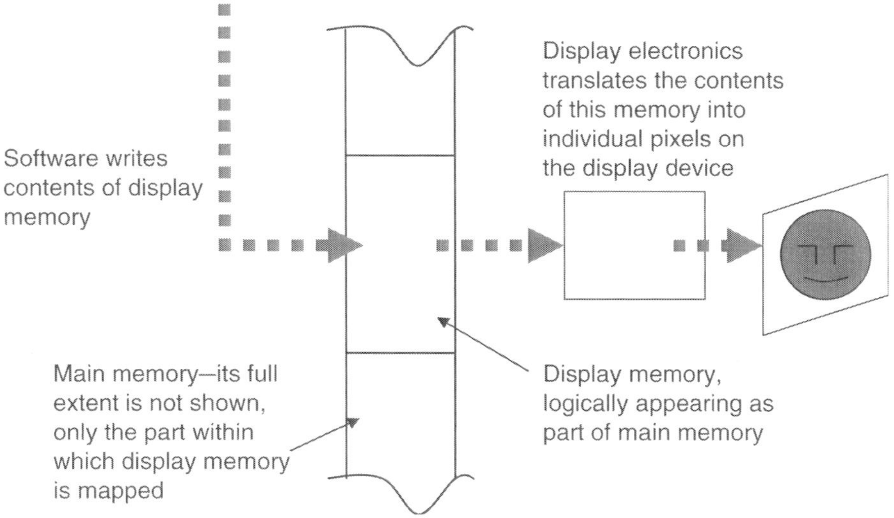

Fig. 11.6 Graphical display sub-system of a computer system

We see in Fig. 11.6 that the display memory is shared by (a) the running program which is using the display, and (b) the display electronics. The program writes pixel values into display memory, while the display electronics transfers and 'translates' the display memory contents for the display device actually being used.

Now consider a more expensive work-station which may have a *color* graphics display of, say, 1200 pixels by 1000 pixels. We know from high-school Physics that colors visible to the eye are made up of three primary colors—red, green and blue. If each of these primary colors is to be given 256 possible shades, then 8 bits are required for encoding the shade of each of the three colors. This means that the color encoding of one pixel now requires $3 \times 8 = 24$ bits.

The total display memory required within this expensive work-station would then be $1200 \times 1000 \times 3 = 3.6$ million bytes. The display electronics would produce the right combination of red, green and blue at every pixel location on the display screen, giving the device a total range of 2^{24} possible colors*.

*The human eye is not in fact capable of distinguishing these many colors.

So far we have discussed only the display of still—i.e. static—images, such as that shown in Fig. 11.5; but today, we want our systems to display also animated images. For us to perceive smooth movement in a sequence of still images, it is necessary that the eyes see about thirty still images per second. This is known as *persistence of vision*, on the basis of which the century-old technique of *cinematography* was developed.

On the work-station we considered above, one full-screen image was seen to require display memory of 3.6 million bytes. If thirty such images—or *frames*—are to be shown in succession in one second, what kind of requirements does this place on the system? Let us consider the answer to this question as it applies to various elements of the graphical display sub-system as shown in Fig. 11.6.

Firstly, the display device—CRT or LCD—should be capable of changing the displayed image thirty times in a second. For CRT devices this has never been a problem, since the 'cathode ray' used inside—i.e. the beam of electrons, as described in the next section—has very little inertia. For the more recent LCD displays, this was a problem in earlier years, but it has since been overcome.

Secondly, for this work-station, the display electronics must be capable of handling the equivalent of $3.6 \times 30 =$ *108 million bytes of data per second*, as this passes through from the display memory to the display screen. The concerned data paths, in other words, should have the capacity to handle data at this rate.

We must also consider the source of the animated displayed images. There are many possibilities, three common examples being:

(a) the images are stored on magnetic or optical disk,
(b) the images are being created by software 'on the fly'—as in a video game, and
(c) the images are being received over the network and displayed 'live'—i.e. without being first fully downloaded on disk.

If the animated images are stored on disk, then the disk-to-memory data path should be capable of sustaining the high data transfer speeds required. To save disk space—and download times over a computer network—video data is usually stored in *compressed format.* The processor must de-compress images before placing them in display memory, and therefore, it must be capable of de-compressing images at the high rates required.

If the images are being created 'on the fly', as in a video game, then clever software techniques are used to speed up the generation and display of moving images. Suppose, a car is to be shown moving against a background. It is then possible that, between two successive frames, only the position of the car changes, not the background. The software should change only that part of display memory which stores pixels of the car; the rest of the image is simply carried forward from one frame to the next.

If the images are being downloaded over a network in compressed format, once again software has to de-compress them at the required rate, so that the user sees the correct number of frames per second. In this case, however, if the network cannot deliver data at the required speeds, the animated image seen will be jerky rather than smooth.

This discussion shows that all the stages of the system—storage, data paths, processor, and network connection—must be capable of the speeds needed for a highly demanding application such as animated graphics. To enhance display quality and speed, computer systems are often provided with specialised *graphics processors* or *accelerators* which take over many of the graphics functions of the kind discussed (see Section 10.11).

11.4 DISPLAY TECHNOLOGY

With a display of 200 × 200 monochrome pixels, and 8 bits per pixel, we have seen that a display memory of 40,000 bytes is required to store one full-screen image. But as long as this 'image' remains in memory, it is not really an image! This is because the display memory contains only 8-bit bytes made up of binary data. These binary values *encode* the shade of grey a particular pixel should have when the 'image' is transferred from display memory to its final destination—i.e. the display device. For a color display, we store three bytes per pixel instead of one, but the basic idea remains the same.

It is the job of special-purpose *display electronics* to transfer the binary-encoded pixels from display memory to the actual display device provided on the system, where suitable display technology makes each pixel visible to the eye. Two main technologies are used today for displaying images: one based on so-called *cathode ray tubes* (CRT), and the other based on *liquid crystal displays* (LCD).

In this section, we shall study in brief the basic principles of operation of CRT and LCD devices*. Note that the basic relationship between software, display memory, and display electronics—shown schematically in Fig. 11.6—holds true for both LCD and CRT devices.

CRT Displays

The term *cathode ray* refers to a beam of electrons—'cathode' being the name given to the element which emits the electrons. The beam of emitted electrons is accelerated and focused using electric and magnetic fields, making it into a 'high-speed electronic pen' which produces the image pixel-by-pixel on a glass surface coated with a phosphorescent substance. Phosphorescence at a pixel position lasts for only a few milliseconds after it is hit by the electron beam, and therefore the displayed image must be *refreshed* some thirty or sixty times a second. Even a static image needs to be thus refreshed, whereas animated images are created by changing the displayed image so many times a second.

Figure 11.7 shows the principle of operation of a CRT display; parts (a) and (b) show, respectively, the side and front views of an evacuated tube of toughened glass.

Consider first part (a) of the figure. The electron beam originates in the small rectangular element shown on the left, travels to the right, and hits the phosphorescent substance—known in brief as *phosphor*—coated on the inside front surface of the glass tube.

Now consider part (b) of the figure, the front view of the display screen. Seen from the front, this surface has an approximately rectangular shape. Electronics inside the tube *deflects* the beam in such a way that it traces out horizontal *scan lines* on the front screen, one after the other, from top to bottom. If a display screen has a resolution of 640 × 480 pixels, for example, the beam will trace out 480 horizontal scan lines across the display screen, from top to bottom, each of which will be made up of 640 pixels.

To create the pixels in each scan line, the beam is *modulated* in time. This means that, as the beam hits the phosphor position corresponding to a pixel, say p, it has exactly the right strength in it to produce the intensity of light required at p. That information—i.e. the intensity of light needed at each pixel—of course comes from display memory.

---

*Both of these technologies are also utilised in televisions, whereas compact, portable devices such as mobile phones and digital cameras make use of LCDs. The picture tube in the older types of televisions is a cathode ray tube (CRT), but these types of televisions use analog video signal, and therefore the concept of pixels is not applicable.

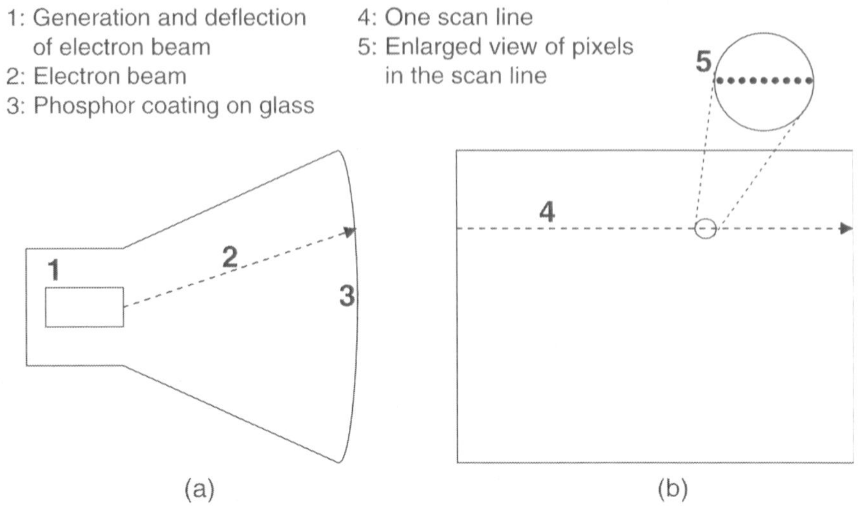

Fig. 11.7 **Principle of operation of CRT display: (a) side view (b) front view**

Therefore, while this may sound complicated, the basic idea is to simply translate the pixel-by-pixel information stored in display memory into an appropriate modulation pattern of the electron beam—so that the beam hits each pixel position with just the right strength. This modulation is the main function of the display electronics mentioned in the previous section, and this is the basic mechanism whereby the beam creates an image on the phosphor coating on the inside surface of the display screen. Since the front surface is transparent, we see the image in front of the screen.

In part (b) of Fig. 11.7, we see one scan line going from left to right, with one tiny part of the scan line enlarged to show the pixels making up that part. The pixels along one scan line, and also scan lines from top to bottom, are placed sufficiently close together for the user to perceive a continuous image on the screen.

In a color CRT display, three electron beams are used instead of one, and pixel positions on the inside of the front glass are coated with spots of three types of phosphor—one for each primary color. Each electron beam is modulated by the encoded image information of one color, and hits only the phosphor spot of that one color.

This means that a pixel in a color display is in fact made up of three distinct sub-pixels, one of each primary color. Since these sub-pixels are packed closely together, the human eye perceives only a single composite color. Display electronics ensures that this perceived color matches the color information stored in the corresponding three bytes of display memory.

Liquid Crystal Displays

CRT displays cannot be made compact, since the electronic elements which generate, accelerate, focus, and deflect the electron beam cannot be miniaturised. In today's world, portability and mobility of devices has assumed great importance, and therefore display technology of a different kind has come into wide-spread use.

Materials known as *liquid crystals* have the property that their transparency to light can be varied by applying a voltage along the path of light. To achieve such controlled transparency to light through a liquid crystal, it is necessary to *polarise* light—which can be done by using a thin plate of a polarising material. Consider a display screen made up of, say, 200 × 200 monochrome pixels. If the transparency of light at each pixel position can be controlled independently, then each pixel can be given the desired shade. The nett effect of such an arrangement is that we see an image made up of 200 × 200 pixels.

Figure 11.8 shows a schematic diagram of how this is achieved. The rectangular grid of pixels is actually made up of thin horizontal and vertical strips of the polarising material, and also transparent electrodes for applying voltage. The liquid crystal forms a thin layer at each pixel position in the middle of this sandwich of strips. The horizontal and vertical strips of transparent electrodes allow voltage to be applied at each pixel position, according to the shade of grey to be produced at that position.

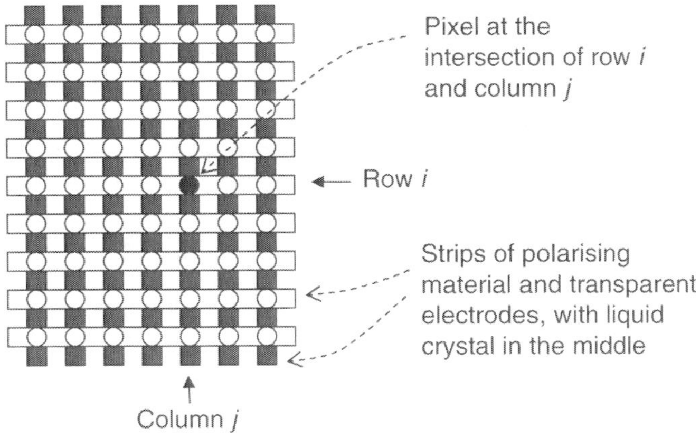

Fig. 11.8 **Principle of operation of LCD display**

Once again, the job of display electronics is to translate the contents of display memory into voltage pulses which must be applied at the right time instants to the row and column electrodes. These voltage pulses control the transparency of the liquid crystal at each pixel position—and therefore the observed intensity of light at each pixel position corresponds to its encoded pixel intensity value stored in display memory.

In a color liquid crystal display, clever optics at each pixel position ensures that the transparency of liquid crystal to the three primary colors can be independently controlled. Once again, therefore, we may say that each pixel is really made up of three sub-pixels, one for each primary color.

Liquid crystal displays are flat in shape, since they do not use anything like an electron beam which must travel from back to front; also, these displays consume less power than CRT displays. Therefore, for portable devices such as mobile phones, laptop PCs, and even wrist-watches, at present there is no alternative to liquid crystal displays. In other respects—such as brightness, contrast, and viewing angle—CRT displays used to perform better, but today LCD devices have achieved comparable performance.

11.5 SOFTWARE FOR USER INTERACTION

In conjunction with an input device, a graphics display can be designed to provide extremely responsive and effective *graphical user interfaces*. For example, when we move a mouse around, the *cursor* on the display screen seems to behave almost as though it is 'tied to the mouse'. In this case the mouse and the display system combine to give us the integrated interface to which we have grown accustomed. Cleverly written software for user interaction achieves this effect, as we shall see briefly in this section.

In hardware, the mouse and the display screen are two distinct devices—one for input and one for output. The right kind of software seems to 'tie together' mouse movement and cursor movement on the screen. The following algorithmic notation describes the iterative steps that a program must execute to achieve this effect:

```
repeat
{
        Read change in mouse position, say Δm
        Translate Δm into change in cursor position, say Δc
        Change display memory for new cursor position
}
```

Many times in a second—sufficiently rapidly to take advantage of persistence of vision—the program reads in the change in mouse position, say Δm. The program translates Δm into a corresponding change in the on-screen cursor position, say Δc. As seen in Section 11.3, the on-screen change in cursor position, Δc, is effected by making appropriate changes in display memory. It is then the job of the display electronics shown in Fig. 11.6 to display the changed cursor position on the screen.

If the basic 'program loop' shown above is sufficiently fast, the user does not perceive any discontinuity between his or her hand movement and on-screen cursor movement—and the two movements appear 'magically' tied together.

In Fig. 11.9, we show an enlarged view of what might be one discrete step of on-screen cursor movement. The background to the cursor is shown in a very light shade; the cursor in its old position is shown slightly darker, while in its new—i.e. changed—position, it is shown in a still darker shade.

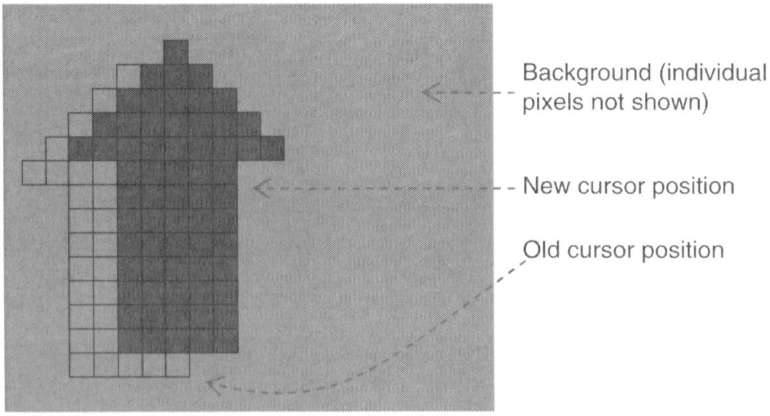

Fig. 11.9 **One step of cursor movement—enlarged view**

Clearly, in order to achieve perceived movement of the cursor, the program should:

(i) replace background pixels by cursor pixels in the new cursor position, and
(ii) replace 'exposed' pixels of the cursor in its old position by background pixels.

These operations are carried out by the program in display memory—and then display electronics does the rest.

The basic mechanism explained above lies at the heart of any graphical user interface—for example, the familiar *drag-and-drop* operation, or the interface to a computer game. If the system response is fast enough, the user sees operations taking place in direct and quick response to mouse movement and mouse clicks. The designer aims to provide the user with an intuitive, friendly, and responsive interface —without which such technology cannot ever achieve wide-spread acceptance among users.

When the keyboard is used to type in text, select commands, or select options within a *dialog box*, similar considerations apply—except for one crucial difference. Keys are necessarily pressed one at a time, so that it is not always possible to create on the screen the effect of a continuous and arbitrary movement of the cursor, an icon, or any other graphical symbol. Most user interfaces on computers today provide an option to the user to rely more on the keyboard or on the mouse.

It is virtually impossible to program even a simple graphical user interface in machine language, by writing programs and functions such as those seen in Chapters 4, 5 and 10. The reason is that machine language programs handle data at hardware level, in bits and bytes. A graphical user interface, on the other hand, uses more complex entities such as the *cursor*, *icons*, *dialog boxes*, and so on. No doubt an icon is nothing but a set of pixels arranged in a certain way; however, the programmer working with an icon does not think about the pixels making up the icon. Instead, the programmer thinks of an icon as an integral entity in itself, on which appropriate operations can be carried out.

For this purpose, therefore, libraries of functions are available to facilitate programming with 'higher level' entities such as icons, dialog boxes, and so on. This makes it possible, for example, to create a new icon with a certain shape, to define some of its properties, and to associate it with another entity or operation on the system. A pre-written library function to move an icon, for example, then also works with the newly created icon.

SUMMARY

User interaction—achieved through a combination of hardware and software—is an important and integral aspect of a modern computer system. Input devices, display technologies, and software work together to provide the graphical interfaces which are in common use today on powerful work-stations, PCs, and hand-held devices.

The keyboard (or keypad) works on the basis of detecting the electrical contact made between a row wire and a column wire when the user presses a key. The touchpad works in a similar way, except that the user's touch changes the capacitance between a row and a column conductor underneath. The mechanical mouse detects motion by the change in values of a pair of potentiometers which turn with the motion of a ball.

The graphics display sub-system consists of the display memory, display electronics, and the display device. Two types of display devices commonly in use today are the cathode ray tube (CRT) and the liquid crystal display (LCD). Resolution, contrast, and speed are some of the key characteristics of a display device. These determine the memory sizes required for static images, and the data rates required to achieve animation.

Software plays a key role in providing the functionality of an intuitive and responsive graphical user interface. User's input—received through the mouse or the keyboard—must be translated quickly into appropriate changes in display memory, so that the display electronics then shows the altered display. In this way, the software in effect seems to 'tie together' the input device and the display.

REVIEW QUESTIONS

1. List the five steps of the complete cycle of user-computer interaction.
2. State in brief how the running program detects that a particular key has been pressed on a keyboard.
3. State in brief how two input 'events' are associated with a single key closure.
4. Describe in brief the basic principle of operation of a mechanical mouse.
5. Describe in brief the basic principle of operation of a touch-sensitive device.
6. List three characteristics which define the quality of a graphics display device.
7. In the context of a display device, what is the meaning of 'monochrome'?
8. In the context of a display device, what is the meaning of a 'pixel'?
9. What is the function of display memory in a display sub-system?
10. A monochrome display provides 64 shades of grey, and has the size of 200 × 200 pixels. What is the size in bits of the display memory required?
11. What is the function of display electronics in a display sub-system?
12. How is color produced in a CRT display?
13. How is color produced in a liquid crystal display?
14. Explain in brief what is meant by 'persistence of vision'.
15. In a computer system, list the three possible sources of animated graphics.
16. On a CRT display, why is it necessary to refresh even a static image thirty or more times in a second?
17. On a CRT display, what is the meaning of a 'scan line'?
18. Why is that CRT displays cannot be made as compact as liquid crystal displays?
19. State in brief how transparency to light is controlled at a single pixel position of a liquid crystal display.
20. Using simple algorithmic notation, show how user interaction software ties together an input device and the display device.

EXERCISES

1. In Section 11.3 we saw that, for a display having 1200 × 1000 pixels, one color image requires 3.6 million bytes of data. Animated graphics would require thirty such frames to be displayed in a second. If the bus along which this data is transferred has a width of four bytes, what is the minimum bus cycle time which will support the nett transfer speed required for animated graphics?
2. It was stated in Section 11.3 that Fig. 11.4 (b) observed from a distance of about eight feet appears the same as Fig. 11.4 (a) observed at normal reading distance. Verify this statement by using rules of geometry and the fact that the size of an object perceived by the human eye is proportional to the angle that the object subtends at the eye.
3. Recall the simple 'repeat loop' described in Section 11.4, which ties together movement of the mouse and movement of the cursor on display screen. Now assume that, instead of a mouse, a simple computer system provides only four arrow keys (left, right, up and down) to control the movement of the cursor on its display screen. Using algorithmic notation of the same type, write the 'repeat loop' which would be required to have cursor movement controlled by these arrow keys.
4. Keyboards on PCs offer an *auto-repeat* feature which operates when the user performs text entry, for example, while using a word processor program. This means that if a pressed key is <u>held down</u>, the system behaves as though the corresponding character is being sent repeatedly as input to the program.
   (a) Try out the operation of this feature on any PC available to you.
   (b) No change is made in the keyboard hardware to support auto-repeat. Explain in brief, what changes would be required in the keyboard software to support this feature.
5. Refine the answer to part (b) of Exercise 3 so as to provide the auto-repeat feature with the four arrow keys.
6. Consider the monochrome graphical object shown in enlarged mode in Fig. 11.10. This object has to be rotated right by 90 degrees around point *p*. Perform this rotation <u>by hand</u> and determine:

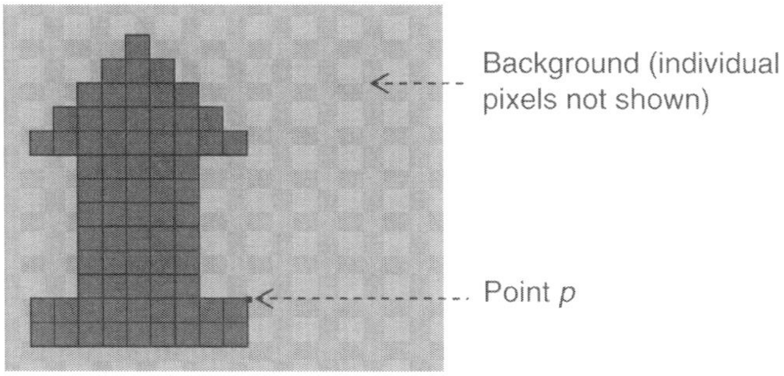

Fig. 11.10 **Graphical object for Exercises 6 and 7**

(i) pixels of the object in its old position which will be replaced by background pixels, and

(ii) background pixels which will be replaced by pixels of the object in its new position.

Note that, for simplicity, we have assumed that all object pixels are of one uniform color, and all background pixels are of another uniform color.

7. Consider once again the monochrome graphical object of Fig. 11.10. This object has to be enlarged by one pixel in height, while it maintains its general shape. Perform this enlargement by hand and determine the background pixels which will be replaced by pixels of the object in its enlarged version. If any technical difficulty is encountered in the process of enlargement, try to identify the cause of the difficulty.
[Of course, it should be clear that, due to the limited resolution available, we cannot enlarge or shrink a graphical object by less than one pixel in height or width.]

8. Repeat the previous exercise, but this time the object has to be enlarged by one pixel in width, while it maintains its general shape. If any technical difficulty is encountered in the process of enlargement, try to identify the cause of the difficulty.

SECONDARY STORAGE AND OTHER DEVICES

12

12.1 INTRODUCTION

In the previous chapter, we studied the hardware and software elements of a computer system which provide graphical user interaction. In the present chapter, we shall take a broad overview of some of the other input, output and storage devices which are used today in conjunction with computer systems.

In Chapter 9, we looked at the memory hierarchy within a computer system, and saw that secondary storage supports the file system as well as virtual memory. For the last several decades, the most commonly used device for providing secondary storage has been *magnetic disk*, although today *flash memory* also plays that role in hand-held systems.

Apart from secondary storage, users also have longer term storage requirements for other functions such as *archival storage*, *backup storage*, and *distribution*. These functions do not require the stored data to remain available *online*; rather, data is stored on *removable media*, of which *optical disk* is the most commonly used example today.

There are also many other useful devices which may be available on a system—such as a *clock*, a *printer*, a *speaker* and *microphone* pair, and a network connection through wired or wireless LAN. We shall take a brief look at the principles of operation and typical applications of some of these devices.

12.2 MAGNETIC DISKS

Magnetic media have been used for non-volatile storage since at least the 1950s*. For example, the *magnetic tape* in a tape recorder stores a piece of music by virtue of the fact that the longitudinal pattern of magnetisation along the tape mimics the sound of the music. The tape is magnetised in this way during the *record* operation, and *playback* means sensing the magnetisation pattern and converting it into sound waves by using an amplifier and speaker(s). A thin, tough plastic gives the tape its mechanical properties, while a coating of magentisable material on the plastic turns it into a medium for recording and playback of sound signals.

---

*Before semiconductor memories came into use, early computers used tiny *ferrite cores* to store individual bits of main memory. The main memory was therefore non-volatile, although that property was not utilised in any way in those early days. For this reason, on these early systems, main memory was also known as *core memory*.

A tape recorder is equipped with two *heads*—one for recording and one for playback; in each case, the operation is performed when the moving tape passes under the appropriate head. The record head, for example, is basically a tiny electromagnet coming in contact with the moving tape, as shown schematically in Fig. 12.1. Current through the coil generates a magnetic field corresponding to the sound signal being recorded, and this field magnetises the moving tape—so that the linear pattern of magnetisation produced length-wise on the tape corresponds to the sound signal.

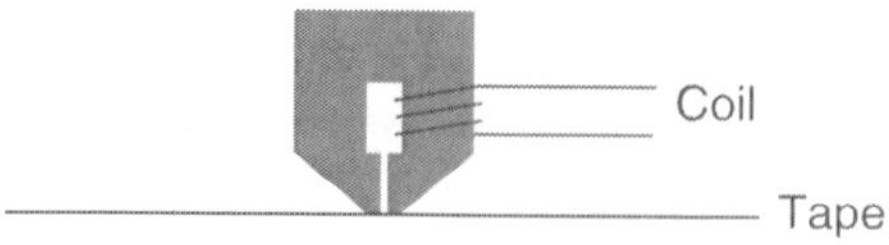

Fig. 12.1 Record head on a magnetic tape

During record and playback operations, the two respective principles of electromagnetics at work are the following:

a. current in a coil generates a magnetic field, and
b. a changing magnetic field induces a voltage across a conducting coil placed in the field.

A magnetic disk makes use of these same basic principles—but, as we shall see, the rest of the design of the disk is very different from that of a tape.

Unlike the conventional tape recorder, the magnetic disk is a *digital* storage medium—i.e. it stores only '1's and '0's, using two directions of magnetisation to represent the two binary values. The magnetic medium itself is coated on a rigid disk, which rotates around its spindle at a high speed. The combined *read/write* head of the magnetic disk is located on an arm which can move radially in and out over the surface of the disk.

Figure 12.2 shows in a schematic way the top view of the surface of a magnetic disk. The *disk arm*, shown on the right, can be moved in and out; the tiny *read/write* head is located on this arm. For a read or write operation on the disk, the *read/write* head is brought to the required radial position with accuracy of the order of a micron (1 micron = 10^{-6} meters). As the disk rotates underneath, one *track* on the disk surface moves under the head in one revolution of the disk. Data is stored longitudinally along each track.

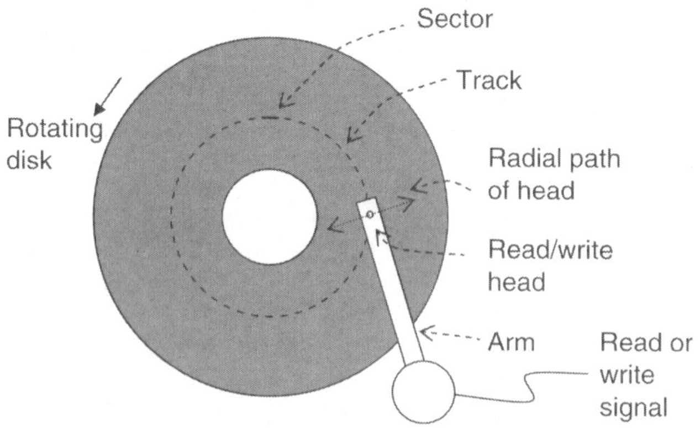

Fig. 12.2 Organisation of one surface of a magnetic disk

The smallest unit of data transfer between magnetic disk and main memory is usually of the order of 512 to 4096 bytes. In fact, this is much smaller than the amount of data which can be stored on a track. Therefore, each circular track is divided length-wise into many *sectors*, which is the smallest unit of data transfer between disk and main memory.

There are two important reasons which dictate this strategy of dividing a track into many sectors: (i) Error detection and correction techniques are more effective on smaller blocks of data, and (ii) Better utilisation of disk space can be achieved by dividing tracks into the smaller units of sectors, since the smallest unit of data transfer also becomes the smallest unit of allocation of disk space to files.

The two examples below clarify these points by means of some typical magnetic disk parameters. Example 12.1 considers the storage capacity of a disk, while Example 12.2 considers its *data transfer rate* and *latency*.

Example 12.1

Consider a magnetic disk which has a radial track density of 10000 tracks/cm, which corresponds to one track per micron. The disk has radial operating distance of 2.4 cm—i.e. the distance between its outermost and innermost tracks. The total number of tracks on one surface is therefore $10000 \times 2.4 = 24000$.

Naturally, the circumference of a track increases as we move radially out. Assume that the average circumference of a track is 15 cm, and that one sector occupies 0.1 cm = 1 mm of length along the track. Therefore, on average, a track is divided into $15/0.1 = 150$ sectors, and the total number of sectors on the disk is $24000 \times 150 = 3600000$.

If each sector stores 512 bytes = 4096 bits of data, then the bit density of data storage along a sector is $4096/0.1 = 40960$ bits/cm. This number gives an idea of the rate at which magnetisation changes along the length of a sector.

The data storage capacity of one surface of this disk is $3600000 \times 512 = 1800$ megabytes. If the disk has six such surfaces stacked together on a common spindle, the total disk capacity is 10800 megabytes = 10.8 gigabytes (ignoring for the present the small difference between 1 megabyte and 10^6 bytes).

Latency of a magnetic disk is defined as the time taken for the required data sector to become available under the *read/write* head on the disk arm. Due to the structure of the disk as outlined in Fig. 12.2, this latency has two components:

(i) *Seek time* is the time taken for the head to be moved radially to the required track. On modern disks, this is in the range of 1 to 10 milliseconds, depending on the radial distance that the arm has to be moved from its previous position.

(ii) *Rotational delay* is the time taken for the required sector on the track to reach a position under the head, so that it can be read or written, On average, this delay is half the time taken by the disk to make one revolution—since the required sector is equally likely to be at any position along the circular track.

Therefore, we can say that *total latency* = *seek time* + *rotational delay*. But it should be noted that both these components of the total latency are random in nature, since they depend on the position of the disk arm prior to executing a read or write command.

Example 12.2

Now let us assume that the disk of the previous example is rotating at an angular speed of 6000 revolutions per minute (rpm), which equals 100 revolutions per second. The time for making one revolution is therefore 10 milliseconds (ms).

One complete track passes under the head in 10 ms, and contains on average 150 sectors. Since each sector has 0.5 kilobytes of data, we can say that 150 × 0.5 kilobytes of data pass under the head in 10 ms. Therefore, the rate at which data is read from or written into disk is $150 \times 0.5 / (10^{-2})$ kilobytes/second, which is 7.5 megabytes/second*.

Note that this is the rate at which data is transferred—but only after the required sector reaches the *read/write* head on the disk arm.

The total latency of the disk can also be estimated. The time of one revolution is 10 ms, and therefore rotational delay is between 0 and 10 ms. Assuming seek time in the range of 2 to 10 ms, we can say that the total latency is in the range from 2 ms to 20 ms. The average latency will then be the average of these two quantities, i.e. 11 ms.

The magnetic disk is known as a *direct access* storage device because any required data sector on it can be accessed directly, without having to access any intervening sectors. In other words, the average latency figure—such as the one calculated in Example 12.2—applies to any data sector on the disk. To perform a read or write operation on a magnetic disk, the program supplies to the disk controller the track number, sector number, and number of sectors to be read or written**.

Tracks and sectors on the surface of the disk are formed by appropriate patterns of magnetisation along the track and between tracks, in an operation known as *formatting* the disk. Sensor electronics associated with the read/write head is capable of locating the required track and sector by its track number and sector number.

Some percentage of space along each track is used for recording sector numbers, providing inter-sector gaps, and so on. Naturally, the nett usable data within each sector—for example, 512 bytes as seen in Example 12.1—excludes all such overhead, and it also excludes additional bits stored with each sector for error detection and correction.

The magnetic disk has become the undisputed storage work-horse of computer industry today. Even within a very small package, disks are capable of storing many gigabytes of data and of making it available to main memory with small latency and high transfer rate. Behind the 'cyber-space' created by the *world wide web* lie millions of rotating magnetic disks, with their millions of

*If the disk has the same number of sectors on inner and outer tracks, the transfer rate as calculated above is uniformly applicable. If the outer tracks contain a larger number of sectors, they will in effect provide faster data rates than the inner tracks. In this case, the transfer rate calculated above becomes the average transfer rate. Note also that the *disk controller* buffers data sectors on their way to and from the disk, and therefore the rate calculated here does not refer to the data transfer rate between disk controller and main memory.

**In contrast, the magnetic tape drive provides a *sequential access* device, because the required data on a tape can be reached only after spooling through the intervening length of tape from its previous position. Earlier generations of computers made heavy use of magnetic tapes for backup, archival storage and distribution. Today, however, these functions are performed using optical disks. Until at least the 1970s, many computer systems also used magnetic tape drives in actual processing of data in sequential mode.

gigabytes of data, made available through *web servers* and the Internet to users around the world. Large websites utilise hundreds of disk drives and high-speed interconnections, which make up so-called 'disk farms'.

For all its versatility, compact size, and storage capacity, there are certain important requirements for which the magnetic disk is not suited. One major reason for this is that the disk is a *non-removable storage medium*. In order to achieve high storage densities and transfer speeds, the disk and head assembly, along with its associated electronics, is built into a sealed package from which the disk cannot be removed.

To meet the requirements of *backup*, *archival storage* and/or *distribution* of data, multi-media content, and software, such a packaged magnetic disk unit is not at all suitable. Earlier generations of computers did make use of removable magnetic disks—and tapes—for these functions, but several better alternatives have emerged over the years.

Today *optical disk* and *flash memory* provide far more suitable media for backup, archival storage, and distribution functions. In particular, for distribution of data, multi-media content, and software, the optical disk is ideally suited because it can be mass produced by 'stamping out' one entire disk at a time; this is not possible with magnetic disk or flash memory, which can only be written sequentially, block by block.

Note 12.1

An interesting recent development in physics has led to the production of far more compact magnetic disks, especially useful for mobile devices; the story forms an interesting case study in the relationship between science and technology.

It has long been known to physicists that, in the presence of a magnetic field, ferromagnetic materials exhibit a very slight change in their resistivity to electric current. This change is, however, too small to be of any practical value.

In the years 1988–89, two scientists in Europe discovered so-called *giant magnetoresistance* (GMR) in elements created out of layers of very finely aligned magnetic and non-magnetic metal crystals. Such elements—which can be produced only in highly controlled conditions—exhibit change in resistivity in a magnetic field which far exceeds similar changes observed in other materials; hence the word *giant* in GMR.

In subsequent years, GMR has been used to design and build highly sensitive read/write heads for magnetic disks, leading to higher storage densities and more compact disks. In the year 2007, the Nobel prize for Physics was awarded jointly to European scientists Fert and Grünberg for their independent discovery of GMR.

The type of technology which allows GMR sensing elements to be built is today described as *nanotechnology*. It requires extremely fine control in processing and manufacturing, which is not possible without the use of very sophisticated computer technology. Thus this case study can also be understood as: Technology leads to new discovery in science, which in turn leads to improved technology*.

*See 'The Discovery of Giant Magnetoresistance', Scientific Background on the Nobel Prize in Physics 2007, at the website www.kva.se of the Royal Swedish Academy of Science.

12.3 OPTICAL DISKS

An optical disk makes use of a narrow beam of laser light, and distinguishes between a '1' and a '0' by the way in which the beam is reflected back by a shiny metallic coating on a transparent polycarbonate disk. A laser beam is basically a coherent light beam of a single wavelength; it can be focused on an area of the disk which is much less than a micron (i.e. 10^{-3} millimeter) across, resulting in very high storage density.

A *compact disk* (CD), the first type of optical disk to achieve wide use, has tiny 'pits' on the inside of its reflecting surface. These 'pits' alter the way in which the laser beam is reflected back, as compared to flat spots without pits (which are known as 'lands'). As the disk rotates, the serial pattern of pits and lands on it moves over the electronic circuit which generates the laser beam and detects its reflection. The detector circuit—i.e. the 'read head' of the optical disk drive—reads the sequence of pits and lands, and generates the electronic '1's and '0's used by the computer system.

A side view of the arrangement of an optical disk drive—i.e. a cross-section—has been shown schematically in part (a) of Fig. 12.3.

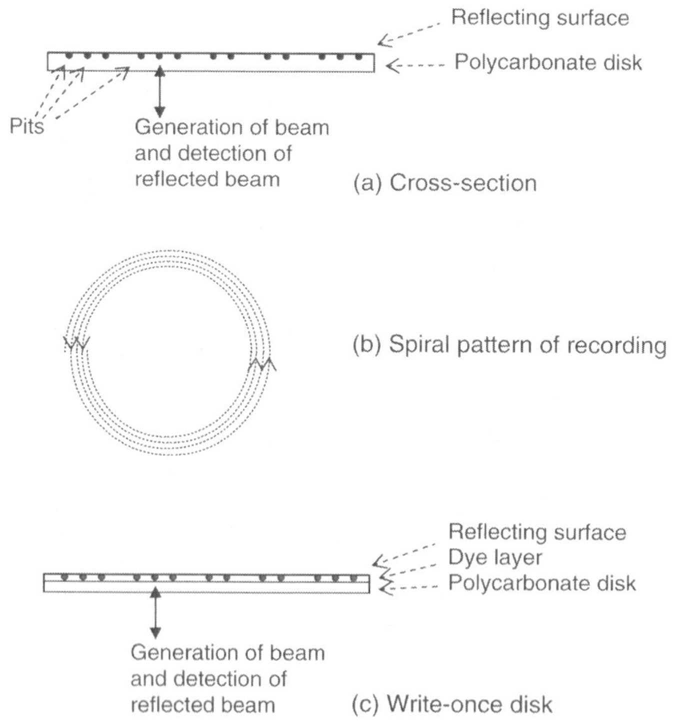

Fig. 12.3 Recording of binary data on an optical disk

Since pits and lands are created mechanically on the disk, the storage on a CD of this type is *read only*—i.e. the CD drive inside the user's PC cannot make any changes in the recorded data. Part (b) of the figure shows the *spiral* pattern of recorded data on the surface of an optical disk. Unlike the concentric tracks on the surface of a magnetic disk, the recording pattern on an optical disk is that of a single long spiral running over the entire recording surface. Because of this, and also because of its slower speed of rotation, the *seek time* of an optical disk is much longer than that of a magnetic disk.

Unlike a magnetic disk, the optical disk is made to rotate about its axis at an angular speed which is inversely proportional to the radial distance at which the read head is positioned. This means that the linear speed with which pits and lands pass over the read head remains constant—and with this the rate at which '1's and '0's are read.

The *compact disk* (CD) format was developed originally for distribution of music, and for that application it has replaced the magnetic tape cassette to a very large extent. The great advantage of such CDs is that they can be 'stamped out' from a master disk at very little cost per piece. A magnetic disk or tape must be recorded serially as the recording surface moves across the head. But a master CD, with the correct pattern of pits and lands on it, can be used to create an imprint CD in one single operation, making the process much more cost-effective for mass production. For this reason, the *read only* CD format is widely used for distribution of music, software, directories, and so on.

The optical properties of laser beams allow very high data storage density to be achieved on optical disks, as illustrated below in Example 12.3 using some typical figures.

Example 12.3

An optical disk has outer diameter of 120 mm. Assuming 80 square centimeters or 8000 square millimeters of storage area, and storage density of 1 bit per square micron, the total number of bits recordable is $8000 \times 10^6 = 8000$ megabits.

The number above includes data bits as well as error correction bits, header bits, etc. Assuming that 50% of all bits are data bits, the data storage capacity of such a disk is 4000 megabits, or 500 megabytes. Compared to the earlier magnetic removable storage media—or 'floppy disks'—this figure is larger by a factor of more than a hundred!

With the numbers as above, the total length of the spiral of pits and lands on the disk can be roughly estimated as $(8000 \times 10^6 \text{ bits}) \times (10^{-6} \text{ meters/bit}) = 8$ km*.

The speed of data transfer to and from such a device depends both on storage density and rotation speed. It should be clear that, for mechanical reasons, a removable rotating storage device must rotate much more slowly than a non-removable device. If the 'press fit' optical disk is rotated on its spindle at the speed of a non-removable disk, it will simply fly off due to the centrifugal forces generated. The speed of a non-removable magnetic disk may be 7200 rpm, but that of a CD is limited to a few hundred rpm.

After CDs achieved widespread use for computer data and software, naturally the need was felt to produce *writable* versions of optical disks. This means that the laser beam in the optical disk drive must somehow alter the reflectivity of a tiny spot on the disk, the spot taking the place of the 'pit' mentioned above.

In *write-once* optical disks, this is achieved by using a layer of a chemical dye to control the effective reflectivity of a spot on the reflector surface, as shown schematically in part (c) of Fig. 12.3. As initially

*The rounded numbers of Example 12.3 have been chosen for illustrative purposes only. For the standard CD format, the actual numbers differ slightly from these.

coated on the layer, the dye is opaque to light, but a laser beam with slightly higher power can break up dye molecules and make a spot transparent rather than opaque. The pattern of opaque and transparent spots corresponds to the mechanical pits and lands seen in part (a) of Fig. 12.3. For reading the disk, the laser beam is given less power, so that it does not break up the dye molecules.

The dye-based disk allows only one write operation on the disk, for the simple reason that once-broken dye molecules at a spot cannot be regenerated. To allow multiple write operations on an optical disk, a different technique is used. Spots on a layer of a specially designed metal alloy can be switched between crystalline and amorphous state by the application of appropriate amount of heat through a laser beam. Optical properties of the material are different in its crystalline and amorphous forms. A layer of such material on the underside of the reflector on the disk therefore allows '1's and '0's to be written in the form of tiny spots with different effective reflectivity.

While the original CD format is in wide use, improvements in technology have led to the development of *digital video disk* (DVD) storage format, with much higher storage density and therefore much higher storage capacity per disk. The speed at which data transfer takes place between the disk and main memory has increased over the years, to keep up with higher demands such as those of video applications. On drives, these speeds are indicated by factors such as 32×, which means that the drive transfers data 32 times faster than the original CD rate (1×) of approximately 150 kilobytes per second.

12.4 FLASH MEMORIES

Semiconductor memory based on transistors switching 'on' and 'off' is necessarily volatile, for the simple reason that transistors cannot operate without power supply. Therefore, since the introduction of semiconductor memories in the early 1970s, critical need has been felt for *non-volatile* semiconductor memory, and also for *read-only* memory. Non-volatile semiconductor memory allows for long-term storage of data, with the advantage over magnetic disk of not having any moving parts. Read-only memory is needed to protect programs and data against accidental deletion and corruption.

The earliest read-only memories (ROMs) could only be 'written' or 'programmed' at the time of their manufacture—since 'writing' in this case involved making physical changes in the array-like circuits of the memories. But this restriction becomes a handicap, since computer companies need to program such memories at a much later stage, at the time of final assembly of computer systems. Therefore *programmable* read-only memories (PROMs) were developed, which allowed computer companies to program the memories as needed for the computer system being built. These PROMs were non-volatile and, after one round of programming, they became read-only.

Later came PROMs which could also be *erased*, by using ultra-violet light, to become ready for another round of programming—and still later came *electrically erasable* PROMs (EEPROMs) which could be erased simply by applying higher voltages to the memory circuits. EEPROMs satisfied the requirements of non-volatility as well as protection against accidental deletion or corruption, since the higher voltages needed for erasing memory contents would not occur during normal computer use.

All these types of memories mentioned—ROMs, PROMs, EPROMS and EEPROMs—followed the same basic organisation of byte-addressable, random-access memory which was described in Chapter 3 (refer in particular to Figs. 3.11 and 3.12).

The development of so-called *flash memories* of today is a follow-up on EEPROM technology, with two important differences:

(i) Far greater density and capacity of storage are now available, because VLSI technology has made it possible to build much smaller memory circuits.
(ii) In view of (i), in many applications flash memory now provides secondary storage, rather than a slice of main memory (as standard EEPROMs do). Therefore flash memories are designed with the *block-oriented* format more suitable for secondary storage, and not the byte-addressable format shown in Figs. 3.11 and 3.12.

The common principle of operation of a semiconductor single-bit cell of an EEPROM and flash memory is illustrated schematically in Fig. 12.4. The darker rectangle in the center of the diagram is a kind of 'metallic island', which is surrounded by insulating material on all sides. Three terminals—labeled 's', 'd' and 'g' in the diagram—are available for the application of appropriate voltages to the device*.

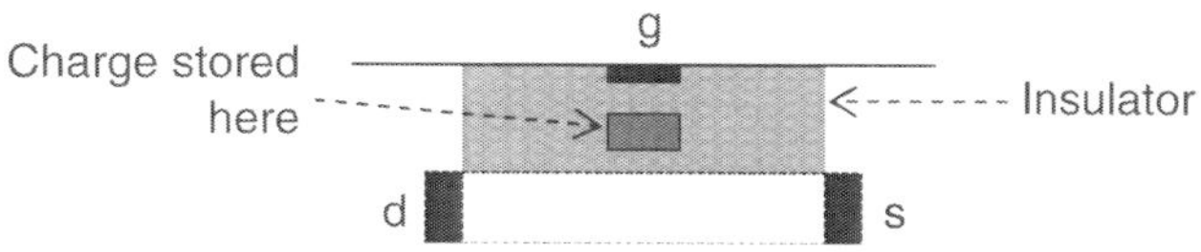

Fig. 12.4 **Semiconductor non-volatile storage of one bit**

With the right combination of voltages, some amount of electric charge can be deposited on the island—or removed from it. However, in the absence of any voltage on the three terminals, the charge remains on the island almost indefinitely, since it is surrounded on all sides by insulating material. The presence or absence of charge on the island indicates a '1' or a '0'—and thus we have here a non-volatile storage of one bit.

For sensing—i.e. reading—the '1' or '0' state of the storage cell, a lower voltage is applied to the terminals. This voltage does not alter the charge present on the island, but its presence or absence can be sensed across the two terminals 's' and 'd'.

For creating larger amounts of storage, a correspondingly larger number of single-bit cells of this type must be connected together. Naturally, this can be done in many ways, giving rise to different memory organisations. Compared to byte-addressable EEPROMs, these memories can be made more compact by allowing *erase* and *write* operations to take place only on a block of bytes, rather than on individual bytes**. For their use as secondary storage devices, this restriction on flash memories does not create a difficulty, since secondary storage operations take place a block at a time in any case.

---

*Source, drain and gate terminals, respectively, of a field effect transistor.

**In flash memories, writing '0' and '1' bits are not symmetric operations. 'Erasing' a block means filling all bits in the block with '1's. Then '0's are written as needed, but a '0' once written cannot be overwritten with a '1' until the whole block is erased again. There is a limit—which is quite large, for practical purposes—on the number of erase and write cycles which a block of memory can support before beginning to lose its storage property.

Example 12.4

The familiar 'memory stick' is a flash memory device which works under the control of a tiny microcontroller provided on the stick. The microcontroller performs all the required operations of the flash memory, and also communicates with the main computer into which the stick is plugged in.

Communication between the microcontroller and the main computer takes place over the *universal serial bus* (USB) which connects the two (see the next section).

Strictly speaking, therefore, the arrangement is that of two computers communicating over the USB link. Since the function performed by the microcontroller is limited—and invisible to the computer user—the memory stick appears to the user to be purely a storage device. The small amount of power needed to operate the device is received by it from the main computer over the USB link.

12.5 COMMUNICATION LINKS AND DEVICES

In the 1950s, it was an extremely difficult and expensive proposition to build or even to operate a computer, and only a small number of computers were in use around the world. When data had to be exchanged between computers, it was done using magnetic tape, or even 'paper tape' or 'punched cards' which recorded '0's and '1's as tiny holes.

In the decades since then, computers have become incredibly less expensive and more numerous. From around the 1960s, scientists and engineers realised that great advantages could be derived if computers could *communicate* with each other—i.e. if they could send and receive data from one another—without someone having to physically carry a magnetic tape, for example, from one computer to another.

In the language of input and output, communication between two computers—say computer A and computer B—requires the following:

(i) A *communication link* which can carry an electrical, electromagnetic, or optical signal from one computer to the other,
(ii) Devices—also known as *adaptors*—on the two computers which translate the user's instructions, to send or receive data, into appropriate operations to be performed over the communication link, and
(iii) *Software* which carries out the functions specific to the task of communication, such as, for example, error detection and correction.

Figure 12.5 shows a schematic diagram of such an arrangement between two computers. In the language of Chapter 10, *send* is analogous to an output operation, and *receive* is analogous to an input operation.

If the communication link is capable of carrying data only in one direction, say from computer A to computer B, but not in the other direction, it is known as a *simplex* link. If the link can carry data in either direction, but only in one direction at a time, it is known as a *half-duplex* link. A *full-duplex* link is one which can carry data in both directions simultaneously—a common example being the ubiquitous telephone.

Use of telephones was widespread around the world in the 1950s, and therefore the earliest communication between computers utilised devices to convert computer data into signals which could be carried over existing *voice grade* telephone lines and exchanges. The telephone network, in other words, provided the communication links of the day.

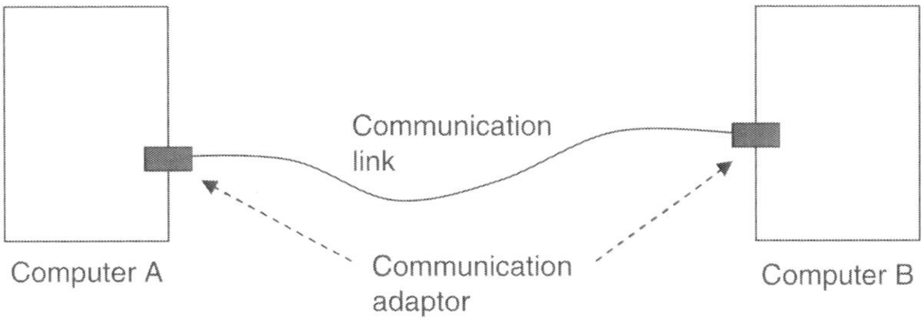

Fig. 12.5 **A communication link between computers**

The electronic process to convert binary computer data into signals for a communication link is known as *modulation*; and the converse process, to convert signals on the link back into binary data, is known as *demodulation*. Therefore the device which connects computers to telephone lines is known as *modulator-demodulator*, or *modem*.

Telephone modems today can send and receive data at the speed of 56 kilobits per second (kbps), whereas the earliest modems communicated at the speed of a mere 110 bits per second (bps). A modem can be used to connect a home PC to other computers, using the simple telephone line to effectively 'plug into' to the Internet, which is a worldwide network of computers and many different types of communication links.

From the time of the earliest communication links between computers, many factors have led to continuing and ongoing development of links with much higher speeds, including *wireless* links which allow user equipment—telephone or PC—to be mobile.

The many inter-related factors driving the growth in computer networks may be listed as:

- higher processing speeds and memory capacities of computers,
- steadily decreasing costs,
- increasing numbers of computers in use around the world, and
- the vast range of applications for which computers are used.

As a result of such growth, today speeds as high as several megabits per second are possible over commonly available and inexpensive communication links.

Computers and different types of communication links combine to form *computer networks*. The familiar Internet can in fact be thought of as network of networks. Based on the communication technology used and the physical reach of the network, we may have a *local area network* (LAN), a *wide area network*, a *wireless network*, and so on.

Recall the discussion in Section 10.7 about modes of data transfer. Unlike the *parallel* mode of input/output used for disks and printers, a communication link operates in *serial* mode—which means that the data being sent or received can be thought of as a bit stream which is carried over the link after the appropriate type of modulation is applied to it.

A typical computer system today has provision for several types of communication links to be connected to it. Typical such devices include: a modem for use with a telephone, a LAN connection, the general-purpose serial link known as the *universal serial bus* (USB), and usually also provision to connect to a wireless LAN.

The communication device—which is also known as *communication adaptor* or *network adaptor*—allows computers to communicate over a link, by performing the following main categories of functions:

(i) ***Buffering of data***—Data is transferred from the computer to the adaptor in parallel, a byte or a word at a time. This data is buffered and then transmitted serially over the link; on the receiver side, the data is assembled and buffered before it is transferred to main memory, a byte or a word at a time. Buffering allows for speed mismatches between the computer and the link to be handled without loss of data.

(ii) ***Modulation and demodulation***—The data being sent or received must be modulated and demodulated, as appropriate to the nature of the link; if an optical fiber link is used, for example, the '1's and '0's of the computer circuits will get converted into extremely tiny pulses of light.

(iii) ***Error detection and correction***—Communication links are prone to data transmission errors, and therefore some technique of *error detection* and/or *error correction* must be provided in the adaptors.

(iv) ***Book-keeping***—This involves keeping track of data which has or has not been correctly sent and received. Some header information is usually added to the data sent on the link, to allow the receiving end to verify its correct reception.

(v) ***Link control***—Functions specific to the communication link must also be performed by the controller, for example, checking the status of the link.

Communication links come in many varieties, and the same variety is reflected in the adaptors required. However, in general, all adaptors must perform the broad categories of functions outlined above. As in the case of the disk controller, a communication adaptor may also have an embedded processor built into it.

Of course, like any other input/output device, a communication adaptor must also perform data transfers to and from main memory, a byte or a word at a time, using either programmed I/O or direct memory access. All of the principles and techniques discussed in Chapter 10 are therefore applicable to communication adaptors as well.

In Chapter 15, we shall take a further look at the working of computer networks, and in particular the kind of software that is required in a network.

12.6 PRINTERS

Use of paper and ink as a medium for recording and conveying information goes back more than a couple of thousand years*. As we have seen, today computer systems handle information in electronic form, encoding all forms of information using the binary digits '1' and '0'. Printers are the devices used to transfer such electronic data from a computer onto paper, basically by producing tiny dots of ink on paper according to the characters or graphics which are to be printed.

**Papyrus* was the writing medium which Ancient Egyptians made from dried plant-matter of a wetland plant of the Nile delta. The English word 'paper' is derived from *papyrus*.

Figure 12.6 illustrates how the three characters **`Tgl`** can be created using a *dot matrix* of 7 rows and 5 columns for each character. Laser printers today can produce a resolution of 1200 dots per inch, and even dot-matrix printers produce better resolution that what is evident in Fig. 12.6, but this low resolution serves us better as an illustration.

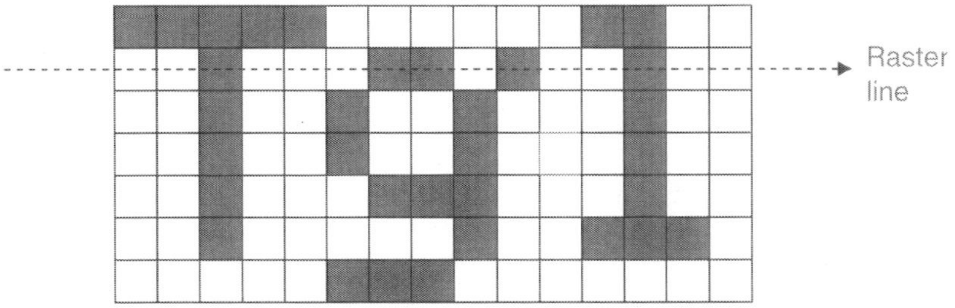

Fig. 12.6 Characters created using rows of dots

We shall now take a brief look at how different types of printers produce the required patterns of ink dots on paper to generate required characters or graphics.

Laser Printers

A laser printer prints a page only after creating in its internal memory a dot-by-dot image of the entire page. This page image is in fact created one row of dots at a time. All the dots making up one row of the page image are said to make up one *raster line* or *scan line*. Thus, before printing a page, a laser printer needs to have in its internal *raster memory* the binary images of all the raster lines making up the page.

Example 12.5

Suppose a sheet of paper of size 8 inches by 11 inches is to be printed on a laser printer with a resolution of 600 dots per inch. We can calculate the size of raster memory required per page as follows:

Number of dots in one raster line = 8 inches × 600 dots per inch = 4800.

Each dot needs one bit of storage to indicate whether or not the dot is to be 'inked' on paper. Thus we need 4800 bits = 600 bytes of raster memory for every raster line.

For paper length of 11 inches, we need 11 × 600 = 6600 raster lines.

Therefore the raster memory needed per page is 600 × 6600 = 3.96 million bytes.

Inside the computer system, the page to be printed is described using a character code (e.g. ASCII), or an appropriate *page description language*. An embedded processor in the printer first converts this page description into a *raster image* of the page, which—as we saw above—is basically a dot-by-dot image of the page as it will be printed.

A laser beam is used to transfer the page image from raster memory to a rotating photosensitive drum. The laser beam determines—at each dot position on the drum—whether or not there will be an electric charge at the dot position. The presence or absence of electric charge at each dot position determines whether or not the dot will be inked. The way in which the laser beam converts the binary '1's and '0's of the raster image into dots of charge on the drum is illustrated schematically in Fig. 12.7.

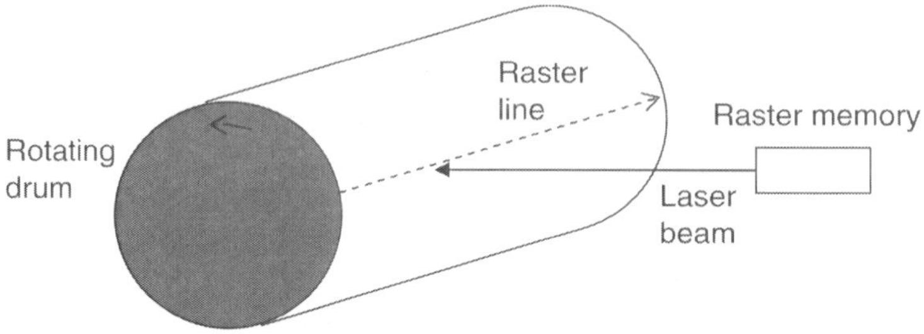

Fig. 12.7 **Laser beam 'writing' one raster line on drum**

In effect, the laser beam 'writes' the page on the drum—one *raster line* at a time—in the form of dots of electric charge.

In place of liquid ink, a laser printer uses *toner*, a very fine powder of plastic and ink. As the drum rotates, toner particles are attracted to the charged dots on the drum. At the end of this stage, therefore, dots of toner particles on the drum correspond to the image to be printed. This image is transferred to paper using physical contact between the drum and paper. By the application of heat and pressure, the toner particles are made to fuse with the paper, producing the final printed page we are familiar with.

Dot-matrix and Thermal Printers

Manual and electric typewriters are *impact devices**. A small 'hammer', with its head in the shape of a mirror-image of the character to be printed, hits the paper at the required spot. A rubber roller behind the paper ensures that the impact does not tear the paper. An inked ribbon intervenes between the striking hammer and the paper, and the force of impact transfers ink from ribbon to paper to create the character on paper.

A dot-matrix printer makes use of a similar mechanism, except that the impact is made by tiny dot-shaped hammers, rather than the character-shaped hammers of a typewriter. Consider Fig. 12.6, and imagine that seven tiny dot-shaped hammers—actually pins of stiff wire—are vertically arranged in the shape of one column of the 5×7 matrix shown. The pins ride on the *print head*. As the head moves from left to right on its carriage, the correct pins for each column hit the inked ribbon with the paper behind it, producing the image required. Printing thus proceeds one line of characters at a time**.

A thermal printer has a somewhat similar mechanism, but uses tiny spots of heat to produce patterns of black dots on the special 'thermal' paper provided for it. Both dot-matrix printers and thermal

*Some features of computer systems today have origins in the humble manual typewriter. ASCII characters *carriage return* (CR) and *line feed* (LF) correspond to two operations on manual typewriters of (i) pushing the entire carriage back from left to right, and (ii) rotating the roller and paper up by one line. The familiar QWERTY layout of the computer keyboard was originally developed for manual typewriters—and has stayed with us ever since.

**Common commercial models of printers use 9 pins or 24 pins.

printers can accept *continuous stationery*, whereas a laser printer prints only on cut sheets. An impact printer can produce multiple copies using multi-part stationery, which comes with intervening sheets of carbon paper.

Pre-printed continuous stationery is used for printing receipts on dot-matrix printers, which allow the *form length* of the stationery to be defined by the user. Today this is the method used to print most journey tickets of Indian Railways. Cash receipts from point-of-sale terminals and receipts of credit card transactions are often printed on continuous rolls of thermal paper, with a 'knife-edge' provided to easily tear off a printed slip.

Ink-jet Printers

In dot-matrix and thermal printers, the print-head comes in physical contact with the paper, to deliver either mechanical impact or heat at individual 'dots'. This requirement places limits on the print quality which can be achieved with these printers. They cannot achieve the resolution of even 300 dots per inch, for example, which is quite low for laser printers. At the same time, due to their basic mechanism, it is not possible to make laser printers as compact and inexpensive as dot-matrix and thermal printers.

Ink-jet printers combine to some extent the advantages of print quality and lower cost. The basic mechanism of printing in these printers is a 'print head' which ejects microscopic droplets of liquid ink towards the paper, without coming into contact with it. The droplets are produced by applying heat or pressure to a tiny chamber of ink behind the print-head. Color can be produced by using three inks of different color.

An advantage of ink-jet printers over other types of printers is that the amount of ink ejected towards the paper can be modulated, to provide better range of colors, or shades of grey. But the print quality depends greatly on the properties of the liquid ink. If the ink thickens even slightly—due to some evaporation of the liquid medium, for example—it will have a major effect on print quality. Similarly, if the microscopic aperture for the ink droplets is partly blocked, the print quality will suffer.

12.7 CLOCK, SPEAKER AND MICROPHONE

Clock

We saw in Section 3.6 that the digital circuits in a computer system require a *clock signal* which drives the sequence of discrete operations that the circuits perform. This clock signal can be viewed as a basic 'low level' requirement of the sequential circuits and data paths of the system, and every computer system has at least one 'master clock'.

User programs running on the system, and also the operating system itself, usually perform several crucial 'higher level' functions which also need the functionality of a clock. Several examples of such functions can easily be cited, such as:

- Time of day is to be shown in a corner of the display screen,
- A program is to be run for a *time slice* of fifty milliseconds at a time, and
- A user program needs to perform *auto-save* every ten minutes.

To allow such functions to be programmed, computer systems are provided with a hardware element known as a *real-time clock*. The real-time clock is basically an I/O device provided on the system, which performs clock and timing functions when appropriate commands are issued to it. Examples of real-time clock functions are: setting time and date, reading time and date, generating an interrupt after a certain time, generating periodic *timer interrupts*, and so on.

Within a computer system—such as a desktop or a larger system—a small battery is typically provided with the real-time clock, so that the clock does not lose its time, date and other information in the absence of power.

Speaker and Microphone

Sound signal as we normally hear it is an *analog* signal carried in the form of sound waves through air. A microphone converts sound waves into an analog electronic signal which mimics closely the variations of the sound wave. Conversely, a speaker converts an analog electronic signal into corresponding sound waves. Thus the output of a microphone and the input to a speaker are both analog electronic signals.

Most PCs today are equipped with microphone and speaker, for audio input to the system and audio output from the system, respectively. While the speaker and microphone in a PC are analog devices, internally the PC represents sound in *digital* form. And devices such as mobile phones and music gadgets—whose main function is audio input and output—also utilise digital technology based on an embedded processor.

In a digital system, any audio information is stored in binary. Depending on the quality of sound required, one second of sound may require storage varying from a few thousand bits to several tens of thousands of bits. Digital audio systems today are also designed using processor and memory, and they use basically the same techniques for audio input and output which is used by computers—as illustrated schematically in Fig. 12.8.

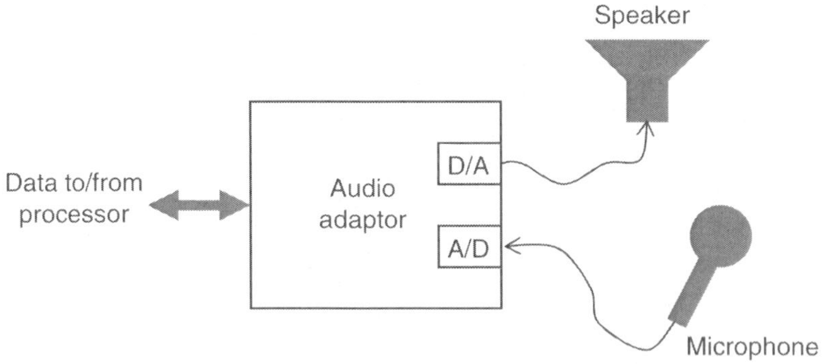

Fig. 12.8 **Connection of audio devices to the system**

As in the case of any other input or output device, audio input and output also requires a specialised device controller—or *adaptor*—to be provided on the system. As indicated in the figure, binary audio data is transferred between memory and the adaptor over the internal data bus. Buffer memory is provided on the adaptor to ensure that the process of recording and playback proceeds at its required rate, since any fluctuations in this rate will adversely affect the quality of audio signal produced.

For playback, the digital audio signal is converted back into analog form by means of an electronic circuit known as *digital to analog converter*, shown as D/A in the figure. An amplifier (not shown) regulates the speaker volume. For recording, the analog signal from the microphone—or another source of sound—is amplified and then converted to digital form by means of an *analog to digital converter*, shown as A/D.

Example 12.6

Suppose a personal computer is used to send and receive audio signals across the Internet, for a net-based phone conversation. For such an application, the system set-up required is as illustrated in Fig. 12.9.

The bit-stream of digitised voice is received from the network, assembled within main memory, and sent to the audio adaptor, where it is converted to analog form and sent to the speaker. In the other direction, analog input from the microphone is digitised in the audio adaptor and transferred to main memory, from where it is sent out to the network using data formats appropriate to the network connection.

A chain is only as strong as its weakest link. In a system of the type shown, all the elements must be capable of processing data at the required rate. If any one element in the system cannot keep up with the data rate, the quality of voice will suffer.

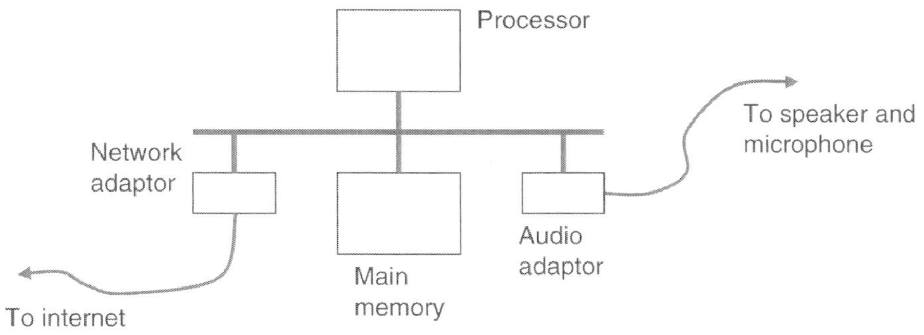

Fig. 12.9 **A network-based phone conversation (one end)**

SUMMARY

No computer system is complete without the input, output, communication, and storage devices which are needed to meet its functional requirements. In this chapter, we studied the basic principles of operation of several such commonly used devices.

Magnetic disk has been the main secondary storage device in computer systems over the last several decades. For distribution and archival storage, today optical disk provides the most convenient option. Flash memory is also finding use for backup storage, exchange of data, and even as secondary storage device which replaces magnetic disk.

A wide variety of communication devices is today available even on low-cost computers, and use of computer networks has become almost inseparable from the use of computers. For communication to take place between two computers, we need a communication link between them, communication adaptors at each end of the link, and the right software. A collection of such computers and links forms a computer network.

We also studied in this chapter the basic principles of operation of laser, dot-matrix and ink-jet printers, real-time clock, speaker, and microphone. And we studied briefly the basic mechanism of audio communication carried out over a computer network.

REVIEW QUESTIONS

1. List two different functions of a storage medium other than providing main memory and secondary storage.
2. Can record and playback functions on a magnetic tape be considered similar to write and read operations on main memory? Justify your answer in brief.
3. What are the two basic principles of electromagnetism which make possible magnetic storage of information?
4. In a magnetic disk, what is the function of the disk arm? What is the meaning of 'track' and 'sector'?
5. List two important reasons why, in a magnetic disk, tracks are divided into sectors.
6. In a magnetic disk, what is meant by latency? What are the two components of total latency?
7. Why is a magnetic disk known as a direct access storage device?
8. Why is a magnetic disk not suitable as a medium for distribution of data, multi-media content, and software?
9. State the basic principles of how a read-only compact disk records and reads back binary data.
10. State the basic principle of how (i) a write-once, and (ii) a read-write optical disk records and reads back binary data.
11. State in brief how an optical disk drive maintains constant linear speed of data passing against the read/write head.
12. State in brief the principle of operation of an EEPROM.
13. State in brief how flash memory differs from an EEPROM.
14. What is the basic principle of storage of one bit in a flash memory device?
15. Why is byte addressability not required in a secondary storage device?
16. State in brief the difference between simplex, half-duplex, and full-duplex communication links.
17. State in brief the meaning of modulation, demodulation and modem.
18. List some of the key factors which have been driving advances and growth in computer networks in recent years.
19. List the main categories of functions performed by a communication adaptor.

20. What is the role of raster memory in a laser printer?
21. State in brief the basic principle of operation of a laser printer.
22. State in brief the basic principle of operation of a dot-matrix printer.
23. List two functions possible with a dot-matrix printer which cannot be performed on a laser printer.
24. State in brief the basic principle of operation of an ink-jet printer.
25. List two examples of clock function required in software.
26. List two examples of functions which can be performed by the real-time clock in a computer system.
27. Explain in brief why A/D and D/A converters are required in the audio adaptor of a computer system.

EXERCISES

1. On the computer system you are using, or on a computer system to which you have regular access, identify the input, output, and storage devices being used. In each case, try to find technical specifications of the devices.

   In particular, try to include in your study the following devices:

   Display screen, mouse, magnetic disk, optical disk, flash memory, laser printer, speaker, and microphone.

   Basic data about some of these devices may be available on the system, and further information may be available (i) in technical specifications provided with the system, and (ii) on the manufacturer's website.
2. On the computer system you are using, or on a computer system to which you have regular access, identify the I/O ports available for exchanging data with removable devices and over communication links. In each case, from the relevant websites, try to find technical specifications of the interfaces.

   For example, for the laptop PC being used by the author, the following information was found readily in the specifications section of the manufacturer's website: *Modem 56K v.92, 1 Gb Ethernet installed via the system board, three USB ports version 2.0.* On each of these, more information is available on the web.
3. In a school, college, or any other organisation, find a manual or electric typewriter which is currently in use. Print a few lines on the typewriter, and observe closely its working mechanism, including the operations of carriage return and line feed.
4. Assume that a user of a word processor program is typing in text at a speed of 40 words per minute, and that an average word has five characters. If the processor spends a total of about 10 microseconds to read in each character, what percentage of processor time is spent on keyboard input?
5. Find the 'form length' and 'form width' of a computer-printed railway ticket issued by Indian Railways. Observe closely and try to identify the size of the dot matrix within which each character is printed.

6. Find the form length and form width of a transaction slip from a bank ATM. Observe closely and try to identify (a) the size of the dot matrix within which each character is printed, and (b) whether an impact printer or a thermal printer is used.
7. For storing the 'soft-copy' of a book, it is found that about 8000 bytes of storage are required per page of the book. If an average book has 500 pages, how many such books can be stored in a magnetic disk of capacity 100 gigabytes?
8. A color laser printer prints 1200 dots per inch, on a paper of size 8.5 inches by 11 inches. Inks of three different colors are available, any combination of which may be deposited at each dot position. Calculate the size of raster memory required.
9. For storing a music file, it is found that about 15 kilobytes of storage are required per second of music. If an average song is of 3 minutes duration, how many songs can be stored in a memory card of capacity 2 gigabytes?
10. Perform a simple experiment to determine the qualitative difference, if any, between the sounds you hear when you play (i) a music file stored on local disk, and (ii) a music file being received over the Internet and played in 'real-time'.

PARALLELISM

13

13.1 INTRODUCTION

In Chapter 6, we saw that the technique of pipelining can speed up the effective rate at which machine instructions are executed. In Chapter 9, we saw that the overall system throughput can be increased through multiprogramming—i.e. by allowing multiple running programs to occupy main memory and run seemingly 'in parallel', even if the system has only one processor. While pipelining can speed up the execution of one program, multiprogramming aims at higher system throughput and resource utilisation.

In a computer system, *parallelism* is defined as any combination of:

(i) two or more processors executing their machine instructions in parallel, and/or
(ii) two or more machine instructions of one processor being executed in parallel.

We have seen that device controllers on systems often make use of an embedded special-purpose processor to implement their internal functions. Even on a system with one main processor, such embedded secondary processors operate in parallel. The above definition of parallelism, however, refers to general-purpose system or application programs executing in parallel. Since embedded processors in device controllers do not execute such programs, they are not usually considered as examples of parallelism.

In the sense defined above, the multiple pipeline stages of a single processor, which operate in parallel, do satisfy the second part of the definition.

Let us consider *multiprogramming*, which was discussed in Chapter 9. On a single processor system, if the processor executes only one instruction at a time, then multiprogramming in itself does not involve true parallelism. Of course, if the single main processor in the system happens to be pipelined, then <u>that</u> system feature satisfies the second part of the above definition—with or without multiprogramming.

The technique of multiprogramming is commonly referred to as *pseudo-parallelism*, since the single main processor on the system is shared between multiple running programs. As opposed to this, a system with multiple processors involves true parallel processing between them, and is referred to as *multiprocessing*.

While pseudo-parallelism is not the same thing as multiprocessing, the two techniques do share some technical issues in common, related to the need for synchronisation between running programs.

In a pipelined processor, only a single instruction stream passes through the N stages of the instruction pipeline. However, the N successive machine instructions occupying the N stages of the pipeline do get executed in parallel. As we shall see, exploiting *instruction level parallelism* and *thread level parallelism* are interesting technical challenges in the efficient utilisation of an instruction pipeline.

Apart from these special forms of parallelism, we shall also discuss in this and the next chapter, some basic forms of true parallelism—namely *vector processing*, *shared memory multiprocessors*, *cluster computing*, and *distributed computing*.

13.2 INSTRUCTION LEVEL PARALLELISM

The basic concept of *instruction pipeline* has been discussed earlier, in Section 6.10. We saw that pipeline *flushes* caused by conditional jump instructions lead to degradation in performance, and therefore attempts must be made to minimise them. In Section 7.2, we saw that pipeline *stalls* caused by cache misses also result in wasted processor cycles.

An instruction pipeline is an example of multiple instructions of the same program executing in parallel, in successive pipeline stages. Following up on our earlier study in Chapters 6 and 7, we shall now see that a processor with an instruction pipeline offers opportunities for the exploitation of so-called *instruction level parallelism* (ILP)—i.e. the potential for parallelism which may be present within a single instruction stream.

To start with, let us consider the following simple sequence of two instructions in a running program:

```
ADD       R1, R3
SHIFTR    R3, #4
```

The result of the **ADD** instruction is stored in destination register R3, and then shifted right by four bits in the second instruction. Thus there is a logical *dependency* between the two instructions—the output of the first is required as input to the second.

Now recall that, in a pipelined processor, the second instruction should be executed just one stage—and therefore just one clock cycle—behind the first. The difficulty here, however, is that it takes one clock cycle to transfer ALU output to R3, and then another clock cycle to transfer R3 content back to ALU input for the right shift, for a total of two clock cycles. Therefore—as things stand—the second instruction above cannot be executed just one clock cycle behind the first.

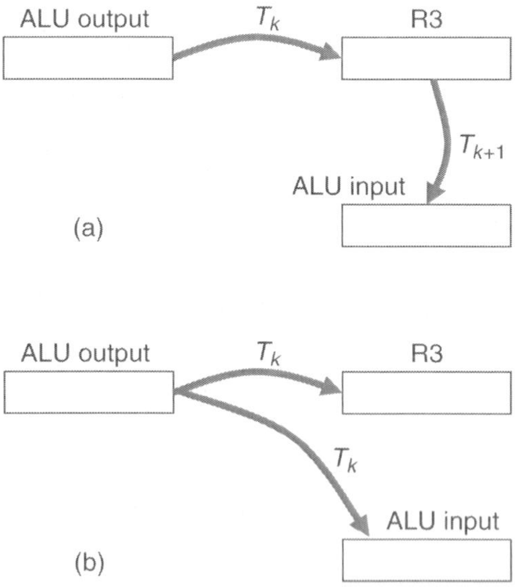

Fig. 13.1 **Two data transfers (a) in sequence and (b) in parallel**

This sequence of data transfers has been illustrated in Fig. 13.1 (a). In clock cycle T_k, ALU output is transferred to R3 over an internal bus. In the next clock cycle T_{k+1}, the content of R3 is transferred to ALU input for the right shift. When carried out in this order, clearly the two data transfer operations take two clock cycles.

But note that the required transfers of data can be achieved in only one cycle if ALU output is sent to both R3 and ALU input in the same clock cycle—as illustrated in Fig. 13.1 (b). In general, if X is to be copied to Y, and in the next cycle, Y is to be copied to Z, then we can just as well copy X to both Y and Z in one clock cycle. If this can be done in the above sequence of instructions, then the second instruction can be just one clock cycle behind the first, which is a basic requirement of an instruction pipeline.

In technical terms, this type of an operation within a processor is known as *operand forwarding*. Basically this means that, instead of performing two or more data transfers one after the other, we perform them in parallel. This can be viewed as parallelism at the level of elementary data transfer operations within the processor. However, the need to fully exploit this type of parallelism is more acute in a pipelined processor, in view of its basic design objective of completing one instruction in every clock cycle.

The above reasoning may apply even if there is an intervening instruction between **ADD** and **SHIFTR**. Consider the following sequence of instructions:

```
ADD       R1, R3
SUB       R5, R6
SHIFTR    R3, #4
```

SHIFTR must be executed after **ADD**, since it is the result of **ADD** which has to be shifted, i.e. there is a logical *dependency* between **ADD** and **SHIFTR**. But note that there is no such dependency between **SUB** and any of the other two instructions—which means **SUB** can be executed before **ADD**, or after **SHIFTR**.

Figure 13.2 shows the dependencies between these instructions in the form of a graph. A *node* in the graph represents an instruction, while an *edge* between nodes represents a logical dependency. Since there is only one dependency in this instance amongst the three instructions, the graph in the figure has three nodes and only one edge.

But the basic question here is: Why should **SUB** be executed in any order other than that in which machine instructions appear in the program, i.e. between **ADD** and **SHIFTR**?

The reason is that, in some instances, this may result in better utilisation of processor cycles. For example, if for some reason **ADD** cannot be executed in a given clock cycle, then the processor may well decide to execute **SUB** before it. In instances such as these, we say that the processor performs *out of order execution* of instructions.

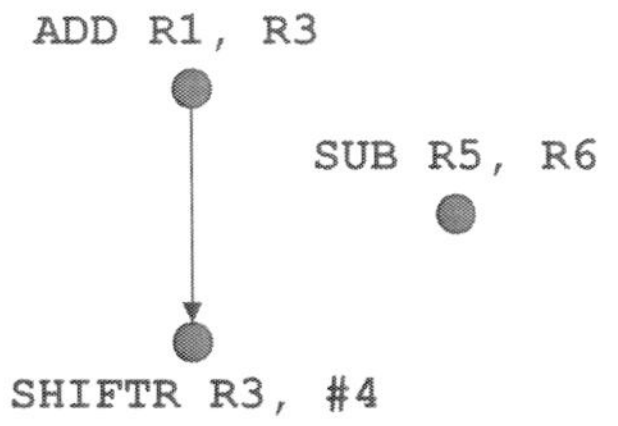

Fig. 13.2 **Graph of dependencies between instructions**

Note 13.1

As we have seen in Chapter 6, in a pipelined processor, an instruction may go through the five typical pipeline stages of instruction fetch, decode, ALU operation, memory access, and storing of result. On processors designed with multiple functional units, internal processor architecture is often structured in the form a *fetch unit*, an *execute unit* which feeds the functional units, and a *load/store unit* responsible for memory operations.

On such processors, *out of order execution* of instructions can be provided in two ways, assuming of course that logical dependencies within instructions are respected:

(i) The processor may allow out of order operations within the execute unit and functional units, while ensuring that memory operations take place in the same order as provided for in the program.

or

(ii) The processor may allow out of order operations within the execute unit, functional units, as well as the load/store unit. In such a system, memory load/store operations may take place in an order other than that provided for in the program.

Compilers which generate code for the processor need to take into account these features of the processor architecture. The interrupt handling mechanism of the processor must also take into account all such features, since several instructions will in general be in different stages of execution at the time of occurrence of an interrupt.

Decisions such as (i) transferring ALU output in parallel to both R3 and ALU input, and/or (ii) out of order execution of the instruction **SUB**—must be made by the hardware 'on-the-fly'. This implies that the control unit of the processor must detect any such possibilities and generate the required control signals. Of course, to achieve such speed-ups, considerable complexity must be added to the control unit—but that is a price which must be paid for faster execution of instructions through the pipeline.

In Chapter 5, we have seen that the machine instructions of a typical processor can be classified into: *data transfer* instructions, *arithmetic and logic* instructions, *comparison* instructions, *transfer of control* instructions, and other miscellaneous instructions.

Of these, only the second group of instructions—i.e. arithmetic and logic instructions—actually alter the values of their operands. The other groups of instructions involve only transfers of data within the processor, or between the processor and main memory, or between the processor and a device controller.

Arithmetic and logic instructions are basically functions to be computed—either unary functions of the form $y = f(x)$, or binary functions of the form $z = f(x, y)$. And these computations are carried out by functional units such as *arithmetic and logic unit* (ALU), or *floating point unit* (FPU). But even to get any computations done by these functional units, we need the transfer of operand(s) to the inputs of functional units, and the transfer of results back, usually to programmable registers.

From the above arguments, we see that data transfers make up a large part of the work of any processor. When a processor is provided with an instruction pipeline and multiple functional units, the need to fully utilise the hardware forces designers to pay very close attention to the data transfers required not only within one instruction, but also across multiple instructions. This is what motivates designers to exploit techniques such as operand forwarding and out of sequence execution.

As we know, within an N-stage pipeline, N successive instructions are in different stages of execution. Logical dependencies between instructions—of the type between **ADD** and **SHIFTR** above—must of course be respected, since they reflect program logic. On the other hand, as we have seen, two independent instructions can be executed out of sequence, if that results in better utilisation of processor clock cycles.

Today most high performance processors are provided with multiple functional units. With two FPUs, for example, two floating point operations can be carried out in parallel. Further, if each of the FPUs is itself designed with an internal pipeline, then each FPU can itself perform multiple floating point operations in its several pipeline stages.

Assume that a processor has multiple functional units; and assume also that, through the use of an internal pipeline, each functional unit is capable of completing one instruction in every processor clock cycle. Then—at least in theory—the total throughput of the processor can exceed one instruction per clock cycle. Such a processor is said to have *super-scalar* architecture. In practice, of course, instruction dependencies as well as pipeline flushes and stalls result in reduced throughput.

13.3 PSEUDO-PARALLELISM

The technique of multiprogramming was discussed in Chapter 9 mainly with a view to study its implications for memory organisation. In Example 9.1, and the discussion that followed, we saw that processor utilisation increases with multiprogramming, and with it also the overall resource utilisation within the system.

Figure 13.3 is a somewhat detailed view of the running of three programs—labeled P1, P2 and P3—in multiprogramming mode. In the top part of the figure, we see that all three programs seem to be running in parallel. With time, each program makes progress in terms of both (a) instructions executed, and (b) input/output performed.

However, the system has only one processor—and therefore only one of the three programs can be executing instructions on the processor at any one time. Thus, in terms of the actual execution of program instructions, there is no parallelism in this system.

In the figure, a 'magnified' view of a small period of time clarifies this point. In this view, a lightly-shaded slice of time indicates that a particular program is actually having its instructions

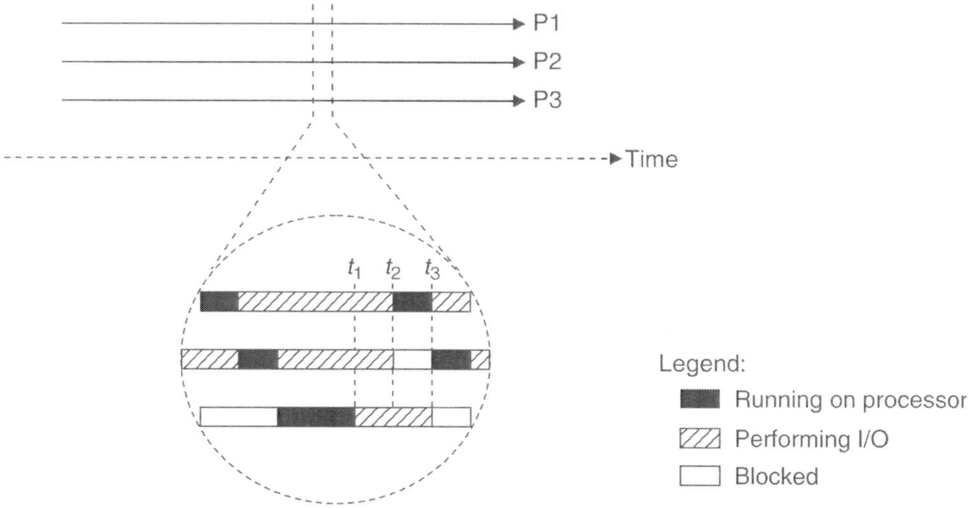

Fig. 13.3 **Three programs sharing a processor—pseudo-parallelism**

executed on the single processor. It may be noted in the figure that, at any time instant in the magnified view, at most one of the three programs is in this *compute phase*. The other two programs are either in *I/O phase* or *blocked*, i.e waiting for the single processor on the system to become available.

A time slice with slanted brown lines indicates that a program is performing in *I/O phase*. At the time instant marked t_1, for example, both P1 and P2 are performing I/O operations. This they can do in parallel either because the system has multiple I/O devices capable of operating in parallel, or because an I/O device allows multiple operations on it to proceed in parallel. In fact, in the time interval from t_1 to t_2, all three programs are performing I/O operations.

We see that, in the time interval from t_2 to t_3, program P1 is running on the processor, P3 is performing I/O, and P2 is doing nothing. This can happen because P2 needs to run on the processor, but the single processor is assigned to P1 during that interval. At time t_3, program P1 'releases' the processor, and P2 resumes its execution.

Thus we see that, in terms of the operation of the single processor, there is in fact no true parallel processing between P1, P2 and P3. In a 'longer term' view, however, all three programs do in fact make progress in parallel, with better overall system utilisation. Therefore this form of apparent parallelism between running programs is known as *pseudo-parallelism*.

Clearly, no single program can run faster under multiprogramming than it would as the only program running on the system. The goal of multiprogramming is to improve overall system utilisation, without however causing too much of a performance penalty in the running time of any one program.

When programs running in parallel—such as P1, P2 and P3 above—do not share any resources or data whatsoever, then the execution of one program can have no bearing on any other program. Such a theoretical possibility can be described by saying that the programs are totally independent of one another.

However this is only a theoretical possibility, because running programs do definitely share the hardware and software resources of the system they are running on. Two programs may need to send their outputs to a common printer, for example. If the system cannot handle even such a simple requirement correctly, printed pages of the two users will get garbled. A different kind of dependency between programs can arise when they share a common item of data.

To understand better such dependencies between running programs, let us consider the following example.

Example 13.1

Two programs, say P1 and P2, which are both working with a shared common item of data. The data item shared by P1 and P2 is someone's bank balance.

At a given time, assume that P1 must add Rupees 5,000/- to the bank balance, and P2 must subtract Rupees 2,000/- from it. Naturally, the combined effect of these two transactions should be that the final value of the bank balance increases by Rupees 3,000/-. If we assume that the initial bank balance is Rupees 20,000/-, for example, then its correct final value is Rupees 23,000/-.

So far so good. This is just simple arithmetic. What is the problem?—The impatient student may well ask.

To see the problem, we need to consider the relevant parts of the two programs which carry out these transactions. We see below the relevant parts of program P1 and P2, in the algorithmic notation we have been using:

Program P1	**Program P2**
.	.
.	.
`read bank balance from memory`	`read bank balance from memory`
`add 5000 to it`	`subtract 2000 from it`
`store bank balance in memory`	`store bank balance in memory`
.	.
.	.

Now it is entirely possible that, after P1 completes its first step, the single processor shared by P1 and P2 begins to execute instructions of P2. If this happens, P2 will also execute its first step—before P1 moves on to execute its remaining two steps.

The combined effect of this particular sequence of operations is that both P1 and P2 read the initial value of the shared variable from memory, which we have assumed is 20,000. At this point, both P1 and P2 have a separate copy of this one data item—each within its own address space. Both P1 and P2 then proceed to work on their own copy of the data, before writing it back in the shared memory location for bank balance.

The nett effect is that P1 changes its copy of the data item to 25,000, while P2 changes its copy to 17,000. Both then proceed to write their computed value back in the shared memory location, with the result that the final value of the bank balance is either 25,000 or 17,000, depending on which program was the last to write its value to memory.

But both these answers are now wrong! As we know, the correct answer is 23,000. We must therefore identify what goes wrong in this computation if steps of P1 and P2 happen to be executed in this particular sequence.

Basically, the erroneous answer is produced because both P1 and P2 are changing the bank balance value in parallel, rather than one after the other. It is easily verified that the correct answer results if P1 completes its three steps before P2—and also if P2 completes its three steps before P1. As we saw, an error can occur only if these three steps of P1 and P2 become 'interleaved' in terms of their execution times.

The way to avoid generating erroneous answers is, therefore, to ensure that the above three steps of P1 and P2 cannot become interleaved in time. For this, we must arrange that, while either P1 or P2 is executing its three steps shown—i.e. changing the value of bank balance—the other program is blocked from doing the same. Only after one program completes making the change is the other program allowed to do so.

This type of *synchronisation* between programs running in parallel can be achieved by ensuring the following condition:

While a program is executing a *critical section* of code—such as the three steps of P1 and P2 shown in Example 13.1—it must complete executing this critical section before another program is allowed to execute its own critical section. In fact, we use this condition as the definition of *critical section*.

Note 13.2

In Example 13.1, we had one program depositing Rupees 5000/- to a bank account, and another program withdrawing Rupees 2000/- from it. Clearly, these two operations must be allowed to occur—and they may occur—in any order. That should not create any logical difficulty in the software or in the final result.

The student should note that the problem arises only when the deposit is attempted while the withdrawal is not yet completed, or the other way around. If we define the complete deposit and withdrawal operations as two different *transactions*, we must impose the condition on the system that one transaction on the bank account must be completed before another is started, but that they may occur in any order.

Such considerations play a very important role in the design of multi-user applications such as those involved in online banking, trading, ticket reservation, etc.

In fact 'running program' is such a crucial entity in a computer system that it is given a name of its own and referred to as a *process*. Henceforth we shall also use that name. In the example above, we can then refer to P1 and P2 as two processes. The problem which we have discussed is thus an instance of *inter-process synchronisation.*

We shall not discuss here the issue of how a *critical section* can be implemented in a program. But we shall see in the next chapter that the solution to this problem is a little trickier on a multiprocessing system, i.e. when the computer system has more than one processor executing instructions in parallel. In such a system, there is truly parallel execution of instructions on multiple processors—rather than the pseudo-parallelism we discussed here on a system with only one processor.

13.4 THREAD LEVEL PARALLELISM

With the aim of achieving increased throughput, a system or application program can be designed in the form of multiple *threads of execution*—usually referred to as simply *threads*. Just as a multiprogrammed system yields increased system throughput, a *multi-threaded program* yields increased throughput of the program.

As a running program—i.e. a process—is performing some task, the successive values of its program counter (PC) define a *thread of execution*. In earlier chapters, we have been assuming implicitly that each process consists of just one thread of execution. But we can now remove that restriction and allow a process to be made up of multiple threads. Processor time is then shared amongst these multiple threads. Of course, for this to become possible, we must assume that the higher level programming language as well as the operating system provide the necessary support.

The basic idea of multiprogramming is that the work being done on a computer system is arranged in the form of multiple processes. In a similar way, the idea of multithreading is that the work being done by a single process is arranged in the form of multiple *threads*. Programming language JAVA, for example, includes *thread* as a basic type of entity in terms of which the program structure can be defined.

Example 13.2

Consider a web server program, which must respond to requests being received over the network from multiple user programs. To achieve higher system throughput, the server program can be designed so that each request received over the network is handled by a separate thread. The servicing of a typical request requires, in general, some processor time and some I/O to access data from disk. With multiple threads executing in parallel, the system will have better resource utilisation and aggregate throughput.

In such a system, creating a separate process to service each request would not be correct, because of the much higher system overhead involved in creating and terminating a process. In fact a thread is often described as a 'light weight process'.

On a single processor system, multi-threading is also a form of *pseudo-parallelism* that was discussed in the previous section. Processor time is shared between the threads making up a process. The threads run independently, in pseudo-parallelism, except when the application requires explicit synchronisation between two or more threads, as was illustrated in Example 13.1.

Given that multi-threading is a useful and established software technique, the question that arises now is: Can the processor be designed in such a way that the parallelism between threads can be supported—and even exploited—in hardware, so as to achieve better system utilisation and aggregate throughput?

We saw in Section 13.2 that a processor can be designed with features to exploit instruction level parallelism (ILP) in a single thread of execution. Now we must explore whether a processor can be designed also to exploit *thread level parallelism* (TLP) in a single process, or even across multiple processes. There are basically two approaches to providing hardware support in a processor for thread level parallelism:

a. In so-called *coarse-grained multi-threading* (CGMT), the processor is designed to switch to another thread when the execution of one thread is held up for access to main memory. Recall here that access to main memory is required on a cache miss, and that it may take a few tens of processor clock cycles. These clock cycles—which would otherwise go idle—can be utilised by another thread. At any given time, the register contents of several threads are present in the processor, but the processor pipeline is occupied by instructions of the one thread that is being executed.
b. *Fine-grained multi-threading* (FGMT) is based on the idea of sharing processor cycles in a regular manner amongst multiple executing threads. Assume that a processor is designed for such fine-grained sharing amongst eight threads. The register contents of the eight threads are present in the processor, and processor clock cycles are allocated in turn to each thread. Therefore, at one time, the various stages of the processor pipeline are occupied by instructions from these multiple threads. In other words, sharing of the processor amongst threads is on the basis of individual clock cycles, rather than few tens of clock cycles as in the case of CGMT.

When a processor provides support for multiple executing threads in either CGMT or FGMT mode, the data paths and functional units of the processor are shared amongst these threads. But registers are provided in multiple sets for the multiple threads in execution. Strictly speaking, this form of multi-threading support involves both (a) true parallelism between pipeline stages and functional units, and (b) pseudo-parallelism between threads, since they share processor data paths and functional units.

In general, a high performance processor will have features to exploit both *instruction level parallelism* (ILP)—described in Section 13.2—and *thread-level parallelism* (TLP). For either coarse-grained or fine-grained multi-threading support in processor hardware, it is necessary to provide within the processor (i) one set of registers for each executing thread, and (ii) a mechanism to switch quickly amongst the register sets of threads.

13.5 FLYNN'S CLASSIFICATION OF COMPUTER SYSTEMS

An *instruction stream* can be defined in a simple way as the sequence of machine instructions as they get executed on a processor. An instruction stream may belong to a process, or it may belong to a single thread in a multi-threaded process.

In an analogous way, a *data stream* can be defined as the sequence of data items as they are brought into a processor from main memory, operated upon within the processor, and then stored back in main memory.

With this understanding of instruction and data streams, it should be clear that a computer system with a single processor—such as the one we studied in Chapters 4 to 7—works on the basis of a single instruction stream and a single data stream. On such a *uniprocessor system*, the single instruction stream operates over time upon the single data stream. All the programs which we have studied so far have been written for such a system.

As early as in 1972, a computer scientist named M J Flynn pointed out that parallelism in a computer system would involve (a) multiple instruction streams, or (b) multiple data streams, or (c) perhaps both*. If this criterion is used as a basis, the resulting classification of computer systems takes the form shown in Table 13.1.

Table 13.1 Classification of computer systems

		Data Stream	
		Single	*Multiple*
Instruction Stream	*Single*	SISD	SIMD
	Multiple	MISD	MIMD

According to Flynn's scheme of classification, a computer system may execute either single or multiple instruction streams. Independently, the system may operate on either single or multiple data streams. The four possible types of systems resulting from this scheme are shown in the table as SISD, MISD, SIMD and MIMD.

A conventional single processor system is classified as *single instruction stream, single data stream* (SISD). We have already studied such a system in some depth, and therefore let us examine briefly the other three possibilities.

(i) *Multiple instruction streams, single data stream (MISD)*

*Flynn's paper "Some Computer Organisations and their Effectiveness" appeared in *IEEE Transactions on Computers* in September, 1972.

Such a computer system is in fact difficult to visualise. The reason is that two or more instructions cannot operate simultaneously upon a single data item common to them. But if multiple instructions operate in sequence—i.e. one after the other—upon a single data item, then there is no essential parallelism in the system.

This point is illustrated in Fig. 13.4, which shows a single data stream—lightly-shaded horizontal arrow going from left to right—being operated upon by *k* instruction streams on *k* different processors. But note that, on any one item of data, the *k* instruction streams are operating in sequence, one after the other, i.e. the arrangement is nothing but *k* sequential stages in processing the data. Therefore there is no essential parallelism in the processing architecture shown in Fig. 13.4—since even a single processor can perform all the *k* stages of processing on the data, one after the other.

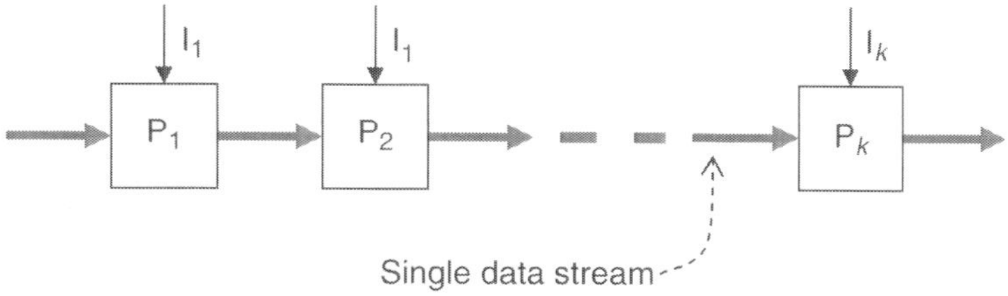

Fig. 13.4 **Single data stream, multiple instruction streams?**

(ii) *Single instruction stream, multiple data streams (SIMD)*

The original SIMD architecture proposed in the 1970s involved multiple processors operating in parallel in a synchronised mode, each processor working on its own 'slice' of data. In the next two sections, we shall look at this original concept of SIMD, and also at one of the ways in which the concept has been re-formulated,

(iii) *Multiple instruction streams, multiple data streams (MIMD)*

Such systems represent true parallelism between multiple processors, since each *instruction stream* in the system operates upon its own *data stream.* Over the years, MIMD systems have been successfully designed in several different basic forms, such as *shared memory multiprocessors*, *cluster computers*, and *distributed computing systems.* Key design issues in such systems are the following:

a. whether multiple processors in the system share common main memory,
b. whether the multiple processors are identical to each other, and
c. the way in which the multiple processors communicate with one another.

Basic concepts underlying these systems will be discussed in the next chapter.

13.6 SIMD ARCHITECTURE

In its original version of the 1970s, SIMD architecture had the form shown schematically in Fig. 13.5. Each of the multiple processing elements (PEs) in the system has its own processor and some local memory. The PEs are connected together with a regular *topology*—which in Fig. 13.5 is that of a rectangular array. For this reason, a system such as that shown in the figure is also known as an *array processor.*

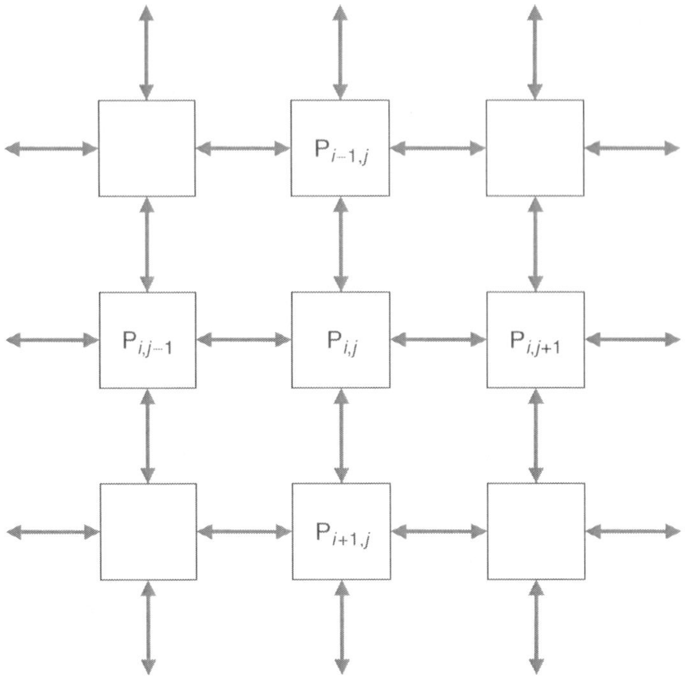

Fig. 13.5 **SIMD architecture—original version**

All the processors execute the same program—i.e. a *single instruction stream* gets executed at each PE. And the execution at PEs is fully synchronised—i.e. at any given time, the processors in all the PEs execute the same instruction. Instructions may be broadcast to the PEs, or they may be pre-stored in local memories of PEs.

Each PE in an array processor processes—i.e. operates upon—a different slice of the aggregate data. This has the obvious implication that the aggregate data on which the system operates must have a structure which matches the topology of the system.

Such aggregates of data are not at all uncommon in practical applications. For example, a weather forecasting system collects data from weather monitoring stations. If the stations are arranged in a grid across a large geographical region, then the aggregate data from all the stations clearly has the structure of a two-dimensional array. Similarly, an experiment in physics or engineering may collect data from an array of sensors.

The heavy processing demands of many such applications cannot be satisfied with a single processor. In theory, therefore, an array of processors of the type shown in Fig. 13.5 can be deployed for such applications.

Since each PE in the system is processing a different slice of the aggregate data, we can say that the aggregate data gets divided into *multiple data streams*, one stream per PE. This is the reason why such a system is described as a *single instruction stream, multiple data stream* (SIMD) system.

In a given instruction, each PE in the array will either (a) operate on some data in a local register or memory, or (b) send and receive data from its adjacent PEs along a row or along a column. If the

PEs are connected in the form of a two-dimensional array, the four adjacent PEs of the PE at array position (i, j) are defined as follows:

(i) along row i, its two adjacent PEs are at array positions $(i - 1, j)$ and $(i + 1, j)$, and
(ii) along column j, its two adjacent PEs are at array positions $(i, j - 1)$ and $(i, j + 1)$.

From this description, it should be clear that such SIMD systems are not meant for general purpose computing applications. Only special problems which can be 'mapped' to the system topology are suitable for such systems. Science and engineering present many such challenging problems, but in each such case the aggregate data as well as the required software must be carefully mapped to the system. Difficulty in achieving this has meant that this original model of SIMD has not achieved acceptance.

On a parallel processing system, different applications have different requirements of inter-processor communication. A major weakness of the architecture of Fig. 13.5 is that the connections between processing nodes are rigid—they cannot be re-configured to meet the requirements of a different application. Another limitation of the system is that the processors must execute the single instruction stream in complete synchronisation.

The SIMD system described here represents the original *array processor* which emerged in the 1970s. In this version, for the reasons mentioned, such a system has not found acceptance. Since the 1970s, however, both processor and interconnect technologies between processors have made tremendous advances, and the basic concept of SIMD has found other forms of expression in computer systems. Vector processing, described in the next section, can be considered as one of the newer forms of SIMD systems.

13.7 VECTOR PROCESSING

Each instruction of the processor we have seen operates on one operand, or a pair of operands; for example, in one instruction we may add two numbers, or multiply two numbers. In science and engineering, however, very frequently we deal with *vectors* of numbers—usually floating point numbers—such that an operation must be performed on each number in the vector.

If X and Y are vectors of 100 numbers each, we may denote this by writing:

$$X = [x_1, x_2, \ldots\ldots x_{100}]$$
and $$Y = [y_1, y_2, \ldots\ldots y_{100}]$$

Now suppose vector X is to be modified by adding respective elements of vector Y to elements of X. On a conventional processor, this requires that the addition be performed in an iterative loop which is executed 100 times, as shown below:

```
for values of i from 1 to 100
{
        replace x_i by x_i + y_i
}
```

Is it possible to imagine a single instruction on the processor which, when executed, would cause these hundred additions to be performed?

If we make the very reasonable assumption that elements of a vector are located in consecutive memory locations, then a *vector addition* instruction will require the following three operand values to be specified:

the starting address in memory of vector X,
the starting address in memory of vector Y, and
the common length of X and Y.

The starting address of a vector is usually also the address of its first element. Therefore a vector addition instruction—say VADD—will have a format such as, for example:

```
VADD        X1, Y1, 100
```

The difference between executing this one instruction, and executing a loop of 100 *scalar* addition instructions, is that VADD requires only a single *instruction fetch*. Once this instruction is fetched and decoded, all hundred additions take place within the *execute phase* of this single instruction. Clearly this results in faster processing of vectors.

Another equally important factor leading to higher performance in this case is that vector operations can make full use of pipelined architecture—within the data paths, and also within the floating point unit (FPU). The basic reason for this is that, while the elements of a vector are being operated upon one after the other, no intervening conditional jumps can occur which would require costly flushing of the pipeline.

In contrast to the original SIMD system shown in Fig. 13.5, vector processing has the major advantage that it does not require a fundamentally different processor architecture. Vector instructions can be provided as enhancements on the basic architecture of a conventional pipelined processor.

So-called *supercomputers* are designed to address the enormously high processing needs of many important applications in science and engineering. All such applications involve very intensive use of floating point operations on vectors and arrays. One approach to supercomputer architecture has been to rely heavily on vector processing, pipelining, and multiple floating point units (FPUs) to deliver the performance required*.

Over the last few decades, VLSI technology has grown enormously in sophistication. As a result, many architectural features originally developed for supercomputers have been incorporated into processors used in workstations and even personal computers. Also, with the advent of sophisticated display technology, a major new application area of higher-end processors has opened up—those involving graphics and animated graphics.

Clearly, vector processing does not resemble the original version of SIMD processing shown in Fig. 13.5. Nonetheless, vector processing can be classified as SIMD, since a single vector instruction does process the multiple data items of a vector.

SUMMARY

For achieving increased performance from a computer system, it becomes necessary to exploit the various forms of parallelism which may be present either in the application program, or within the hardware building blocks of the system. In this chapter, we looked at various forms of parallelism which can thus be potentially exploited.

*The two names most closely associated with early supercomputers are Seymour Cray and his Cray series of supercomputers. The company started by him today builds supercomputers of the so-called *massively parallel processing* (MPP) architecture (see www.cray.com).

Pseudo-parallelism is achieved through multiprogramming—i.e. when multiple running programs share space in main memory and processor time on the single processor. As against this, instruction level parallelism (ILP) may be present in the instruction stream of a running program, while thread level parallelism (TLP) exists between multiple threads of one or more running programs. High performance pipelined processors have features which aim to exploit both these types of parallelism.

Parallelism which may be present in a computer system may be classified in terms of whether it involves (a) single or multiple instruction streams, and (b) single or multiple data streams. The resulting classification—known as Flynn's classification—therefore has four possible types of system architecture.

With rapid advances in processor and interconnect technologies, SIMD and MIMD types of systems have been developed in several different ways. In this chapter, we took brief overviews of the original array processor type of SIMD architecture, and also the vector processing version of this architecture.

REVIEW QUESTIONS

1. State in brief the meaning of parallelism in a computer system.
2. Why is multiprogramming considered as *pseudo*-parallelism?
3. State in brief the meaning of multiprocessing.
4. Explain with an example the meaning of logical dependency between instructions.
5. State in brief the meaning of instruction level parallelism.
6. State in brief the meaning of operand forwarding.
7. Data transfers make up a large part of the work of any processor. Justify this statement in brief.
8. State in brief the meaning of super-scalar architecture.
9. State in brief the meaning of critical section.
10. What is the difference between a program and a process?
11. State in brief the meaning of (i) thread of execution, (ii) multi-threaded program, and (iii) thread level parallelism.
12. What is the basic difference between coarse-grained and fine-grained multi-threading support in a processor?
13. State in brief the meaning of instruction stream and data stream.
14. Describe in brief Flynn's classification of computer system architecture.
16. Describe in brief the concept of an array processor. What proved to be some of the key limitations of this architecture?

EXERCISES

1. At the beginning of this chapter, it was stated that: "While pipelining speeds up the running of one program, multiprogramming results in higher system throughput and resource utilisation". Justify this statement in brief.

2. A processor has 8 ns fetch cycle and 12 ns execute cycle. On a non-pipelined version of the processor, 1000 machine instructions are executed. Clearly the total execution time is $(8 + 12) \times 1000$ ns $= 20$ μs.

   A five-stage pipelined version of the same processor completes one instruction every 4 ns with a full pipeline. Calculate the time taken to execute 1000 instructions assuming (a) no pipeline flushes, and (b) a pipeline flush after every 50 instructions.
3. Consider the following sequence of instructions on a processor:

```
MOV      R1, R3
MOV      R3, R5
SUB      #4, R3
STORE    2000, R1
```

   Draw the graph of logical dependencies between these four instructions, in the manner of Fig. 13.2.
4. For the sequence of instructions shown in the previous exercise, show a different order of execution which produces the same results in terms of register contents.
5. Consider the following sequence of instructions on a processor:

```
MOV      R1, R3
MOV      R3, R5
SUB      #4, R3
STORE    2000, R5
```

   Assume that R1 contains value 255 before the first instruction is executed, and determine which other registers in the processor receive this value over the course of these four instructions. Using the operand forwarding strategy of Fig. 12.1 (b), find the smallest number of clock cycles required to transfer the value in R1 to its various destinations.
6. Consider the following sequence of instructions:

```
MOV      R1, R3
MOV      R1, R5
SUB      #4, R3
```

   In how many different ways can this sequence be re-ordered while producing identical result in terms of the contents of various registers?
7. Computing ('C') and input/output ('I/O') requirements of a running program are shown below, over its duration of nine time units T1 to T9. Each time unit is of duration 10 ms.

T1	T2	T3	T4	T5	T6	T7	T8	T9
C	I/O	I/O	C	I/O	I/O	C	I/O	I/O

   Three identical programs of this type are run in multiprogramming mode on a system with one processor; assume that I/O operations can occur in parallel. Show that the total work of the three programs can be completed in eleven time units.
8. Consider now four running programs, each of the type seen in Exercise 4. Calculate the total running time of the four programs in multiprogramming mode, on a system with (a) one processor, (b) two processors, and (c) four processors.

Do you think that, on the system with four processors, some other part of the system can become the 'performance bottleneck'?

9. A seat reservation program performs the following steps for each reservation:

```
1. read seat status from memory
2. if a seat is free
   2.1 mark the seat as booked
   2.2 send e-mail to customer
   2.3 store seat status in memory
```

Two copies of this program are running in parallel with shared memory. Show that, if steps of the two programs become interleaved, they can produce an inconsistent result.

10. An 8 × 8 array of elements, such as the one shown in Fig. 13.5, is required for solving a computational problem. However, the only system available has linear topology with 64 processors. Therefore the computational problem must be mapped to the linear topology of the available system, such that array element (1,1) gets mapped to the first processor, and array element (8,8) gets mapped to the last (64th) processor.

Find a general expression for the processor to which array element (i, j) gets mapped.

MULTIPROCESSOR SYSTEMS

14

14.1 INTRODUCTION

Why must a computer system be provided with multiple processors?

The answer is really quite simple: So that the system can process data at a higher effective rate. For highly demanding computing applications, the overall system throughput is often limited by its processing capacity. And one possible solution to the problem of insufficient processing power is to provide multiple processors on the system.

On such a multiprocessor system, each processor can independently execute the instructions of a program. With N processors on the system, we can have N programs running on the system in truly parallel manner. Of course, as we saw in the Section 13.3, special care must be taken when the need arises to achieve synchronisation between two or more programs running in parallel.

Computer systems with multiple processors, which execute their programs in parallel, have been designed in many different ways. Since each processor in such a system has its own instruction stream and data stream, such systems should be classified as *multiple instruction stream, multiple data stream* (MIMD) systems.

The systems described in this chapter are all generally of MIMD type—but, as we shall soon see, even in such systems considerable variation in design is possible.

A key question pertaining to the architecture of such a system is: Does each processor in the system have its own main memory, or are the processors sharing common main memory? Depending on the answer to this question, a system with multiple processors will fall into one of two broad categories:

(i) *Shared Memory Multiprocessors*

If the processors are sharing a common main memory, then the processors and main memory communicate over the processor-memory bus (recall the architecture shown in Fig. 6.1). Communication between programs running on the processors can also take place through the use of shared memory locations. Technical issues related to such *shared memory multiprocessors* are discussed in Sections 14.2 to 14.4.

(ii) *Cluster Computing and Distributed Computing*

If each processor in the system is provided with its own main memory, then each such processor-memory pair becomes a computing element in itself—since the two basic requirements of a running program are processor and main memory. In such a system, the processor-memory bus does not extend from one computing element—or 'node'—to another. Communication between computing nodes then takes place in the form of input/output over communication links between nodes, i.e. through appropriate communication controllers provided with the nodes, as discussed in Section 12.5.

Depending on certain other system characteristics, such a system is known as either a *computing cluster* or a *distributed computing system*. Technical issues related to these systems are discussed in Section 14.6 to 14.8, while Section 14.5 discusses the message-passing model of communication which is employed in such systems.

At this point, it is important for us to note some major shifts which have taken place in computer technology over the last two decades or so:

(a) *Speed of Communication Links*

Relative to main memory speeds, the speeds of communication links between computers have increased by a huge factor. Earlier, the processor-memory bus was several orders of magnitude faster than communication links—but that is no longer the case. Therefore, today no performance gain is achieved by designing a multiprocessor system with shared memory and bus, as opposed to a system in which processing nodes communicate over high speed communication links.

Today communication links with speeds in gigabits per second are commonly available, and this has had a major impact on the way in which multiple processors in a system are inter-connected. *Cluster computing* and *distributed computing* are two ways in which such multiprocessing architecture is realised.

(b) *Advances in VLSI Technology*

However, over the last few years, yet another technological development has resulted in a new incarnation of shared memory multiprocessors. Advances in VLSI technology—and also certain limitations of VLSI technology—have led to the development of *multi-core processor chips* which follow the shared memory model. Each processor core in such a multi-core chip is pipelined, and is also provided with features to exploit instruction level and thread level parallelism, as we discussed in the previous chapter. Thus several forms of parallelism, as well as MIMD processing, are combined in such a processor chip.

But we start our study with a discussion about the standard model of a shared memory multiprocessor system.

14.2 SHARED MEMORY MULTIPROCESSORS

The typical organisation of a *shared memory multiprocessor* system is shown schematically in Fig. 14.1.

The N processors shown in the figure are assumed to be identical, in terms of their instruction set, external bus interface, and so on. The processors access a common shared main memory for instructions and data. The processor-memory bus shown in the figure is a crucial system component, since all *read* and *write* operations are performed between the processors and main memory over this bus.

Naturally, this bus must have the cycle time and width to support the combined memory accesses of the N processors. But, with today's processor speeds, this becomes a difficult condition to fulfill. For each and every *read* and *write* operation, if the N processors must access main memory over the common bus, then *contention* between processors for access to the common bus certainly becomes a severe performance bottleneck.

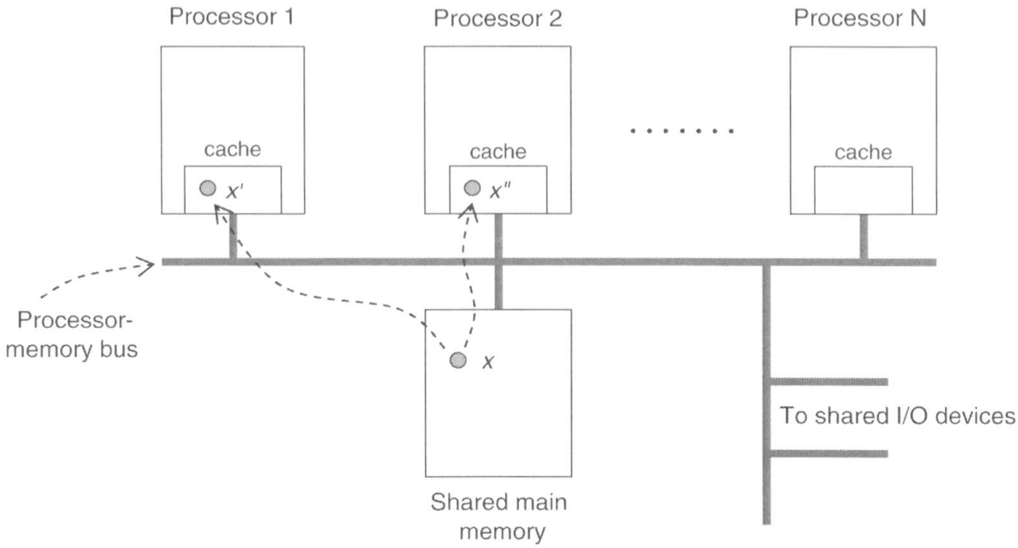

Fig. 14.1 **A shared memory multiprocessor**

This performance bottleneck arises from the fact that, in a given clock cycle of the bus, only one processor can make use of the bus for a *read* or *write* access to main memory. If two or more processors need to use the common bus at the same time, a *bus arbitration* mechanism ensures that one processor uses the bus, while the other processor(s) wait for one or more bus cycles (see Section 14.4). Naturally, if a processor is waiting to use the bus, its processor cycles will be wasted for the duration of the wait.

If memory requests of all N processors must necessarily involve use of the bus, then such wasted processor cycles are inevitable, as the following simple calculation illustrates.

Example 14.1

Recall from earlier chapters that, for every instruction executed by the processor, one memory access is required in the fetch phase of the instruction. Let us assume that, on average, 40% of the instructions executed require a second memory access in execute phase. Recall that the second memory access will be required for instructions such as load, store, function call, and return.

Thus we may say that the average number of memory accesses required per instruction is 1.4, and this is true for each of the N processors in the system.

Now if each processor is to be designed to execute one instruction in every clock cycle, then the total number of memory references required in each clock cycle is $1.4 \times N$. Even with a small value of N such as $N = 4$, for example, this yields 5.6 memory references in each processor clock cycle, which is not sustainable either over the bus or in main memory.

Thus we see that contention for shared bus and main memory becomes significant with even a small number of processors.

But fortunately there is a way out: If separate cache memory is provided on each processor, then main memory access by a processor is required only on a cache miss. If we assume the cache miss rate to be 5%, for example, then the number of memory accesses required is reduced by a factor of 20—and the shared memory multiprocessor system with a common bus becomes viable again.

So we conclude that each processor in the system must have its own separate cache—a fact which has already been anticipated in Fig. 14.1. Further, with present-day designs, each processor would also be built to exploit instruction level parallelism (ILP) and thread level parallelism (TLP), as was discussed in Chapter 13.

In such a shared memory multiprocessor system, clearly it is the common processor-memory bus which plays the central role in achieving effective utilisation of all system resources. Some key technical issues related to the operation of the processor-memory bus are discussed in Sections 14.3 and 14.4.

Another important issue on such systems is that of *load balancing*—i.e. as far as possible, dividing the total processing workload equally across the N processors. The workload consists of both operating system and application programs. Clearly, the potential benefits of having multiple processors will not be realised if, for example, one processor becomes overloaded while another one spends its time in 'idle' mode.

Closely related to load balancing is the issue of *process migration.* If processor A is over-loaded while processor B remains under-loaded, is it possible to migrate one or more processes from processor A to processor B? To achieve process migration, we need to (i) identify the process to be migrated, and (ii) transfer the full context of that process—i.e. registers, memory map, and so on—from processor A to processor B.

In recent years, semiconductor manufacturers have introduced so-called *multi-core processors*—which means two or more processors on a single VLSI chip. Each processor has its own L1 cache, and the system configuration is essentially that of a shared-memory multiprocessor. The word *core* derives from *processor core*, referring to the processor part of a larger VLSI system which includes I/O capability as well*.

The development of multi-core processors can be attributed to the need to squeeze more processing power out of available VLSI technology. Until recently, processors with increased processing power could be built by making their circuits smaller and driving them at higher frequencies. Since further progress using that strategy has become harder to achieve, the alternative approach of multi-core processors is being tried out.

14.3 CACHE COHERENCE

We have seen that, in a shared memory multiprocessor system, each processor must be provided with its own cache memory, to reduce bus contention and to speed up effective access by the processor to its required instructions and data. However, this arrangement—which is essential for achieving high performance—creates a difficulty when programs running on two or more processors share items of data in main memory.

*Often described as 'system on a chip'.

The following example illustrates the nature of this difficulty.

Example 14.2

In Fig. 14.1, a data item labeled x is shown as being shared by the two programs which are running on processors 1 and 2, respectively.

If both these programs make use of x over a period of time, a copy of x will remain in the cache memory of each of the processors. In the figure, these two copies of x have been labeled as x' and x'' respectively.

Now suppose the program on processor 1 modifies the value of this shared variable. The change is initially made in its cache memory copy of the variable, labeled x'. Standard cache memory mechanism will ensure that the main memory copy x of the variable is also modified accordingly, either immediately or when x' is removed from cache.

But recall that the program on processor 2 is also sharing this variable. After x' is modified, it is necessary to reflect this change in its copy x'' of the variable as well, otherwise the program on processor 2 will see a wrong value of this variable.

In the ideal situation, the three copies x, x', and x'' of the same variable should reflect the same value at all times. This means that whenever any processor changes the value of the shared variable in its copy, the change should be reflected in all copies.

In technical terms, the requirement illustrated in Example 14.2 is known as maintaining *cache coherence*, and it must be addressed correctly in any shared memory multiprocessor system. We shall consider here one relatively simple approach to achieving cache coherence in a shared memory multiprocessor system.

Note that cache coherence is lost only when a processor modifies the value of a shared variable in its cache—e.g. when processor 1 modifies x' in Fig. 14.1. When this happens, all other copies of x, such as x'' in processor 2, are said to become *invalidated.* When x'' is thus invalidated, and the program on processor 2 tries to read its value, the cache memory sub-system should return a *cache miss*, since the value it has is invalid.

How does a cache sub-system know that a variable within it has become invalidated?

Suppose the cache memory sub-system in each processor *snoops* on the common processor-memory bus—i.e. monitors the bus—for any memory *write* operations. When a *write* operation is detected on the bus, the memory address on the bus is matched with the cache content—using the same single-cycle associative search which the cache uses on all memory references by the processor (recall Sections 9.8 and 9.9).

When the cache detects that a copy of a variable shared by it is being modified—i.e. written into main memory—by another processor, it *invalidates* its own copy. The next reference to this variable by the processor will generate a cache miss, and thus force the variable to be accessed from main memory. An assumption made here is that the cache memory on each processor is working in *write-through* mode, i.e. each memory write operation results in the main memory copy of the data being modified immediately.

The cache coherence mechanism outlined above—known as *snooping cache*—is fairly simple and straightforward. An obvious improvement in it is this: When a cache memory detects on the bus a memory write operation on a shared variable, it picks up from the bus the value being written into memory, and updates its own copy of the variable. Thus, in this case, its copy of the variable is updated rather than invalidated.

Other algorithms have also been proposed and designed to maintain cache coherence. One approach makes use of a so-called *directory* of the aggregate cache content of all the N processors.

The directory, which is built using fast associative memory, maintains the status of all the cache content, and updates it on all *writes* to main memory. Thus, instead of each cache memory snooping on the bus to maintain its cache status, the directory provides a centralised mechanism for maintaining cache coherence.

14.4 SYNCHRONISATION AND ARBITRATION

In Section 13.3, in the context of a uniprocessor system, we discussed the necessity of achieving synchronisation between processes which are running in parallel, and sharing data or other resources. We saw that the mechanism of *critical section* can be employed to achieve inter-process synchronisation. Clearly, even in a multiprocessing environment, when programs are running on separate processors, this issue must be addressed.

In Section 13.3, we did not discuss how the mechanism of critical section can be implemented in a computer system. On a multiprocessor system, however, with true parallelism between processes, the problem of achieving inter-process synchronisation becomes more acute—and we are forced to examine in some more detail the way in which hardware must be designed to support inter-process synchronisation.

We shall see that a fundamentally different kind of processor instruction must be provided to serve as 'building block' of synchronisation. This instruction—which is known as *test and set lock* (TSL)—carries out a *read* and a *write* operation on main memory as one *indivisible* combination of the two operations.

In earlier chapters, we have studied and used the instructions LOAD and STORE—the first for a *read* operation from main memory, and the second for a *write* operation to main memory. In both cases, the second operand of the instruction is a programmable register. However, we can never create in software an *indivisible* combination of LOAD and STORE instructions in a program, for the simple reason that the processor may be interrupted after it executes LOAD, but before it executes STORE.

The *test and set lock* (TSL) instruction, on the other hand, does perform a *read* and a *write* operation on memory in an indivisible manner—since any interrupt signal arriving during the execution of TSL will only be acted upon after TSL completes its execution.

Let LOCK represent a memory location shared by two or more running programs, and let us arbitrarily select R0 as the register operand in the example TSL instruction below:

```
TSL LOCK, R0
```

The operation of this instruction is: The value in memory location LOCK is read into R0, and the value '1' is written into the same memory location.

After executing TSL, the program typically tests the value in the register. A value of '0' indicates that the shared data item or resource is *unlocked*, i.e. the program can proceed to perform the required operations on it. Since TSL also sets the value of memory variable LOCK to '1', any other program subsequently checking its value will see a '1'—i.e. it will find the shared data item or resource *locked*.

The program which first locked the data or resource can unlock it simply by setting the memory variable LOCK to '0'. The initial value of LOCK should be set to '0', and then onwards only one running program at a time will 'hold the lock' which permits access to the shared data item or resource. The TSL instruction can be used as a basis to implement the synchronisation mechanism of *critical sections* which we saw in Section 13.3.

Now let us turn our attention to how the instruction TSL itself can be implemented on a shared memory multiprocessor system.

In its *execute phase*, clearly TSL requires two bus cycles over the processor-memory bus—one for memory *read* and one for memory *write*. Therefore, for TSL to be indivisible, it is necessary that the bus should not be used by another processor while one processor is executing TSL. The processor-memory bus must therefore be designed in such a way that it can be locked for the duration of the *read* and *write* memory cycles of TSL.

A very closely related issue in the design of the bus is that of *bus arbitration*. Suppose two or more of the *N* processors need to make use of the bus in the same clock cycle. The address and data lines of the bus are, however, designed to be used by only one processor in a given clock cycle. Clearly, in such a case, only one processor must be granted use of the bus, and the other processor or processors must wait.

The bus must therefore be designed with an arbitration mechanism in hardware, so that if multiple processors make *bus requests* at the same time, only one of them receives the *bus grant* signal. But note also that processor cycles are wasted when a processor has to wait for use of the bus—and thus there is a possible negative impact of bus contention on system performance. When multiple processors contend for the bus, it may not matter which of them uses the bus first—as long as only one processor at a time does so.

Recall that bus contention was first discussed in Section 14.2. There, we reached the conclusion that, since it has a negative impact on system performance, bus contention must be reduced by providing each processor with its own cache memory. Now, we have seen that bus arbitration is required to resolve the inevitable contention for the bus which remains even after each processor is provided with its own cache memory.

14.5 MESSAGE-PASSING MODEL

As we saw in Section 14.1, a fundamentally different model of parallel processing emerges if the various processors in the system do not share a common main memory. In such a system, each processor has its own local memory for instructions and data, and at least sufficient I/O capability to send and receive *messages* to/from other processors. A processor with its local memory and I/O capability is then referred to as a *processing node*, or simply *node*. To identify the communicating nodes in such a system, each node in the system is provided with a unique *node ID*.

An application running on such a system is designed as a set of processes which are running on the *N* processing nodes, exchanging *messages* amongst each other as required by the application. Compared to shared memory multiprocessors, such systems offer the very important advantage of *scalability*, which means that this model of multiprocessing is effective even for larger values of *N*. The reason is that, in such a system, there is no single element which becomes a 'bottleneck' in scaling up system performance.

As compared to machine instructions such as LOAD and STORE, sending and receiving messages are *higher level* operations—in the sense that many machine instructions must be executed to accomplish a *send* or a *receive*. Typically, *send* and *receive* are functions (recall Chapter 5) which must be called by a program as needed. Such functions are made available to the programmer as part of the operating system; arguments to these functions include *message address and length*, *receiving node ID*, and so on.

Since *send* and *receive* are functions rather than machine instructions, on such a system we should not say that a processor executes a *send* or a *receive* operation. A processor executes a machine instruction such as CALL, but it is the running program—i.e. *process*—which invokes and executes functions such as *send* and *receive*.

This altered terminology reflects a very important shift of perspective. Earlier, we made statements such as:

Processor 1 performs a *write* operation on location LOCK in shared memory.

Now we shall say, for example:

Process 1 sends a message to process 2.

In other words, the entities performing *send* and *receive* are not processors but *processes*.

We can thus visualise our multiprocessing system as a *set of processes* which send and receive messages from one another. In other words, the overall processing workload in a typical such system is to be realised in the form illustrated in the simple example of Fig. 14.2, which shows a set of four processes.

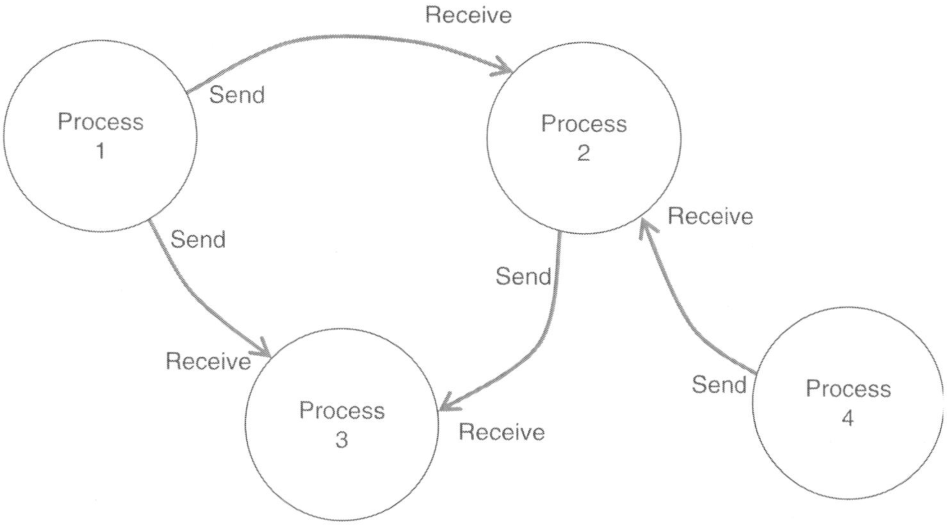

Fig. 14.2 Message-passing model of parallel processing

In moving our perspective from *processor* to *process*, we have performed an act of *abstraction*. As a consequence, we speak of functions such as *send* and *receive*, rather than machine instructions such as LOAD and STORE. And we also stop thinking in terms of physical attributes of processors such as address size, word size, or registers. Of course we must make the very reasonable assumption that functions *send* and *receive* can be programmed on every processor in the system. Beyond that, however, we need not even assume that the processors at various nodes in the system are identical.

Abstraction also means that we think about *processes* in terms of the functions they perform, rather than machine instructions they execute. As long as processes perform their functions correctly, and they *send* and *receive* messages correctly, the system as a whole will also perform its function correctly. The overall system application is made up of the functions performed by its constituent processes, and naturally these functions include *send* and *receive* operations amongst processes.

This in essence is the *message-passing model* of parallel processing. Note that the degree of true parallelism in the system is determined by N, the number of processing nodes. But note also that the number of *processes*, say M, need not be equal to the number of processing nodes. We can only say that $1 \leq N \leq M$, since the system needs at least one processing node, but not more than M. If two or more processes are running on the same node, then the standard technique of multiprogramming can accommodate them.

The overall *throughput* of such a system will certainly depend on the number and processing power of the nodes being put to work, but note that the correctness of the results produced does not depend on the number or power of processing nodes.

Even the type of communication provided between nodes may be different. Two nodes in the same room may communicate over a very fast link, while two nodes separated by a few hundred kilometers may communicate over the Internet. As long as *send* and *receive* operations work correctly between processes, integrity of the system is assured.

Thus message-passing provides us with a very general, robust, and consistent model of parallel processing. The model is so general that, depending on specific system features, two broadly different types of systems can be defined using this model:

(i) If the N processing nodes in the system are of identical type, and are interconnected locally over high-speed communication links, the resulting system is known as a *computing cluster*, and this model of computing is known as *cluster computing*. In Sections 14.5 and 14.6 below, we shall discuss this model of multiprocessing.

(ii) If the processing nodes are not necessarily of one type, and are interconnected using network links of variable speeds which span over larger distances, the resulting model of computing is known as *distributed computing*. We shall discuss this model of multiprocessing in Section 14.7.

Both *cluster computing* and *distributed computing* can be viewed as variants of MIMD multiprocessing, without common shared memory between nodes.

At this stage the student may wonder: What happens on such a system when $N = 1$, i.e. there is only one processing node? With a single processing node, we have the M processes running in pseudo-parallelism on the single node. But, even on such a uniprocessor system, the M processes can use message-passing for synchronisation.

In fact, note that even on a shared memory system with $N > 1$, processes can use message-passing for synchronisation. The message-passing model is general enough to be applicable in such cases as well. However, in such cases, synchronisation based on lock variables in main memory tends to be more efficient than message-passing.

14.6 CLUSTER COMPUTING

As we have seen above, this model of multiprocessing is characterised by *N* identical processing nodes being connected over a high-speed network, which usually spans a limited distance, i.e. it is 'local' in some sense. Each node consists of components—i.e. processor, memory, network adaptor—which are essentially the same as those used in desktop computers or servers. Of course, keyboard and display are required only on nodes through which a user interacts with the system. Figure 14.3 illustrates schematically this version of the multiprocessing architecture.

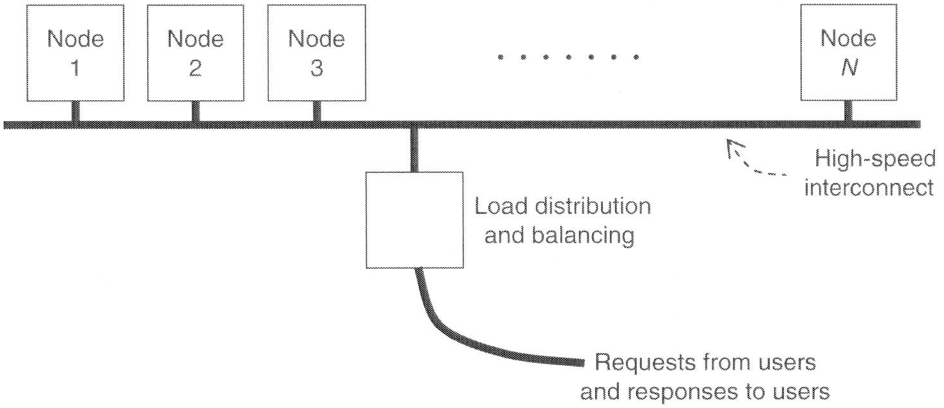

Fig. 14.3 **A computing cluster**

This architecture has the advantage of being highly *scalable*—i.e. it can be built with just a few processing nodes in a small room, or with many hundreds of processing nodes for large applications. In the ranking of the most powerful computers around the world, today cluster computing systems make up the single largest fraction, since they offer a simple and less expensive model for achieving high processing power. In fact, today such systems have completely replaced the specialised and expensive supercomputers which were in use as recently as a couple of decades ago*.

In a system of the type shown, often the *N* processors execute the same application program—but each processor operates on a different 'slice' of the aggregate data being processed by the system. Message-passing provides the required synchronisation between the processes which make up the application. Typically, a separate processing node can provide the coordination needed—e.g. handling system functions such as user requests and responses, load distribution, load balancing, and so on.

With message-passing architecture, the interconnected processors of a computing cluster are relieved from the restrictions imposed by a rigid communication structure (such as that seen in Fig. 13.5). Therefore it becomes easier to map the topology of any computational problem—i.e. any user application—to the computing cluster. This makes the system much more *versatile* in handling different types of applications, and explains the success of this model of parallel processing in recent years.

*The website www.top500.org provides plenty of related information.

Many examples can be cited of scientific applications of such systems. Sophisticated experiments in physics generate enormous amounts of data which must be processed to reveal interactions which might have occurred between sub-atomic particles. In biology, massive amounts of genome data must be processed to correlate sequences.

In the commercial domain, popular web-based applications require 'back-end' servers with huge processing capacity and secondary storage, so as to handle thousands of requests per second. Such servers are built using a number of processors in a computing cluster. Processing load on such a system consists of the large number of user requests which must be serviced with acceptable response time. Multiple user requests can be distributed and processed in parallel across the processors.

Thus we see that *scalability* and *versatility* are major advantages of this model of multiprocessing. In addition, this model offers two other significant advantages which explain its huge success. One is the *low cost per processing node*, which is due to the fact that each node is made up of components—processor, memory, network adaptors, etc.—which have low cost and are readily available. The other major advantage is that of *fault-tolerance*; if one processing node out of a hundred fails, for example, the system can continue to operate without any fault becoming apparent at the application level.

14.7 INTERCONNECTION STRUCTURES

Figure 14.3 shows a computing cluster with a simple interconnection scheme amongst its processing nodes—viz. all the nodes are connected using a single communication link. Over this common link, at a given time, a single node can send a message to one or more recipient nodes. Any message sent on the link is 'seen' by all the other nodes, but only the intended recipients actually 'pick up' the message from the link. Such a link is known as a *broadcast link*, since any message sent by one node is 'seen' by all other nodes.

Over such a *broadcast link*, at a given time, any processing node i can send data to any other node j (or even a group of nodes), regardless of the physical location of the nodes on the network. Of course, if node i is sending data to node j, then at the same time another node m cannot send data to node n—since all the nodes share the common communication link. But this restriction does not cause a performance limitation if the overall speed of the communication link is sufficiently high.

Note that a *broadcast* type of interconnect does not place any restriction on the pattern of communication between connected processors. Unlike in the array processor of Fig. 13.5, the physical location of a node in the system has no bearing on its role as a sender or a recipient of messages. The resulting flexibility in the system is a great advantage—different applications can make use of the broadcast link in different ways.

Many computing clusters in use today do in fact make use of a broadcast interconnect of the type shown in Fig. 14.3. However, over the past few decades, alternatives have also been sought to the use of a single, common broadcast link amongst the N processing nodes of the computing cluster.

Basically, an alternative to a broadcast link is a *point to point link*—i.e. a link with exactly two nodes connected to its two ends. A message sent along such a link by the node at one end, say node A, is only received by the node at the other end, say node B. We shall also assume here that each such point to point link is *full duplex*—i.e. it can simultaneously carry a message from node A to node B, and from node B to node A.

The question now is: With N processing nodes in a computing cluster, and with the use of such point to point links between pairs of nodes, what type of interconnection scheme can we come up with for our computing cluster?

In Fig. 14.4, we see some possible schemes of interconnection between the N nodes of a computing cluster. Part (a) of the figure shows a broadcast interconnection, of the type which we have already discussed above.

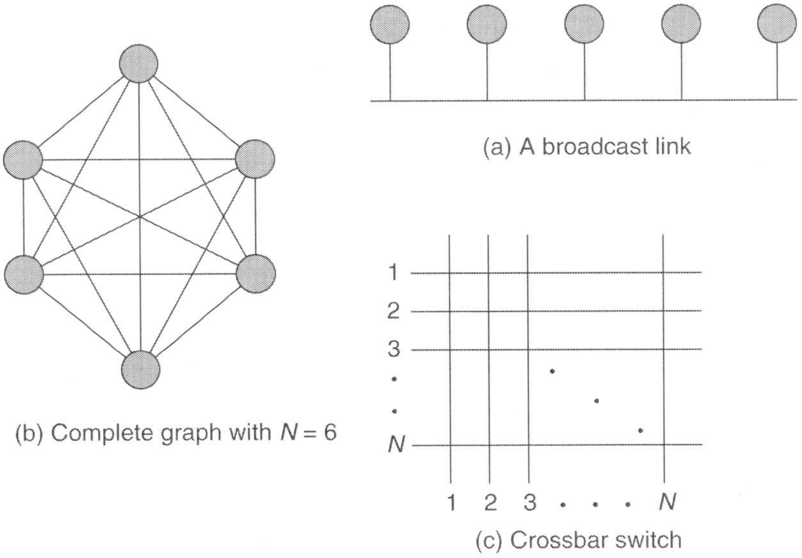

Fig. 14.4 **Possible interconnections in a cluster**

In part (b) of the figure, we see a *fully connected cluster* of $N = 6$ nodes, in which there is a point to point link between every pair of nodes. It is a simple exercise to verify that such a cluster contains a total of $N \times (N - 1)/2$ links. At one time, any node can send or receive a message to/from any other node—since there is no question of any contention amongst nodes for access to a link. But such a configuration is impractical because it is not *scalable*—since, for large N, the number of links required grows as N^2.

In part (c) of Fig. 14.4, we see a so-called *cross-bar switch* to which the N nodes are connected. Note that the same N nodes occur along the rows of the switch (as shown at the left), and also along the columns (as shown at the bottom). At any one time, any node i can be connected to any node j—but, if these two nodes are so connected, then at that time, no other node can be connected to either i or j. Thus, at one time, $N/2$ connections are possible, between distinct pairs of nodes. The pattern of interconnections amongst nodes can be switched electronically as needed*.

*Old-fashioned telephone exchanges worked by using a giant electro-mechanical 'cross-bar switch' which operated in response to digits dialed by subscribers. A connection could only be set up between two subscribers—and therefore there was no concept of 'conference calls', which became possible only with computerised digital telephone exchanges.

Figure 14.5 shows a 2 × 2 *switch*, i.e. a switch with two input links and two output links. At one time, each input link can be connected to exactly one output link. The resulting two possible interconnections between inputs and outputs are shown in the figure using arrows inside the switch. The input signal at the bottom of the rectangle is the control signal which determines the interconnection. Multiple such switches can be used for connecting *N* processing nodes (see Exercises 14.6 and 14.7).

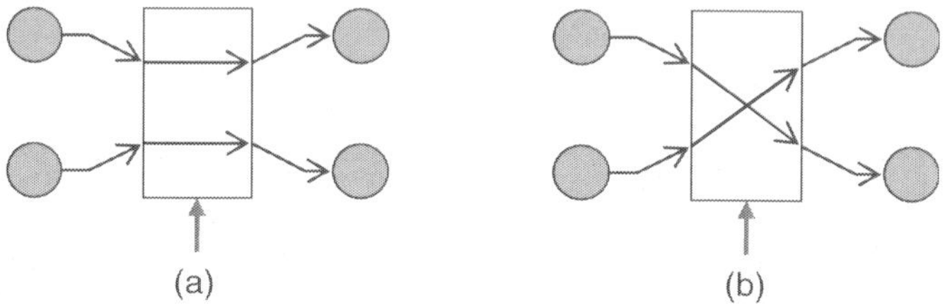

Fig. 14.5 A 2 × 2 switch in two possible configurations

In a computing cluster, as we have seen above, the processing nodes do not share common memory. Communication between processing nodes takes place in the form network I/O, with network interconnections taking one of the various possible forms seen. Amongst all these forms of interconnection, a high speed *local area network* (LAN) provides a proven broadcast type of interconnection, which very often serves the purpose and is commonly employed.

In Section 14.2, we saw that the common processor-memory bus in shared memory multiprocessor system can become a performance bottleneck, limiting the scalability of such systems. A natural question arises here: In a similar way—i.e. due to contention amongst the *N* processing nodes for access to the single, shared LAN—will the LAN not also become a performance bottleneck in a computing cluster?

The answer is: Not necessarily, and the reason is this:

We have seen in Section 14.5 that message *send* and *receive* operations amongst processes are higher level operations as compared to *read* and *write* operations to main memory. In a running program, each machine instruction may generate an average of, say, 1.4 accesses to main memory (see Example 14.1 above). As against this, a message *send* or *receive* operations in a running program may occur once for every 10^5 or even a much larger number of machine instructions. Also, application designers usually have design options available to keep message lengths relatively short.

It is for these reasons that the shared high-speed LAN in a computing cluster is less likely to become a performance bottleneck, compared to the processor-memory bus in a shared memory multiprocessor system; and the result is greater scalability in a LAN-based computing cluster.

14.8 DISTRIBUTED COMPUTING

Network technology today makes it possible to design a computing application consisting of multiple processes, running in parallel on processing nodes which are inter-connected over large distances. Message-passing primitives are employed for communication and synchronisation between processes.

Such a model of computing is known as *distributed computing*, because such a system is not restricted to a single computer system or even a cluster. The computing task is well and truly distributed over multiple systems, and its integrity against network delays is assured by the message-passing model.

It is natural to model such a distributed computation as a set of processes. For this purpose, in fact even details of the computer system available at each computing node of the system are not relevant. Recall that in a computing cluster, we have assumed the processing nodes to be homogeneous. But that is no longer a constraint in distributed computing. Interactions between processes are defined only in terms of *request* and *response* messages exchanged, with no constraint placed on the hardware or software which produces the messages.

Figure 14.6 illustrates schematically the concept of distributed computing. Note that the network supports inter-process communication by ensuring reliable message delivery.

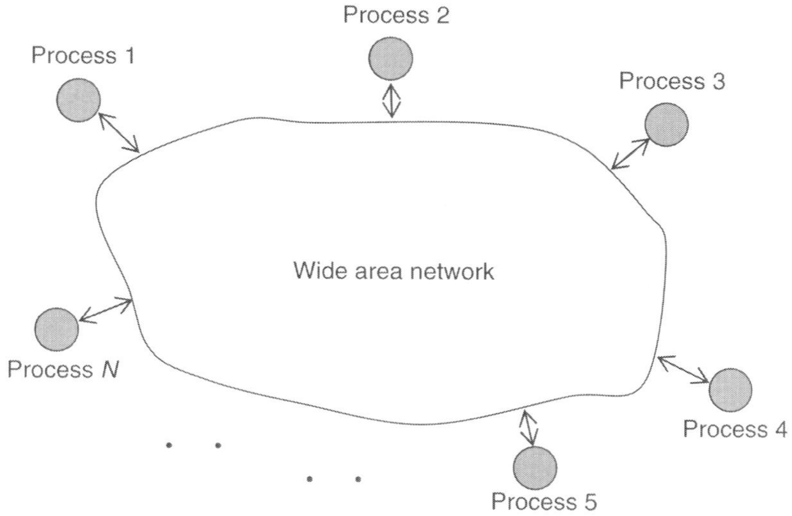

Fig. 14.6 Concept of distributed computing

Under this distributed model of computation, we must assume that the single application consists of, say, N processes, running on a certain number of computer systems connected to the network. The distributed nature of the single application allows us to classify the computation as an instance of distributed computing*.

The message-passing primitives *send* and *receive* are asynchronous, in the sense that no synchronisation is required between the sending and receiving processes. *send* and *receive* primitives are built on the basis of reliable delivery of messages by the network—but their functionality is independent of the type and speed of network links, random delays encountered, and other such factors. As a result, the model of distributed computing based on message-passing is robust, and is widely used.

*In the absence of this criterion of a single application, any set of computer systems—whether networked or not—would qualify as an instance of distributed computing or MIMD, a conclusion which clearly does not make any sense.

Many of today's web-based applications can be considered to be in this category. Such web-based architecture usually divides processes into *clients* and *servers*, and sometimes even a *middle layer* between these two. The simplest such architecture has one server and many potential clients, since any node on the web can become a client by connecting to the server through the network. If aggregate load on the server is heavy, the server may even take the shape of a computing cluster.

Thus network technology and message-passing primitives together provide the required building blocks of distributed computing. This model of distributed computing is robust and versatile enough for the enormously vast range of today's web-based applications. In Sections 15.4 and 15.5, we shall discuss briefly some related aspects of computer networks and the structure of typical applications.

SUMMARY

We have studied in this chapter the various ways in which the MIMD model of multiprocessing can be realised.

In a shared memory multiprocessor system, the processors and the common shared memory are connected over the single processor-memory bus. Cache coherence, inter-process synchronisation, and bus arbitration are some key issues to be addressed in the architecture of such a system. Scalability of the system is limited by the fact that excessive contention for the bus leads to degraded performance.

The message-passing model allows processes to communicate through *send* and *receive* operations. These higher level operations are implemented using communication amongst processing nodes, regardless of whether there is shared memory between nodes. Cluster computing and distributed computing are two forms of multiprocessing which utilise this model of inter-process communication.

In a computing cluster, the processing nodes are of one type, and the high-speed network linking these nodes together extends over a limited distance. In the distributed computing model, there is no restriction on the type or location of nodes, or type of network links. In practice, both cluster and distributed computing models of multiprocessing have been found suitable for different types of applications.

REVIEW QUESTIONS

1. List the main forms in which MIMD system architecture has been implemented in practice.
2. Which are the two main advances in technology which have had a major impact on the implementation of MIMD system architecture?
3. Describe in brief the concept of a shared memory multiprocessor.
4. List in brief the technical requirements of the processor-memory bus in a shared memory multiprocessor.
5. Every processor in a shared memory multiprocessor must have its own cache memory—Justify this statement in brief.
6. State in brief the meaning of load balancing in a shared memory multiprocessor.

7. State in brief the meaning of process migration, and what is required to implement it in a shared memory multiprocessor.
8. What is the basic reason leading to the development of multi-core processor chips?
9. Describe in brief the problem of maintaining cache coherence in a shared memory multiprocessor.
10. Describe in brief the snooping cache mechanism of maintaining cache coherence.
11. State in brief the basic operation of *test and set lock* (TSL) instruction.
12. In a shared memory multiprocessor, what is the meaning of bus contention and bus arbitration? Which bus feature is required to support TSL instruction?
13. Describe in brief the message-passing model as a basis of parallel processing, and its advantage over shared memory multiprocessors.
14. Explain in brief the difference between cluster computing and distributed computing.
15. State in brief the advantages of cluster computing and its two possible applications.
16. Which is the communication mechanism commonly used in a computing cluster?
17. Explain in brief why a computing cluster is more scalable than a shared memory multiprocessor.
18. Describe in brief the basic model of distributed computing.

EXERCISES

1. In a shared memory multiprocessor system, programs on two different processors are reading and updating the value of a shared variable x. The initial value of x is 1, which both processors have read from main memory into their respective cache memories. Processor 1 then updates the value of x to 2; at a subsequent time instant, processor 2 adds 10 to this updated value of x.

   The cache memories work on the basis of *write-through* of updates, and *snooping* to maintain coherence. In a step-wise manner, trace the successive values of x in main memory and in the two cache memories.
2. A shared memory multiprocessor system is operating with eight processors, each executing instructions at the rate of 0.5×10^9 instructions per second. Every instruction makes on average 1.5 accesses to main memory, and a cache hit rate of 98% is maintained. Calculate the aggregate traffic on the processor-memory bus. State clearly any additional assumptions that you need to make.
3. Assume that a main memory module offers read and write access time of 50 nanoseconds. If the memory has a width of K bytes—i.e. if K bytes are read or written in one cycle—the total throughput of the memory is K bytes per 50 nanoseconds. Show that this is equivalent to $20K$ megabytes per second.

   What must be the value of K such that the main memory throughput equals the aggregate bus traffic of the system in the previous exercise? Does the answer seem feasible? In this case, will it be useful to provide a separate cache memory between main memory and the processor-memory bus?

4. A computing cluster of 8 processing nodes is created in such a way that there is exactly one full duplex communication link between every pair of nodes. How many communication links does the network have?
5. A computing cluster of N processing nodes is created in such a way that there is exactly one full duplex communication link between every pair of nodes. Show that the cluster has a total of $N \times (N - 1)/2$ communication links.

   If one more processing node is added to the cluster, how many new links will have to be added so that it continues to be 'fully connected'? Note that this question is related to scalability.
6. Note that the 2×2 switch shown in Fig. 14.5 can be viewed as a cross-bar switch having 2 inputs and 2 outputs. Show how six of these 2×2 switches can be connected together to function as a 4×4 cross-bar switch.

   Hint: Arrange the six 2×2 switches in the form of two rows of switches, in three stages (or columns) as we go from left to right; outputs of the two switches of the first stage should become inputs of the second stage, and so on.
7. In continuation of the previous exercise, show that four of the 2×2 switches do not suffice to function as a 4×4 cross-bar switch.

   Hint: Compare the number of permutations required, of the four inputs, with the number of possible configurations of the four switches.
8. A computing cluster is built around a high-speed local area network having throughput of 100 megabytes per second; the average message size sent and received is 100 bytes. A processor executes 0.5×10^9 machine instructions per second, and on average sends one message for every 10^6 machine instructions executed. What is the fraction of time the processor spends in sending messages? State clearly any additional assumptions that you need to make.

   Note: The higher this fraction is, the higher will be contention for the common bus.

SOFTWARE

15

15.1 INTRODUCTION

A computer system performs only the actions which it is programmed for—and that only when the instructions making up a program are executed. Clearly therefore, to get any useful work done on a computer system, the right program or combination of programs must be executed. *Software* refers to the collection of programs available on a computer system. In a different context, as for example in the phrase *software industry*, the word also refers collectively to any and all computer programs.

Of course any system must have the necessary hardware for programs to run. Hardware and software are in fact two essential and inseparable parts of a computer system. Since most of the content of this book is concerned with hardware, we shall devote this chapter to redressing the balance somewhat by taking a brief overview of software.

We saw early on—in Fig. 1.6—that software consists of *application software* and *system software*. Application software refers to programs which carry out some useful function on behalf of a user—such as the typical functions listed in the beginning of Chapter 1. System software makes it possible for applications to be developed, stored, and executed on a single system or on a network of systems.

The range of applications of computer systems is virtually limitless. Given some data about the real world—or even about a *virtual world* such as the world of a computer game—just about any function that can be imagined on the data can be programmed into an application. For this reason, application software, in a generic sense, can never be a suitable subject for a book, let alone a single chapter in a book. Therefore, we shall attempt in this chapter only a brief overview of the various elements of system software, and a very brief discussion of the typical structure of application programs. Along the way, we shall also discuss in brief the process of software development.

15.2 OPERATING SYSTEM

The central and key component of system software is the *operating system* (OS). The OS can be viewed as intervening between system resources and users with the following two broad and complementary objectives:

(i) management of system resources for their sharing and effective utilisation, and
(ii) making system resources accessible to users, including software developers.

Figure 15.1 illustrates this dual role of the operating system.

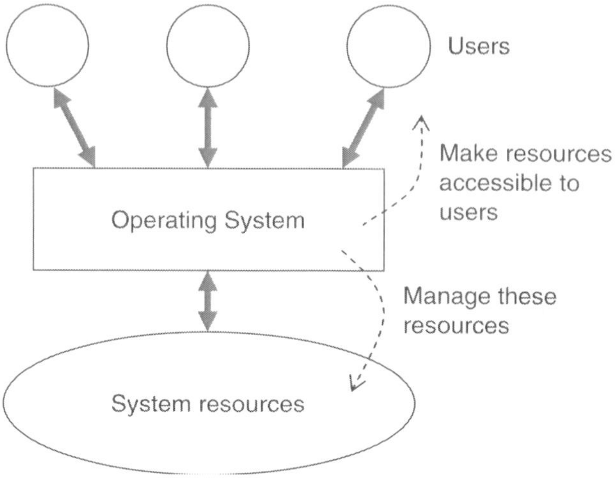

Fig. 15.1 **Dual role of the operating system**

System resources which must be managed by the OS include processor(s), main memory, secondary storage, and communication and other input/output devices. In earlier chapters, we have seen that each such system resource has its own characteristics.

Space on a magnetic disk, for example, is organised and addressed in the form of tracks and sectors. But the user on a PC may wish simply to store and view 'picture files', without having to learn about tracks, sectors, and read/write heads. Similarly, a display is made up of tens of thousands of pixels, but the user may simply wish to open a 'dialog box' or double-click an icon. In both cases, the user is in general unaware of 'lower level' entities such as sectors and pixels which make up the resource being used.

User requirements are both (a) *functional*—i.e. specified as functions to be provided by the operating system, and (b) *abstract*—i.e. specified in terms of entities such as *files*, *icons*, and *processes*, which are not physical. The OS must incorporate effective and efficient techniques to manage system resources, satisfy user requirements, and provide a *user interface* which helps in achieving higher productivity with the system.

Processes

We have seen in Chapter 13 that a *process* is nothing but a running program. As its execution proceeds in time, a process makes explicit or implicit requests to the OS for system resources. An explicit request may be, for example, to *open a file* from which data is to be read. An implicit request will occur for additional disk space when the size of the user's file grows. While Fig. 15.1 shows that the OS makes resources accessible to *users*, in many cases it is more accurate to say that the OS makes resources available to *processes* in response to explicit or implicit requests.

As a process requests and makes use of resources, it goes through different *states*. When a process is actually running on a processor—i.e. its machine instructions are being executed—it is said to be in *running* state. When a process requests for a resource or an input/output operation, it is changed to *blocked* state, since it will not use processor time in this state. On completion of the input or output, the process changes to *ready* state—i.e. it is ready to run if a processor is available on which it can be *scheduled.*

Figure 15.2 shows these process states, and the events causing a process to change state.

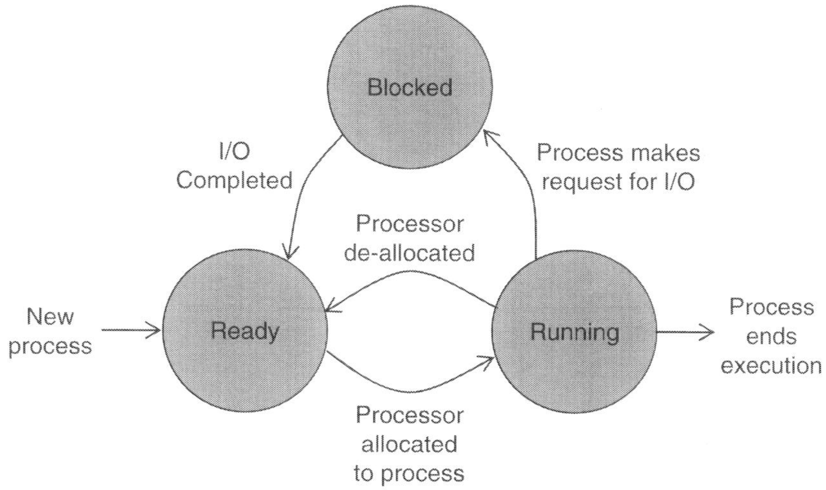

Fig. 15.2 **Process states and state transitions**

Clearly, the number of processes in *running* state cannot exceed the number of processors available on the system. Processes in *blocked* state are waiting for a resource to be allocated, or an input/output operation to complete, while processes in *ready* state are waiting to be *scheduled* to run on an available processor. The OS maintains a queue (or multiple queues) of *ready* processes, and schedules them on available processor(s) in such a way as to balance the twin requirements of high resource utilisation and acceptable response time to users.

When a new process is created, it is in *ready* state—because it is given, at the time of creation, all the resources it needs to execute its first instruction. When process in *running* state executes the operating system function *exit*, the process is terminated.

Main Memory

We saw in Chapter 9 that, in a multiprogramming system, *memory management* requires a significant degree of hardware support. The memory management unit (MMU) of a processor has the precise function of providing this support.

However, there are important higher level functions which cannot be performed by the MMU, but must be performed by the *memory manager* component of the OS. The logical to physical address map of each process on the system must be maintained, and decisions must be made about the physical *page frames* to be allocated to a process. Memory must be allocated to a process at the time of its creation, and de-allocated at the time of its termination. Similarly, while the MMU can flag a memory access violation, the OS must take appropriate action in response.

We can summarise the division of work between the hardware MMU and the *memory manager* component of the OS in this way: The MMU provides for efficient logical to physical address translation on behalf of the running process, while the *memory manager* ensures efficient overall utilisation of main memory for all the processes in the system.

Files and Directories

User data and programs are stored on secondary storage in the form of *files*. A file may contain, for example, a technical report, a spreadsheet with business information, an audio or video clip, or an executable program. A file is identified by its *file name*. The *size* or *length* of a file—defined as the number of bytes stored in it—may vary from zero bytes to millions of bytes. Apart from its name and size, it is necessary to record within the *file system* several other *attributes* of every file—such as file type, date of creation, owner's name, access rights, and so on.

A typical computer system today may store thousands or even tens of thousands of files on its secondary storage. Apart from the files created by users, a large number of files are placed in secondary storage by the operating system and by the application software. For effective and efficient organisation of information, it is necessary to group related files together into a structure of *directories** and *sub-directories*.

A *directory* is nothing but a special type of file which records information about other files and sub-directories. Figure 15.3 shows a typical directory structure; note that, since directories can contain sub-directories, the resulting structure becomes a *hierarchy* of directories. Only a few files are shown in the figure, but in practice the *directory hierarchy* may grow both in depth and in breadth.

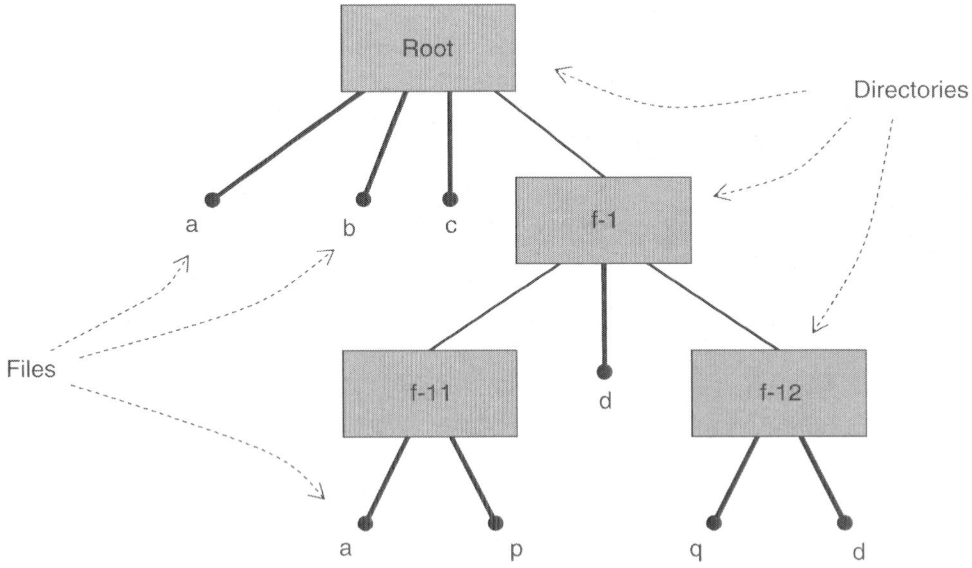

Fig. 15.3 Hierarchical structure of files and directories

*Also known as *folders*.

A file name must be unique within the directory containing the file, but two different directories may have files with the same name. Apart from file names, a directory also stores all the relevant attributes of each file—such as its size, type, date of creation, name of owner—and also the physical address of the file on the secondary storage device. On a magnetic disk, this physical address takes the form of track and sector numbers.

The function of the *file system* is to map the *logical* directory and file structure—such as that shown in Fig. 15.3—to the *physical* structure of the secondary storage device. In the case of magnetic disk, for example, the hierarchical file structure must be mapped to the tracks and sectors making up the physical disk. In general, for any secondary storage device, this mapping must be done in such a way as to satisfy the twin requirements of effective utilisation of space and efficient access to required files.

Input and Output

As we have seen in Chapters 11 and 12, input/output and storage devices for computer systems span a wide variety. Earlier, in Chapter 10, we have seen the general techniques available to interface I/O devices with computer systems. Of course, detailed interface design varies from one device to another, because devices vary in terms of their internal design, functionality, transfer speed, timing, and unit of data transfer. Writing software for a specific device is the work of a specialist, and not the general user of a computer system as shown in Fig. 15.1.

But clearly every user must be allowed the use of input/output and storage devices on a system. Therefore such devices must be made accessible to users by providing abstract, higher level functions. A user may wish to copy 'file A' to 'folder B', for example. To accomplish this function, the user thinks in terms of function *copy*, and entities of the type *file* and *folder*—but clearly he or she cannot be expected to think in terms of disk controllers, tracks, sectors, and so on. With a graphical user interface (GUI), the user may only think of *icons*, and operate on them using intuitive *drag and drop* functionality.

A user must be provided with a standard interface for such functions—either graphical or text-based—which is *device independent*, so that different I/O or storage devices can be accessed by the user in a consistent and uniform manner. Two PCs, for example, may be using different types of display. A program which runs correctly on one PC will run correctly on the other PC only if the two display drivers present a common device independent interface to the program. Clearly this is a critical requirement when the variety of available computer hardware and add-ons keeps increasing.

An important part of the operating system—the *input/output subsystem*—makes this possible. In order to operate correctly the various input/output and storage devices, this part of the operating system has the *device drivers*, including *interrupt handlers*, for each device. The job of a device driver is to initiate a device operation in response to a request by a running program. An interrupt handler takes care of any hardware interrupt received from the device, which may happen when the initiated operation completes successfully, or when an error is encountered during the operation.

15.3 SOFTWARE DEVELOPMENT

We know that a program is a sequence of machine instructions, but we have not yet paid much attention to the process by which programs are developed. In the very early days of computers, programs were written in machine language by specialists, who put in '1's and '0's into main memory using switches provided on the system.

But very soon it became clear that the binary machine language is not the right way to program computers. Higher level programming languages were developed and—since the early days—much progress has been made in the design of higher level programming languages. Modern concepts such as *object-oriented programming* arose from decades of thought given by computer scientists on how computer programs should be written.

Consider the program below, which is written in programming language C:

```
/* Sample program in C */
#include <stdio.h>
main()
{
  int i;
  for (i=1;i<=10;i++)
    printf("%d\n", i);
}
```

It should be a fairly simple matter for a student to understand that this program, when executed, will write out integers from 1 to 10 on the display screen. But the question we are interested in is: How does a program such as this one get ready to be executed—i.e. to be run—on a computer system?

The first line of the program is a *comment line*, which documents and communicates information about the program. The remaining lines of this program determine the actions which will be taken when the program is run. But since this program is not in machine language, in its present form it cannot be run on a computer system.

In order to convert this higher level language program into an executable machine language program, the program itself must go through a couple of processing steps, which have been illustrated in Fig. 15.4.

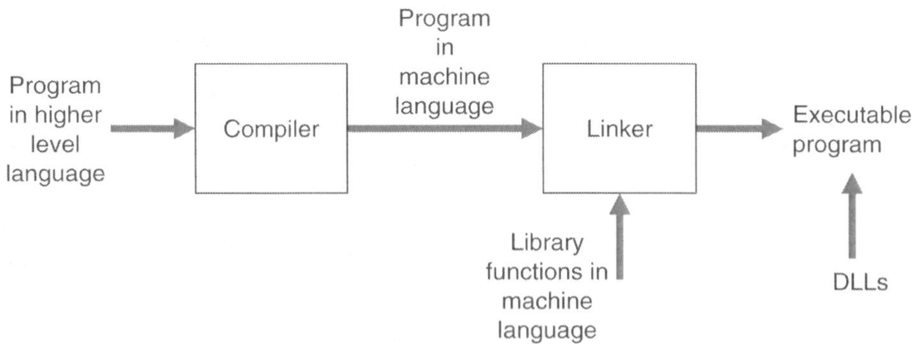

Fig. 15.4 Program development process

The program in the form seen above is known as *source program*—presumably because this is the initial 'source' from which the executable program eventually develops. Another program, known as a *compiler*, converts the source program into an equivalent machine language program, known as the *object program*.

While the object program is in machine language, it cannot be executed on a computer system—the reason being that the object program is in an important sense 'incomplete'. To understand this, we must first note that many functions useful to a running program are in fact provided by the system software and the operating system. This ensures that the user does not have to learn, for example, how to program a disk controller.

In the program above, one such function is being used. Towards the end of the program we see the program statement:

```
printf("%d\n", i);
```

This program statement results in a function named *printf* being invoked—i.e. called, as we saw in Chapter 5—for an integer value to be written out to the display screen. The user is not expected to learn how *printf* performs this action, but the user must know what actions this function performs. Within the pair of parentheses after the word *printf*, the arguments to the function are specified.

Since function *printf* is not written by the user, we do not see in the program above the instructions making up this function. But clearly the function must exist somewhere within the final executable program, so that it can be called. We have seen in Chapter 5 that the machine instruction CALL needs a target address within the same program.

Many such functions useful for program development are provided with the operating system, or with the programming language compiler. For example, a function to open a file for reading would be provided with the operating system, while a trigonometric function would be provided with the compiler.

These functions are made available to the software developer in the form of *function libraries*. As shown in Fig. 15.4, a process known as *linking* combines the user's object program with the library functions which are used by the program, to produce the final executable version of the program.

Use of *dynamically linkable libraries* (DLLs) of functions makes it possible to link library functions with an executable program at the time of its execution. In this way, with DLLs, the choice of linked functions is postponed to the execution time of a program. This makes it possible, for example, to run an older program with a newer version of a graphical user interface, or a newer type of I/O device.

It is the final executable version of a program which runs when the user either double-clicks on an icon, or types in the program name from a command line. A new process is created by the operating system at that time, and necessary resources allocated to the process for it to begin execution, as explained in the previous section.

When additional software is made available on a computer system, the functionality of the system is enhanced. Thus, even while the hardware components of a system remain unchanged, its usefulness is increased by the newly added software. Thus it is true to say that productive work on any computer system is done by software, but it is equally true that without the right kind of hardware support, the software cannot be run.

Note 15.1

Interdependence between software and hardware in fact goes much deeper than the previous paragraph suggests. All engineering design and manufacturing today requires very sophisticated software for *computer-aided design* (CAD), *simulation*, *design verification*, and *automated manufacturing*. Design and production engineers today are therefore heavy users of highly sophisticated software tools. Since these software tools require powerful hardware platforms to run on, we can say that hardware and software are like the two wheels of the progressing cart of technology.

15.4 COMPUTER NETWORKS

Use of communication devices and links has become the common norm with any computer system today—from single-user personal systems to very large systems used within organisations. In Chapter 12, we have taken a very brief look at how a computer system is provided with the capability to communicate data with other systems.

When multiple computers are connected together using communication adaptors and links, the resulting interconnected structure is known as a *computer network*. When a user today opens the website of a bank, the user's *client* computer and the bank's web *server* may be located thousands of miles away—but they become connected through the Internet, which is a vast computer network spanning the globe.

Two specific computer networks most commonly used by us today are *local area networks*—within an office building or a campus—and *wide area networks* which span the globe. Through the use of standard protocols such as *TCP* and *IP*, the Internet reaches across all such networks. The vast reach and scope which the Internet has achieved is increasing even further with the growing use of cellular and other forms of wireless technologies, which allow a network user to be mobile.

In a modern computer network, data is exchanged between computers in the form of *packets* of data, which may vary in size from a few tens of bytes to several kilobytes. On its way from one computer to another, a packet will in general need to be *routed* over the intervening computers and links. For this purpose, the packet contains the network address of the destination computer which is to receive it.

In Fig. 15.5 we see that, from the point of view of any data exchanged between computers A and B, the intervening computer network serves as just another 'link'—which is in some sense similar to the link shown earlier in Fig. 12.5. But one fundamental difference between the two types of links must be noted:

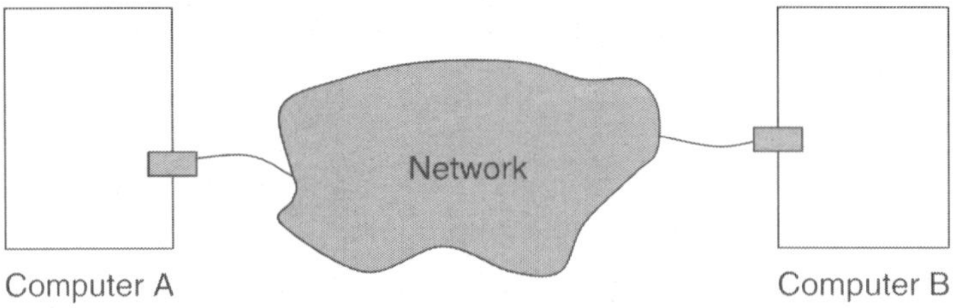

Fig. 15.5 Computer network provides the link between computers

The link of Fig. 12.5 is a *physical* link—it may even consist of a pair of wires connecting the two computers, for example. However, the 'virtual link' of Fig. 15.5 is in general made up of several intervening physical links in the network. This 'virtual link'—called a *connection* in the language of computer networks—is set up on demand, and it lasts only for the duration of data exchange between the two computers; in this sense, therefore, a network *connection* is analogous to a phone call.

Applications—such as a railway reservation system or e-mail—make use of such connections to perform their required functions. These connections are known as *end-to-end* connections, because they stretch between two ends of an application running on the network. The point at which an application attaches to the network is known as an *end*; at this point, data delivery by the network ends, and the work of the application begins.

The component of the network which provides end-to-end connections is known as the *transport layer*. Its primary function is to transport data faithfully and reliably from one end of the network to the other. Applications make use of this functionality, and are therefore usually depicted as being 'above' the transport layer. Figure 15.6 depicts schematically this relationship between an application and the transport layer.

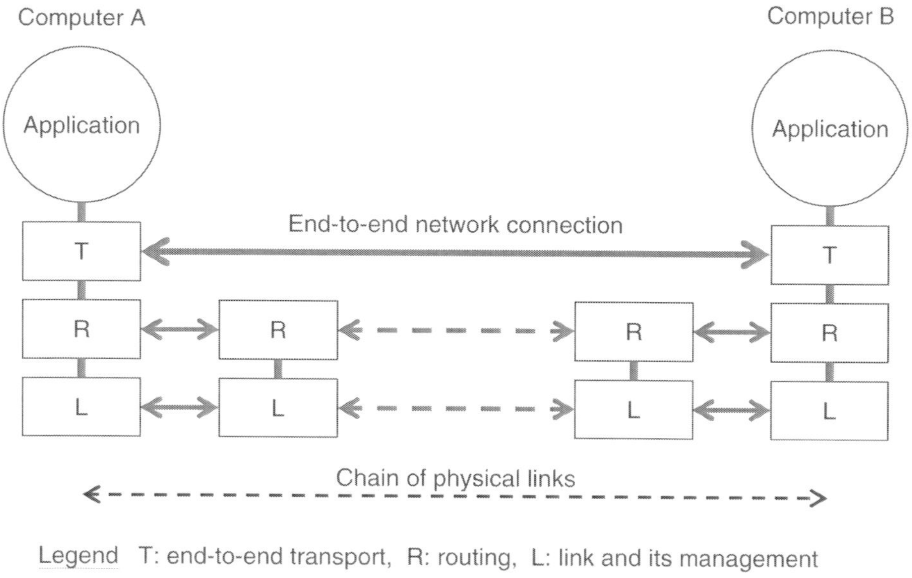

Fig. 15.6 **Structure of end-to-end connection over computer network**

For the data transport function to operate faithfully and reliably, it must rely on 'lower level' *routing* functions of the network. Data packets originating at one end must be *routed* through intervening nodes to the destination computer, and acknowledgement packets must be routed in the reverse direction. In Fig. 15.6, this has been indicated by the use of rectangular boxes with letter 'R' inside; clearly, the routing function must be present at every intervening node on the path of the data packet.

Routing of a packet from one node to the next assumes that:

a. there is a communication link between the two nodes, and
b. correct software runs at both ends of the link to send and receive data packets reliably across the link.

In Fig. 15.6, this function is shown as 'link and its management', in rectangular boxes with letter 'L' inside. Overall, this figure shows the structure of an end-to-end connection over the network—and in that sense it is a detailed view of what is shown in Fig. 15.5.

Software plays a crucial role in link management, routing, and end-to-end transport functions. At each of these layers of functionality, the two communicating entities must follow a common *protocol*, so that an incoming packet is received correctly and—as required—processed or forwarded correctly. For example, *TCP* and *IP* protocols which were mentioned above are central to the functioning of the Internet.

Use of standard protocols has a very significant implication which must be noted. If a network node is performing its function according to its protocol—which is defined in terms of its incoming and outgoing data packets—then it is irrelevant which specific hardware and software is at work within the node.

In other words, a network node is defined by the functions it performs, and not by its internal details*. The Internet today has millions of nodes connected to it, with a vast variety of hardware and software. But the network operates correctly because the nodes follow their defined network protocols.

At the application level, the most logical and convenient communication model is the *message-passing model* which we looked at in Section 14.5. The model is *asynchronous*, in the sense that it does not demand any specific timing relationships involving the two communicating processes. This makes the model ideally suited to be applied across a network, since its logical correctness is not affected by network delays.

With the world-wide reach and sophistication of modern computer networks, it is not at all surprising that applications have been developed with similar reach and sophistication. The *world-wide web* and its associated protocols have made possible the deployment of many *web applications* which could not even have been imagined a few years ago.

With reliable and efficient data transport available, network applications today provide many innovative *value added services*. Web-based e-mail was an early innovation of this kind, and today it is a simple matter for a customer to operate his or her bank accounts and make purchases over the web. *Search engines* can bring us the results of keyword or content based searches made across millions of documents stored on the web.

It is also possible today for users to maintain and share documents and data on servers within the network, instead of storing them on their personal computers. A vast range of applications is also available on the web. Therefore, with such possible modes of operation, the network can be viewed by users as one giant multi-user and multi-functional system—a view sometimes described by saying: 'The network is the computer'.

15.5 APPLICATIONS

A typical application program on a single computer system has the structure shown in Fig. 15.7. One part of the program interacts with the user, as shown on the left, while another part accesses and stores data on secondary storage, as shown on the right. To take but two examples, a word processor program saves the edited document as a file, and an accounting program saves relevant data in a *database management system* (DBMS).

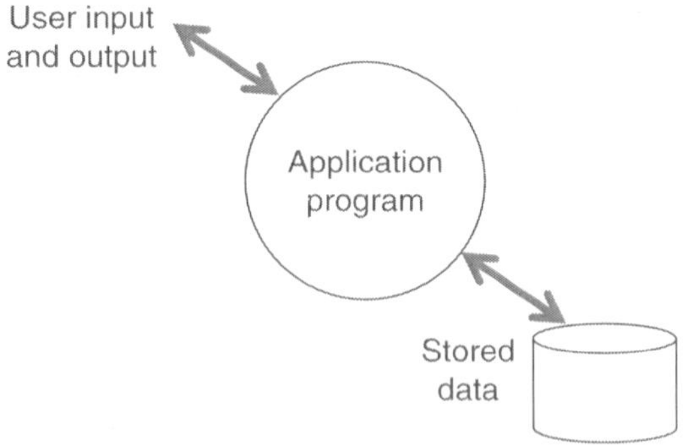

Fig. 15.7 Typical application on a single computer system

*This is another example of abstraction—see Section 14.5.

If such an application is designed for multiple users operating on common data, then appropriate synchronisation has to be provided between user processes, so that changes made to the shared data do not result in inconsistent results; recall that this issue was discussed in Section 13.3 on Pseudo-parallelism.

When an application is designed to work across a network, it has the typical structure shown schematically in Fig. 15.8. Two processes are shown in the figure, with a network connection established between them.

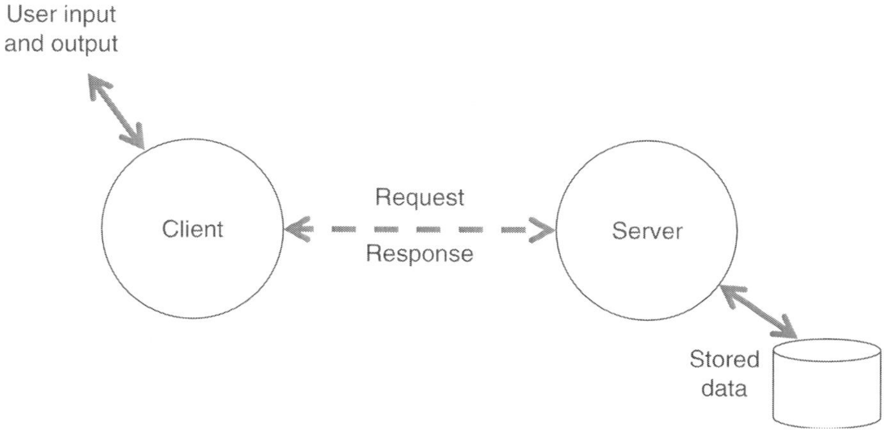

Fig. 15.8 **Typical network application**

The process shown on the left in Fig. 15.8 accepts input from a user and provides output to the user; this process is known as the *client* process. The process shown on the right is responsible for managing data on secondary storage and for making data available to client processes over the network; this process is known as the *server* process.

The application structure shown in Fig. 15.8 is the so-called *client-server model*; today it is the most commonly utilised model for network applications. For a large application—such as airline reservation—there may be millions of potential users across the world, and at any time thousands of users may be using the application over the Internet, connecting as *clients* to the application *server*. On the server side, clusters of processors and disks may be employed to keep up with the demands of such large applications.

A conceptually simple, consistent and robust technique for building such applications is to use the message-passing model which was described in Section 14.5—with *request messages* going from a client process to the server process, and *response messages* returning from the server process to the client process. Libraries of useful functions are available for developing such network-based applications.

As discussed above, protocols are important at every level of network functionality. The most widely used protocol for web applications today is the *hypertext transfer protocol* (HTTP). 'Hypertext' here refers to the *hypertext markup language* (HTML), which is a technique to enrich text with special markers, so as to define the displayed formats of documents stored and accessed using the world-wide web.

Using the HTTP protocol, a *web browser* program is able to access an HTML document from the *web server* on which the document is hosted. Within this basic model, an application running on a web server can define its user interactions using HTML, or one of its variants or extensions. Thus a simple web browser program on the client system becomes the common window through which web applications can be accessed, illustrating the enormous power of this simple application level protocol.

SUMMARY

System and application software play a vital role in the effective and productive utilisation of any computer system. In recent decades, the widespread availability of computer networks has enlarged enormously the scope of computer applications. In this chapter, we took an overview of some key aspects of system and application software, including with it a brief look at the process of software development.

Key functions of the operating system include the management of processes, main memory, secondary storage, and the input and output devices available on a system. Software development is carried out using higher level programming languages, and associated tools and utilities such as compilers and function libraries.

An application running on a computer network needs reliable, end-to-end transport functionality—which in turn depends on 'lower level' functions such as routing and link management. Standard protocols such as TCP and IP play the central role in the operation of the Internet, which connects together millions of computers around the world.

Network applications make use of the message-passing model and appropriate application level protocols; applications on the world-wide web rely on HTML and HTTP, along with their variants and extensions.

REVIEW QUESTIONS

1. What are the two broad objectives of an operating system?
2. In the text, you read the statement: User requirements are functional and abstract'. Justify this statement in brief.
3. Give one example each of explicit and implicit request for system resource made by a process.
4. Which are the three states of a process? Describe them in one line each.
5. List the main functions of the memory manager part of an operating system.
6. What is a 'file'? Which of its typical attributes does the file system store?
7. What is a 'directory'? Why do directories form a hierarchy?
8. What is the function of the file system part of the operating system?
9. Why is achieving device independence important in I/O device management?
10. State in brief the function of a device driver and interrupt handler.
11. Explain in brief what is meant by (i) source program, (ii) object program, and (iii) library of functions.
12. Hardware and software are like the two wheels of the progressing cart of technology. Justify this statement in brief.
13. Explain briefly the meaning of a computer network.
14. What is the difference between a physical link between two computers and a network connection?
15. What is the role of routing in a computer network?
16. Comment briefly on meaning of the statement: The network is the computer.
17. Outline the structure of a typical application on a single computer system.
18. Outline the basic structure of a typical network application.

EXERCISES

1. Identify the operating system running on the computer system which you use most often. Find the names and brief descriptions of any six different functions of the operating system which are available to a program developer.
2. On the computer system which you use most often, explore and learn how to list the status of various running processes. By double-clicking on an icon, or through a command line, create one more process. Check again the status of processes.
3. By double-clicking on an icon, or through a command line, create one more process. Make a list of steps which *you think* the operating system must have carried out to create the process.
4. On the computer system which you use most often, explore and learn features of the file system. What are the attributes of each file that the system records? How many seconds does it take to copy a ten megabyte file from disk to a memory stick?
5. Learn the steps required to compile, link, and execute the simple C language program shown in Section 15.2. Give the source program any name of your choice. What is the name and size in bytes of the executable machine language program produced?
6. Find the network address of the computer system you use for accessing the Internet.
7. The following is a small example of an HTML document. Note that it consists of simple text characters, and note the use of HTML markers. Create an HTML document with this text, and open that document using a web browser.

```
<html>
<head>
<title>PAGE TITLE</title>
</head>
<body>
<p><font size="5">PROJECT REPORT</font></p>
<p><font size="4"><u>Abstract</u>:</font></p>
<p><font size="4"><u>Executive Summary</u>:</font></p>
<p><font size="3">Text of executive summary goes here ...
</font></p>
<p><font size="4"><u>Conclusions</u>:</font></p>
</body>
</html>
```

8. Repeat the previous exercise, after changing the title of the web page to 'MY WEB PAGE', and removing all the colon characters (':') from the page.

CASE STUDIES

16

16.1 INTRODUCTION

We have studied in this book many of the *principles* and *techniques* which govern the design and operation of modern computer systems. Like any other complex system, a computer system is also built from several different functional sub-systems. We have seen that the processor plays the central role in a computer system, because instructions executed within it determine the actions of all other sub-systems.

In the previous fifteen chapters of the book, we have consciously and carefully avoided making any explicit references to hardware or software products which are commercially marketed. The main reason behind this approach is that principles and techniques of computer system design are valuable in themselves. To bring out clearly an essential principle or technique, it is necessary to avoid slipping into specific product details which may distract the student from understanding and appreciating the main point.

If a commercial product is to be chosen as a running example in the main text, it is difficult to avoid being biased in the choice of product. In today's highly competitive computer industry, any successful product must necessarily represent excellence in one or more aspects of design, manufacturing, and business strategy. But such products are also very complex—and it is therefore not a simple matter to make an unbiased choice of the one product which best represents the various design principles and techniques.

About Intel's 'x86' family of processors, for example, there may be different opinions amongst experienced persons in the academic world or in computer industry. However, for a student learning computer system organisation for the first time, such differences of opinion are not of primary concern. The student's aim is to understand clearly the design issues involved—so that not only can he or she work with any specific product, but also, when the time comes, make the right design choices.

In the last chapter of the book, however, we do present a few case studies based on products which have made a mark on computer industry. We describe, in particular, two different processors, a 'virtual' processor, a microcontroller family, and the popular PC family of computer systems. The main criterion in the selection of these case studies has been widespread adoption and use of the products in their respective applications.

Needless to say, another dozen such case studies can easily be prepared—not only on other processors, but also on other elements of computer systems such as memories and interconnect standards. However, we must draw the line somewhere—and hope that the few case studies presented here will prove useful to the student.

16.2 THROUGHPUT

In earlier chapters, we have referred at times to the *throughput* of a computer system. It should be clear from the context that, in broad terms, throughput refers to the capability of a computer system to process data. Very often, two or more computer systems are compared for performance, and for such purposes the concept of *throughput* needs to be quantified. However, since a system is made up of several different types of elements—processors, memories, pipelines, data paths, and so on—very careful thought is required for such quantification.

One method of quantification could be based on the application load. If a system is designed for a bank, for example, then its throughput could be measured in the maximum number of transactions that could be processed in a second. In a system designed for graphics, throughput could be measured in the number of graphics vectors processed per second, or in the number of picture frames processed per second.

But sometimes we may need to quantify system throughput without reference to any particular application. This would certainly be the case if the mix of applications running on the system is expected to be quite broad. Or we may also wish to compare two or more processors for throughput, without reference to any particular application. The need in this case would be to quantify in some way the throughput of the processors, when all other elements of the systems are made identical, or at least comparable.

One way to characterise a processor is to determine, based on its design, the theoretical maximum rate at which the processor can execute instructions. This rate can be expressed in *instructions per second.* In units of *million instructions per second*, this measure is usually abbreviated as *mips*.

However, many compute-intensive applications make heavy use of floating point operations, and therefore a more useful measure of performance would be *floating point operations per second*, abbreviated as *flops*. With prefix *mega* (10^6) or *giga* (10^9), this is written as *megaflops* (*mflops*) or *gigaflops* (*gflops*).

Example 16.1

A processor is capable of completing one instruction in every processor clock cycle of 2 nanoseconds, assuming no pipeline stalls and flushes. The maximum throughput of this processor is thus $1/(2 \times 10^{-9}) =$ 500 million instructions per second (*mips*).

Suppose, however, that the above processor throughput is not applicable to floating point instructions—because the floating point unit of this processor can only complete one operation in every four processor clock cycles. Then, in terms of floating point operations, the throughput of this processor is only 125 million floating point operations per second (*mflops*).

For the next version of this hypothetical processor, one can imagine research efforts proceeding in several different directions. Let us consider here a few examples.

Firstly, for higher overall processor performance, higher processor clock speed must be achieved. Secondly, for further performance gain specifically in floating point operations, the designers can also aim for (i) execution of floating point operations in smaller number of clock cycles, and (ii) provision of multiple floating point units in the processor. In addition, the designers can also attempt to provide better branch prediction, larger cache, and exploitation of instruction and/or thread level parallelism.

Since programs are written in higher level languages, compilers play a crucial role in determining the performance of machine language programs. Because of frequent pipeline flushes and stalls, the actual processor performance in practice is usually much less than the theoretical maximum for which the processor may have been designed.

Therefore, in an attempt to quantify the actual processor performance which can be expected in practice, use is made of standard *benchmark programs*. If processor P runs a standard benchmark program twice as fast as processor Q, for example, then that may be judged to be a fair reflection of their respective processing powers.

A widely used set of benchmark programs is developed by System Performance Evaluation Corporation (SPEC)*. SPEC has developed a range of standard benchmark programs for integer and floating point performance of processors, graphics, parallel processing in message-passing or shared memory model, different types of applications developed on JAVA platforms, mail servers, file servers, and others.

16.3 INTEL PENTIUM® FAMILY OF PROCESSORS

Of all the companies in the world, the name of semiconductor manufacturer Intel** is most closely associated with the microprocessor revolution which has swept across the world over the last few decades. In the early 1970s, Intel produced the first ever microprocessor on a single chip, a 4-bit processor which was given the Intel part number 4004†. This processor was soon followed by its 8-bit version 8008, and then the successively improved versions 8080, 8086 and 8088.

Around 1980, Intel's 8088 processor was selected by IBM†† for use in its Personal Computer, known simply as the PC. Even though other companies—including Apple—had earlier come out with their own path-breaking versions of the personal computer, IBM PC and its 'clones' soon became the largest selling computers around the world (see Section 16.7).

Intel 8088 was a 16-bit processor with 20-bit physical address, i.e. total physical address space of 1 megabyte. Logical memory space consisted of four segments—namely, *code*, *data*, *stack* and *extra* segments. A 16-bit segment offset meant that each segment was limited to 64 kilobytes. The PC which was built around this processor made use of Microsoft‡ operating system DOS, which in its original version was distributed and run from 5¼" *floppy disks*, each of which had a storage capacity of 360 kilobytes.

Subsequent processors in Intel's 'x86' processor family were numbered 80286, 80386 and 80486. As VLSI technology advanced, these successively upgraded members of the processor family had larger memory address space, 32-bit word size, higher clock frequencies, on-chip cache and memory management functions, and additional instructions, including floating point instructions.

Successive models of the immensely popular PC were built around these processors. Therefore, maintaining *backward compatibility* of instruction set with earlier processors of the x86 family has always been a non-negotiable design requirement of any processor of the family. Note that this requirement follows from a *business strategy*—that all software written for earlier versions of the PC must also run with its subsequent versions. This critical business requirement pushed Intel processor designers to the

*Founded in 1988 as Standard Performance Evaluation Cooperative; see www.spec.org.

**Intel Corporation, with headquarters in Santa Clara, California, USA.

†All the product numbers and names used in this chapter are registered trademarks of the respective corporations named.

††IBM Corporation of Armonk, New York.

‡Microsoft Corporation of Redmond, Washington. DOS was the company's first product.

limits of their ingenuity—since they had to achieve higher processor performance with every model, while maintaining at all times full backward compatibility of instruction set.

When the 8088 processor was introduced, the concept of RISC had not yet made its appearance, and instruction pipelines had been implemented only on very expensive supercomputers. Given the state of computer technology of the day, the 8088 instruction set was comparable to that of other similar microprocessors. And, in any case, having an inexpensive 16-bit processor on a chip was so 'cool' that the relative merits and demerits of competing instruction sets had not yet become 'hot' research topics!

With rapid advances in IC and VLSI technology, it became possible to build enormously more powerful single-chip microprocessors—and then the spotlight turned on the critical role of the instruction set in achieving high performance. Benefits of the RISC approach soon became clear to processor designers, and all new processor designs benefited from the new ideas. But the only way for the x86 family to maintain backward compatibility in instruction set was to continue with its opposite CISC approach.

Designers at Intel pushed the frontiers of VLSI technology to achieve higher processor performance while maintaining backward compatibility. The original Pentium and its successors were introduced as advanced sequels to the Intel 80486 processor. Even with the inherited CISC instruction set, these processors combined standard RISC design techniques in their internal architecture—such as a *micro-operation* pipeline, multiple functional units, and out-of-order sequencing.

Figure 16.1 is an overview of the architecture of the Pentium 4 processor.

Note first of all that the processor has two levels of cache memory—level 1 (L1) and level 2 (L2). The faster but smaller L1 cache is divided into 8 kilobytes of instruction cache and 8 kilobytes of data cache, while the larger L2 cache is a combined instruction and data cache of 256 or 512 kilobytes, depending on the processor model. The required instruction or data bytes are accessed from L1 cache and L2 cache, in that order. If a cache miss occurs in both L1 and L2, the required bytes are accessed from main memory, which may also be provided with an additional off-chip L3 cache.

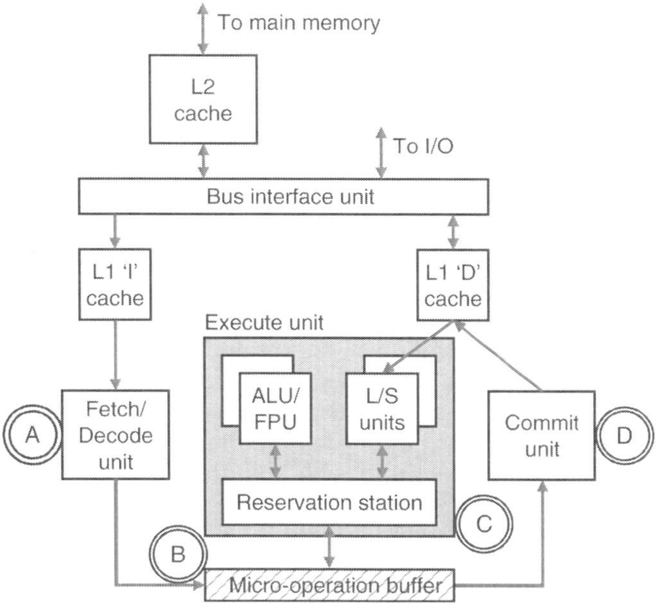

Fig. 16.1 **Internal architecture of the Pentium 4 processor**

The Fetch/Decode unit (marked 'A' in the figure) is connected to the L1 instruction cache. This unit fetches and decodes successive instructions, producing several so-called *micro-operations* corresponding to each machine instruction. These micro-operations are forwarded to the *micro-operation buffer* (marked 'B'), in which micro-operations produced by multiple machine instructions are buffered.

For execution by specific functional units—such as the integer ALU or the FPU—micro-operations are forwarded to a *reservation station.* An operation is performed in a unit when its operands become available and the functional unit becomes free. Execution of micro-operations need not follow the order in which machine instructions are fetched. Data load and store operations on memory are carried out by the *load unit* and *store unit*, respectively, which operate as functional units connected to the L1 data cache.

The reservation station and the functional units together make up the *execute unit* of the processor (marked 'C'). Within this execute unit, hardwired control is provided for the simpler instructions of the processor, whereas complex instructions of the CISC type are provided with microprogram control. This is one of the ways in which RISC and CISC approaches have been combined in the internal architecture of the processor.

When all the micro-operations of an instruction have been performed in the execute unit, the instruction is *committed* (or *retired*) to main memory. This work is carried out by the *commit unit* (marked 'D'), which ensures that completed machine instructions are committed in the order in which they are fetched, as the programmer expects.

Fetch/decode unit ('A'), *execute unit* ('B') and *commit unit* ('D') operate in parallel, sharing the common *micro-operation buffer* ('C'). Thus these three units can be said to form a 'high-level' pipeline through which instructions pass. But each of these units is also implemented as a pipeline, so that multiple instructions can be in each of these units at one time, each in a different stage of processing. Branch prediction logic, which is required with the instruction pipeline, is also provided.

Figure 16.2 shows the set of programmable registers on Pentium processors. Note that, of the total 32-bit width of each register, the left half has been shaded in light color. Starting with the 80386 processor, the register size was extended from 16 bits to 32 bits. The shaded portion denotes this extension, while the un-shaded portion on the right shows the 16-bit registers as they existed from the time of the 8088 processor.

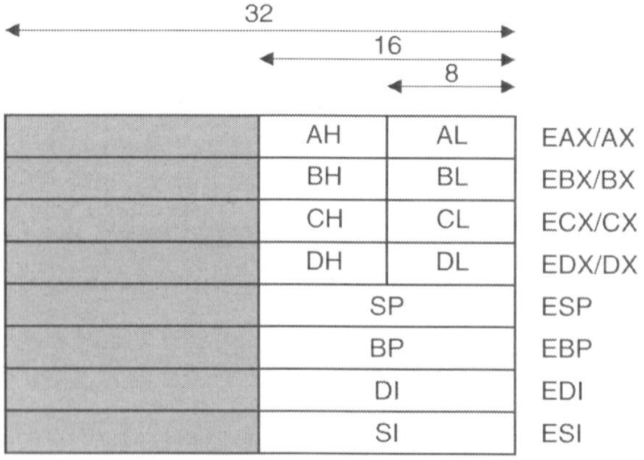

Fig. 16.2 Programmable registers on Pentium processors

To achieve backward compatibility, names of the registers are chosen to indicate whether an operation is to be performed on 8-bit, 16-bit, or 32-bit register operands. For example, 'AH' and 'AL' denote the higher and lower order bytes, respectively, of the 16-bit 'AX' register, and 'EAX'' denotes the 32-bit extension of the 'AX' register. The registers are not alike in their functionality, and therefore in this sense they are not general-purpose registers; it is not surprising then that the instruction set is not *orthogonal*.

Memory management functions on the processor provide support for virtual memory using paging and/or segmentation, as well as memory protection for user programs and the operating system; segments may be shared between running programs.

The *instruction set architecture* (ISA) of the 32-bit Intel processors is known as IA32. This is the processor 'seen' by an assembly language programmer or a compiler writer, and it should be distinguished from the internal processor architecture shown in Fig. 16.1. In theory, the instruction set provided on a processor can be changed without changing its internal processor architecture. However, companies such as AMD* do exactly the opposite—they design and build processors with the IA32 instruction set, but develop their own proprietary designs for the internal processor architecture.

16.4 SUN ULTRASPARC T2® PROCESSOR

The concept of *reduced instruction set computing* (RISC) became widely known with the work done by David Patterson at the University of California, Berkeley, and by John Hennessey at Stanford University. The work done at Berkeley led to the development of the Sparc processor by Sun Microsystems** in the late 1980s.

As we have seen in earlier chapters, the basic idea of RISC is that, with a 'reduced' instruction set, a processor can be designed to perform more useful work per second. We have seen that the two key elements of processor architecture which make this possible are the instruction pipeline and the cache memory.

The original Sparc processor is a 32-bit RISC processor with load-store architecture, relatively simple addressing modes, and register-to-register arithmetic/logic machine instructions in three-address format. Separate registers are provided for integer and floating point operands. Of the 32 integer registers, some play a special role in passing arguments during function calls from the calling to the called function.

UltraSparc is the 64-bit enhanced version of Sparc, and UltraSparc T2 is the newest *multi-core*, *system on a chip* version of UltraSparc with extensive on-chip support for multithreading, networking, I/O, and much else.

Even on a reduced instruction set processor, the constant need to squeeze maximum performance out of it introduces complexity in the processor architecture. We have already seen this in the case of Intel's Pentium IV processor, and it should be clear that the basic technical constraints are no different in the case of a RISC processor.

For increased processor performance, one design option for processor designers is to maximise *instruction issue rate* by increasing the number of stages in the instruction pipeline. The idea is that—with each pipeline stage doing relatively less work in a clock cycle—it is possible to drive the processor with a higher clock frequency. However, the problems of pipeline flushes and stalls do not go away, and the

---

*Advanced Micro Devices, with headquarters in Sunnyvale, California, USA.

**Sun Microsystems has headquarters in Sunnyvale, California, USA. Before Sparc, the company used Motorola's 680x0 series processors in its workstations.

total power consumption of the chip increases very rapidly with frequency. As a result, total power consumption of the chip becomes a limiting factor in achieving higher performance.

In this connection, the following observation is of interest*:

Power and memory latency considerations place additional obstacles to improving single-thread performance. While recent attempts at improving single-thread performance, through even deeper pipelines, have led to impressive clock frequencies, these clock frequencies have not translated into demonstrably better performance over less aggressive designs.

UltraSparc T2 and its predecessor UltraSparc T1 are designed to achieve higher processing throughput by adopting a different strategy. The architecture of these multi-core chips is designed for those highly demanding applications which exhibit a large degree of thread level parallelism (TLP), but not necessarily much instruction level parallelism (ILP). The strategy adopted in UltraSparc processors is referred to as *chip multi-threading* (CMT). As we have seen in Section 13.4, this means that the compute time and memory latencies of multiple executing threads are interleaved in time.

UltraSparc T2 has eight processor cores on the chip, with each supporting eight-way fine-grained multi-threading (FGMT, see Section 13.4). Overall, therefore, the chip supports sixty-four parallel threads. The chip also contains a crossbar switch, shared L2 cache, and extensive support for I/O and networking—and therefore it is referred to as a *system on a chip* (SoC), rather than 'just a processor'. In fact, since the threads run independently of each other and share hardware resources, each thread behaves as a processor in its own right; therefore the single chip can be said to support 64 *virtual systems* on it.

Figure 16.3 depicts schematically the architecture of UltraSparc T2.

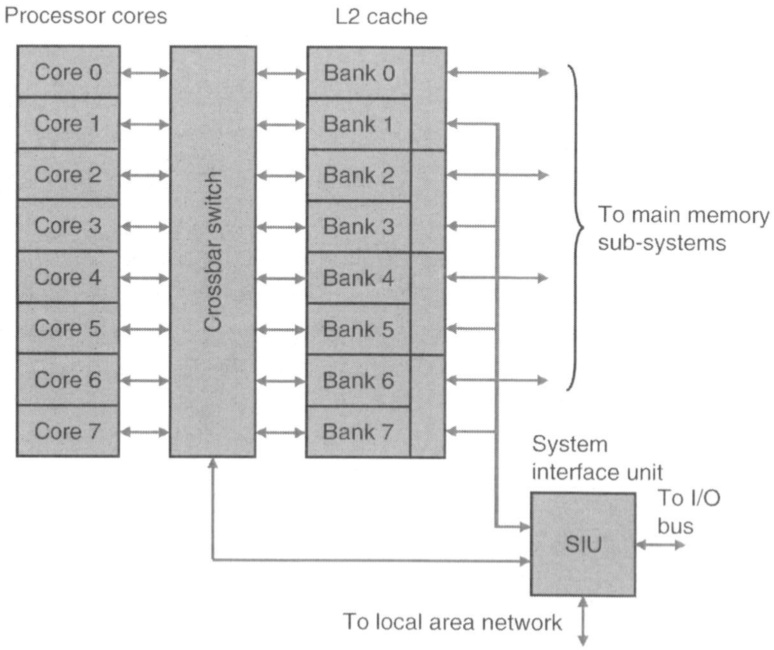

Fig. 16.3 **Architecture of UltraSparc T2 'system on a chip'**

*From "Chip Multithreading: Opportunities and Challenges", by L Spracklen and S G Abraham of Sun Microsystems, *IEEE International Symposium on High-Performance Computer Architecture* (*HPCA-2005*), 2005.

Physically, the T2 chip has an area of just under 3.5 cm^2, with about 500 million transistors on it. A simple calculation shows that, on average, there is one transistor on the chip for every 0.7 square micron (i.e. micrometer) of area. This is made possible by a VLSI process which can create geometries which are 0.065 microns in width. The chip can operate at 1.4 gigahertz with 1.1 volt supply, and has 1831 pins on its underside for connection to the rest of the computer system. Nominal power consumed by the chip is 95 watts; on the basis of power per cm^2 of chip area, this is greater than that of an iron. However, on a per thread basis, this power consumption works out to be quite low.

Note 16.1

As we have seen, a transistor can be thought of as a basic building block of digital circuits. In an analogous way, let us think of a brick of size 10 cm $\times$ 10 cm $\times$ 20 cm as a single physical building block, and calculate the area we could cover with 500 million such bricks laid out in a plane.

The area covered by one brick is $10 \times 20 = 200$ cm^2, and therefore 500 million bricks would cover an area of 10^{11} cm^2. Since one km equals 10^5 cm, one km^2 equals 10^{10} cm^2. The area covered by the bricks therefore equals 10 km^2; if this area had a square shape, each side of the square would be slightly more than 3 km in length.

To put it differently, if a single transistor had the size of a brick, area of the UltraSparc T2 chip would be about 10 square kilometers.

Each of the eight processing cores on the T2 has its own data paths, register sets for multiple threads, two integer operation units, and a floating point unit. This part of the core is in essence somewhat similar to the architecture shown in Fig. 16.1. But, in addition, each core has hardware provided for cryptography and graphics and—the important point—support for eight-way fine-grained multi-threading.

These hardware resources—as also the per core L1 instruction cache and data cache—are shared by eight threads executing on each core.

At the level of the 'system' on the chip, other hardware resources such as the 4 MB L2 cache are made available to the cores by means of a cross-bar switch. For faster access, the L2 cache is organised in the form of eight parallel 'banks'. Memory interfaces, I/O interfaces, and networking are also shared amongst the cores. Networking capability consists of two network interfaces of 10 gigabits per second; this could be very useful, for instance, when multiple such systems are to be connected to build a computing cluster (recall Section 14.6).

Design of UltraSparc T2 is targeted towards compute-intensive applications with a high degree of multi-threading. Apart from back-end servers, these include network devices such as packet routers (see Section 15.4), switches for local area networks, graphics and imaging applications, and so on.

In addition to multi-threading support, such applications require very high reliability and availability from the system. At the design stage of the chip, this requires very intensive verification and simulation—so that all the elements of the 'system on a chip' are verified to be logically correct, and are also balanced for the aggregate throughput expected. For higher reliability, sub-systems and data paths of the UltraSparc T2 are provided with error detection and correction.

A unique feature of the UltraSparc T2 chip is that its complete design has been made available on the web to researchers and developers under an 'open source' arrangement. The stated objective behind this decision by Sun Microsystems is to encourage innovations around the world in processor design and applications.

16.5 JAVA VIRTUAL MACHINE

JAVA is a higher level programming language, developed originally by Sun Microsystems, for writing programs which can run on any computer on the Internet. Computers connected to the Internet span a vast variety in hardware as well as software. Clearly therefore, for a program to be executable on any computer on the Internet, it must not be made up of machine instructions of any one particular processor, or of system functions of any one operating system.

As a companion to JAVA, Sun Microsystems therefore developed a *JAVA virtual machine* (JVM)—a processor built not on a silicon chip but simulated in software, on which compiled JAVA programs would run, and which could be made available as a software download on any computer on the Internet*.

Once JVM is available on a computer, a compiled JAVA program—known as *applet*—can be downloaded from a server on the Internet and executed locally. This capability enhances tremendously the power of the Internet—since it allows not only multi-media information but also program functionality to be shared on the world wide web.

Specifically, JVM works as an *interpreter* for the JAVA program which has been compiled into the 'machine language' of JVM. This means that 'machine instructions' in the compiled JAVA program are *interpreted* by JVM—i.e. executed one by one in software. The compiled JAVA program is also known as *bytecode*.

Figure 16.4 depicts the relationship between the computer hardware, operating system, JVM, and an applet. Typically, JVM functionality is available with the web browser program, which is also responsible for downloading the applet over the Internet. The browser, with its built-in JVM and the applet running over it, make up just one of several applications which may be running on the system at a given time.

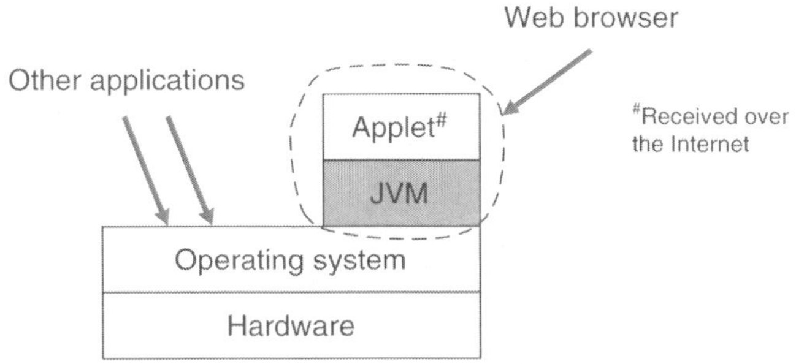

Fig. 16.4 Role of JVM

The arrangement depicted in Fig. 16.4 ensures that functionality of the applet downloaded over the Internet remains independent of the local hardware and operating system. For obvious reasons, this is a key requirement for applications which can be deployed across the Internet. Bytecode is designed to be compact, so as to reduce its download time, and several features of JVM are designed to protect the local system against erroneous or malicious bytecode.

---

*JAVA Virtual Machine is also known as JAVA *Runtime Environment*. Support and downloads are available at www.sun.com/java. See also the book '*The Java Virtual Machine Specification*', by Tim Lindholm and Frank Yellin, at java.sun.com/docs/books/jvms.

In keeping with the 'strongly typed' nature of JAVA programming language, JVM also provides support for *data types* and *classes*. For example, when a JVM instruction refers to an operand, the instruction *opcode* appears in different variants for integer, 'long' integer, single-precision operands, double-precision operands, and so on.

All JVM opcodes are one byte in length, and most do not have any explicit operands, because JVM instructions are designed to work with operands on a runtime *operand stack*. This stack-oriented instruction set means that JVM has no programmable registers such as the ones we have used in earlier chapters*.

Operands of JVM opcodes are variables which have been brought from memory to the runtime stack. When an arithmetic or logic operation takes place, its operands are removed from the runtime stack; after the operation, the result is again placed on the stack. Thus the result of one operation can again be used as an operand of another.

As mentioned above, operations are type-specific; opcode prefixes are therefore used, such as *i* for an integer operation, *c* for a character operation, and so on. Floating point data types and operations are compatible with the IEEE Floating Point standard—see Section 2.6—but with a few minor simplifications.

Support is provided in JVM for *classes*, in terms of which JAVA programs are written. For example, there is a JVM instruction to create a new instance of a class. This is a 'higher level' or 'more abstract' instruction, as compared to those which we have studied in Chapters 4 and 5. Therefore, when such a JVM instruction is simulated on a hardware processor, it will result in the execution of several machine instructions.

Memory on JVM is not conceived as a linear sequence of bytes, as was shown in Fig. 3.12. Rather it is viewed as a collection of variables of various types occupying different memory areas. Variables and objects of different types are located not by their binary memory addresses, but by *references* which are also type-specific.

Multiple threads executing on a JVM can access shared variables through the use of locks. Each thread is provided with its own simulated 'program counter'. Note here that a multi-threaded JVM program should run correctly on a processor, regardless of whether the underlying processor has hardware support for multi-threading.

16.6 INTEL 8051® MICROCONTROLLER FAMILY

In Chapter 1, a *microcontroller* was defined as a processor with memory and some input/output capability, in a compact package, especially designed for use in embedded applications. While the PC has brought about a revolution in our lives which is all too visible, many millions of microcontrollers are also embedded in systems and appliances in use all around the world. Through the use of embedded microcontrollers, such systems and appliances provide improved and enhanced functionality to the user—but the presence of the microcontrollers in the system usually remains hidden.

*The *stack-oriented* instruction set of the JVM is to be contrasted with the *register-oriented* instruction set of *NICE*, the processor which we have used, and also of most other commercial processors including the Pentium, Sparc, and the Intel 8051 (see ahead).

Intel's 8051 and other 8-bit single-chip microcontrollers of the family—known as the MCS® 51 family—have been used by system designers for well over two decades*. Intel has produced several microcontrollers in the family—such as 8031, 8751 and 87C51—with the same basic architecture and instruction set, but with differences in on-chip memory and other features. In fact several other semiconductor manufacturers have also produced competing products which offer additional features, while maintaining *pin-compatibility* and software compatibility with the 8051 microcontroller.

The original 8051 microcontroller is produced in a 40-pin package. Of these forty pins, two are used for power supply and ground, and two for connecting an external crystal which is required to generate the processor clock signal.

The remaining pins of the chip provide four bidirectional 8-bit wide I/O ports, and control signals for externally connected memory and devices. But this assignment leaves no pins for the 16 address lines and 8 data lines required for external memory and other devices. These external address and data lines are therefore not provided on separate pins, but share the same pins as two of the four 8-bit I/O ports. Similarly, interrupt lines, serial receive and transmit lines, and a few other control signals are provided as alternate functions of pins of the third I/O port.

Recall that Fig. 10.6 shows how a parallel input/output controller is used to read the switches and control the lights in a very simple laboratory application. The 8751 microcontroller provides a total of $8 \times 4 = 32$ input/output lines and also on-chip EPROM for the program. Therefore a single such microcontroller chip can replace the components shown to the right of 'interface electronics' in Fig. 10.6, including the processor.

Relevant part of the simpler microcontroller-based system would thus be as shown in Fig. 16.5. Use of a microcontroller would result in lower chip count in the system, and therefore lower cost of production as well as a more compact and reliable design.

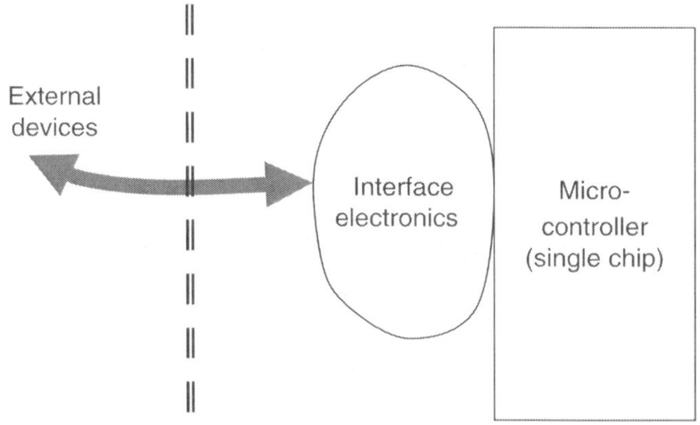

Fig. 16.5 **Use of microcontroller (compare with Fig. 10.6)**

In the design of a 'one-off' laboratory experiment—such as the one described in Chapter 10—these may not be considered major issues, since even a 'spare' PC lying around can be used for the

*A predecessor of the 8051 microcontroller was the Intel 8048 microcontroller, which was used internally in the keyboard of the original IBM PC.

experiment. But appliances are today produced, marketed, and serviced in very large quantities. In such systems, lower chip count, cost, and reliability can certainly make the difference between a successful product and a failed product.

The 8051 processor architecture has separate memory address space for the program and for data—each allowing for up to 64 kilobytes of external memory through the 16 address lines and 8 data lines mentioned above. Program memory—both on-chip and external—is *read only*. Different members of the microcontroller family have on-chip RAM of either 128 bytes or 256 bytes; of these, the lower 128 bytes include four banks of byte-wide registers R0 to R7. Several addressing modes of the processor are designed specifically for the effective use of this on-chip RAM.

Other useful functional devices—such as two 16-bit timers/counters and a full duplex serial communication port—are provided along with the processor in the same package, as are two external interrupt lines.

The application program running on a microcontroller system is often organised in the form of multiple *tasks* which are invoked through external or internal interrupts. Input and output devices connected to the system—such as measuring instruments or actuators—may require attention from the processor either in response to interrupts, or at regular time intervals, say ten times a second, depending on the application*.

To allow faster access to registers and to cater to the needs of multiple tasks, the 8051 architecture provides four banks of 8-bit registers R0 to R7—within the lower 128 bytes of the on-chip RAM. This allows different register banks to be used by the different tasks making up the application program. When execution switches from one task to another, the processor can be simply switched to use the appropriate register bank, to enable faster access to working variables of the task.

The instruction set of the 8051 processor family is fairly simple and compact—but it is definitely not orthogonal. To enable effective use of on-chip as well as external data and program memory, various different addressing modes are provided for accessing data and also for transfers of control.

Microcontroller applications often require manipulation of individual bits which may reflect the status of various devices controlled by the system. To facilitate this, the 8051 instruction set provides a number of useful *bit manipulation* instructions.

Consider the following instruction as an example:

```
LDB  C, bit     //Load addressed bit into C
```

Here **bit** is an eight-bit address pointing to one of 256 bits in the on-chip RAM which are directly bit-addressable. The instruction shown here copies—i.e. loads—the addressed bit into the carry bit C of the processor.

Other instructions—such as **BB**, for 'branch on bit'—allow a transfer of control based on the value of the addressed bit. Similarly, each single input or output line of the four 8-bit I/O ports can also be read or written individually.

Parameters of the timers/counters, serial port, and so on, are set by the programmer in so-called *configuration registers*. Low power versions of the processor—such as 87C51—provide *power down* and *idle modes* of operation which are invoked by software and result in reduced power consumption by the microcontroller.

---

*Recall in this connection the two versions of the program of Section 10.6—one which uses timer interrupts, and one which keeps time in software using a program loop.

Microcontroller application software can be developed either in assembly language or in C language. Accordingly, a *cross-assembler* or a *cross-compiler* is used—i.e. one which runs on a PC, but produces the corresponding machine language program for the microcontroller, to be downloaded into it over the serial port.

16.7 THE PC

As we have seen in Chapter 1, computers were first developed in the 1940s. Since then, computer technology has witnessed advances which seem incredible even when seen in retrospect. One important milestone in this journey was reached around the year 1980 when, soon after the advent of single-chip microprocessors, it became possible to build computers which could be considered 'personal'.

Let us reflect for a moment about what it takes for a computer to be accepted as 'personal'. Some key features which immediately come to mind are: *cost*, *size*, *ease of use*, *ease of maintenance*, *choice of applications*, and *choice of hardware add-ons*. Without these features, we would find it difficult to accept a computer as being personal. The importance of such a personal computer arises from the fact that, in a knowledge-based society, a PC becomes an inseparable part of the user's life.

When we say 'PC' today, we refer to a member of a very large family of computer systems. Many, many millions of PCs are in use around the world, and many millions have also gone out of use since the time the first PC was introduced.

The first member of this family was introduced by IBM in 1981*. It employed the Intel 8088 processor, which had 20 address lines, 8 data lines, and a clock speed of about 5 megahertz. The system could be operated with a minimum of 256 kilobytes of memory. The operating system DOS was distributed—and ran—from 5 ¼" removable magnetic 'diskettes' with capacity of 360 kilobytes each. While the system fetched a file from such a disk, the user could hear the 'clicks' in the drive and enjoy a few sips of coffee or tea.

There was virtually no graphics capability in the original PC, and no graphical user interface. The command line option which is still available on present-day PCs was the only means of system interaction available to the user on the original PC.

For the PC, IBM followed from day one the *open architecture* policy of making the entire hardware design of the system freely available. The aim behind this policy was to allow a wide range of 'third party' hardware and software to become available for the PC. This would provide added value to users, and would also lead to increased demand for the PC itself. This policy worked like a charm—not only third-party hardware and software, but also third party PC 'clones' became readily available in the ensuing years.

The PC family has since prospered, evolved, and grown to an extent which could not have been predicted by any computer *gurus* in 1981. Many key factors have played a role in this process, including: steady advances in VLSI technology for processors, memory, display, multi-media and networking technology; improved batteries, better packaging and lower costs; and an almost unlimited range of applications.

*The first personal computer to achieve wide-spread acceptance was produced by the garage start-up Apple Computer, of Cupertino, California, a couple of years earlier. But IBM Chairman's 2007 Annual Letter to Shareholders includes the statement: *We exited businesses like PCs and hard disk drives—businesses that we had invented.* For the type of hardware and software technologies on which IBM is focusing today, see this letter at www.ibm.com.

In any technology product, production in large volumes leads to lower costs, and lower costs lead to higher demand for the product. Since the PC is made and sold globally on a competitive basis, and the demand amongst users has been growing steadily, the worldwide 'PC market' has seen thousands of product innovations and innovative products.

The PC we use today is very different from the first IBM PC of 1981. In terms of any of the system elements—processor, memory, secondary storage, display, I/O, networking, or software—there is nothing in common between the two. However, as a basic business strategy, IBM—and therefore also Intel and Microsoft—have maintained full *backward compatibility* in the PC family from the original Intel 8088-based PC to the present-day Pentium-based and other compatible systems. In theory, any program which ran under DOS operating system on the original PC should run on a present-day PC.

The processor in today's PC is a member of Intel's Pentium family, or a compatible processor made by a company such as AMD (see Section 16.1). Memory, magnetic disk, optical disk, and display may be made by any of a number of manufacturers around the world. The PC itself may be assembled in a country where none of these components are made, and the software may originate from several different countries.

Figure 16.6 shows a typical organisation of a PC. The main I/O bus shown in the figure is the *PCI bus*—where *PCI* stands for *Peripheral Component Interconnect*. This standard bus was developed by Intel in 1993; it has recently been upgraded to *PCI Express*, but *PCI* is still available on PCs because of its widespread use in the industry.

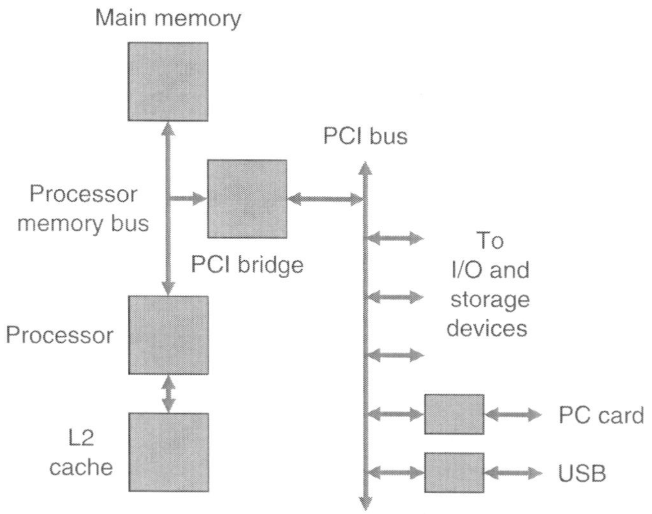

Fig. 16.6 **Typical organisation of the PC**

A system element is shown in Fig. 16.6 with the label *PCI bridge*. The word *bridge* here refers to the fact that this element 'bridges' the differences between the specific data transfer mechanisms of the two data busses connected to it. In this way, the *bridge* makes it possible to send and receive data between devices connected to two different busses. In the case shown in the figure, one of these two busses is the high speed processor-memory bus, while the other is the PCI bus. Also seen in the figure is another high speed bus which connects the processor to the off-chip L2 cache.

For connecting a variety of I/O and storage devices to the PC, provision is made for the so-called *PC card* interface, and one or more *Universal Serial Bus* (USB) ports. The former is technically known as PCMCIA* interface. It is provided so as to extend the PCI I/O capability for devices which can be plugged in and out by the user. USB has also been developed with the same objective—except that it is a serial interface, and therefore is more compact, less expensive, and provides lower data transfer speeds.

The original open architecture concept of the PC has ensured that—even if its originator IBM Corporation has left the PC business—hundreds of manufacturers of PCs are in business today, in dozens of different countries around the world. The number of vendors of PC components, hardware add-ons, and software is probably uncountable.

SUMMARY

In this chapter, we have looked at a sample of processors, and one computer system, which have found wide-spread acceptance and use. The successful products described here have been designed for different end-uses, and represent different facets of a rapidly changing technology. The main objective behind these case studies has been to round off and to complement, with a few practical examples, the principles of computer system organisation presented in earlier chapters.

Successful products—of the kind seen here—certainly require correct application of principles of computer system design. But they also require much more: understanding of customer needs; excellence in design, engineering, manufacturing, distribution and support; business and marketing strategy, and so on.

Around the world today, there must be hundreds of millions of large and small computer systems at work, including those which are 'embedded'—and therefore invisible to the user. The processors in these systems are of many different types, and the systems themselves have been put to work for an uncountable number of different applications. How does one 'cover' in one book a subject whose scope is as vast as this? Indeed, is it even possible to 'cover' such a subject? These are not easy questions to answer.

Fortunately, however, the basic principles of computer system organisation do not change much from one system to another. The aim in this book has been to introduce these basic principles with some clarity and simplicity, and the case studies have also been selected with the same objective. The specific systems described in this chapter are excellent examples of human ingenuity, business strategy, and hard work. Each has made a name for itself in the history of computers—but it is also true that there are many other equally noteworthy systems which could have been selected as our case studies.

Certainly it is true that no computer product—hardware or software—can be successful unless careful attention is paid to basic design principles and good engineering. Over the last few decades, advancing computer and communication technologies have

*Personal Computer Memory Card International Association.

brought about a revolution in human society. Technology—i.e. human ingenuity at work—and business instinct have fuelled this particular revolution. This process has generated keen interest in subjects such as computer system organisation, and we close with the hope that the student has found this study enjoyable and fruitful.

REVIEW QUESTIONS

1. List three different ways in which the throughput of a computer system can be measured and/or specified. For an application of your choice, determine how you would like to specify the system throughput.
2. As we saw, the 5¼" 'floppy' disk of 1981 had a storage capacity of 360 kilobytes. A DVD today has storage capacity of around 4.5 gigabytes. Estimate (i) the required number, and (ii) the volume in cubic meters, if the original 'floppy' disks of 1981 are used to store 4.5 gigabytes of data.
3. List the features introduced in Intel's 'x86' processor family as it progressed from the 8088 processor to the 80486 series.
4. Explain in brief the meaning of 'backward compatibility' of instruction set in a processor family. In which way is it related to a business requirement?
5. In the Pentium IV processor, the fetch/decode unit, execute unit, and commit unit operate in parallel, sharing the common micro-operation buffer. Explain this statement in brief.
6. In Intel 'x86' processor architecture, what is the difference between registers denoted in assembly language as AH, AL, AX and EAX?
7. Explain in brief the chip multi-threading provided on the UltraSparc T2 processor.
8. A single UltraSparc T2 chip can be said to support 64 *virtual systems* on it. Explain this statement in brief.
9. On the basis of power per cm^2 of chip area, power consumption of the UltraSparc T2 is greater than that of an iron. Verify this statement using approximate figures for power consumption and area of a household iron.
10. List three typical applications towards which the UltraSparc T2 is targeted.
11. What is an applet? What role do the Internet browser and JVM play in running an applet?
12. Outline very briefly the operation of stack-oriented processor instructions, as opposed to register-oriented processor instructions.
13. Outline in brief the role of operand references in JVM.
14. List three possible advantages of using an embedded microcontroller in a system.
15. List in brief the I/O functionality provided on the Intel 8051 microcontroller.
16. Explain in brief, with an example, the bit addressability feature in the instruction set of the Intel 8051 microcontroller.
17. What is the role of the cross-compiler and/or cross-assembler in developing a microcontroller application?
18. List some of the key factors which have led to the growth and success of the PC family.
19. Outline with a diagram the basic architecture of the PC.
20. Identify the country of manufacture of three different hardware elements on the PC to which you have regular access.

APPENDIX: BINARY ENCODING OF *NICE* MACHINE INSTRUCTIONS

A

By using a variable number of bits to encode the opcode in the instruction, we can reduce the number of unused bits in the encoded instructions. For this purpose, instructions need to be grouped together based on broad function. As a rule of thumb, a smaller number of bits should be used to encode an opcode, if a larger number of bits are required to encode the rest of the instruction, and *vice versa*.

NICE machine instructions have been divided into five groups, based on similarity of action and operands, as shown in Fig. A.1.

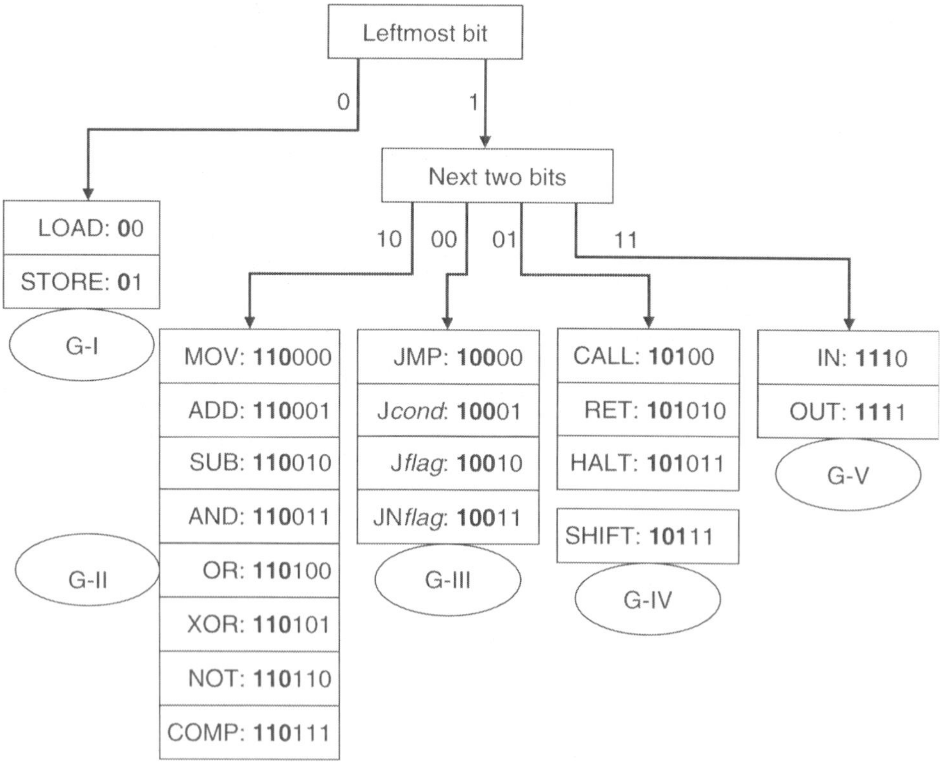

Fig. A.1 **Groups of *NICE* machine instructions**

Group G-I (Load/Store) is defined by leftmost bit being '0'. The remaining three groups are defined by the leftmost three bits of the instruction. The respective instruction opcode is shown in Fig. A.1 with each instruction, including the bits which define each group.

SHIFT instruction should really be in group G-II, along with other arithmetic and logic instructions. But this would result in nine instructions in G-II, requiring one extra bit to encode instructions of the group. Therefore, since group G-IV has only three other instructions, SHIFT has been moved to G-IV.

For efficient fetch and decoding, machine instructions are encoded into an integer number of bytes. Therefore, in some instruction formats there may, in general, be a few unused bits, as we shall see in the examples below.

A.1 GROUP G-I: LOAD, STORE

1. **Direct mode:** 24-bit address specified in instruction.
2. **Indirect Mode:** A register contains memory address.
3. **Indexed Mode:** 19-bit base address and index register are specified; five '0' bits are appended to base address at the time of execution.

Opcodes:	As in Fig. A.1
Modifier:	Byte/Word: 0/1
Addressing modes:	Direct: 0
	Indirect: 10
	Indexed: 11

Examples

1. LOAD byte, in direct mode, from memory address 1234 (hex) to R5:

   00 0 0 0101 000000000001001000110100

   Total instruction length: 32 bits.
2. STORE word, in indirect mode using R5, from source register R4:

   01 1 10 <u>000</u> 0101 0100

   Total instruction length: 16 bits (including three unused bits).
3. LOAD word, in indexed mode using R7 and the 19-bit base address shown, into R9:

   00 1 11 0110011000010000000 0111 1001

   Total instruction length: 32 bits.

A.2 GROUP G-II: MOV, ADD, SUB, AND, OR, XOR, NOT, COMP

1. **Register mode:** Performs register to register operation.
2. **Immediate mode:** Specified 20-bit quantity is used as one operand, and only destination register is specified in instruction.

Opcodes: As in Fig. A.1
Modifier: Byte/Word: 0/1
Addressing modes: Register: 0
Immediate: 1

Examples

1. MOV immediate constant 134 (hex) into R5:

   110000 1 1 0000000000100110100 0101

   Total instruction length: 32 bits
2. ADD word in R11 into R12:

   110001 1 0 1011 1100

   Total instruction length: 16 bits
3. Logical **AND** of rightmost byte of R5 into R4:

   110011 0 0 0101 0100

   Total instruction length: 16 bits
4. Unlike other instructions in this group, instruction **NOT** has only one register operand, and only one modifier: byte/word. Thus, for logical complement of the word in register R7, we will have the encoding:

   110110 1 00000 0111

   Total instruction length: 16 bits (including five unused bits)

A.3 GROUP G-III: JMP, J*COND*, J*FLAG*, JN*FLAG*

Opcodes: As in Fig. A.1
Codes for jump conditions in **J***cond*:

GT: 000, GE: 001, LT: 010, LE: 011, EQ: 100, NE: 101

Codes for condition flags in **J***flag* and **JN***flag*:

Z: 000, N: 001, O: 010, C: 011, P: 100

Examples

1. Unconditional transfer of control to location 1134 (hex):

   10000 000 000000000001000100110100

   Total instruction length: 32 bits (including three unused bits)

2. Jump if less than (JLT) to location 654321 (hex):

   10001 010 011001010100001100100001

   Total instruction length: 32 bits
3. Jump if Z flag not set to location 789ABC (hex):

   10011 000 011110001001101010111100

   Total instruction length: 32 bits

A.4 GROUP G-IV: CALL, RET, HALT, SHIFT

CALL instruction has the same format as JMP (see above), except that the opcode is different. RET and HALT instructions have no explicit operands. The opcodes assigned to these two instructions in Fig. A.1 have seven bits, and therefore, with one unused bit, each of these two instructions has length of one byte.

SHIFT

Opcodes: As in Fig. A.1

Modifiers	Byte/Word:	0/1
	Left/Right:	0/1
	With/Without carry:	0/1

First operand in the instruction specifies the register. Second operand is a 4-bit unsigned integer signifying the shift count.

Example

1. Shift right content of register R8 by 4 bits, with carry:

   10111 110 1000 0100

   Total instruction length: 16 bits

A.5 GROUP G-V: IN, OUT

Opcodes: As in Fig. A.1

Source or destination register is specified as the first operand.
Second operand specifies the 8-bit I/O address of the input or output device.

Example

1. Read a byte IN from device at I/O address 71 (hex) into R5:

   1110 0101 01110001

Of course, there is nothing sacrosanct or final about this particular binary encoding of *NICE* machine instructions. In this context, the student should recall the possible criteria listed in Chapter 6 for binary encoding of machine instructions, namely: (a) compactness of encoding, (b) reducing the gate delays in the control unit, and (c) reducing the number of combinational gates needed in the control unit.

The encoding scheme described above has not been optimised for any of these criteria. Rather, it has been chosen on the basis of simplicity, so that a student should be able to understand some of the issues involved. Also, this particular encoding has been used to build an assembler-cum-simulator for the *NICE* processor, which is available at the website accompanying the book.

INDEX

C

D

E

F

G

H

I

J

K

L

M

N

O

P

R

S

T

U

V

W

X